FIN DE SIÈCLE AND ITS LEGACY

FIN DE SIÈCLE

AND ITS LEGACY

EDITED BY

MIKULÁŠ TEICH

Emeritus Fellow, Robinson College, Cambridge

AND

ROY PORTER

Senior Lecturer in the Social History of Medicine, Wellcome Institute

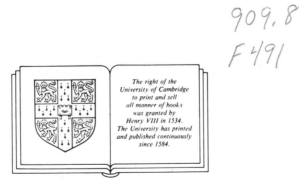

The right of the
University of Cambridge
to print and sell
all manner of books
was granted by
Henry VIII in 1534.
The University has printed
and published continuously
since 1584.

CAMBRIDGE UNIVERSITY PRESS

Cambridge
New York   Port Chester
Melbourne   Sydney

Published by the Press Syndicate of the University of Cambridge
The Pitt Building, Trumpington Street, Cambridge CB2 1RP
40 West 20th Street, New York, NY 10011, USA
10 Stamford Road, Oakleigh, Melbourne 3166, Australia

First published 1990

Printed in Great Britain by The Bath Press, Avon

British Library cataloguing in publication data
Fin de siècle and its legacy.
1.   European civilization, 1870–1899
I.   Teich, Mikuláš   II.   Porter, Roy, 1946–
940.2'87

Library of Congress cataloguing in publication data

Fin-de-siècle and its legacy edited by Mikuláš Teich and Roy Porter,
p.   cm.
ISBN 0 521 34108 6 – ISBN 0 521 34915 X (pbk)
1. History. Modern – 19th century.   2. History, Modern – 20th
century.   I. Teich, Mikuláš.   II. Porter, Roy. 1946–
D395.F55   1990
909.8--dc20   89-22347   CIP

ISBN 0 521 34108 6 hard covers
ISBN 0 521 34915 X paperback

SE

CONTENTS

vi

❧

ILLUSTRATIONS

viii

NOTES ON CONTRIBUTORS

KURT BAYERTZ studied philosophy, German literature and social sciences at the Universities of Frankfurt, Düsseldorf and Bremen. His main interests lie in philosophical and ethical problems of science. His last major publication in this area is a book on ethical problems of human reproductive technology which came out in 1987 under the title *GenEthik*. He has also done a lot of research in the social history of science in nineteenth-century Germany, especially on the philosophical, ideological and cultural reception of the theory of evolution. He is presently working at the Center of Science Studies at the University of Bielefeld.

JENNIFER BIRKETT is Professor of French Studies at the University of Strathclyde. Her main area of interest is ideology and fiction, with special reference to the late eighteenth and late nineteenth centuries. Her latest book *The Sins of the Fathers: Decadence in France 1870–1914* was published by Quartet Books in 1986. She is currently engaged in editing a collection of essays in Contemporary Women's Studies (*Determined Women*), in preparing the Macmillan *Guide to French Literature*, and in writing another book for Quartet on *Sexuality, Politics and Fiction in the French Revolution*.

PATRICK BRANTLINGER, editor of *Victorian Studies* and Professor of English at Indiana University, is the author of three books: *The Spirit of Reform: British Literature and Politics 1832–1867*; *Bread and Circuses: Theories of Mass Culture as Social Decay*; and *Rule of Darkness: British Literature and Imperialism 1830–1914*.

ALFRED D. CHANDLER, JR, taught at Massachusetts Institute of Technology and Johns Hopkins and has been the Strauss Professor of Business History at the Harvard Business School since 1971. He is the author of books, chapters in books and articles on business and economic history. His books include *Strategy and Structure: Chapters in the History of the Industrial Enterprise* (1962) which received the Newcomen Award; *The Visible Hand: The Managerial Revolution in American Business* (1977) which was awarded the Pulitzer Prize in History, the Bancroft Prize and the Newcomen Award, and the forthcoming *Scale and Scope: The Dynamics of Managerial Capitalism*. His article in this volume is based on the last book.

ENZO COLLOTTI is Professor of Contemporary History at the University of Florence. His primary interest has concerned German and Austrian contemporary history, the history of the international labour movement, the comparative history of fascism, and the history of the Second World War. His latest publications include *L'internazionale operaia e socialista tra le due guerre* (ed.) 1985; *Fascismo, fascismi* (1989).

HENNING EICHBERG is a cultural sociologist having received a Ph.D. in history from the Ruhr University Bochum in 1970. Since 1984 he has been doing research on sport sciences at the University of Copenhagen. He has lectured in history, sociology and sport sciences at many of the major European universities. His twenty-two published books cover the history and cultural sociology of sports and body culture, military technology, nationalism, and also Indonesian social studies. He has recently edited *Nordic Sports, History and Identity* (Helsinki, 1989).

ANNE HARRINGTON is Assistant Professor in the History of Science Department at Harvard University. She received her D.Phil. from Oxford University in 1985. She was a Wellcome Trust Fellow at the Wellcome Institute for the History of Medicine in London in 1985–6, and an Alexander-von-Humboldt Fellow at the Institut f. Geschichte d. Medizin, Freiburg University from 1986 to 1988. Her book, *Medicine, Mind and the Double Brain: A Study in Nineteenth Century Thought*, was published by Princeton University Press in 1987. She is currently working on a book-length study of the wider cultural and ideological meaning of holistic psychobiology in the German-speaking countries, *c.* 1918–33.

ALISON HENNEGAN graduated from Girton College, Cambridge (where she read English) in 1970 and embarked on a Ph.D. thesis entitled *Literature and the Homosexual Cult, 1890–1920*. Formal research was permanently interrupted by her increasing involvement with gay politics. She was National Organizer of the gay counselling organization, FRIEND, and Vice-Chair of the national Campaign for Homosexual Equality from 1975 to 1977. From 1977 to 1983 she was Literary Editor of *Gay News* and now works for the feminist publishers, The Women's Press, where she acts as an editorial consultant and as Editor of their Bookclub. She was a regular contributor to the *New Statesman* from 1984 to 1988 and has published numerous articles on the relations between gender, sexuality and literature. Recent publications include contributions to *Writing Lives: Conversations between Women Writers*, edited by Mary Chamberlain (Virago, London, 1988), and *Sweet Dreams: Gender, Sexuality and Popular Fiction*, edited by Susannah Radstone (Lawrence & Wishart, London, 1988).

ERWIN N. HIEBERT is Professor of the History of Science at Harvard University. His major teaching and research interests are in the history and philosophy of the physical sciences since 1800. He is currently working on a volume entitled *Lise Meitner: A Portrait in Letters*.

BARBARA LESÁK attended the University of Vienna where she pursued theatre studies and read history of art and philosophy. She has published numerous scholarly articles on the history of theatre and art in the twentieth century. She acted as adviser to various art exhibitions. Publications include *Die Kulisse explodiert. Friedrich Kieslers Theaterexperimente und Architektur-projekte 1923–1925* (Vienna, 1988).

RICHARD OVERY is Reader in modern European history at King's College, London. He has published extensively on the history of air power, including *The Air War 1939–1945*. He is currently writing a history of the Nazi economy.

ROY PORTER, formerly Lecturer in History at Cambridge University, is currently Senior Lecturer in the Social History of Medicine at the Wellcome Institute for the History of Medicine, London. His current research interests focus largely on the history of psychiatry and of medicine in the eighteenth century. Recent publications include *In Sickness and in Health* (Fourth Estate) and *Patient's Progress* (Polity) – both co-authored with Dorothy Porter – and *Health for Sale* (Manchester University Press).

ROMAN SANDGRUBER is Professor of Economic History at the University of Linz. His books and other writings are on agrarian history, on history of Austrian industrialization, history of everyday life, and environmental history.

MIKULÁŠ TEICH is Emeritus Fellow of Robinson College, Cambridge. His publications include work on the history of chemistry and biomedical sciences, social and philosophical aspects of the development of science, historical relations of science, technology and the economy, and on the history of scientific organizations. His *A Documentary History of Bio-chemistry* (with the late Dorothy M. Needham) will be published by Leicester University Press (1990).

ALICE TEICHOVA is Emeritus Professor of Economic History at the University of East Anglia and Honorary Fellow of Girton College, Cambridge. Her interests concern the history of finance, industry and international relations in the twentieth century. Her recent publications include *Kleinstaaten im Spannungsfeld der Grossmächte* (1988) and *The Czechoslovak Economy 1918–1980* (1988).

FRITZ WEBER, research fellow of the Creditanstalt-Bankverein in Vienna, is an economic historian by profession, who, since his youth, has had a marked interest in music. His fields of research range from banking to labour and political history and, recently, the history of music as a social phenomenon. His various publications include the book *Der Kalte Krieg in der SPÖ 1945–1950* (Vienna, 1986). During 1989–90 he is Monnet Fellow at the European University Institute, Florence.

INTRODUCTION

MIKULÁŠ TEICH AND ROY PORTER

It appears that the expression *fin de siècle* was launched upon the world when the play with the same title by two French authors, F. de Jouvenot and H. Micard, was performed first in Paris on 17 April 1888. Whereas the Brockhaus Encyclopaedia describes the play as a comedy, Eugene Weber in an highly informative work on *fin-de-siècle* France points out that it 'turns around shady deals, adultery and murder'.[1] The play certainly is not a comedy if by this genre is meant a dramatic work of amusing character possibly with a happy ending.[2] As to E. Weber's description, it is too brief to convey the message of the play though it is true that shady deals and adultery run through it ending with the murder of the main character, the corrupt and adulterous Richard Trévor. Trévor is shot by his brother-in-law Roger Bridière, who takes personal and family revenge for having been by Trévor first deluded, then falsely declared insane and put into an asylum from which he manages to escape.

The play is Schnitzleresque but badly crafted and hence miles away from the brilliant critical artistry with which Arthur Schnitzler dissected the duplicity of morals and the part it played in the bourgeois-aristocratic world of the Austrian *fin de siècle*. Nevertheless, what emerges from the French play is a chronicle of shallow and rotten morality permeating the pores of a society in which, as the broker Filagand states, 'in order to succeed, it is better to be a *canaille* than an unknown honest man'.

For decades *fin de siècle* implied a 'go to the dogs' feeling that was thought to pervade European 'civilized' society in the years around 1900. This mood of malaise certainly affected individuals and sections of aristocratic as well as bourgeois social background towards the end of the nineteenth century. Underlying it was a cocktail of lamentations for the past and fears of the future, countenancing the notion that human progress was being brought to a halt, if not to an end. This evaluation now, as we ourselves approach another turn of the century and look back, appears distinctly simplistic.

F. DE JOUVENOT & H. MICARD

FIN DE SIÈCLE

PIÈCE EN QUATRE ACTES

PARIS

PAUL OLLENDORFF, ÉDITEUR

28 *bis*, RUE DE RICHELIEU, 28 *bis*

1888

Tous droits de traduction, de reproduction et de représentation réservés.

1   Title page of *Fin de Siècle: Pièce en Quatre Actes*
by F. de Jouvenot and H. Micard, 1888

Indeed, there are several good reasons for treating the later years of the nineteenth century and the early years of the twentieth century as a watershed in many areas. They are the period of the rise of the giant corporation, mass production and mass consumption. They are the period of the development of generation and distribution of electrical energy, of the spread of motor vehicles and aviation. They are the period of the emergence of novel social features such as mass politics, mass media and mass sport, by way of which the body of ordinary people, denoted as 'the masses', was growing into a major participant in public affairs, popular culture and leisure activities. They are the period which engendered in the arts, literature, aesthetics and philosophy complex reactions to contemporary social reality. Last but not least they are the period which has given birth to quantum mechanics and relativity physics, when the exploration of mental processes was given fresh impulses, and the systematic study of genetical processes began. The purpose of this volume is to consider these aspects of the *fin de siècle*, broadly and interpretatively, in separate historical essays.

The *fin-de-siècle* phenomenon has, of course, received considerable attention from historians in the recent past – a testament to its appeal. On the whole treatments, however, give privileged consideration to its cultural – literary and artistic – manifestations, to the relative neglect of other elements. They also tend to concentrate on individual as well as social alienation as particularly characteristic of the *fin-de-siècle* feeling. This volume aims to break new ground by surveying in parallel a diversity of fields while taking into account their historical, social and geographical dimensions.

Perhaps the first thing to note is that most contributors acknowledge explicitly that the matters they deal with are in some way related to changes in the system of capitalism, industrial and liberal, since the close of the nineteenth century.

In the economic sphere these are associated with transition of the free market economy to one regulated and dominated by large corporations. Its business, social, organizational and technological contexts are discussed by Alice Teichova and Alfred Chandler in the first two essays. What emerges from their pages is how vital to this process was the materialization of the mass market, as its factor and outcome. Commensurate to altered scale and scope of economic activity, the mass market supplied by tolerably cheap mass-produced goods was indicative of industrialism entering a new phase by 1900.

Advancing and sustaining it were electrification and the internal combustion engine – technological developments taken up in the essays by Roman Sandgruber and Richard Overy respectively. The *fin-de-siècle* theme has largely turned into one of the relationship between culture and society in which it arises and operates. That this has become so has much to do with

Carl Schorske's influential account of politics and culture in the capital of the Habsburg Empire at the turn of the century.[3] Sandgruber's contribution points to an overlooked aspect of the *fin-de-siècle* phenomenon in Austria by highlighting electrification as being just as much a part of technological, social and economic history as of cultural history. Austria is not generally thought of as a country with a long aviation past. Yet, as Overy records, in Vienna the world's first aeronautical institute was founded in 1880 and the first international air exhibition took place in 1912. It is neither intended nor appropriate to follow here in detail what the authors say in their particular essays. Even so, in Overy's contribution there is one item regarding the social consequences of the mass-produced internal combustion engine on wheels[4] which merits attention at this point. He believes that 'the democratization of motor-car ownership and motor transport matched the corresponding political shifts towards mass politics and greater equality'.

Behind the evolution of twentieth-century mass politics lay major social and economic changes, associated with the nineteenth-century industrialization of Europe and America and the recession known as the 'Great Depression' (1873–96). This is the starting point of Enzo Collotti's wide-ranging examination of four forms of politicization of the masses: nationalism, anti-Semitic racism, socialism and political Catholicism. He has a good deal to say on the issue of what it was that turned these movements, after 1900, into powerful forces of politics – in terms of numbers and influence. Thus with respect to nationalism Collotti identifies its wellspring with the mythos that 'Nation' and 'strong State' constitute, in effect, supra-class societal entities in which social conflict and democracy have no place. This kind of nationalism flowed not only into fascism but 'facilitated the penetration of racism into the European political world' of which the anti-Semitic variant became fateful. As to the socialist movement, Collotti stresses all its programmes 'were reacting to conditions of real exploitation, of real attempts to isolate the masses, of real opposition between classes, even when conflicts were spirited away or denied outright'. Lastly, Collotti considers political Catholicism as a move – historically strongly indebted to Leo XIII's encyclical *Rerum novarum* (1891) – brought into play in order to counteract socialism.

Underlying these movements, it is well to remember, were the political aspirations and hopes of diverse sections of the lower middle class and working class, and the new ways and means to channel them. Here is the historical connection, since the close of the nineteenth century, with the changes in the cultural life of the lower income groups of the population. They have been taking place under the pervasive impact of developments in communications of which the popular press, the cinema, radio and television are the most potent components. This problematic, encapsulated in the terms 'mass culture' and 'mass media', is dealt with in the essay by Patrick

Brantlinger. Brantlinger juxtaposes mass culture and the artistic avant-garde and sees in these two phenomena dialectical opposites, historically originating in, and bound up with, what he describes as 'advanced capitalism between the 1880s and 1914'. Brantlinger's unease with the negative influences of the mass media upon society is challenging when he writes: 'The extent to which journalism, film, radio and television can or cannot promote social intelligence and democracy is perhaps the central unanswered question of modern history.'

No less challenging is that the growth of sport during the last hundred years – historically significant for its social, commercial and political repercussions – has received little attention. This development is most poignantly symbolized by the Olympic Games, first held in their modern and international form in Athens in 1896. Thus Henning Eichberg's essay in this volume on their history, albeit a critical one, is a 'natural'. A point made by Eichberg is that ever since Athens 'race' – in the sense of a contest of timed speed – has moved into the centre of the games and sporting scene where traditionally activities undertaken rather in a spirit of light-heartedness used to prevail. Part of the interest of this approach lies in the fact that Eichberg pinpoints the historically common socio-economic context in which the stopwatch emerges as the principal instrument for timing performance both in sports and production. Of no less interest are the passages which deal with those elements in the history of Olympics rooted in colonialism and racism.

It is now time to move on to four contributions looking into cultural aspects which, as mentioned, have been the main focus of *fin-de-siècle* historiography. Here it is worth referring to an observation made by Norman Stone in a perceptive review of Schorske's book some time ago: 'Cultural history is probably impossible to do satisfactorily because, except perhaps in architecture and the cinema, links between society and individual cannot be made clear.'[5] Behind this sceptical position really looms the large question of precisely how the turn-of-the-century artists and writers perceived the world around them and their own place in it. There is no simple answer because society, nature, individuals – which make up the world – are complex phenomena and so are the relations between them. Yet, for all that, in the four 'cultural' contributions to this volume something of these links is revealed. This is an issue to which their authors are sensitive although they may differ in their approaches and concerns.

Before coming to the first of the contributions concerned with specific fields of artistic activity mention has to be made that an essay on architecture was planned but has, very much to our regret, not materialized – the prospective author was taken seriously ill while he was preparing it. But the cinema, apart from Brantlinger, receives attention from Barbara Lesák in her essay exploring the historical relationship between photography, film and the theatre.

One way of summing it up is to say – rather banally – that what united them was that they were after 'mirroring reality'. Here, as Lesák stresses, photography and its progeny, cinematography, set new standards which eventually left the theatre behind as a social, cultural and economic force. 'Along with photography', wrote S. Krakauer in a major study, 'film is the only art which leaves its raw material more or less intact.'[6] This throws considerable light on why millions the world over have taken to them as their favourite pastimes offering unmatched accessibilities to and possibilities of interpreting reality. Indeed, in this century photography and film have become the mass art forms *par excellence*.

In contrast, a considerably lesser number of people had been reached by the visual arts, literature and music. Nevertheless, also here the situation had begun to change since the 1870s and 1880s, not least because the introduction of zincography and photography into printing made all types of illustration cheaper. Already before 1900 a market for reproductions of paintings was developing though it was hardly capable of keeping the artist's body and soul together. '[He] had to sell to the wealthy', writes Jennifer Birkett, 'before he reached the masses.' In probing the complexities of *fin-de-siècle* painting Birkett affirms interrelationships between the painters' creations and their political and social ideas and ideals, including their sexist and patriarchal attitudes which she exemplifies chiefly through the works of Moreau, Redon and Rops. She also follows up the intricate passage from *fin-de-siècle* painting to the surrealist canvas and screen of the twentieth century.

Some of the themes and personalities around which Jennifer Birkett's survey of the painting scene in *fin-de-siècle* France is organized can also be found in Alison Hennegan's scrutiny of the literary setting in *fin-de-siècle* England. This should not be surprising in view of the then lively cultural toing and froing across the waters of what in Dover is called the English Channel and in Calais La Manche. 'London's sulphurous yellow fogs', writes Hennegan, 'acquired for French eyes a glamour as potent as any Englishman's wistful fantasies of sinful Paris.' This certainly was not what attracted Oscar Wilde, the key figure in Hennegan's account, to take refuge there after his release from jail, only to die three years later (1900). Wilde emerges from her essay as a man of abiding stature – 'of writers produced by the British Isles only Shakespeare has been more written about' – whose imprisonment (1895) signals that '[i]n England the *fin de siècle* all but ends'. Hennegan points out that Wilde's 'trials became a very public debate on the nature of the morality of art, the relations between art and life, the social obligation of artists and the nature of society's claims upon them . . . The examination . . . in effect put Wilde on trial for aesthetic, philosophical and moral ideas painfully elaborated over half a century by artists and writers on both sides of the Channel.'

Widely acknowledged, the subject of the social relations of music is most controversial. In the fourth and last essay dealing with an artistic topic Fritz Weber grapples with the problem through a nuanced approach which he describes as 'a socio-historical approximation' and brings to bear on a wide range of music's specifics: compositions, composers, orchestras, conductors, tonality, instrumentation and so forth. Thus regarding 'classical' *fin-de-siècle* music he has this to say:

We do not know in detail which and how many of the new social challenges the composers of the time consciously recognized (and whether they did at all). However, we can assume that they grasped the new phenomena in society by intuition. And although music was not part of any political movement, it was – in general – 'critical': hostile to the world of money-making, of commercial, technological and scientific rationality.

But Weber stresses that this kind of music forms only a small part of *fin-de-siècle* music. Discussing other elements of *fin-de-siècle* music he discovers closer relations between them and technology, economics and other factors of social life. To take two examples: electrical bright light as a prerequisite of the revue; the revue girl as the factory girl of the theatre whose synchronized movements recall Taylor's thinking regarding the precise manner in which work in the factory is to be performed.

Finally, there are four contributions in which the authors address some historically substantive scientific issues and topics which came to the fore around 1900. Of these Erwin Hiebert's essay is on the transformation of physics often described as 'a revolution in physics', set off by the trinity of discoveries – X-rays (1895), radioactivity (1896) and the electron (1897) – which 'paved the way for the study and theoretical interpretation of radiation and spectra, atomic and molecular theory, quantum theory and relativity'. While Hiebert uses terms such as 'abrupt' or 'genuine and brisk' to characterize the transformation from 'classical' to 'new physics', he also states with respect to the latter's 'decisive anchor points' that 'most if not all . . . can be linked with components embedded in late nineteenth-century classical theory and practice'. Hiebert discounts the influence of backward-looking thinking associated with *fin-de-siècle* mentality, on the transformation of physics at the turn of the century. It took place 'in a relatively unbroken and tranquil but reformist and spirited manner'.

Hiebert broadly concentrates on 'internal' developments in physics as they affected it as a 'scientific discipline' after 1895. Anne Harrington's contribution, on the other hand, is concerned with the 'external' influence of a philosophical trend, holism, on a branch of medicine – clinical neurology. Harrington traces the holistic reaction of neurologists since the 1890s to their growing dissatisfaction with the inadequacy of mechanistic cerebral localization thinking to explain 'the simple fact that brain-damaged people can get better over time – can regain lost speech and movement'. Beyond that she thinks that the rise of the influence of holism has to be viewed in socio-economic, cultural and geographical contexts. It was part of the

concern with the fatal loss of humanity caused by the mechanization, industrialization and super-compartmentalization of modern living. Once this is understood, one sees too how it is hardly coincidental that a so-called 'holistic biology' should have taken root in the German-speaking countries during a period when these elites had turned references to 'wholeness', 'oneness', the 'whole' . . . into slogans for their fight against the shallow individualism of modern life and their effort to reclaim the essential spiritual values of German *Kultur*.

A rarely discussed topic of *fin-de-siècle* cross-border relations is the challenge to aesthetics posed by the nineteenth-century growth of science and its institutionalization. The problem was how to reconcile aesthetic and scientific criteria regarding truth about nature which Friedrich Nietzsche, for one, viewed as incompatible with each other. This is the general term of reference of Kurt Bayertz's essay in which he discusses 'evolutionary aesthetics', a theory of art variously indebted to the theory of evolution, as part of wider social history. Bayertz's analysis involves a critical look on monistic pantheism subscribed to by Ernst Haeckel – a great name in late nineteenth-century biology – through which he erected a construct in which Evolution and Beauty co-existed peacefully. In this context Bayertz puts forward the view that Haeckel's monistic pantheism 'can be taken as a "philosophical *Jugendstil*" above all because it expresses conceptually the artistic practice of the *Jugendstil*'.

In the concluding essay on a scientific topic Mikuláš Teich addresses human genetics as an historiographical issue that has been neglected. In particular, he attempts to explore the hitherto overlooked methodological elements within human genetics. They grew, since the rediscovery of Mendel's work in 1900, out of the amalgam of Weismannian and Mendelian approaches to heredity. It was this latter, Teich believes, that was at the root of validating scientifically the control of human heredity in desired racial and mental directions.

It goes without saying that such a volume as this cannot include everything that could be said on the *fin-de-siècle* phenomenon. Even so the contributions make abundantly clear that it is more complex than it appears from presentations of the subject. The issue becomes one of the evaluation of the common framework of developments in the particular spheres which the authors discuss. They can now be seen as interrelated and interacting manifestations as well as factors of a major change affecting broadly all facets of life and thought that had evolved under the conditions of industrial and liberal capitalism during the nineteenth century. The understanding of this process, different from anything man previously knew, carries reverberating implications for the comprehension of the tangled and turbulent transformations which the twentieth century has been passing through.

NOTES

1 E. Weber, *France, Fin de Siècle* (Cambridge, Mass. and London, 1986), p. 10.
2 *Oxford Dictionary of Current English*, repr. (Oxford, 1985); *Brockhaus Enzyklopaedie* (Wiesbaden, 1968), vol. VI, pp. 266–7.
3 C. E. Schorske, *Fin-de-siècle Vienna: Politics and Culture*, repr. (Cambridge, 1985).
4 This expressive term appears in the title of J. B. Rae's article 'The internal-combustion engine on wheels', in M. Kranzberg and C. W. Pursell, Jr (eds.), *Technology in Western Civilization* (New York, 1967), vol. II, pp. 119–37.
5 See N. Stone, 'Depression over Austria', *The Times Literary Supplement*, 16 May 1980, 545–6.
6 S. Krakauer, *Nature of Film: The Redemption of Physical Reality* (London, 1961), p. x.

❧

ONE

A LEGACY OF *FIN-DE-SIÈCLE* CAPITALISM: THE GIANT COMPANY

ALICE TEICHOVA

I

As the end of the twentieth century is approaching giant companies spreading their business interests all over the world and operating in a global market are a legacy of the growth in the size of enterprises set in motion at the end of the last century and the early years of this one.

Fortune's annual compilation of the fifty biggest industrial companies shows that in 1987 they employed 8.8 million people, more than the population of Sweden; their sales totalled $1.5 trillion and their profits $56 billion, involving sums greater than the national income of many an industrial state. At the head of this roll-call of industrial giants have been producers of cars, oil and chemicals – General Motors, Royal Dutch/Shell, Exxon, Ford, Toyota, DuPont, Unilever – year after year roughly in the same order. Close on their heels follow electronics companies which, in the 1980s, advanced into the list of the 'Top 50'. Of these fifty companies, twenty were domiciled in the USA, twenty were West European-based and eight were Japanese. 'These companies set the styles, invest the money, build the plants – sometimes altering the economies and ecologies of vast regions.'[1] When one surveys the world's leading companies since the 1960s, the rising impact of science-based technology in their international production programmes embracing atomic energy, microelectronics and genetic engineering is striking[2] and is, at the same time, part of a development in our age which can be called the scientific-technical revolution.[3]

In this context practically insurmountable difficulties appear at the present time by the demands to fulfil the aims of the much propagated 'enterprise culture' destined to revive the 'competitive spirit' in entrepreneurship which is expected to make the Western capitalist economy even more prosperous. However, the historical reality of contemporary capitalism, far from giving a multitude of independent entrepreneurs a chance of competing in the market to satisfy consumers, confers advantages on the strongest, most forceful companies pursuing oligopolistic and monopolistic aims and competing among themselves for ever bigger market shares. Indeed, business firms have expanded since the turn of the century by persistently seeking to increase profits through reducing costs and relentlessly integrating the processes of mass production with those of mass distribution,[4] and by seeking to raise efficiency through scientific management of labour, finance and marketing. At the same time, their capacity to survive and prosper has depended on their success in controlling the markets in which they work and in bringing as many markets as possible within their sphere of influence, preferably concentrating market power fully into their own hands in pursuit of advantages through internalization. They have become international, transnational, supranational or multinational in the sense that their production has spread to several countries through a network of subsidiary firms dependent on them as parent companies.[5] But their headquarters are in most cases in one country where the home-base of the whole organization is situated and from where its world-wide interests are controlled, although international, even global, aspects are central to the business policies of the large companies. Thus, for instance, the Dutch electronic group, Philips, sees its objectives for the 1990s in gearing its production to 'a single world concept' and wishing to be a 'global' rather than an international company.[6]

The scramble for markets accelerated the growth of mergers and takeovers within and across national borders, that is, the struggle taking place between the large companies to outbid each other in order to gain an increasing share of total international investment and by ousting competitors to tighten corporate control of markets.

At the time of writing this essay the economic and financial pages of the press are brimming over with reports of 'raids' by 'predators' in the 'recent surge of cross-border takeovers in Europe' when the rate of merger activities is quickening in preparation for the establishment of the single common European market in 1992. Giant American and Japanese companies are buying up shares or entire enterprises in western Europe to gain access to the prospective unified European market; in answer to this threat mainly British, French and German companies are drawn together into mergers, joint-ventures and alliances to secure the advantages expected from the requirements of 250 million people in the European market-place. West European industry is set on a path to even greater concentration into giant concerns.[7]

The manner and method in which the concentration and merger movement has developed in anticipation of the borderless European market is evidence of the paramount importance of market control. Fusions of companies have reached records in recent years: in the United States the number of takeovers rose threefold to 4,000 within eight years. Taking the European Community as a whole international joint-ventures involving its 1,000 largest companies doubled in 1987 as compared with 1986, while mergers rose by one-third with most of the activity in food and drink, vehicles and transport equipment industries. Of the 303 that took place, nearly 60 per cent involved mergers with sales exceeding $1 billion. Thus the trend is towards mega mergers.[8]

Although the most noticeable development took place in the United States during the 1960s, the cradle of large-scale business such as national and international cartels, big companies and their international and multinational development is nevertheless to be found in Europe at the end of the nineteenth century. Three periods of rapid growth connected with foreign expansion of large enterprise emerge: the initial stage of conspicuous expansion fell clearly into the last two decades of the nineteenth century; a further remarkable increase in concentration and multinationality of companies occurred in the 1920s and 1930s; and the most intensive global reach has come about since the 1960s.[9]

Thus takeovers and acquisitions to increase market shares have for decades been prevalent throughout the entire range of industries, from producer to consumer goods production. This is why by comparing changes in concentration with the time pattern of merger activity in Britain Leslie Hannah could identify the first period for which sources are available as the 1890s and then peak periods in the 1920s and again in the 1960s.[10] The most recent merger wave of the 1980s reached new heights creating a broad international web of mergers, joint-ventures and alliances from power generation through heavy engineering and space equipment to food, drink and publishing.[11]

As a result of the recurrent waves of mergers throughout the twentieth century the process of concentration of corporate ownership has accelerated. Investigating the period 1870–1939 economic historians have shown that the path of expansion started by the merging of domestic firms into local monopolies which was accompanied or followed by acquiring subsidiary companies abroad through foreign direct investment. Thus concurrent with the peaks in the number of mergers the amount of foreign direct investment increased as companies were building up international combines.[12] Among the most spectacular examples were: the formation of the big American oil trusts and the great mergers and cartels of the American and German electrical companies in the last decade of the nineteenth and the first decade of the twentieth century;[13] then in the aftermath of the First World War European firms accelerated acquisitions at home and abroad, such as in the 1920s Ivar Kreuger's Swedish Match company,[14] and the combination of the entire German chemical industry into IG Farbenindustrie in 1925,[15] followed in 1926 by the creation of Imperial Chemical Industries in Britain,[16] as well as the biggest industrial amalgamation in European history until that time which occurred in 1929–30 when the powerful trust of Unilever was formed.[17]

After the Second World War a global capital market has been emerging where the decisive buyers and sellers of shares in joint-stock enterprises are the giant companies. Thus by the early 1980s half of the total share capital in Japan was held by companies, not by private individuals as investors;[18] and after the stock exchange crash of October 1987 virtually 'the only one type of buyer of stocks in the US . . . are corporations, both foreign and domestic'.[19] British large companies have since 1985 annually increased their foreign direct investments by acquiring US and west European firms. Discussing the structure of international investment, Eneko Landaburu, the Director of the Institute for Research and Information on Multinationals, remarked that in the 1980s new investment in many countries is more likely to come from foreign multinationals than from domestic companies, therefore 'the main issue of the eighties seems to be the struggle of nation states for an adequate share in the investment cake which multinational companies are still distributing'.[20] Doubtless, states and the giant companies contend for control over investments but they also co-operate in acquiring, securing and defending their long-term investments. This is part of the wider question of the relationships between governments and the large international companies which have perennially been influenced both by conformity and by conflict of interests.

Historically foreign direct investment is closely bound up with the development of global business and has become the most effective instrument in establishing the dominance of giant multinational enterprise in the international economy. In the 1980s the decisive share of the total stock of foreign direct investment is owned, controlled and operated by multinational companies whose headquarters are situated in their various home countries. Geographically the giant companies of the USA, the European Community (EC) and Japan have established a veritable triangular power base which so far has not been seriously challenged. The industrially developed economies not only export the largest share of total direct foreign investment (97.3 per cent in 1983) but they also absorb its greatest share (74.2 per cent in 1983) investing in each other's enterprises, while the developing areas of the world receive a relatively small percentage of total direct foreign investment (25.8 per cent in 1983) and they obviously are only marginally engaged in exporting capital (2.7 per cent in 1983).[21]

Economically and politically foreign investment became one of the crucial factors in the international capitalist economy and in international relations. Thus the changes in the rank order of the leading countries of origin of foreign direct investment represent also some measure of their power and influence; at the same time they reflect the economic strength of the giant companies radiating their direct investments from those countries.

A prolific stream of economic, political, social and historical publications has recently accumulated regarding the nature of multinational companies and the phenomenon of direct investment they engender. Authors examine and attempt to interpret the reasons why large companies invest in production abroad. Usually only a multicausal explanation can provide satisfactory answers. Most frequent among many motives in the earlier period are access to and control of raw material sources, overcoming of customs barriers, breaking out of narrow home markets, while in the second half of the twentieth century further considerations come to the fore as reasons for expanding production abroad, such as utilizing to the full the advantages of research and development, of diversifying from a common base to reduce costs and increase profits, of gaining from differences in labour costs, of making profitable use of world-wide trading and financial networks as well as of differences in exchange values.[22]

Overall, surveyed historically, the underlying motive of capitalist enterprise to expand generally and to invest in foreign companies in particular can be traced almost invariably directly or indirectly to the consolidation of acquired markets and to the defence of already occupied market positions or to the penetration and opening up of new profitable markets. As the leading companies increased the scale and scope of their production[23] and their business activities flowed across national borders the imperative requirement of their mass production was mass markets.

II

Within the framework of capitalist market economies the dynamic process of business development was powerfully generated in the course of the twentieth century by the increasing interactions between science and technology on the one hand and industry, transport and communications on the other. These relationships facilitated rationalization, normalization and standardization of products as a vital component of the spread of mass production.[24] At the same time, they significantly furthered the process of concentration of which the giant company and its global reach is, at present, the most advanced structure.

David Landes in his *Unbound Prometheus* has depicted the changes in economy and society during the late nineteenth century as climacteric, seeing in them a shift from a one-nation to a multi-nation industrial system. And Eric Hobsbawm writes: 'By 1900 . . . the foundations of modern large-scale industry had been laid . . . The last major change was the increase in the *scale* of economic enterprise, the concentration of production and ownership, the rise of an economy composed of a handful of great lumps of rock – trusts, monopolies, oligopolies – rather than a large number of pebbles.'[25] Among their peers there exists general consensus that momentous changes had indeed begun to take place by the turn of the century; however, opinions differ about their historical significance.

Contemporaries were aware of the rise of large-scale enterprise, of cartels, combines and trusts, of concentration of production, capital and business organization. They observed the new phenomena, described them, theorized about them, made assumptions about the advent of a new stage of capitalism and speculated about its future trend; they voiced anxieties about excessive concentration of economic power and sought remedies for the ill effects they saw and they feared would yet ensue. How historical reality was perceived is reflected in the rising number of publications since the 1880s which during the interwar period turned into a swelling stream; above all since the 1960s literary output has become immense as journalists, politicians, sociologists, economists and historians have tried to gauge the impact of giant enterprise on the life of society. This literature itself has been historically conditioned, and in the following an attempt will be made to discuss this aspect by selecting certain writings which described the new organizations and offered explanations about the path capitalism has taken since the turn of the century.

It may seem improbable that the very first book on cartels, published in 1883, was written in the Bukowina, a backward region of the Habsburg Empire where there was hardly any large industrial enterprise, by Friedrich Kleinwächter, who as Professor at the University of Czernowitz (now Cluj in Romania) observed new developments in the industrial world. He did not conceive his book as an analysis of cartels as such but as a defence of the institution of private property in face of the demand of socialism for collective ownership. Responsibility for the social misery of his times he places not on private property but on the anarchic organization of the economy where the entrepreneur becomes a victim of the community because he is left to the vagaries of competition. Not collective property but regulation of the economy is for him the answer. He argues: as cartels (about which he gathered information by correspondence with German and Austrian entrepreneurs) aim at bringing order into the chaos caused by limitless competition and at fitting production to demand,[26] they could fulfil the function in the modern economy which guilds had in the Middle Ages.[27]

Kleinwächter's description of the first cartels, as agreements among producers to limit output and to raise prices, provides an insight into the embryonic character of the new business organization which at first covered a relatively small locality, such as a district or a town. In his book he identifies probably the oldest cartel agreement concluded in 1862 among the Rhenish producers of tinplate, but connects the real rise of cartels with the crisis of 1873 so that from the end of the 1870s their numbers increased remarkably, especially in beer-brewing and in iron production.[28] Looking back nostalgically at the 'idyllic' economy of the mediaeval guilds he attributes to cartels the capability of acting in the interests of the community, if they were legalized and controlled by the state.[29]

Parallel to the proliferation of cartel agreements, combinations and amalgamations of firms in Europe and the formation of trusts in the United States, organizations of the socialist movement experienced a rapid growth in the last three decades of the nineteenth century. And it was also during this period that Marxism fundamentally influenced the continental socialist movement. Next to the historical approach to capitalism as a socio-economic formation which has a beginning and inevitably progresses to an end, one of the pillars of Marx's analysis of capitalism is that the logical outcome of competition is the tendency to concentration and centralization of capital.[30] While the historical development of capitalism was the subject of writings by academics, as for instance in the voluminous work by Werner Sombart, *Modern Capitalism*, which examines the 'genetics' of capitalism from its birth to its 'threatening end',[31] the dynamic aspects of business development were largely ignored by contemporary economists so that in economic theory there was no important place for changes in organizational structures. All the more attention to this aspect of capitalist development was paid by socialist authors.

When in 1910 Rudolf Hilferding's *Finance Capital: A Study of the Latest Phase of Capitalist Development* appeared in Vienna it was regarded as a continuation of Marxist economic theory. Hilferding, who belonged to the Left interested in *fin-de-siècle* economic problems, viewed socio-economic developments through the eyes of the Austro-Marxist school. As one of its leading theoreticians, he was involved in debates with distinguished academic representatives of *fin-de-siècle* economic theory in Vienna, in the course of which he engaged in polemics in defence of the Marxist conception of society and social relations as a starting point in assessing economic phenomena against criticisms coming from the marginalist school which begins economic analysis with the individual.[32] Acutely aware of new facets in society, Hilferding pursued as his main aim the investigation and analysis of the 'most characteristic features of "modern" capitalism', that is, 'those processes of concentration which, on the one hand, "eliminate free competition" through the formation of cartels and trusts, and on the other, bring bank and industrial capital into an ever more intimate relationship. Through this relationship . . . capital assumes the form of finance capital, its supreme and most abstract expression.'[33] In a closely argued and documented treatment Hilferding appraises the main tendencies in the contemporary stage of capitalism: above all, the role of banks in financing joint-stock companies which stimulates the centralization of capital; this at the same time favours the growth of giant corporations which tends to lead to their eventual control of whole branches of industry nationally and internationally; he also discusses how the control over social production is increasingly put into the hands of a small number of capitalist associations which separate the management of production from ownership and can gain dominance over a large number of companies – again furthering concentration and centralization.[34] The outcome of the interweaving of bank and industrial capital, of the personal union established by interlocking directorships and the striving of large bank–industry complexes for domination of markets, spells the end of the period of free competition; it is replaced by the next stage of development which Hilferding terms 'finance capitalism'.

In later writings he returned to the concept of finance capitalism as a transitional phase which would be followed by a further stage characterized by tighter centralization and partial planning of production to mitigate its anarchic character within the capitalist system. This further phase he termed 'organised capitalism' from which the transition to a socialized economy and society could, in his opinion, be made more easily.[35]

The concept of the evolution from a capitalist to a socialist society was criticized by V. I. Lenin who nevertheless considered Hilferding's *Finance Capital* to be 'a very valuable theoretical analysis'.[36] From it and from the book by J. A. Hobson on *Imperialism*[37] he drew information for his influential publication *Imperialism, the Highest Stage of Capitalism*, because he believed that these two authors summed up the state of knowledge about the latest phase of capitalist development existing around 1912.[38]

Since the beginning of the twentieth century the term 'imperialism' had been commonly used to describe the contemporary era, which is reflected in the title Hobson gave to his book. Lenin adopted it as a sign of the time 'when the new capitalism definitely superseded the old' at the beginning of the twentieth century, 'when capitalism "grew" far more rapidly than before' and when 'competition becomes transformed into monopoly'.[39] Therefore, Lenin argues, in its 'economic essence imperialism is monopoly capitalism which grew out of competition'.[40] Writing in 1916, in the midst of the Great War, Lenin was chiefly interested in the political implications connected with the stage of development the capitalist economy had reached and how this affected social relations. Here one finds most clearly the influence of Hilferding's analysis, who establishes a link between the export of capital and the rapid expansion of capitalism which, in effect, 'leads to the expansionist policy of imperialism'.[41] Lenin argues that only in its highest stage can capitalism become capitalist imperialism when, as a consequence of concentration of economic and political power, not only world markets are divided among monopolistic capitalist associations but the world is divided among the strongest capitalist powers,[42] resulting, on the one hand, in imperialist war, and on the other, in social revolutions.[43] As to the fate of 'capitalism in transition', Lenin declares it to be 'moribund' and finds fault with Hilferding for not seeing the decay of capitalism in its final stage.[44]

Capitalism in transition also occupied the mind of the renowned economist Joseph Alois Schumpeter. A contemporary of both Hilferding and Lenin, he, like Hilferding, was confronted with the Viennese *fin-de-siècle* marginal utility theory. But he adhered neither to Marxist nor to marginal utility economic thinking. His approach to economic theory was historical as he saw 'economic life as one unique process which takes its course in historical time and in a troubled environment'.[45] Since his first book which appeared in 1911[46] Schumpeter worked on the manifold problem of the theory of economic development. With regard to the latest development of 'monopolistic competition' he remarked in 1930 that neither classical economics nor economics of marginal utility was able to provide explanations of phenomena between 'the limiting cases of perfect competition and "pure" monopoly, i.e. the whole reality of markets'.[47] Schumpeter's answer lies in his interpretation of the economic system in which the characteristic feature of capitalism is – similar to the Marxist view – the continuous revolutionizing of production the rate of which accelerated at its later stages by credit-financing of industry through specialized financial institutions. This is also the driving force propelling competitive capitalism into a monopolistic stage of the giant corporation during which capitalism engenders a new dynamic quality. Indeed, far from decaying, according to Schumpeter, the demise of capitalism will not occur because of its failures but because of its great successes which were achieved by its *primus agens*, the individual entrepreneur. With the rise of the giant company the individual entrepreneur becomes increasingly obsolete and is substituted by the managerial team – the most destructive force in Schumpeter's view – which heralds the end of capitalism.[48]

In his article on 'The Instability of Capitalism' Schumpeter considers his diagnosis of the life of capitalism 'no more sufficient as a basis for prediction than a doctor's diagnosis to the effect that a man has no cancer is a sufficient diagnosis that he will go on living indefinitely'. 'Capitalism', he writes in 1928, 'is . . . so obvious a process of transformation into something else, that it is not the fact, but only the interpretation of this fact, about which it is possible to disagree . . . Capitalism . . . will be changed . . . into an order of things which it will be merely a matter of taste and terminology to call Socialism or not.'[49]

Less theoretically and more practically directed were the researches of Robert Liefmann, Professor at Freiburg-im-Breisgau, who devoted almost half a century to the study of business organizations.[50] His books appeared in many consecutive editions which he indefatigably enlarged and revised to include the new organizations of modern enterprise as they happened, on both a national and an international scale. In chronological order they present a historical typology of organizational changes of the modern firm.[51] In 1918

Liefmann observed that the Great War significantly furthered large monopolistic organizations[52] and, as a consequence of technical innovations, which
made mass production possible, and improvements in transport, which made
mass distribution possible, the modern entrepreneur must see to it that his
machines are permanently in use to produce for the market.[53] With expanding
markets, he surmises, the significance of international cartels and trusts
increases, and competition on world markets becomes submerged at the same
time as national frontiers become blurred.[54]

Fundamentally, Liefmann regards cartels and trusts as symbols of the
'height of modern capitalism' whose contemporary stage, in view of the
financing of joint-stock companies and trading of shares and securities on the
stock exchanges, he terms 'impersonal' capitalism or *Effektenkapitalismus*.[55]
In this connection he finds Sombart's concept of 'modern capitalism',
pronounced in 1902, and Hilferding's concept of 'finance capitalism', formulated in 1909/10, related to his own thoughts about a new stage of capitalism
which he voiced in his *Beteiligungs- und Finanzierungsgesellschaften* and
which seemed to him to confirm that awareness of a new stage of capitalism
was, in the first decade of the present century, 'in the air'.[56] A few years later
he came back to this question when he disputed that this denotes a
transitional stage to socialism for, as capitalism constantly creates new
organizational structures to conform with economic change, its lifespan has
by no means been spent.[57] He realizes, however, that as large business strives
for monopoly the most likely to suffer is the consumer. Therefore, in order to
prevent the consumer from becoming the victim of monopolistic organizations, Liefmann advocates a sensible and judicious monopolies policy by
governments as neither socialization nor nationalization seem to him the best
solution of the problems connected with misuse of economic power.[58] The
ultimate remedy of social ills he sees in an extension of shareholding among
the population to enable a greater number of persons to participate in the
profits of the large enterprises.[59]

As the preceding survey has attempted to show, contemporary authors on
socio-economic phenomena of their era contributed substantially to our
knowledge of the process which set the changes in the economy and society in
motion.

By the 1920s public disquiet about the excessive concentration of economic
power and the international operations of big business was widespread and
demands for the control of large-scale enterprise became louder. Not
unconnected with this public mood was the decision taken by the League of
Nations to devote a whole section of its International Economic Conference,
which met in Geneva in 1927, to cartels. For the first time in history the
problem of amalgamations, trusts and cartels became a topic of discussion on
an international forum. Among the criticisms raised in the discussions there

were also hopes expressed for greater international co-operation of governments in controlling international combines – a hope that remained as
unfulfilled as the role of the League of Nations in preventing wars. The papers
occasioned by the World Economic Conference give 'a great background of
direct international capitalism created by the ramifications of "Concerns"'.[60]
As the most experienced long-term observer of the process of cartelization,
the task to prepare a general introduction and to publish the record of the
proceedings fell to Robert Liefmann.[61] Its content documents that post-war
rationalization – the word 'rationalization' was considered to have become a
magic formula denoting what in pre-war language was 'monopolistic organization' – went hand in hand with a formidable extension of the combination
movement, on the one hand, and with a strong public desire for concerted
legislation to curb the market power of the combines, on the other.[62]

   Much greater concern was voiced over the unprecedented concentration of
economic power in a comparatively small number of giant enterprises during
the prolonged economic crisis of the 1930s. Evidence of the greatest agglome-
ration of industrial capital came from the results of a research project on *The
Modern Corporation and Private Property* in the USA conducted by Adolf
Berle and Gardiner Means, who came to the conclusion in the early 1930s that
'we are at present passing' through a 'corporate revolution. The translation of
perhaps two-thirds of the industrial wealth of the country from individual
ownership to ownership by the large, publicly financed corporations vitally
changes the lives of property owners, the lives of workers, and the methods of
property tenure. The divorce of ownership from control consequent on that
process almost necessarily involves a new form of economic organization of
society.'[63]

   The fact that questions were being asked about the changing character of
the American corporation reflected apprehensions about the fate of individuals among a series of huge industrial oligarchies. One of the results of this
deepening apprehension was F. D. Roosevelt's initiative in appointing the
Temporary Economic Committee[64] in 1938 to investigate the concentration
of power in the US economy and to propose measures for protecting and
furthering competition. The basic assumption underlying the investigations
was that competition should be resuscitated and that the operations of
monopolistic organizations should be controlled by legislation. Thus by
contrasting competition and monopoly, the first was considered socially more
acceptable. When during the Second World War it was revealed by Congressional hearings and court proceedings against leading American and British
trusts that by conspiring with German concerns they had violated the national
interest, opposition to monopolistic practices became stronger. However, the
illusion on the part of the protagonists of a free market economy about the

return to a state that had existed in the nineteenth century was at that time, and is even more today, anachronistic.

Already Berle and Means were pointing out, as did writers mentioned above before them, that capitalism was changing rapidly. For them the most important aspect of corporate development seemed to be the rapidly spreading separation of ownership and control: 'In the case of management control, the ownership interest held by the controlling group amounts to but a fraction of the total ownership.'[65] Coming to certain speculative conclusions of their study, Berle and Means suggest that in the hands of those who exercise control over the modern corporation – that is, the managers who could develop into a 'neutral technocracy' – such enormous economic power becomes concentrated that they 'can compete on equal terms with the modern state – economic power versus political power'.[66] Means pursued the question of separation of ownership from control further in the early 1960s and suggested that capitalism changed to 'collective enterprise' in which owners, workers and consumers have been separated from direct control over the instruments of production, and management becomes the arbiter between investors, workers and consumers.[67]

While Berle and Means drew attention to the new role of management, the first writer to use the term 'managerial revolution' was James Burnham who made it the title of his book published in 1941.[68] Like previous authors, he too speaks of 'our time' as a period of transition from one type of society to another. However, he does not look only at the giant corporation but at society as a whole and predicts that capitalist society will be replaced by 'managerial society'. Reacting to Berle and Means, he disputes that ownership is separated from control but argues that 'the mechanism of the managerial revolution is the shift of ownership to the new controlling, the new dominant class' formed by the managers.[69] 'Indeed', Burnham writes, 'the development of modern industry places them in the key positions of production even before the transition to managerial society takes place. Before the managerial structure is consolidated, the managers function throughout enterprise, both private and governmental. With the consolidation of the managerial structure, which includes the state monopoly of all important enterprise, the position of the managers is assured.'[70] Burnham's theory of transition goes beyond capitalism and does not necessarily refer to the transition from one phase to another within the capitalist system, but his managerial society can also fit the case of transition from capitalism to a soviet-type system.

After the Second World War the idea of a return to free market competition as a panacea has again been taken up by politicians who have embraced the monetarist theory. As, however, the most intensive and conspicuous expansion of the giant companies has occurred since the 1960s, when also the term 'multinational corporation' came into common usage around the world, writing on this phenomenon has burgeoned.[71] The vast amount of literature has been controversial both in defence of and opposition to international business; at the same time it is evidence of the unease which like a red thread goes through previous and present publications about the increasing control of world markets by giant companies and about their relations to governments in general.[72] Yet, moral speculations about 'competition versus monopoly' or about 'controlling concentration of power to mitigate the abuse of it' are of limited value for scientific analysis.

As the process of concentration and centralization has irresistibly been taking place since the turn of the century the most rewarding approach to an understanding of the historical context of economic change has been serious empirical research. This has made impressive strides in recent times. Among the many publications some of the most comprehensive studies have come from the pen of Alfred Chandler, above all, his *The Visible Hand: The Managerial Revolution in American Industry* which has greatly influenced the course of economic and business history. In relation to the topic of this essay two points need to be made: in the first place, Chandler's giant multi-unit company representing the present form of business organization derives its strategy and structure from its response to the market; and in the second place, Chandler's researches led him to the conclusion that American capitalism in which corporate business was most advanced became from about the 1920s managerial capitalism[73] and that this stage of capitalist development has been penetrating into all advanced economies.

In historical context the present advances in business organization since the 1880s, in which the giant company stands at the centre of mass production, distribution, employment and consumption and operates in a global market, signify indeed a new stage in capitalist development. Various aspects of these changes were recognized by contemporaries and substantiated by empirical evidence in time. The vast scale of the continuing transformations in every walk of life is involving millions of people, their impact reaches the whole human society and in this sense a process of 'socialization' is taking place which qualitatively changes capitalism itself.

NOTES

1 F. H. Katayama and W. Bellis, 'The world's biggest industrial corporations', *Fortune International*, D1.

2 *The Times 300* (London, 1967); *The Times 1000, 1986–1987* (London: 1988).

3 Mikuláš Teich discusses this historical development in his article 'The scientific-technical revolution: an event in the twentieth century?', in R. Porter and M. Teich (eds.), *Revolution in History* (Cambridge, 1986), pp. 317–30.

4 A. D. Chandler, Jr and H. Daems, 'Introduction – The rise of managerial capitalism and its impact on investment strategy in the Western world and Japan', in H. Daems and H. Van der Wee (eds.), *The Rise of Managerial Capitalism* (Louvain and The Hague, 1974), p. 25.

5 I share Mira Wilkins' view that these terms are interchangeable whereas the characteristic feature of such a company at the centre of a geographically widespread combine is in most cases that direct participations in subsidiary enterprises located in different host countries are controlled and dominated from the parent company's headquarters situated in its home country. Cf. M. Wilkins, 'Modern European economic history and the multinationals', *Journal of European Economic History*, 6 (1977), 577.

6 Peter Large cites the Philips president Cornelius van der Klugt at the group's headquarters in Eindhoven, 'Philips in "global company" strategy', *Guardian*, 27 February 1987.

7 Cf. Sir James Ball, 'Mergers, takeovers and the market for corporate control', *First* (n.d.), 9–10; 'Raiders target the continent', *Sunday Times*, 7 February 1988; F. O'Boyle, 'Urge to merge stirs in board rooms of German firms', *Wall Street Journal of Europe*, 24 March 1988; 'Why the companies are taking over', *Financial Times*, 23 April 1988; 'How companies and countries fend off foreign predators', *Financial Times*, 19 May 1988; C. Lorenz, 'When the choice is buy or be bought', *Financial Times*, 31 May 1988; J. Plender, 'The choice of corporate gluttony', *Financial Times*, 21 November 1988; M. Bleackley and G. Devlin, 'Strategic alliances in highly technical industries', *Acquisitions Monthly*, March 1989, 18.

8 Figures are taken from *Acquisitions Monthly* (1988), 'What merger policies companies need from Brussels', *The Wall Street Journal*, 20 August 1988; 'Firmen-Akquisitionen/Acht Regeln für erfolgreiches Planen und Realisieren', *Handelsblatt*, 14 November 1988; 'Über tausend Fusionen im vergangenen Jahr', *Frankfurter Allgemeine Zeitung*, 4 January 1989.

9 There exists a large consensus on this periodization. For the most recent attempt to present a pattern of stages see J. Cantwell, 'The changing form of multinational enterprise expansion in the twentieth century', in A. Teichova, M. Lévy-Leboyer and H. Nussbaum (eds.), *Historical Studies in International Corporate Business* (Cambridge, 1989), pp. 15–28.

10 Cf. L. Hannah, *The Rise of the Corporate Economy* (London, 1976), pp. 105–15.

11 The biggest merger battles have been taking place in West Germany and in Britain. The dailies and weeklies have been paying great attention to these negotiations which involved the largest companies and governments. Cf. K.-H. Büschemann and Klaus-Peter Schmid, 'Unter schlechtem Stern', *Die Zeit*, 11 November 1988, 25–7; 'Siemens und General Electric wollen Plessey kaufen', *Frankfurter Allgemeine Zeitung*, 17 November 1988; W. Kratz, 'Das grosse Fressen', *Die Zeit*, 13 January 1989; 'Companies and markets', *Financial Times*, 20 January 1989; J. Jay and J. Bird, 'GEC powering into Europe', *Sunday Times*, 19 March 1989, D24; 'Raiders target the continent', *Sunday Times*, 7 February 1988; 'A Europe-wide mergers policy', *Financial Times*, 26 May 1988.

There are many examples of mega mergers in the consumer goods industries in the history of concentration and the rise of giant companies. Appropriate to this theme is the story of cigarettes told by Phil Shepherd, 'Transnational corporations and the denationalisation of the Latin American cigarette industry', in Teichova *et al.* (eds.), *Historical Studies*, pp. 201–28. To cite an example from publishing: writing about the takeover of the British publishing house Collins by the publishing empire *News International* one of Collins's editors wrote: 'It seemed to be the final demise of the independence argument. We had to look at the competition. Penguin Viking is a global operation. Random House is a global operation. Bertelmans is a global operation. Unless you are up with the big boys, you can't compete.' *Guardian*, 23 January 1989.

12 Cf. L. G. Franko, *The European Multinationals. A Renewed Challenge to American and British Big Business* (London, 1976), pp. 90–7.

13 Cf. M. Wilkins, *The Emergence of Multinational Enterprise* (Cambridge, Mass., 1970); H. C. Passer, *The Electrical Manufacturers, 1875–1900* (Cambridge, Mass., 1953).

14 H. Lindgren, *Corporate Growth. The Swedish Match Industry and Its Global Setting* (Stockholm, 1979), pp. 100–33.

15 T. Meer, *Die I. G. Farbenindustrie Aktiengesellschaft. Ihre Entstehung, Entwicklung und Bedeutung* (Düsseldorf, 1953); R. Sasuly, *I. G. Farben* (New York, 1947).

16 W. J. Reader, *Imperial Chemical Industries: A History* (London, 1971).

17 C. Wilson, *The History of Unilever* (2 vols., London, 1954).

18 'Japan's new empire', *Sunday Times*, 5 March 1989.

19 R. Atkins, 'Spending on US acquisitions "doubled"', *Financial Times*, 13 January 1988.

20 E. Landaburu, 'Foreword' in J. H. Dunning (ed)., *Multinational Enterprises, Economic Structure and International Competitiveness* (Chichester, 1985), p. xi.

21 Cf. J. H. Dunning and J. Cantwell, *IRM Directory of Statistics of International Investment and Production* (Basingstoke, 1987), tables B15 and B16.

22 For more detailed information see the contributions based on empirical research in A. Teichova, M. Lévy-Leboyer and H. Nussbaum. (eds.), *Multinational Enterprise in Historical Perspective* (Cambridge, 1986), and *idem* (eds.), *Historical Studies*.

23 A. D. Chandler, Jr, 'Technological and organizational underpinnings of modern industrial multinational enterprise: the dynamics of competitive advantage', in Teichova *et al.* (eds.), *Multinational Enterprise*, pp. 30–54.

24 M. Teich, 'Zu einigen Fragen der historischen Entwicklung der wissenschaftlich-technischen Revolution', *Jahrbuch für Wirtschaftsgeschichte*, 2 (1966), 52.

25 D. S. Landes, *The Unbound Prometheus* (Cambridge, 1969), p. 247; and E. J. Hobsbawm, *Industry and Empire* (Harmondsworth, 1969), pp. 176–7.

26 F. Kleinwächter, *Die Kartelle. Ein Beitrag zur Frage der Organisation der Volkswirthschaft* (Innsbruck, 1883), pp. 34, iv–viii, 87, 126–7.

27 *Ibid.*, p. vi.

28 *Ibid.*, pp. 138–41.

29 *Ibid.*, pp. 160–206, 244–5.

30 K. Marx, *Capital: A Critique of Political Economy*, vol. I (Chicago, 1926), pp. 685–7. The first German edition was published in 1867.

31 W. Sombart, *Der moderne Kapitalismus. Historisch-systematische Darstellung des gesamteuropäischen Wirtschaftsleben von seinen Anfängen bis zur Gegen-*

wart, 5th edn (2 vols. in 4 half-vols., Munich and Leipzig, 1922; 1st edn Berlin, 1902). The author entitled the last, 71st, chapter 'Das drohende Ende des Kapitalismus'.

32 For one of the best-known encounters see P. M. Sweezy (ed.), *Karl Marx and the Close of His System by Eugen von Böhm-Bawerk and Böhm-Bawerk's Criticism of Marx by Rudolf Hilferding* (Clifton, 1973).

33 R. Hilferding, *Finance Capital: A Study of the Latest Phase of Capitalist Development* (London, 1981), p. 21.

34 *Ibid.*, pp. 199, 367.

35 Cf. *ibid.*, p. 370; and H. A. Winkler, 'Einleitende Bemerkungen zu Hilferdings Theorie des Organisierten Kapitalismus', in Winkler (ed.), *Organisierter Kapitalismus* (Göttingen, 1974), pp. 9–18, who cites R. Hilferding, 'Arbeitsgemeinschaft der Klassen?', *Der Kampf*, 8 (1915), 322, and 'Probleme der Zeit', *Die Gesellschaft*, 1 (1924), 1–17.

36 V. I. Lenin, 'Imperialism, the highest stage of capitalism: a popular outline', in V. I. Lenin, *Selected Works in Three Volumes*, vol. I (Moscow, 1975), p. 641. First published in 1917.

37 J. A. Hobson, *Imperialism: A Study* (London, 1902).

38 Lenin, 'Imperialism, the highest stage of capitalism', 641.

39 *Ibid.*, cf. pp. 645, 649, 728.

40 *Ibid.*, p. 726.

41 Hilferding, *Finance Capitalism*, 365.

42 Lenin, definition of imperialism, 'Imperialism, the highest stage of capitalism', p. 700.

43 Lenin, 'Imperialism is the eve of the social revolution of the proletariat', *ibid.*, p. 640.

44 *Ibid.*, p. 708.

45 J. A. Schumpeter, *Beiträge zur Sozialökonomik* (Vienna, 1987), p. 368.

46 J. A. Schumpeter, *Theorie der wirtschaftlichen Entwicklung. Eine Untersuchung über Unternehmergewinn, Kapital, Kredit, Zins und Konjunkturzyklus*, 2nd edn (Munich and Leipzig, 1926; 1st edn 1911).

47 J. A. Schumpeter, 'Preface' to F. Zeuthen, *Problems of Monopoly and Economic Warfare* (London, 1930), pp. vii–xi, viii.

48 Cf. J. A. Schumpeter, *Capitalism, Socialism, and Democracy* (London, 1943), 'capitalism is being killed by its achievements', p. x, and part II, 'Can capitalism survive?' pp. 61–163. Cf. also F. März, 'The economic system of Joseph A. Schumpeter. Historical roots, theoretical structure and sociopolitical relevance', in A. Teichova (ed.) *Economic Concepts and European Thought in Historical Perspective*, Special Issue of *History of European Ideas*, 9, no. 2 (1988), 211–12.

49 Schumpeter, *Beiträge*, p. 67. From his article 'The instability of capitalism', *Economic Journal*, 38 (September 1928), 361–86.

50 R. Liefmann, *Die Unternehmerverbände* (Leipzig, 1897).

51 *Idem, Die Unternehmungsformen mit Einschluss der Genossenschaften und der Sozialisierung* (Stuttgart, 1903; 4th edn 1928); *Kartelle und Trusts und die Weiterbildung der volkswirtschaftlichen Organisation* (Freiburg-im-Breisgau, 1905), *Kartelle, Konzerne und Trusts*, 8th edn (1930); *Beteiligungs- und Finanzier-*

ungsgesellschaften. Eine Studie über den modernen Kapitalismus und das Effektenwesen in Deutschland, den Vereinigten Staaten, der Schweiz, England, Frankreich und Belgien (Jena, 1909), *Finanzierungsgesellschaften. Eine Studie über den modernen Effektenkapitalismus . . .*, 4th edn (1923). These books and their many reprints and revised and extended editions represent, as the author himself emphasizes, a complete description and categorization of modern enterprises, their fusions and their combinations (*Konzernbewegung*), Cf. *Die Unternehmungsformen* (1928), p. vi.

52 Liefmann, *Kartelle*, 3rd edn (1918), p. 16.

53 *Ibid.*, p. 29.

54 *Ibid.*, p. 16.

55 Liefmann, *Finanzierungsgesellschaften* (1923), pp. 18, 21.

56 *Ibid.*, p. 18.

57 Liefmann, *Kartelle* (1930), p. 410. In the Foreword to his 4th edition of *Unternehmungsformen* published in 1928 Liefmann claimed that for many years he had waged a struggle against socialist ideas, and he blamed economic theorists for neglecting the structure and organization of enterprise, for he maintained that only by analysing the principle of organization can Marxist theories be refuted; already before that in the 4th edition of his *Finanzierungsgesellschaften* (1923) Liefmann advocated the refutation of Marxist teaching because of the influence of 'Marx's *Kapital* das Hauptwerk dieser Lehre, das wie kein anderes wissenschaftliches Buch das politische und gesellschaftliche Leben bestimmt . . .' (pp. 2–4).

58 Liefmann, *Die Unternehmungsformen* (1928), pp. 312, 326–7.

59 *Ibid.* Liefmann cites the census of 1913 according to which only 2 per cent of the total of taxpayers in Prussia owned shares (p. 132). Cf. also Liefmann, *Kartelle* (1930), pp. 419–20. How legislation against misuse of economic power could be formulated he demonstrates by appending a decree by the Weimar government of 2 November 1923: *Verordnung gegen Missbrauch wirtschaftlicher Machtstellungen*, pp. 423–8.

60 D. H. Macgregor, 'Recent papers on cartels', *Economic Journal*, 37 (1927), 248.

61 R. Liefmann, *International Cartels, Combines and Trusts* (London, 1927).

62 Report on meeting of 10 May 1927 addressed by the Right Hon. Sir Alfred Mond, Bart, MP, 'International cartels', *Journal of the Royal Institute of International Affairs* 6 (1927), 265–83.

63 A. A. Berle, Jr and G. C. Means, *The Modern Corporation and Private Property*, 6th repr. (New York, 1937), pp. vii–viii (first published 1932).

64 Temporary National Economic Committee (TNEC), Descriptions of hearings and monographs, 31 vols. and 6 additional vols., 42 monographs (Washington, D. C., 1941).

65 Berle and Means, *The Modern Corporation*, p. 5.

66 *Ibid.*, pp. 356–7.

67 G. C. Means, 'Collective enterprise in economic theory', in Helmut Arndt (ed.), *Die Konzentration in der Wirtschaft*, 2nd edn, vol. I (Berlin, 1971), p. 97.

68 J. Burnham, *The Managerial Revolution* (Harmondsworth, 1945; first published 1941).

69 *Ibid.*, p. 83.
70 *Ibid.*, p. 234.
71 Cf. D. K. Fieldhouse, 'The multinational: a critique of a concept', in Teichova *et al.*
    (eds.), *Multinational Enterprise*, pp. 9–29.
72 This finds expression in the volumes edited by Helmut Arndt, *Die Konzentration
    in der Wirtschaft*, 2nd edn (2 vols., Berlin, 1971).
73 A. D. Chandler, Jr, *The Visible Hand: The Managerial Revolution in American
    Industry* (Cambridge, Mass., 1977), pp. 11, 483.

❧

TWO

FIN DE SIÈCLE: INDUSTRIAL TRANSFORMATION

ALFRED D. CHANDLER, JR

I

The last decades of the nineteenth century were marked by as profound a transformation in the process of production and distribution as had yet occurred in the history of mankind. During the 1880s and 1890s a surge of technological innovations swept through western Europe and the United States – innovations that reshaped existing industries and created new ones. That transformation has been properly termed by historians the Second Industrial Revolution.

The new technologies brought into being a new type of industrial enterprise, a new subspecies of economic man, a new structure of industries and a new system of capitalism. They did so because the full exploitation of these technologies required the recruitment of teams of salaried managers who participated with and increasingly replaced the owners of industrial enterprises in making decisions concerning current product and distribution and those concerning investments for future production and distribution.

The basic reason for the coming of the new managerial enterprise, the new managerial class and, therefore, what I term managerial capitalism was that the new technologies permitted for the first time in history the exploitation of the economies of scale and those of scope. That is, the new technologies permitted large production facilities to produce at lower unit costs than smaller ones.

But to benefit from those cost advantages of the new technologies, entrepreneurs had to make three sets of investments. The first was an investment in production facilities large enough to exploit a technology's potential economies of scale or scope. The second was not in production, but in building a national and international marketing and distributing network so that the volume of sales might keep pace with the new volume of production. Finally, to benefit fully from these two investments the entrepreneurs had to invest in management. They not only had to recruit and train managers to administer the enlarged facilities and personnel in both production and distribution, but also to monitor and co-ordinate those two basic functional activities and to plan and allocate resources for future production and distribution.

It was this three-pronged investment in production, distribution and management that brought into being the large managerial enterprise, the managerial class and managerial capitalism. Moreover, these industries where the new technologies offered the cost advantages of scale and scope became capital-intensive. That is, their creation and operations called for a much higher ratio of capital to labour than did the older established industries such as textiles, shoes, furniture, iron making and shipbuilding.

The powerful cost advantages of the economies of scale and scope in such capital-intensive industries can be illustrated by two well-known examples. The Standard Oil Company, one of the very first modern industrial enterprises in the United States (its successor, Exxon, is still the nation's largest oil company) provides a dramatic example of the economies of scale. The oldest and still largest German chemical companies provide as striking an example of the economies of scope.

In 1882 the Standard Oil 'alliance' formed the Standard Oil Trust. The purpose was not to obtain control over the industry's output. That alliance, a loose federation of forty companies each with its own legal and administrative identity but tied to John D. Rockefeller's Standard Oil Company through interchange of stock and other financial devices, already had a virtual monopoly.[1] The members of the alliance of that time produced 90 per cent of America's output of kerosene. Instead the Trust was formed to provide a legal instrument to rationalize the industry so as to exploit more fully economies of scale. The Trust provided the essential legal means to create a corporate or central office that could, first, reorganize the processes of production by shutting down some refineries, reshaping others and building new ones and, second, co-ordinate the flow of materials, not only through the several refineries, but from the oil fields to the refineries and from the refineries to the consumers.

The resulting rationalization made it possible to concentrate close to a quarter of the world's production of kerosene in three refineries, each with an average daily charging capacity of 6,500 barrels, with two-thirds of their product going to overseas markets. (At this time, refined petroleum products were by far the nation's largest non-agricultural export.) Imagine the diseconomies of scale, that is, the increase in unit costs, that would result from placing one-quarter of the world's production of shoes, or textiles or lumber into three factories or mills! The administrative co-ordination of the operation of miles and miles of machines and the huge concentration of labour needed to operate these machines would make no economic or social sense.

This reorganization of the Trust's refining facilities brought a sharp reduction in average cost of production of a gallon of kerosene. It dropped from 1.5 cents a gallon before reorganization to 0.54 cents in 1884 and 0.45 cents in 1885. Profit margin rose from 0.53 cents in 1884 to 1.003 cents in 1885. (That increase was the source of at least three of the largest industrial fortunes in modern times.) The costs at the giant refineries were still lower – costs far below those of any competitor. However, to maintain this cost advantage required that these large refineries have a continuing daily throughput of from 5,000 to 6,500 barrels or a three- to fourfold increase over the earlier daily flow of 1,500 to 2,000 barrels with the resulting increases in transactions handled and in the complexity of co-ordinating the flow of materials through the process of production and distribution.

In the same years that Standard Oil was investing in its large refineries to exploit the economies of scale, German dye makers were making an even larger investment to permit them to exploit fully the economies of scope. The enlarged plants came to produce literally hundreds of different dyes and in addition many pharmaceuticals from the same raw materials and the same set of intermediate chemical compounds and processes. The first three enterprises to make the investment to exploit, first, the cost advantages of scale and, then, those of scope – Bayer, Hoechst and BASF – were able to reduce the price of the new synthetic dye, red alizarin, from 270 marks per kilo in 1869 to 23 marks in 1878, and to 9 marks in 1886 *and* to make comparable price reductions in their other dyes.[2] The addition of a new dye or pharmaceutical to their total product line added little cost for the production of that dye and at the same time reduced the unit cost of the other dye products. On the other hand, each addition involved the development of a specialized product – one requiring constant supervision to assure the necessary quality. Thus each addition increased the need for organizational co-ordination.

These stories of Standard Oil and the three German chemical firms are by no means unique. Indeed in the last two decades of the nineteenth century comparable investments were made in new production technologies in nearly all the industries where the modern industrial enterprise would continue to cluster for the next century – in the refining, distilling, processing and packaging of food products, in the production of a wide variety of chemicals, rubber, glass, abrasives and other materials; in the making of steel, copper and other non-ferrous metals; and in the production of machines made through the fabrication and assembling of interchangeable parts, and also in heavier machinery, including electrical equipment, that provided the furnaces, refineries and a wide variety of processing equipment used in the many new industries.

The three-pronged investment that created the modern industrial enterprise also transformed the structure of capital-intensive industries and the nature of competition between firms in those industries. For, as soon as a handful of enterprises made such investments, they dominated their markets. Their industries quickly became and remained oligopolistic and occasionally monopolistic; for the first to make the three-pronged investment acquired powerful competitive advantages.[3] To compete with such first movers rivals had to build plants of comparable size and to make the necessary investment in distribution, and in some industries in research. They also had to recruit and train a managerial hierarchy. However, the construction of a plant of the size needed to achieve comparable economies of scale or scope often meant that the total capacity of an industry came to exceed existing demand. If newcomers were to maintain capacity utilization essential to assure competitive unit costs, they had to take customers from the first movers.

This was a challenging task. While the newcomer's production managers were learning the unique characteristics of a new or altered technology and while its sales forces were being recruited and trained, the first movers often had already begun to work out the bugs in the production processes and had taken strides in assuring prompt delivery, in meeting customers' special needs and in providing the basic marketing services. In branded packaged products, where advertising was an important competitive weapon, the first movers were already investing some of the high profits resulting from high volume throughput into massive advertising campaigns.

The first movers had other advantages. In the more technologically complex industries the first to install research laboratories and to train technicians in very product-specific development skills had a comparable advantage, one that was usually reinforced and expanded by patents obtained on both product and process. Moreover, in most of the new industries the late-comers had to make much larger initial capital outlay than did their predecessors, for they could not finance the initial increases in the scale of production or expand their marketing networks from retained earnings as could the first movers. Not only did the late-comers' investment have to be larger, but it was also riskier, precisely because of the first movers' competitive strength. Thus, the first to make the three-pronged investments were not only the first to exploit the cost advantages of scale and scope, but their head start in developing capabilities in all functional activities – production, distribution, purchasing, research, finance and general management – meant that they were often well down the learning curve in each of these functional activities before the newcomers were in full operation.

Although these barriers to entry were intimidating, newcomers did appear, particularly when new sources of supply were opened, when rapid demographic changes altered existing markets and when technological change created new markets and diminished old ones. However, in those industries where scale and scope provided cost advantages the number of major players always remained small. There was little turnover among the leaders of these capital-intensive industries between the 1890s and the 1960s.

In these industries a few large integrated firms competed for market share and profits in national and often world markets in what was a new, oligopolistic manner. That is, they no longer competed, as firms had done previously and as firms continued to do in the more fragmented labour-intensive industries, primarily on price. In the new capital-intensive industries the largest (usually the first to make the three-pronged investment in production, distribution and management) became the price leader, basing its prices on the estimates of demand in relation to its plant capacities and those of its competitors.

Although price remained a significant competitive weapon, these firms competed more forcefully for market share and increased profits through functional and strategic efficiency. That is, they competed by attempting to carry out more capably the several processes of production and distribution, by developing and improving both product and process through systematic research and development, by locating new and more suitable sources of supply, by providing more effective marketing services, by product differentiation (in branded packaged products primarily through advertising), and finally by moving more quickly into new and expanding markets and out of old and declining ones. The test of such competition was changing market share, and in nearly all the new oligopolistic industries market share and profits changed constantly.

Such competition for market share and profits tended to sharpen the capabilities of the middle managers responsible for each of the functional activities. It also tested and enlarged the skills of the top managers in co-ordinating the functional departments and in strategic planning and resource allocation. Their combined capabilities can be considered those of the organization itself. These highly product-specific and process-specific organizational capabilities and skills affected, indeed often determined, the direction and pace of the continuing growth of the industrial enterprise and of the industries and the national economies in which they operated.

II

Transformation of enterprise and industries came with surprising swiftness and came primarily in two nations – the United States and Germany. Between 1870 and the Great Depression of the 1930s three nations – Great Britain, Germany and the United States – accounted for two-thirds of the world's industrial output.[4] The output of the second two quickly surpassed that of

Great Britain, the home of the First Industrial Revolution. In 1870 Great Britain accounted for 32 per cent of the world's industrial output, the USA 23 per cent and Germany 13 per cent. For the period 1896–1900 the figures were 20 per cent, 30 per cent and 17 per cent. By 1913 Britain's share had fallen to 14 per cent; that of the United States had soared to 36 per cent; and Germany had stabilized at 16 per cent. In the 1926–9 period the figures were 9 per cent for Britain, 42 per cent for the United States and 12 per cent for Germany. What is more significant than these percentages of total output was that the output of the United States and particularly Germany was more in the new capital-intensive industries of the Second Industrial Revolution, while those of Great Britain remained in long-established labour-intensive industries. Why then did the industrial transformation begin in the last decades of the nineteenth century, and why was that transformation concentrated in the United States and Germany?

The reasons for the timing of the transformation are clear enough. The cost advantages of the economies of scale and scope in the new capital-intensive industries could only be realized by having a regular, steady, high-volume flow of materials into and processed goods out of production facilities. Such flows are only possible after the completion of modern systems of transportation, those based on the steam railroad, steamship, telegraph and cable. Transportation and communication that depended on the power of animals, wind and current was too slow, too irregular and too uncertain to permit the daily volume of output necessary to achieve the potential economies of the new technologies.

Such flows, however, required more than just the building and operating of railroad, steamship, telegraph and cable lines. They called for creating integrated systems that permitted a continuous, steady, high-volume movement of goods on schedule from hundreds of different locations to hundreds of others. On the railroads such integration required not only the standardization of tracks (that is, of gauges) and equipment, but also the development and standardization of accounting procedures such as the through bill of lading and the car accountant office that permitted fast, scheduled through freight shipments across the lines of several railroad corporations. Such standardization and integrating procedures, carried out by associations of railroad managers, accountants and engineers, were in place in both the United States and Europe by the 1880s.[5] In Europe the creation of such an international continental network was largely the work of the managers of German railroads. Thus by the 1880s entrepreneurs in the United States and Europe, particularly Germany, had the opportunity to commercialize improved and new technologies that exploited the economies of scale and scope, and so transformed existing and created new industries by making the required three-pronged investments.

One other factor stimulated the burst of technological innovation in the 1880s and 1890s. That was the coming of electricity.[6] The inventions of Thomas Edison, George Westinghouse, Elihu Thomson in the United States, Joseph Swan in Britain, and Werner von Siemens and his associates in Germany not only provided modern lighting for homes, offices and factories, and power for industrial establishments and urban transportation, but also transformed many processes of production, particularly in chemicals and metals. In metals, for example, the new electrolytic processes created a new industry – aluminium – and transformed an ancient one – copper. Nevertheless, both the new power and light systems and the factories producing equipment to generate, transmit and use electricity required the railroad and steamship to assure a steady supply of coal for the power plants and of a variety of materials needed to produce electrical equipment.

The reasons for the timing of the Second Industrial Revolution also help to explain why the new technologies were so much more successfully exploited in the United States and Germany than in Britain, the first industrial nation. For in the two continental nations the entrepreneurial opportunities created by the completion of modern transportation and communication networks and the coming of electricity for power, light and industrial processes were greater than those in Britain. In both Germany and the United States the very building of railroad and telegraph systems created new markets for machines, metals and other industrial products. In both countries the coming of the industries based on the new technologies and the rapidly growing cities continually enlarged the demand for industrial products. At the same time the rapid growth of population in the United States (that nation had the fastest rate of population growth of any major nation) and increasing per capita income provided incentives for large-scale investment in consumer goods industries. German industrialists, the major European supplier of railroad and telegraph equipment, moved as quickly as their American counterparts, into making of machinery, metals and other materials for the new industries and the growing cities in the European continent, particularly central and eastern Europe. But because per capita income in most of Europe was much less than the United States and Britain, and distribution of income was more skewed, the opportunities on the continent for investment in consumer goods was much more limited than in the United States and Britain.

On the other hand, by the 1870s Britain was already an urban, industrial economy. There railway building provided much less of a new market. The completed British network consisted of 20,000 miles of track as compared to 240,000 in the United States and over 60,000 miles in the German-supplied systems. In the 1870s established industries were still profitable and cities were growing more slowly than in the United States and in the European continent. Indeed, as T. R. Gourvish writes: 'With the basic industries well established in 1830, the railway could do little more than cement the existing patterns of settlement and industrial location.'[7] On the other hand, 'retailing was transformed' with the coming of new mass marketers – the department stores, chain stores and co-operatives. As the world's first industrial nation Britain became also the first consumer society. The triangle between London, Cardiff, Glasgow, remained from the 1850s to the 1950s the world's richest and most concentrated consumer market. Here new business opportunities came primarily in the production and distribution of branded, packaged, semi-perishable consumer products such as soap, cigarettes, chocolate, margarine, whisky and beer.

A closer look at the entrepreneurial responses to the industrial opportunities created in the three countries by the coming of modern transportation and communication and of electricity emphasizes the profound industrial transformation that occurred during the last two decades of the nineteenth century. That transformation was particularly dramatic in metals. In the United States Andrew Carnegie, a first mover in steel, completed the giant Edgar Thomson works in Pittsburgh in 1879 and obtained the nearby Homestead works in 1881 and the Duquesne works in 1891. The increasingly high throughput of these works drove down costs and with them prices. In 1880 the price of steel rails at Pittsburgh was $67.50 a ton.[8] By 1889 it was $29.95 a ton. By 1898 Carnegie's cost to produce steel rails had dropped to $11.25 a ton. In the 1880s Carnegie began to move into structures for factories and offices including the new skyscrapers. In the 1880s the application of the electrolytic process for making aluminium dropped the price of that once precious metal from $12.00 a pound to $2.00. Once Arthur Vining Davis and Alfred E. Hunt formed the Pittsburgh Reduction Company (it soon changed its name to the Aluminum Company of America) and made in the early 1890s the essential three-pronged investment in manufacturing, marketing and management the price fell to 32¢ a pound. In 1891 the adoption of electric generators powerful enough to refine copper electrolytically soon transformed that industry into a global oligopoly dominated by American first movers.

In heavy machinery American strength lay in the production and distribution of electrical equipment. Within ten years after Edison had completed the world's first central power station in New York City in 1882 the first movers – General Electric and Westinghouse – dominated American markets and were moving aggressively overseas.[9] It was, however, in light machinery mass produced through the fabricating and assembling of interchangeable parts that the Americans excelled. In sewing machines, office machines (typewriters, cash registers, adding machines, and the like) and complex agricultural machines American enterprises quickly achieved close to global monopolies. In the 1880s both Singer Sewing Machine and McCormick Harvester moved into full interchangeable parts productions. By the mid-1880s Singer's plant at Elizabethport, New Jersey and the one near Glasgow, Scotland were each producing 8,000 to 10,000 machines a week; and by 1891 McCormick's Chicago works were making over 75,000 machines a year.[10] By 1910 Singer and International Harvester (the successor to McCormick Harvester) completely dominated European markets. The latter had built a large plant in Germany and then, as had Singer, in Russia. Indeed, in 1913 subsidiaries of these two companies were the two largest commercial enterprises in Imperial Russia. In that year Singer produced 400,000 machines annually in its Moscow factory, with a workforce of 2,500 wage earners and 300 salaried employees; while its sales force of 27,439 covered the vast territory from the Sea of Japan to the Baltic.

In consumer goods American entrepreneurs led the way in the mass production of branded packaged products.[11] In 1885 Proctor & Gamble built its large soap-making machinery works in Cincinnati – a factory that became the model for William Lever's similar works in Britain. In the same year Quaker Oats, Diamond Match and James B. Duke's cigarette company built comparable mass production works. With commercializing of the new high-speed canning processes in the mid-1880s such first movers as Borden Condensed Milk, H. J. Heinz and Company, and Campbell Soup quickly invested in large plants and began to distribute nationally and internationally. In all these American industries the first movers of the 1880s and the early 1890s continued to dominate their industries for decades.

In the 1880s German entrepreneurs were responding to similar opportunities, but almost wholly those in the production of industrial goods. In steel the Krupp, Thyssen and Haniel families were building plants smaller than the Americans, but still large enough to drive the cost of steel well below that of their British and continental competitors. Indeed by the first decade of the new century, one historian has noted, German steelmakers 'produced cheaply enough to export . . . Even with free trade, Germans would have regularly imported only tin plate and special types of pig iron.'[12] In aluminium the German-financed and German-managed first mover quickly became the leading producer in Europe. In copper, Metallgesellschaft immediately adopted the new electrolytic refining processes. In order to be closer to the sources of ore and blister copper, it preferred to invest in such works in the United States rather than in Europe, and so quickly became the only non-American firm in the industry's global oligopoly.[13]

It was in heavy machinery and chemicals that the Germans developed their greatest competitive strengths. In both industries they did so by exploiting the economies of scope. In chemicals the producers of man-made dyes built during the 1880s and 1890s the huge plants that permitted them to make several hundred lines of dyes, a smaller number of pharmaceuticals, and then film from the same intermediate products and processes.[14] At the same time they established world-wide marketing and distribution organizations, for makers of thread, woven goods, apparel, shoes and other cloth and leather products had to be taught how to apply the new man-made dyes and druggists and pharmacists to use the new man-made pharmaceuticals. The industrial laboratories they established became the largest and most productive in the world; and the managers they recruited as professional as any in the world. By the turn of the century managers rather than owners made the decisions in this industry about current production and investments for the future. In non-electrical machinery German entrepreneurs built facilities that used the same metals and other semi-finished materials and the same forges, furnaces and stamping, grinding and shaping equipment to produce an extraordinary variety of machines employed in the products and processes of nearly all the new industries of the Second Industrial Revolution, and also those in a number of the older, established industries. In electrical machinery Siemens & Halske, Europe's leading producers of telegraph equipment, and Allgemeine Electricitäts-Gesellschaft (AEG) formed in 1883 had by the end of the century created enterprises that competed effectively in global markets with General Electric and Westinghouse. These four giants continued to dominate the global oligopoly in electrical equipment until well after the Second World War.

British entrepreneurs soon found themselves unable to compete with American and German first movers in chemicals, machinery, metals and other new or transformed industries. So British industrial activities continued to be concentrated in the older labour-intensive industries such as textiles and shipbuilding. Only in the production of branded packaged products were they able to hold their own in the newer industries. In chemicals, for example, British entrepreneurs had pioneered in developing man-made dyes. The British textile industry long remained the world's largest market for dyes. Dyes were made from high-grade coal of which Britain had a larger, more available supply than did Germany. Nevertheless, British dye makers failed to make the essential three-pronged investment in production, distribution and management. So by 1913, of the 160,000 tons of dyes produced, 140,000 were made in Germany. (Bayer, BASF and Hoechst accounted for 77 per cent of this output.)[15] Three Swiss neighbours produced 10,000 tons and the British pioneers 4,000 tons. In the other most technologically advanced industry of the day – electrical equipment – two-thirds of the British output produced in the British factories just prior to the First World War was made by the subsidiaries of General Electric, Westinghouse and Siemens.[16] In steel by 1913 British producers had not only lost the European markets to the Germans (who, except in Germany itself, had to pay the same tariffs as did the British), but also those in Latin America and Asia.[17] By then Britain was importing steel (15 per cent of the world's steel exports). Of these imports 58 per cent came from Germany, the rest from Belgium and the United States. In copper no British enterprise ever made the investment necessary to compete in the global oligopoly with Metallgesellschaft and the four American leaders. The one British aluminium producer never became more than a secondary player in its global oligopoly.

By the turn of the century, therefore, the largest industrial enterprises in the world's first industrial nation were not producing metals, machinery or chemicals. Instead they were makers of branded packaged products such as Lever Brothers (now Unilever) in soap, Ricketts & Sons in starch and blueing, Distillers Ltd in whisky, Guinness in beer and Cadbury in chocolates.[18] Of all the new capital-intensive industries, those producing branded packaged products used the simplest technologies of production, enjoyed the smallest economies of scale and scope, and required the lowest product-specific investment in marketing and distribution. And in branded packaged products industries only a tiny number of British companies adopted before the 1930s the high-speed canning processes commercialized in the United States in the 1880s.

III

The evolution of the modern industrial enterprise in Britain differs from that in the United States and Germany not only because fewer obvious entrepreneurial opportunities resulted from the transportation and communication revolution and the coming of electricity, but also because of the predilections of British entrepreneurs to retain personal and then family management of their enterprises. They disliked the weakening of control that could result from the making of the large investments in production and distribution essential for competing abroad and even at home. They hesitated to turn even part of the management of their enterprises to non-family salaried managers. In sharp contrast with their American and German counterparts, they rarely elected salaried managers – to whom they had given the term, company servants – to their boards of directors. Precisely because the production of branded packaged products enjoyed smaller economies of scale or scope and required less in the way of investment in production and distribution, the family firm was able to continue to compete at home and to some extent abroad. Even in the few other capital-intensive industries where family enterprises did make the investment needed to compete internationally – Pilkington Brothers and Courtaulds are examples – the owning family was reluctant to recruit large managerial hierarchies. And both Pilkington and Courtaulds suffered in international competition from a lack of managerial strength.[19]

As a result of the combination of less obvious entrepreneurial opportunities and an unwillingness of British entrepreneurs to make the investments required to compete, Britain became in many of the new or transformed capital-intensive industries 'a late industrializer', to employ Alexander Gerschenkron's widely used term. During the interwar years enterprises in some of these industries were able to catch up and to compete in the existing oligopolies; but they did so only after entrepreneurs and enterprises made the essential three-pronged investment in manufacturing, marketing and management. This was done in chemicals by Imperial Chemical Industries, in oil by Anglo-Persian Oil (now British Petroleum), in rubber by Dunlop, in canning machinery by Metal Box, in steel tubes by Stewarts & Lloyds, and in records and radio by Electrical & Musical Industries (EMI).[20] In the 1930s Pilkington and Courtaulds regained their earlier strength by improving their facilities and enlarging their managerial hierarchies. In the 1920s British automobile firms began to challenge American first movers, and British electrical equipment companies began to challenge both American and German first movers in British markets and in those of the Empire; but they failed to develop the organizational strength necessary to remain long-term players in international markets.

Because British industrialists failed to make the investments and to recruit the managers needed to exploit the technologies of the Second Industrial Revolution, Great Britain remained a bastion of personal capitalism well after Germany and the United States had begun to move towards managerial capitalism. In Germany, as in the United States, founding entrepreneurs in the new capital-intensive industries recruited sizeable teams of managers. In Germany, however, the founders and large investors continued to share top management decisions longer than was the case in large American industrial enterprises. In France and southern Europe the relationship between owners and managers remained closer to that in Britain, while those of central and northern Europe became closer to that of Germany.[21]

After the Second World War European enterprises became increasingly managerial, much as a few leading British firms had done during the interwar years. The Japanese firms that moved into the global oligopolies in the 1960s and 1970s were even more management-intensive than the pre-war American enterprises. By the 1960s the managerial enterprise and managerial capitalism had become the norm in major capital-intensive industries. The structure of industrial enterprises, the ways in which they competed and continued to grow, the structure of the industries in which they operated, the impact they had on competitive abilities and long-term growth of the nations in which they were based – all these ways of modern industrial organization had their beginnings in the last years of the nineteenth century. They are among the most significant legacies of the many *fin-de-siècle* transformations that ushered in a new age in the west.

NOTES

1 A. D. Chandler, Jr and R. S. Tedlow, *The Coming of Managerial Capitalism: A Casebook on the History of American Economic Institutions* (Homewood, Ill., 1985), pp. 346–60, summarizes the Standard Oil story. This review of Standard Oil and the leading German chemical firms follows closely one first given in my 'The emergence of managerial capitalism', *Business History Review*, 58 (Winter 1984), 479–84.

2 J. J. Beer, *The Emergence of the German Dye Industry* (Urbana, Ill., 1959), p. 119; L. F. Haber, *The Chemical Industry during the Nineteenth Century* (Oxford, 1958), pp. 128–36. S. Kaku, 'The development and structure of the German coal-tar dyestuff firms', in A. Okochi and H. Uchido (eds.), *Development and Diffusion of Technology* (Tokyo, 1979), p. 78.

3 This analysis of first mover advantages follows closely the statement given in chapter 2 of my *Scale and Scope: The Dynamics of Industrial Capitalism* (Cambridge, Mass., 1990).

4 W. W. Rostow, *The World Economy: History and Prospect* (Austin, Tex., 1978), table 11:2, pp. 52–3.

5 For the United States see A. D. Chandler, Jr, *The Visible Hand: The Managerial Revolution in American Industry* (Cambridge, Mass. 1977), pp. 124–33. For Germany see *Scale and Scope*, ch. 9.

6 The significance of electricity is reviewed in *Scale and Scope*, chs. 3, 7, 9 and 12.

7 T. R. Gourvish, *Railways and the British Economy, 1830–1914* (London, 1980), pp. 30–1.

8 P. Temin, *Iron and Steel in Nineteenth-Century America: An Economic Inquiry* (Cambridge, Mass., 1964), pp. 170–5, 179–83; Chandler, *The Visible Hand*, pp. 259–66. For aluminium see G. Smith, *From Monopoly to Competition: The Transformation of Alcoa, 1886–1986* (New York and Cambridge, 1988), chs. 1–3; for copper my *Scale and Scope*, ch. 4.

9 H. F. Passer, *The Electrical Manufacturers, 1875–1900* (Cambridge, Mass., 1953), ch. 20.

10 Chandler, *The Visible Hand*, pp. 305–7; F. V. Carstensen, *American Enterprise in Foreign Markets: Studies of Singer and International Harvester in Imperial Russia* (Chapel Hill, N. C., 1984), pp. 65, 80, 193–5, 208. Particularly useful on the dominance of American light machinery firms in Germany, the home of Europe's most sophisticated machinery production, is F. Blaich, *Amerikanische Firmen in Deutschland 1890–1918: US – Direktinvestitionen im deutschen Maschinenbau* (Wiesbaden, 1984).

11 Chandler, *The Visible Hand*, pp. 290–9.

12 S. B. Webb, 'Tariffs, cartels, technology, and the German steel industry, 1879–1914', *Journal of Economic History*, 40 (1980), 310, 312. The German story is reviewed in *Scale and Scope*, ch. 12.

13 The story of Metallgesellschaft is reviewed in *Scale and Scope*, ch. 12.

14 The histories of the leading German chemical, electrical and non-electrical machinery are also covered in *Scale and Scope*, ch. 12.

15 L. F. Haber, *The Chemical Industry 1900–1930: International Growth and Technological Change* (Oxford, 1971), pp. 121, 123, 145.

16 I. C. R. Byatt, *The British Electrical Industry 1875–1914: The Economic Returns of a New Technology* (Oxford, 1979), pp. 150–2. In addition, imports of electrical equipment from Germany largely from AEG, rose from £121,000 in 1904 to £348,000 in 1910.

17 P. Temin, 'The relative decline of the British steel industry, 1880–1913', in H. Rosovsky (ed.), *Industrialization in Two Systems* (New York, 1966), p. 148.

18 As told in *Scale and Scope*, chs. 7 and 9.

19 D. C. Coleman, *Courtaulds: An Economic and Social History*, vol. II, *Rayon* (Oxford, 1969), pp. 232–3; and T. C. Barker, *The Glassmakers – Pilkington – the Rise of an International Company, 1826–1976* (London, 1977), ch. 19.

20 The details on these companies are given in *Scale and Scope*, chs. 8 and 9.

21 France, the fourth largest industrial producer, like Britain, fell behind the United States and Germany. In 1870 France accounted for 10 per cent of the world's industrial output. From the late 1890s to the end of the 1920s it accounted for from 6 to 7 per cent of output: Rostow, *World Economy*, p. 52. The story of the modern industrial enterprise in France is concisely told in M. Lévy-Leboyer, 'The large corporation in modern France', in A. D. Chandler, Jr and H. Daems (eds.), *Managerial Hierarchies: Comparative Perspectives on the Rise of the Modern Industrial Enterprise* (Cambridge, Mass., 1980), ch. 4.

THREE

✌

THE ELECTRICAL CENTURY: THE
BEGINNINGS OF ELECTRICITY
SUPPLY IN AUSTRIA

ROMAN SANDGRUBER

The late nineteenth century was characterized by the spread of three new forms of power supply: mineral oil, gas and electrical energy. As a result of the technical advancements which it induced and the structural changes which resulted from it, electricity was undoubtedly the most successful of these new energy forms for further economic, social and cultural developments. The immediate consequences associated with the use of electrical power range from the easy handling of light and dark, the new perception of lightness and the banishment of darkness from the streets, from shop windows, dwellings and factories to the new rhythms at home and at work, as well as the changes in housework and leisure habits brought about by the new equipment and technology. On the one hand, there was the increasing social entwinement and interlacement of society, as well as the growing trend towards monopolization. On the other hand, there were the new opportunities offered by decentralization with their effects on the competitiveness and productivity of small and medium-sized companies, on the location of the works, the internal organization of work (assembly line, horizontal arrangement, greater flexibility) and the creation of innumerable new products which, taken as a whole, introduced a new phase of economic growth on a new wave of industrialization.[1] The half-century between 1880 and 1930 represented the constituent years in the history of the electrical power supply system: an enormous network of power lines came to criss-cross the industrial society.

The indirect consequences, especially in the fields of communications, regulation and control engineering, have by no means been fully exhausted or assessed. Not only was the traditional organizational structure of factory production – i.e. the arrangement of moving machines, transmission mechanisms and machine tools – turned completely upside-down by electricity. It was also supplemented by a fourth, fully new element: the control system.[2]

Experiments with electrical current were started in the seventeenth and eighteenth centuries. As in so many cases, the application of electricity began as a pastime or pleasure. Among the small delights of the gallant age was, for example, the sight of 180 soldiers of Ludwig XV's guard or 200 Carthusian monks linked together by wire. To amuse the court society, they were given a proper fright and made to jump as if on command or demonstrate the 'electrical kiss'. For physical reasons, however, this was never successful because the spark which sprang over would cause even the most courageous cavalier to shrink back before contact was made.[3] Around 1800, a professor of physics pitched his tent in the Prater, Vienna's famous amusement park, and demonstrated electrical experiments on payment of a fee.

The nineteenth century, the great century of mechanics and thermo-dynamics, saw the decisive research and development work on electricity, which at the beginning was only remotely linked with economic requirements of any kind. The first business requirement which electricity helped to meet was created by the railways. Here there was a need for an efficient and fast-acting system of information: the solution was the telegraph. Telegraphy had been a central feature of information transmission since the middle of the nineteenth century. In the case of the telephone, there was practically no demand for it before it was discovered. The situation was similar with wireless communication. Beforehand, nobody had given the remotest consideration to such a possibility. In 1831 Faraday's transformation of mechanical movement into electrical current completed the series of scientific discoveries necessary for the industrial generation of electrical energy. Nevertheless, fifty years were still to pass before his discovery could actually be put to use. At that time, there was no real demand for electricity and, in turn, because there was no supply of electricity available, no equipment which could have used this power in any quantity.

Electrical power was first used industrially in the 1830s and 1840s for electro-silver plating. This encouraged improvements to be made to the generators. Then the lead was taken over by electric lighting with arc lamps. However, arc lamps were only suitable for applications demanding strong light. It was not until the invention of the incandescent lamp and, with it, the possibility of parcelling out light into small amounts, that electricity became a genuine consumer good. As a consumer goods industry, it made a major contribution to the great prosperity of the 1890s. The investment goods industry followed suit: with railways, with electro-chemical and metallurgical processes, and with engines.[4]

The upturn in the Austrian electrical power and equipment industries began in the mid-1880s. At the opening of the Vienna Electricity Exhibition in 1883, Crown Prince Rudolf coined the idea of a 'sea of light' which would spread from Austria across the whole world, and spoke of the progress which could be expected to ensue from it.[5] Although many things tend to take longer in Austria, it was not long before foreign companies were playing a dominant role in the electrification of the country. No one has better described the Austro-Hungarian monarchy than Robert Musil.[6] Lifts, electric light, modern mechanical aids – the old Emperor, Franz Joseph, mistrusted them all. A brief conversation which he held with the Mayor of Gastein during the opening of the Tauern railway is typical of the style of this monarch: 'Much is being done, particularly with a view to improving this health resort?' – 'Yes, your Majesty. Last year, we installed a new water main and, this year, we are getting electric light.' –'So', came the incredulous reply, 'electric light, too!'[7]

Perhaps he presaged that his kind would be swept away by this new age. As Count Chojnicki says in the book by Joseph Roth:

'We are the last of a world in which God still bestows grace on majesties while lunatics such as I make gold. Do you hear? Look!' And Chojnicki rose, went to the door, turned a switch and the lamps sparkled from the chandelier. 'Look!' said Chojnicki. 'This is the age of electricity, not of alchemy. Chemistry, too. Don't you understand? Do you know what that thing is called? Nitroglycerine', he said emphasizing every syllable individually. 'Nitroglycerine' he repeated. 'No more gold! In Franz Joseph's castle, they still burn candles! Don't you see? Nitroglycerine and electricity mean the end for us! It won't take much longer, not very much longer!'[8]

Electric lighting was something that left a lasting impression on everybody. 'On arriving in Berlin', reported Arthur Schnitzler, 'I stayed at the recently opened Hotel Continental where, for the first time, I had a room with electric light. In 1888, this was still something rather new – not only for me but for the whole population of Central Europe.'[9] The absence of the fumes which used to be caused by the pinewood splinters and gas light delighted contemporaries. In the second half of the nineteenth century, soot was a much discussed subject not just in London but also in Vienna. It was comfort, however, for which particular praise was reserved.[10]

The revolution in public and private lighting – which, beginning with the Argand lamp, followed with gas lighting and reached its initial high point with arc lamps and light bulbs – had consequences that we are no longer conscious of because they are so much a part of everyday life today. It is an expression of the release from the restraints of darkness, as well as a symbol of increased state supervision. After all, it was for good reason that the street lamps were always the first target of revolutionary activities in the nineteenth century.[11]

Artificial light provides improved vision. It means more information – and loss of anonymity. Light takes away intimacy. Artificial light made possible a complete reversal of the established order, firstly as a social privilege of the upper classes. For members of the baroque court society, life only really began at night. If the night sparkled through enchanting festive illuminations, it could become the setting for a second life, far removed from the harsh reality of day. The later someone could start his or her day, the higher was their standing in society.[12]

Festive illuminations were an essential part of all baroque spectaculars, for the monarch's birthday celebrations as well as for royal marriages and births.[13] The tradition of such illuminations remained intact until the end of the monarchy. At the celebrations for the marriage of Franz Joseph and Elisabeth on 29 April 1854, the whole of the *Hauptallee* (main boulevard) of the Prater was illuminated while a huge electric sun shone from the middle of the *Rondeau*.

The year 1886 not only marked the start of the electrical era in Austria, it was also the year in which the Austrian Auer von Welsbach invented the incandescent gas lamp, an innovation which represented a decisive improvement over the previous gas lighting. Because the incandescent gas lamp cost only a fifth to a sixth of the price of an electric lamp, von Welsbach's invention once again made gas lighting a serious competitor for electricity. The existence of powerful gas companies, which wanted to amortize their plants, was a serious obstacle to the expansion of electrical power supply in the big cities. Hence, the electrification of Graz – which had been started by the Viennese Gas Industry Company (*Wiener Gasindustriegesellschaft*) – remained restricted to a quite inadequate direct current network until well into the First Republic.[14]

Before the First World War, the light of the poor man was neither gas nor electricity. Up to 1914, the number of household connections and the extent of electrification in Vienna and Austria was extremely limited. In 1900 only 8.6 per cent of Viennese apartments were connected to the gas supply and only 2.9 per cent could boast an electrical connection.[15] People saved on everything that could be regarded as a luxury: electricity from more than one light bulb, gas and water, a full bath, a bathtub or a gas water-heater. At that time, personal hygiene was dominated by the washstand with washbasin and bucket.

In the interests of more rational household management, women wanted above all more adequate home amenities. According to a survey conducted in 1930, 18 per cent of working women in Vienna had neither electric light, nor gas, nor water in their apartments. Exactly the same percentage had all three. Only a fifth had running water in their homes. Roughly half had gas and almost a third electricity. 'Petroleum lamps and candles are still burnt, the stove must be lit every day and water brought continuously from the staircase.' Among Vienna's working women, the definition of luxury was a municipal apartment with running water, light and gas. However, only 10 per cent of those interviewed actually lived in such a municipal dwelling.[16]

Electricity promised ease of use, a broad spectrum of applications and a host of benefits. Electric motors were smaller and handier than any previous engines. As small motors, they were even suitable for use in private households so that a start could be made on mechanizing them. In his book *Women and Socialism* (1909), August Bebel enthused about an electrical paradise of the future (*Elektrokultur*). However, although they had already been conceived in the late nineteenth century, it was not until after the Second World War that household appliances powered by electricity – such as vacuum cleaners, washing machines, irons, electric cookers and dishwashers – made an appearance in larger quantities.[17]

Rational housekeeping was the new catchword from America. Taylorism conquered the kitchen. Electrical appliances became the new leitmotifs. The catalogue of the 'New Household', a very well attended exhibition in Vienna in 1925, shows a kitchen sink instead of a water tub, a gas or electric iron instead of a heated steel insert (*einschiebbares Stahl*), a dish-drying device instead of a dishcloth, an icebox or a modern refrigerator instead of the cold storage area in the basement, not to mention a vacuum cleaner instead of a broom, electric heating and a warm-water heater. Another thirty years were to pass before all of this became reality for working-class households.[18]

Gas engines, internal combustion engines and electric motors were the new forms of industrial motive power which entered into competition with the water wheel and steam engine at the end of the nineteenth century. The advantages of the internal combustion engine lay in its mobility, in the low weight of the engine and the fuel, and also in the ease with which the fuel could be fed automatically into the engine: it saved the fireman. Gas as an energy carrier could also be distributed automatically. However, the investment required was enormous. As a secondary form of energy, electricity combined the possibility of transportation without significant losses – even over long distances – with the extreme flexibility of being able to be transformed effectively into other forms of energy such as heat, light and motive power.

These new engines changed the face of factories. They meant that the motor could now be attached to the tool, thus making the assembly line and the Taylor system possible. Thanks to arc lamps, the big halls became as light as day. The structure of the buildings and the work flows had to be adapted to the new, individual drives: flat, long-stretched-out halls replaced the five- and six-storey factories characteristic of the nineteenth century. Completely new big businesses developed out of the gas works, electrical engineering firms and electricity companies.

A steam engine could only power an area of a relatively few square metres because transmission over longer distances was expensive and uneconomical.

To operate efficiently, a gas works needed monopoly rights over a large supply area. This was even more true of the supply area of an electricity power station, which covered several square miles. Electric power supply companies are almost by necessity monopolistic businesses. The end of the energy-supply independence of the individual home had arrived, and that of the small commune was already in sight after 1918.

The majority of large-scale enterprises, however, produced their own electricity so that, for the electric power supply companies, small customers were much more important at first. Small-scale industry became the mainstay of the infant electricity industry. On the other hand, electricity can be divided up into small units. Internal combustion engines and electric motors gave a new impulse to the decentralized home and workshop industry, with a new division of labour between small and big companies. Naturally, it was not possible to speak of a predominance of electric motors in small enterprises in 1902, the result primarily of an inadequate supply network. Even though it had the densest network of power stations, not even Vienna could boast a large number of electric motors in small workshops. It was not until after the turn of the century that the increased construction of municipal and district power stations contributed to the widespread use of electric motors. In Vienna between 1902, when the municipal power station was put into operation, and 1913, the number of electric motors in the manufacturing crafts and in industry supplied with electricity from central power stations, rose from 1,366 to 19,076, i.e. about fourteen times as many. In the clothing industry, a trade dominated by small firms, the number shot up by a factor of 20. The trend towards electric motors was most pronounced in Vienna while, outside urban centres, municipal power stations were much slower in coming.[19]

In agriculture, the use of electricity involved many difficulties. At the beginning, only a few machines (bruising mills, straw cutters and threshing machines) were suitable for use with stationary electric motors. However, owing to their peak power requirements, they constantly overloaded the inadequately dimensioned power lines. Furthermore, the decentralized structure of agriculture meant that installing a supply network was very expensive. Hence, electrification in rural areas moved ahead only slowly and, at first, was often restricted to lighting.

In the field of transportation, electrification did not produce the results predicted in the euphoria of the pioneer years. As early as 1883–4, there was an electric tram running between Mödling and Vorderbrühl. A study published in 1891 proposed an electric railway for the Vienna to Budapest line with a maximum speed of 250 km per hour. In 1900 electric cars seemed to have a great future, with double as many electric vehicles being produced in the USA as petrol-driven versions. Despite all of these positive signs, little progress was made in the electrification of transportation with the exception of the tram where, for environmental reasons, there were difficulties with steam power and a direct transition took place from horses to electricity.[20]

A number of Austrian companies, e.g. Krupp in Berndorf, Schindler in the Voralberg town of Kennelbach and Werndl in Styria, had already made a start on their own electricity supply at the beginning of the 1880s. When it comes to municipalities, however, it is the little town of Scheibbs in Lower Austria that holds the title of pathfinder, after the electricity station for the festive lighting – in which the local male voice choir had indulged itself to celebrate its 25th anniversary on 18 July 1886 – was taken over by the Town Council in a festive act on 10 November following several months of trial operations. This was extremely early because it was only four years previously that Edison had opened the world's first power station in New York. In Austria, Scheibbs's example was followed by Salzburg in 1887. However, it was not until 1889 that the capital, Vienna, followed suit. In 1890 there were six electricity works in Austria. Bregenz started work on the installation of an electricity network in 1891, Graz in 1894, Linz in 1898 and Klagenfurt in 1902. By 1907, there were 188 power stations within the boundaries of present-day Austria. By the end of 1914, the number had climbed to 358 and, by 1928, to a total of 627.[21]

The municipal electricity stations in Vienna were built by a variety of different companies founded in 1887, 1889, 1890 and 1901. Up to 1924, the communes and industrial plants were served primarily by individual electricity works. It was only in Upper Austria and Styria that a limited form of group supply developed in the early years of the twentieth century. A serious attempt to provide a uniform electricity supply in a larger area was made in Lower Austria in 1907, when it was decided to build the power station Wienerbruch an der Erlauf and a diesel power station in St Pölten as a reserve. The primary task of the latter was to supply current to the Mariazell Railway, as well as the villages and enterprises along the railway line. Construction was prevented by the First World War.

The integration of the individual power-supply plants into a uniform electricity network did not get under way until after the First World War.[22] Before 1914, electricity was primarily produced by burning coal. However, with the disintegration of the Austro-Hungarian Empire and the loss of the coal resources in the Czech Lands, water power came to hold a position of greater significance in the minds of the energy experts.[23] Indeed, many sides doubted that the new state could even survive for long. One of the main arguments put forward time and again by the doubters was Austria's lack of coal. In 1918 the railways had to stop running almost all passenger trains because of a coal shortage and restrict freight traffic to food transports.

Coal for home use had to be stopped completely. In Upper Styria, the blast furnaces had to be extinguished. The industry and the economy of the new republic could only be kept running through the import of a large quantity of fuel. In 1920 coal imports accounted for a seventh of all imports into Austria.[24]

In view of this dependence on foreign resources, it was only too natural that attention should have been focused on the wealth of water in Austria and its potential economic significance. Hence, an 'Office for Water and Electricity Supply and Distribution' (*Wasser- und Elektrizitätswirtschaftsamt*) was set up in January 1919. This was followed in March of the same year by the foundation of the 'Office for Electrification of the State Railways' (*Elektrifizierungsamt bei den Staatsbahnen*). In this way, it was hoped to counter regional particularism in the field of water and electricity supply and distribution, as well as create a stable basis for financing the massive investments involved. As rich as the new Austria was in potential reserves of water power, it was equally poor in installed capacity.

Although Austria's big banks had maintained their investments in Czechoslovak coal mining after 1918, they could not be interested in financing a large-scale programme of expansion for Austrian hydro-electricity. Hence, in comparison with the ambitious plans of the immediate post-war years, the actual growth of power between 1918 and 1938 was extremely modest. In 1928 there were 627 electricity companies in Austria with a total average annual output of 943,660 kW. More than half of this total output was generated by nine power stations. Of all electricity power stations, 59 per cent were driven by water and 28 per cent by steam. The rest were powered by other forms of energy. In 1929 the construction of power stations was practically at a standstill. Even the electrification programme of the railways was stopped. Despite the high level of employment, the fall in the price of imported coal made the economic exploitation of water power and the electrification of the railways appear pointless.

Although electrification opened up completely new possibilities for using energy, the consumption of all forms of energy in Austria did not rise during the interwar years. On the one hand, improvements in the converters (steam engines, turbines, generators) resulted in an increase in the effective output of electricity while, on the other hand, the structure of production had shifted to less energy-intensive branches of industry. There were no new energy consumers in the consumer-goods sector. Additionally, because it was restricted almost exclusively to lighting and hardly any energy-intensive household appliances found their way into Austrian homes during the interwar years, the electrification of Austrian households did not lead to any significant increases in electricity consumption.

On the whole, the interwar years were less characterized by large-scale investments in energy production than by energy-saving measures and a rearrangement of the country's industrial structure which was too energy-intensive. The gross national product was approximately the same in 1937 as in 1929 but energy consumption fell by roughly 30 per cent in that period.

Following the 'Anschluss' of Austria into the Third Reich, Austria's energy reserves were subordinated to the needs of National Socialist policy and expansion forged ahead.

The construction of power stations begun or continued after the Second World War was in sharp contrast to that of the interwar years. The Glockner-Kaprun power station in the Tauern mountains became the mighty symbol of Austria's determination to rebuild after 1945. A pioneer feeling prevailed in the barracks of the building workers. Between 1947 and 1985, electricity consumption in Austria rose by a factor of 12. The annual rates of growth which amounted to over 10 per cent in the 1950s have now fallen back to around 3 per cent. Given this enormous expansion, it is interesting how respectable was the prediction made by an expert in 1910 of the consumption of electrical energy in 1970: his estimate of 7.87 billion kW against actual consumption of 24.6 billion kW.

The expectations of electricity held at the beginning of the twentieth century are best characterized by Lenin's well-known pronouncement: 'Communism is Soviet power plus the electrification of the whole country.' This has a variety of meanings, not all of which could have been appraised by Lenin: electrification created a wave of productivity increases and economic growth. However, although it opened up the possibility of technical progress to small enterprises, it also boosted the trend towards industrial concentration and monopolization, increased the access of the community and the state to the private sphere and paved the way for comprehensive instruments of super-vision and manipulation.

Although it was meant differently, what Krzhizhanovsky, Lenin's adviser on power questions and a pioneer of Soviet industrialization, wrote in 1929 has acquired a new, oppressive topicality: 'The age of steam is the age of capitalism. The age of electricity is the age of socialism. The age of the exploitation of the internal energy of the atom is the age of developed communism.'[25]

Symbolized by the kitchen stove around which the family gathered, the whole house of old European society had collapsed. Gas and electricity are symbolic of the collapse of this 'whole house' which now became dependent on a central system of supply for lighting, cooking, heating and many other household activities and functions. The end of the symbolic significance of the stove fire was given visible expression by the transition from open fire to electric cooker, by the end of the formal independence of the house with its connection to the gas, water and electricity networks.

Electricity interlinks society, creates dependency on a central system of supply and opens up new perspectives for the future, which can also offer the house new functions and significance. Parallel to that of the nineteenth century, the modern vision is of the new information technologies bringing work into the home instead of workers into factories (a nightmare for trade unionists), the landscape into the home instead of the people into the landscape, the conference on to the monitor screen instead of in conference centres. Indeed, few other developments if any during the last hundred years can be compared with electricity in the close interrelation between social and economic factors on the one hand, and scientific and technical ones on the other.

NOTES

1 T. P. Hughes, *Networks of Power, Electrification in Western Society, 1880–1930* (Baltimore, Md, 1983); L. Wolfgang, *Geschichte der Elektrizitätswirtschaft in Württemberg*, vol. I, *Grundlagen und Anfänge* (Stuttgart, 1982); H. Lindner, *Strom, Erzeugung, Verteilung und Anwendung der Elektrizität* (Reinbeck, 1985); H. Ott *et al.*, 'Historische Energiestatistik am Beispiel der öffentlichen Elektrizitätsversorgung Deutschlands', *Vierteljahrschrift für Sozial- und Wirtschaftsgeschichte*, 68 (1981), 325–48; W. Schivelbusch, *Lichtblicke. Zur Geschichte der künstlichen Helligkeit im 19. Jahrhundert* (Munich, 1983); J. Steen (ed.), *Die Zweite Industrielle Revolution. Frankfurt und die Elektrizität 1800–1914* (Frankfurt, 1981).

2 M. Teich, 'Zu einigen Fragen der historischen Entwicklung der wissenschaftlich-technischen Revolution,' *Jahrbuch für Wirtschaftgeschichte 1966*, 2, 34ff.

3 J. Teichmann, 'Frühe Experimente', pp. 1ff, Joseph Braunbeck, 'Das elektrische Jahrhundert', pp. 17ff, in *Lichtjahre. 100 Jahre Strom in Österreich* (Exhibition Catalogue, Vienna, 1986).

4 *100 Jahre Elektrotechnik. Zum 100. Jahrestag der Gründung des österreichischen Verbandes für Elektrotechnik*, published by the Technisches Museum Wien (Vienna, 1983); H. Sequenz, 'Die erste elektrische Kraftübertragung bei der Wiener Internationalen Ausstellung im Jahre 1873', in *Elektrotechnik und Maschinenbau* 84, no. 9 (1967), 377–9.

5 *Elektrizitätsausstellung 1883* (catalogue, reports); A. von Urbanitzky, *Die elektrischen Beleuchtungsanlagen* (Vienna, 1883); *idem, Die Elektrizität im Dienste der Menschheit* (Vienna, 1885).

6 R. Musil, *Der Mann ohne Eigenschaften* (Hamburg, 1952).

7 G. Stadler, *Von der Kavalierstour zum Sozialtourismus. Kulturgeschichte des Salzburger Fremdenverkehrs* (Salzburg, 1975).

8 J. Roth, *Radetzkymarsch*, 7th edn (Nördlingen, 1988), p. 56.

9 A. Schnitzler, *Jugend in Wien* (Vienna, 1968); Viktoria Arnold, '*Als das Licht kam'. Erinnerungen an die Elektrifizierung* (Vienna, 1986).

10 I. Schnitzer, *Die Elektriker*, Operetta (1906).

11 Schivelbusch, *Lichtblicke*, pp. 81ff.

12 R. Sandgruber, 'Zeit der Mahlzeit. Veränderungen in Tagesablauf und Mahlzeiten-einteilung in Österreich im 18. und 19 Jahrhundert', in *Wandel der Volkskultur in Europa, Festschrift G. Wiegelmann* (Münster, 1988), pp. 459ff.

13 R. Alewyn, *Das Grosse Welttheater* (Hamburg, 1959).

14 S. Karner, 'Das Jahr 1918 als Wendepunkt für die Energiewirtschaft der Steiermark und Sloweniens', *Blätter für Heimatkunde*, 52 (1978), 107ff.

15 *Statistisches Jahrbuch der Stadt Wien*, 1900.

16 Käthe Leichter, *So leben wir. 1320 Industriearbeiterinnen berichten über ihr Leben* (Vienna, 1932).

17 E. Viethen-Votruba, 'Mother's little helper – Entwicklung und Nutzen der Haushaltstechnik', in *Lichtjahre*, pp. 133ff; F. Niethammer, *Elektrizität im Hause* (Berlin, 1929). V. Mueller, *Vergleich Elektrizität und Gasverbrauch im Haushalt* (Berlin, 1929); M. Ried, *Gegenwart und Zukunft der Elektrizitätswirtschaft* (Berlin, 1917).

18 R. Sandgruber, 'Vom Hunger zum Massenkonsum', *Die 'wilden' fünfziger Jahre. Gesellschaft, Formen und Gefühle eines Jahrzehnts in Österreich*, published by G. Jagschitz and K. Mulley (St Pölten, 1985), pp. 112ff.

19 F. Hoppe, *Die Elektrizitätswerkbetriebe im Lichte der Statistik* (Vienna, 1916); C. Brückner, 'Die Bedeutung der elektrischen Energie für die Industrie', *Jahresbericht der Neuen Handelsakademie* (Vienna, 1911–12); *Jahrbuch der Elektrizitätsgesell-schaften Österreichs* (14 vols., Vienna, 1905–18); J. Langer, *Denkschrift über Elektrizitätswirtschaft* (Vienna, 1918); *Elektro-Bureau-Compass* (Vienna, 1916); P. Gilles, *Die Elektrizität als Triebkraft in der Grossindustrie* (Berlin, 1910); E. Honigmann, *Die öst.ung. Elektroindustrie* (Berlin, 1917); F. Broch, *Gestehungs-kosten und Verkaufspreise elektrischer Arbeit* (Vienna, 1930); A. Wilke, *Die volkswirtschaftliche Bedeutung der Elektrizität* (Vienna, 1913); H. Schreiber, *Elektrizität in Recht und Wirtschaft* (2 vols., Leipzig, 1913); A. Buchleitner, *Promemoria zur Frage der Elektrizitätsversorgung* (Innsbruck, 1917); M. Ried, *Gegenwart und Zukunft der Elektrizitätswirtschaft* (Berlin, 1917).

20 H. Stockklausner, '50 Jahre Elektro-Vollbahnlokomotiven in Österreich und Deutschland', special issue of *Eisenbahn* magazine (Vienna, 1952); E. März, *Österreichs Bankpolitik in der Zeit der grossen Wende 1913–1923* (Vienna, 1981), pp. 519ff.

21 W. Györgyfalvay, *Die Geschichte der Gas- und Elektrizitätsversorgung der Stadt Linz* (Linz, 1979); S. Koren, 'Struktur und Nutzung der Energiequellen Österreichs', in W. Weber (ed.), *Österreichs Wirtschaftsstruktur gestern – heute – morgen* (Berlin, 1961); J. Ornig, *Österreichs Energiewirtschaft* (Vienna, 1927); R. Sandgruber, 'Energieverbrauch und Wirtschaftsenwicklung', *Beiträge zur Histor-ischen Sozialkunde*, 12 (1982), 79ff; R. Sandgruber, 'Die Energieversorgung Österreichs vom 18. Jahrhundert bis zur Gegenwart,' *ibid.*, 100ff; Sequenz, '100 Jahre Elektrotechnik in Österreich, 1873–1973', *Schriftenreihe der Technischen Hochschule Wien*, 3 (1973); O. Vas, *Grundlagen und Entwicklung der Energie-*

wirtschaft Österreichs. Offizieller Bericht des österreichischen Nationalkomitees der Weltkraftkonferenz (Vienna, 1930); *idem, Ergänzungsband 1930–1933* (Vienna, 1933); *idem, Wege und Ziele der österreichischen Elektrizitätswirtschaft* (Vienna, 1952); W. Weber (ed.), *Österreichs Energiewirtschaft* (Vienna, 1957); F. Weigl, *Die Entwicklung der oberösterreichischen Elektrizitätswirtschaft von den Anfängen bis zu Jahre 1938* (Linz, 1981); J. Kluger, *Ein halbes Jahrhundert kommunaler Elektrizitätsversorgung* (Vienna, 1952); *Die Elektrifizierung Österreichs* (1st edn Vienna, 1925, 2nd edn Vienna, 1930); M. Schwaar, 'Stromzeiten', in *Lichtjahre*, pp. 177ff.

22 S. Karner, 'Der Kampf zwischen "weisser" und schwarzer Kohle. Zu den Anfängen einer gesamtsteirischen Elektrizitätswirtschaft', *Blätter für Heimatkunde*, 51 (1977), 122ff.

23 E. Kurzel-Runtscheiner, *Österreichs Energiewirtschaft und die Ausnützung seiner Wasserkräfte* (Vienna, 1923); statistics of the power supplied by hydro-electric stations from 1921 in 'Entwicklung, Struktur und Tendenzen der österreichischen Energieversorgung', *Monatsberichte des österreichischen Instituts für Wirtschaftsforschung* (1960).

24 März, *Österreichs Bankpolitik*, pp. 504ff.

25 Teich, 'Zu einigen Fragen', p. 41.

❧

FOUR

HERALDS OF MODERNITY: CARS AND PLANES FROM INVENTION TO NECESSITY

RICHARD OVERY

Of all the inventions from that great age of scientific engineering in central Europe in the later nineteenth century, none has had a more profound effect than the internal combustion engine. The motorization revolution to which it gave rise is one of the major hallmarks of modernity, transforming social life, the economic system, even warfare. The practical application of the new engine created new opportunities and expectations, provided the technical dimensions for the 'age of the masses' and marked a pronounced break with the nineteenth-century world from which it developed. Not even the railway, which has progressively given way to the motor car and the aeroplane, made such an impact. Important though railways were, they did not replace the ship and the horse, which had dominated mobility and communication for a millennium, nor did they transform the economy and environment in the way that modern motorized transport has done. In a very real sense, those writers who saw the birth of the motor vehicle and the aeroplane as the coming of a new age, the triumph of human ingenuity over the constraints imposed by nature herself, did not exaggerate. To imagine a Second World War fought with marching soldiers and cavalry, or a modern industrial economy dependent on delivery by horse or cart is to see how very different the modern world might have been.

FROM VISION TO INVENTION

Yet it is just as difficult to imagine that the internal combustion engine would not have been invented. The pursuit of a mechanical means of propulsion went back to at least the seventeenth century. The principles governing motor transport by road or in the air were already understood in the eighteenth. Experiments with successful steam-driven road vehicles matched the growth of rail locomotion. Aviation experiments in balloons, airships and gliders were widespread in Europe and America throughout the nineteenth century.[1]

When the German aeronautical pioneer Otto Lilienthal began his experiments in the 1870s, the eventual conquest of the air was a possibility widely supported. It was the next frontier for a confident, imaginative, technically ambitious scientific community, for whom the technical limitations of steam locomotion – which was even applied with a very limited success to aircraft – were clear. While the heavy and expensive vehicles could be used in agriculture or for haulage, they could not easily be applied to long-range transport, and indeed, with the railway, did not need to be. The technical limitations in aviation were even greater. Lilienthal, the founder of modern aeronautical science, spent his energies perfecting the glider; 'it appears obvious', he wrote 'that in order to discover the principles which facilitate flight, and to eventually enable man to fly, we must take the bird for our model'.[2] Wilhelm Kress, the inventive Viennese piano-maker, devoted a lifetime to aviation experiments, but powered his aeroplane models with rubber bands. The first generation of Austrian and German aircraft were derived, somewhat incongruously, from the work of the Austrian scientist Friedrich Ahlborn, who demonstrated the inherent stability of the winged seeds of the vine *Zanonia Macroparpa*, and whose findings were adapted to the problems of flight by Igo Etrich, an Austrian businessman. So enthusiastic was the support in Vienna for the idea of manned flight that the city boasted the world's first aeronautical institute, the Wiener Flugtechnische Verein, founded in 1880. In 1885 the balloonist Viktor Silberer founded the Wiener Aeronautische Anstalt, and the Wiener Aero-Club in 1901. Later, in May 1912, Vienna hosted the first international air exhibition.[3]

What all these experiments failed to solve was the problem of power. Until the technological threshold made possible an engine of sufficient power and efficiency the breakthrough could not be made. For all the development of aeronautical theory, which was important enough, a light engine with sufficient lifting power was the answer to powered flight. This breakthrough depended in turn on developments in the manufacture of high-quality materials, and of mechanical parts with high tolerances and durability, and the discovery of an effective fuel. The technical and scientific framework to permit this breakthrough emerged in Europe, particularly in Germany and France, during the twenty years after the 1848 revolutions. In 1860 Etienne Lenoir produced a working gas engine which he applied, unsuccessfully, to a motor vehicle in 1862, the year that Beau de Rochas discovered the four-stroke engine cycle. But the real source of the modern internal combustion engine lies in the experiments carried out in the laboratories, technical schools and engineering firms of the German Confederation. A combination of traditions of rigorous physical experimentation, high standards of workmanship and the opportunities provided by an extensive technical education sector, provided the ideal climate for engine research. It was here that Otto and Langen produced a gas engine in 1867 which was developed into a full four-stroke engine in the 1870s, and which provided the basis for the future internal combustion engine using petrol. It was in this atmosphere that Karl Benz and Gottlieb Daimler undertook their scientific apprenticeship.[4]

Benz, the son of a German engine-driver, was educated at the Karlsruhe Polytechnic in the 1860s, where his teachers, Grashof and Redtenbacher, experimented on perfecting the Lenoir engine. He worked for the Karlsruhe Maschinenbaugesellschaft where he was able to continue his experiments on gas engines, concentrating on the effort to vaporize petrol so that it could be used as an effective fuel. By the 1880s he succeeded in producing first a workable engine, then, in 1885, the first successful motor vehicle employing a small internal combustion engine. Daimler, son of a German trader, began as an apprentice to a gunsmith in 1848, moving five years later to a machine-building works, and in 1856 to two years of advanced education at Stuttgart Polytechnic. In 1869 he became technical director of the Karlsruhe works where Benz had been employed, and three years later moved to the Deutz works run by Otto and Langen, where he was able to carry out his own research in gas engines using a number of different combustible fuels. In 1882 he established his own engine-building company at Canstatt with Wilhelm Maybach (inventor, in 1893, of the first modern carburettor), where a year later he produced the first true petrol-driven engine from which all subsequent development was derived. Two years later he applied the engine first to a motor cycle, then to a motor car, and in 1888 he powered a dirigible with an internal combustion engine. Both the Benz and Daimler designs proved to be technically efficient and within a matter of a few years cars built around the engines were produced in quantity for a European-wide market.[5]

The development of an efficient internal combustion engine using petrol as fuel solved the central problem in the evolution of motor transport. The technical milieu in Europe and America permitted the application of the engine to a wide variety of needs, and led to its rapid refinement and improvement. There was never any question that this process would be reversed or would stagnate. The discovery released all those scientific energies that had been devoted to other sources of power, steam or electricity, to be concentrated on taking the internal combustion engine to its technical limits. Improvements in materials and production techniques made the engine more reliable and efficient, while the development of modern gearing and trans-mission systems gave motor vehicles the high levels of performance that the small cars of Daimler and Benz lacked. Much of this work was continued in Germany, though by no means exclusively so; Rudolf Diesel perfected the heavy-oil engine in 1897, which allowed the development of heavier vehicles for haulage, and Robert Bosch the production of high-quality electrical components.[6]

The reception and rapid evolution of the motor vehicle, car or aeroplane, needs little explanation. The technology became international very quickly – the spread of Daimler's patents for his car into Austria, France, Britain and the United States is a good example – and in terms of the current state of engineering was not particularly complex. The most difficult technical stage was the application of the engine to powered flight, which began some twenty years after the first successful motor cars were produced. Improvements in engine efficiency, which permitted lighter engines of high power output, and the accelerated development of aeronautical science (important for the design of the airscrew, wings and tailplane) produced something of a scramble among the engineering community to get a self-propelled aeroplane off the ground. The Wright brothers in the United States succeeded in making the first powered flight in 1903 lasting for a few seconds, and the first true flight two years later. The first flights that did not require some kind of launching apparatus were made in Europe in 1908, the culmination of a great wave of experimentation, particularly in France, encouraged by the Wright's early experiments with gliders. Within less than five years the first tentative flights gave way to sustained journeys over distances of fifty miles or more.[7] The sheer weight of scientific and engineering resources devoted to aviation provided progress on a broad front. There were no major technical thresholds to cross until the coming of jet propulsion thirty years later.

THE SPREAD OF MOTORIZATION

If the technical reception of motor transport was widespread and irrepressible, its wider application depended much more on the economic and social environment. This wider reception varied in detail from country to country, though there were many features in common. The economic context affected the development of motor transport in several ways. It was necessary to move from invention to production, a process that depended on the current state of industrial technology, the willingness of businessmen to take risks and the nature of the market for the new products. Before the First World War there were very few limitations on entry into the new industry. The inventors themselves – Benz, Daimler, etc. – produced their own motor cars, but the bulk of the new entrepreneurs came from a variety of industrial and commercial backgrounds. No particular scientific skill or knowledge was required, but a solid background in practical engineering was difficult to forgo. The bicycle industry, a pioneer of early mass assembly techniques, gave rise to a great number of motor-car makers – Morris in Britain, Opel in Germany, the Duryea brothers in America – but so too did coach-building – Panhard in France, for example – and specialized or precision toolmaking.[8] Since much of the early production was carried out by buying specialized parts from individual suppliers, it was also important to have well-developed engineering industries from which to draw supplies and skilled labour. The centres of car production were to be found in the traditional artisan engineering regions: in Britain around the Midlands, in France in Paris and Lyon and the region of the Vosges, where Peugeot used the traditional skills of the local craftsmen to produce cars of high quality, in Germany in the southern states and the Rhenish towns, in Austria around Vienna and Graz.[9] In the United States the situation was different, partly because of geography, partly because it lacked the settled and traditional communities of craft workshops on which to draw. The developments in America favoured large-scale production from the start, based on the output of cheap standard components produced by general engineering companies, which were then simply assembled by the car manufacturers using semi-skilled labour. While this produced cheap, light cars in quantity much sooner than in Europe, it meant that the United States played little part at first in the early technical development of motor cars, or in the production of successful racing cars and cars of large capacity and high levels of luxury.[10] French, Austrian and German cars dominated these fields precisely because their makers could rely on very high levels of craftsmanship and a steady input from engineers and managers with a high standard of technical education and scientific knowledge.[11]

Two examples illustrate these very different traditions. Ferdinand Porsche, the son of a German tinsmith from Maffersdorf (Vratislavice nad Nisou) in Bohemia, was trained in the local technical school in engineering, before moving to Vienna to join the Vereinigte Elektrizitäts AG in charge of the test and experimental department. Here he worked on electrical engines for motor vehicles, moving in 1898 to co-operate with the Viennese coach-builder to the Emperor, Ludwig Lohner, to produce electric-powered carriages. After doing military service in Archduke Franz Ferdinand's regiment, accompanied by one of his own electric-powered cars, Porsche switched his research from electric to internal combustion engines, joining the Daimler company at Wiener-Neustadt as technical director in 1906. Here he designed and developed high-quality cars which won regular racing trophies, while developing the 'Maja' Daimler for the fashionable rich. He developed aero-engines as well, which were used in Austrian aircraft throughout the Great War, and after the war continued his work on luxury and racing cars. It was from this background of high-quality engineering and scientific capability – he was an indifferent businessman – that Porsche conceived the idea of a cheap reliable mass car, the *Volksauto*, based around a revolutionary new design, the forerunner of the *Volkswagen* he later designed for Hitler.[12] Henry Ford, son of a farmer, had none of Porsche's formal technical education, and learned his engineering working for the Edison Company in the 1880s. In the 1890s he began to assemble bicycles, then his first car, built up from components bought in from other producers. In 1903 the Ford Motor Company was set up with the help of a wealthy Detroit coal merchant, and Ford began assembling cars in quantity using the same system of buying the major components from the cheapest supplier in order to keep the price as low as possible. For Ford the key factors were not to do with quality or technical development, but with finance and selling. Costs were kept down to a minimum by the use of rational assembly methods. All efforts were devoted to selling just one major model, the Ford Model-T, through a nationwide network of Ford distributors and with widespread publicity. After the First World War Ford began to diversify, the major component suppliers were bought up, development and scientific application became more important. The product range was widened to include not only the small family car but the luxury limousine as well (President Coolidge began a tradition of using Ford cars), at exactly the same time as Porsche was moving away from racing cars to the *Volksauto*.[13]

In the early stages the same was true of aviation development. Given the enormous strides American aviation was to make later in the century it was something of an irony that the initial development of high-performance aircraft was concentrated in France and Austria–Hungary. But again it was the traditions of high standards of precision engineering and the close links between science and industry that explains at least some of the discrepancy. These were essential qualities in the early stages of aeroplane construction, more so than with cars. By 1912 France held forty-five aviation world records, Austria eighteen, but America only eight and Britain only one.[14] Not until the war was much of the ground made up, and then largely due to the dissemination of the technology to allied powers – the famous German Taube aircraft was the Austrian Etrich aircraft produced under licence in Germany by the Rumpler Company – and the British had to depend for their early aircraft development on the supply of higher-quality French aircraft. When the United States entered the First World War it had virtually no modern aircraft industry and had to be supplied almost entirely by Britain and France.[15]

The different pattern of development between countries depended very much on the nature of the market as well. For much of the first thirty years of motor-car development the market was confined to the very rich. There were obvious reasons for this. Motoring costs were very high, not only the initial cost of a motor car (well over £1,000 in Britain in the early 1900s, an average of $1,000 in America in 1900, 15,000 marks for the Benz 'Rennwagen'), but also the running and maintenance costs. In Britain the tax on a car of over 60 horsepower before 1914 was £42 a year. Petrol was taxed in most countries, and did not become a cheap fuel until the oil discoveries of the 1920s.[16] For many customers the car was simply another addition to the carriages and horses, and was looked after by the servants in the same way. Many aristocrats and wealthy bourgeois not only bought cars but also invested in their production and development, or raced them as one might race horses. The nature of the early clientele encouraged the emergence of a whole range of small producers, providing custom-built cars at high price. Many motor manufacturers produced the engine, chassis and mechanical parts, but left the bodywork to specialized coach-builders who could meet the exacting requirements of wealthy customers more easily. The association of early motor-car ownership with wealth gave the motor car a special kind of status as a product. The link between power (both economic and political) and the motor car was immediately recognized, for the car was altogether a more convenient vehicle than horse or carriage, and could be made to display rank and wealth just as easily. The first head of state to buy a motor car was the Sultan of Morocco, who bought a Daimler car at the Paris World Fair in 1889, and the habit spread rapidly. Wilhelm II was an avid collector with twenty-five vehicles by 1912, tended in his stables by a staff of thirty-one. Franz-Joseph was fascinated by both cars and aeroplanes and Tsar Nicholas II owned twenty-one, including two Rolls-Royce cars bought in 1914, which had already succeeded in establishing a reputation as the aristocrat among cars; so much so that Henry Ford himself bought one, and Lenin commandeered those of the Tsar for his official use.[17]

The initial stage of fashionable car-buying was important in laying the foundation for the development of specialized car industries and the infrastructure of services and supplies on which the motor car depended. It also helped to foster habits of consumption that could, and did, filter rapidly down the social scale. Luxury consumption was also accompanied by more mundane applications. Very rapidly the commercial advantage of motor vehicles over horse-drawn vehicles was demonstrated. The motorized taxi became a general feature of most major cities by 1914; a Daimler taxi worked from Stuttgart railway station as early as 1888. Commercial bus companies sprang up rapidly after 1900, subject only to the vagaries of local carriage legislation.[18] Lorry transport, for convenient local delivery rather than for longer hauls, also developed generally after 1900, particularly with the advent of the Diesel engine, challenging the monopoly long enjoyed by the horse. Agriculture was one area of economic activity that promised particular and immediate gains, not only through delivering its products more effectively, but in replacing horses and hand or steam equipment with petrol-driven 'tractors'. The first modern tractors appeared in 1902, and by 1920 there were over 200,000 in the United States alone. Motorization developed first in two very different environments, among the world's conspicuous consumers and among the firms and farms of the most advanced economies.[19]

These developments did not take place smoothly. Although the spread of motorization was not, and indeed could not, be reversed, it was uneven and hampered by restrictions, some deliberately imposed, some imposed by circumstances. For all those aristocrats who welcomed the new mechanical toy, there were those who deeply distrusted the new invention, especially its challenge to the horse, still, in many parts of Europe, the symbol of status and wealth. For all those businessmen who welcomed the new petrol-driven lorry, there were carriage owners, livery stablers and railway managers who saw a direct threat to their livelihood, and who attempted to obstruct its development. In Britain the notorious Red Flag Act, which restricted the speed of motor vehicles to 2 m.p.h. (3 km.p.h.) in towns, and insisted that at least three people should accompany any powered vehicle with red flags of warning, was only repealed in 1896, when the maximum speed permitted was raised to 14 m.p.h. (22 km.p.h.) Other regulations on the maximum size of commercial vehicles and low maximum speeds – 5 m.p.h. (8 km.p.h.) for vehicles over 2 tons in weight – were withdrawn in 1903 and 1904. The British example was the most restrictive, but was by no means the only one. Motorization posed new problems of regulation of traffic, and of competition for established businesses which had to be solved before further expansion was possible.[20]

But there were other restrictions that were not deliberate. The standard of roads in most of Europe and America, even of those with tarmac surfaces, made it difficult to use motorized transport. Until the development and general use of rubber pneumatic tyres, invented by John Dunlop in 1888, journeys were uncomfortable and unreliable. Even the new tyres were unable to withstand the impact of rough and poorly made roads, so that the connection between the spread of motorization and the construction and maintenance of an adequate road network was established well before the coming of mass motoring.[21] Finally the cost of motoring and the unreliability of many early cars acted as something of a brake on development. The absence of anything like the later infrastructure of motoring made the activity in its early days hazardous and expensive. Demand came, of course, to secure its own supply, in the growth of a network of garages and repair shops, petrol pumps and specialist car dealers, but again this was a slow process, very much at the whim of the market. Before the coming of mass motoring and mass production the cluster of small, financially weak firms was prey to regular business failure, which, while it led by a process of 'natural selection' to the survival of large and successful firms, inhibited the growth of the market at first by placing large numbers of expensive cars on sale with no guarantee of an effective after-sales service or the supply of spare parts. The financial risks tended to be high both for producer and customer.[22]

THE AGE OF MASS MOTORING

The real transformation came with mass motoring. The very name chosen to describe the next stage of motorization, when the second generation of producers moved from servicing the rich to selling to the 'masses', indicates how fundamental a transformation this represented. It was a shift produced not simply by the gradual technical improvements in the vehicle itself, although this was significant in reducing running costs, nor by the slow spread of motor-car ownership among the next layer of wealthy consumers, but was a deliberate and sudden shift from specialized luxury production to catering for a mass market of ordinary consumers. That this change occurred when it did, and in the way that it did, reflects wider changes in political attitudes and social perceptions. It was no accident that mass motoring developed first in the United States, where society was more mobile and less bound by class conventions and patterns of status, or that it spread first and fastest among those societies – America, Britain and France – where industrial society and political democracy had both made the greatest strides. There is a very real sense in which the democratization of motor-car ownership and motor transport matched the corresponding political shifts towards mass politics and greater equality.

This was a self-conscious development among motor manufacturers themselves. The populist conceptions of a Henry Ford or William Morris are an important part of any explanation for the sudden transformation of motorization. Ford set out to produce a car for the poor mid-westerner, cheap enough so that workers and farmers could afford both the initial price and the upkeep. The Model T Ford that resulted sold over 15 million.[23] Morris formed his vision of a 'car-owning society' before the First World War: 'from the first I set out to cater for the "man in the street"'. The list of major producers with the same ambition could be extended – Renault in France, a great admirer of the French peasants who bought his small two-cylinder cars, or Porsche whose real ambition was not to race fast cars but to make a 'small economic car of good performance' to 'popularize motoring'. Porsche's search produced the archetypal car for the masses, the 'People's Car'. The second generation of car producers came from very different backgrounds from the engineer-inventors of the first. Morris was the son of a farm manager, Renault of a button-maker, and if Ford, grandson of an Irish immigrant, did not quite come from the log cabin, he was certainly typical of poorer, small-town, small-farm America.[24] Mass motoring for them represented the advent of democratic consumption, giving the ordinary man mobility, not merely aping the rich, but extending his own horizons. It was also another kind of triumph, the victory of the practical man, of technology, a fulfilment of the social promise contained in the emancipating effects of modern science.

In this sense mass motoring has to be seen against the background of sustained economic growth and the application of the machine. Belief in the potential of the machine and in the triumph of a rational scientific order was shared by all shades of political opinion. It was part of the mentality of an age when possibilities were opening up on all sides, political, cultural, economic. The example of Henry Ford, the most successful of the mass producers, gave rise to the movement for 'Fordism' in America and Europe, the application of new standards of efficiency to production and a new view of the worker as customer.[25] Fordism promised a rational economic order, replacing the chaos of the market-place with industrial planning and the rule of enlightened technocrats in place of the old elites of birth and status. It was for these reasons that Henry Ford was read widely, and his practices and personal philosophy argued over, in regimes as far apart as Communist Russia and Nazi Germany. Ford established close relations with the Soviet regime in the 1920s. What interested Soviet leaders was Ford's view on the rational organization of labour, which could be made to fit Soviet views of socialist efficiency under the slogan 'Do it the Ford way because it is the best way'. Ford's *My Life and Work* was used in Russian technical universities, and the 'Fordization' of Russian factories was pursued in the early 1920s. Soviet apprentices were trained at the Henry Ford Trade School; and Stalin used Ford expertise and equipment when he launched Russia's own motor industry under the First Five-Year Plan. The first tractors in the Russian countryside were Ford 'Fordson' models, 25,000 of them between 1920 and 1926. The tractor became the symbol of modernization in the villages. The Motor Tractor Stations set up under the First Five-Year Plan in Russia were designed to revolutionize productivity and to link the peasant with the new machine age made possible through the Soviet industrialization drive.[26]

This association of motorization with modernity, with a functional view of technology and technical elites and with popular consumption, was what attracted fascism to the motor car. Interestingly both Morris and Ford flirted with the new radical Right. Morris gave Oswald Mosley £50,000 to help set up the New Party on the grounds that some kind of sound corporative order was preferable to the old class conflicts and party bickering.[27] In Italy Mussolini gave state encouragement to the motor industry. The building of the first motorways, begun in Italy in the 1920s, and the sharp increase in Italian car ownership were hailed by the regime as evidence of the energy and modernism of the new fascist age. In Germany the link was even more explicit. Hitler was an admirer of Ford, whose autobiography (one of over 200,000 copies sold in Germany) he read in Landsberg prison.[28] Hitler remained throughout his life a firm exponent of 'rationalization', of techno-logy at the service of the *Volk*. He disapproved of the restricted upper-middle-class character of car ownership in Germany, brought about partly by the poor economic conditions after 1914 and the effects of hyper-inflation, and had a personal commitment to spreading car ownership among the working classes. One of his favoured inner circle was the Daimler-Benz salesman Jakob Werlin, with whom Hitler spent hours discussing motor-racing and the technical details of motor cars. In 1932 Hitler gave 20,000 RM to Daimler-Benz to develop a racing-car to beat the dominant Italians. His commitment to the *Volkswagen* concept predated 1933, and once in power he introduced a range of measures to speed up motorization in Germany and initiated the search for a people's car, 'a sort of low-priced family car in which one could go on weekend trips'.[29] It was at this point that he met Porsche, a fellow Old Austrian and already committed to such a project himself, who was authorized to design and build the first prototypes. They were completed in 1938, but the war interrupted the onset of mass production in what was to have been Europe's largest motor-car assembly plant at Wolfsburg. The propaganda significance of the *Volkswagen* and of the new German motor-ways, the *Autobahnen*, along which they were to run, lay in their demon-stration of the unity of German society, the new spirit of co-operation in the age of the common man, and 'a monument', Hitler said, 'to technical progress'.[30]

There were, of course, limits to these developments. Except in the United States and Canada, the new wave of consumers was in fact largely drawn from the middle classes and farmers rather than the 'masses'. Even skilled workers were more likely to own a bicycle than a car, or at most a motor cycle, whose sales also increased sharply after the First World War. Much of the new production was bought up by businesses or the self-employed rather than private customers. Large firms bought fleets of cars for their salesmen or vehicles for delivery. But the shifting pattern was clear enough if it did not quite match the propaganda claims, as table 4.1 shows. By 1938 the stock of motor cars and lorries in the world was 23 times greater than in 1914, 43 million compared with 1.83 million. The greatest absolute increase in car ownership came after 1950, but the widespread use of motor vehicles and expectations about general car ownership were both well established before then.

In explaining the coming of mass motoring it is important to distinguish clearly between cause and effect. At least part of the explanation lies in the sustained rise in living standards from the 1890s through to the 1930s, particularly in the United States, but widely evident in Britain, France and other European countries too. The rise was most marked for professional and white-collar workers, but was not confined to them. Falling food prices, rising

Table 4.1 *Total stock of cars and commercial vehicles in selected countries, 1905–70 (000s)*

Date	USA	UK	France	Germany[a]	Italy
1905	77.4	32.0	21.5	11.3	n.a.
1910	458.5	143.8	53.9	42.0	n.a.
1913	1,194.2	209.0	91.0	70.6	24.0
1920	8,225.8	363.0	236.4	90.9	49.5
1925	17,512.6	903.0	721.0	254.6	117.6
1930	26,531.9	1,504.0	1,521.0	658.0	245.1
1935	26,221.0	1,997.0	2,005.0	1,054.0	326.1
1938	29,211.6	2,542.3	2,250.0	1,707.5	389.4
1950	49,161.6	3,290.0	2,440.0	1,059.1	571.0
1960	73,768.5	7,017.0	7,180.0	5,618.0	2,451.0
1970	108,977.0	13,209.0	15,804.0	16,342.0	11,085.0

Note: [a]From 1950 figure for East and West Germany.
Sources: Calculated from B. Mitchell, *European Historical Statistics 1750–1970* (London, 1975), pp. 350–1; Society of Motor Manufacturers and Traders *The Motor Industry of Great Britain 1939* (London, 1939), p. 118, 144; J. Rae, *The American Automobile* (Chicago, 1965), p. 238; J. Morice, *La demande d'automobiles en France* (Paris, 1957), p. 119; *Statistical Abstract of the United States* (Washington, D.C., 1936, 1971).

productivity, increased union bargaining, all pushed up the level of real incomes and made possible the change in consumer habits of the interwar years. Not just cars, but radios, kitchen furniture, the clothing trade, the leisure industries, all benefited from the growth of incomes. Without a favourable economic environment the spread of the motor car would have been much slower, as the poorer economic performance of post-war Germany showed. Mass motoring was also helped by the growth of government regulation of motorized transport, and higher levels of road investment designed to meet the new requirements of the motor vehicle, although government restrictions could also operate adversely through high levels of taxation or the regulation of goods traffic in favour of the railways.[31] Mass motoring was also made possible by the spread of motor services and the infrastructure of motoring (from better road signs to driving schools) in the interwar years, though this, too, was perhaps as much effect as cause.

The fundamental explanation for the sudden revolution in car ownership lies in the nature and price of the product. Mass motoring required cars that were both cheap and reliable, and neither of these things was guaranteed until the introduction of mass production and the simplification and standardization of design that this required. The link between cost and the quantity of output, though it involved something of a financial risk, was evident to those car-makers who deliberately set out to change the nature of the market. Ford did this successfully before the First World War. The fall in price of his

Table 4.2 *Sales and price of the Model-T Ford, 1908–16*

Year	Total sales	Retail price (touring car)
1908	5,986	$850
1909	12,292	$950
1910	19,293	$780
1911	40,402	$690
1912	78,611	$600
1913	182,809	$550
1914	260,720	$490
1915	355,276	$440
1916	577,036	$360

Source: J. Rae, *The American Automobile: A Brief History* (Chicago, 1965), p. 61.

Model-T was directly proportional to the rise in sales, as table 4.2 shows.[32] The success of William Morris after 1919 lay in effective price competition, which increased sales and permitted further price reductions through economies of scale. In 1920 his cheapest car was £465, in 1930 it was £125, while total sales rose from 1,932 to over 60,000. In 1938 British car prices reached their lowest point, only 48 per cent of average prices in 1924.[33] The initial gamble on higher sales became self-sustaining, as higher levels of output produced high profits for reinvestment in new cost-cutting equipment and better-run factories.

The distinctive feature of the successful mass producers was the revolution in production methods or 'rationalization', a technical breakthrough that had implications far beyond the motor industry. Ford had full conveyor-belt assembly methods before 1914; Morris pioneered 'rational' flow-production methods in Britain in the early 1920s. New methods of production cut the overall production time per car at Ford's from 12 hours to 1½ hours per car in two years.[34] If Ford's performance was exceptional, no producer could afford to ignore it and survive. The effect of mass production was not only to produce a cheaper and better product, but to eliminate rapidly all the lesser producers and to concentrate production in a few major firms.[35] This process generated its own form of rationalization of personnel and sales outlets, making it almost impossible for the smaller producers to remain in the market unless, like Rolls-Royce, they produced a very specialized product.

The result was that the mass producers, starting out with one or two standard cheap models, gradually moved to producing a wide range of cars, including the luxury models that smaller companies could no longer supply.

The larger companies were also able to provide better distribution of their products – American cars were sent to all parts of the world in the 1920s – and were also able to offer credit terms to customers. The hire-purchase schemes introduced in the interwar years made it possible to tap a whole additional layer of demand, and became the standard form of private car purchase. Advertising and publicity stunts were also widely used by the industry, which was at the forefront in developing professional techniques of promotion. The rising demand for cars in turn produced further economies. It speeded up the search for more oil resources, and the price of petrol fell steadily. Rubber output tripled between 1920 and 1938, and the price per pound fell by 60 per cent. New methods of producing sheet steel and pressed steel parts led to reductions in the price of major components.[36] Though the price of vehicles rose steadily after the Second World War, the rise was more than offset by the rise of income and the sustained post-war boom. Price competition was still important, but other factors such as reliability, after-sales service and design governed consumer choice to a greater extent than in the early days of mass motoring. Car ownership on a scale envisaged by Ford or Porsche became a practical possibility. Car manufacture was fully internationalized, and the output of all the major producers measured in millions rather than thousands.[37]

THE RISE OF 'AIR POWER'

The development of aviation, though it also led to an age of mass flying, was slower and dependent on different factors altogether. The primary stimulus to the expansion of aviation was the First World War. Not only did the urgent needs of war speed up the research and development of air technology, financed with government subsidies, but the war produced a pool of trained pilots and mechanics (and surplus aircraft), which could be transferred into commercial aviation after the war. The war also turned what had been a growing enthusiasm for aviation before 1914 into the concept of 'air power' itself. It was a term manifestly appropriate to the very great changes that occurred after 1914. In 1913 the major states possessed only a few military aircraft, mainly for reconnaissance or artillery-spotting, with the famous exception of the Russian Sikorsky multi-engined aircraft which became the world's first heavy bomber in 1914. By the end of the war Britain had produced 55,000 aircraft, the French 51,000, Germany over 47,000. The United States was in the early stages of a production programme to put over 200 squadrons into the campaign in 1919, some of which were destined to join the Inter-Allied Independent Air Force set up in October 1918 to carry out a large-scale strategic bombing campaign against German industry and towns in 1919 which might, some airmen hoped, bring the war to an end on its own.[38] Moreover, the aircraft of 1918 had an overall performance and level of technical sophistication remarkably different from 1914. The exercise of air power independent of the other military services was widely regarded as a technical possibility, and was supported by military thinkers as the core of 'modern' warfare.

The legacy of the war was a developed aviation industry, though unlike the car industry it contracted everywhere after the war, and because of high initial capital and research costs, was never far from financial collapse until the design of aircraft capable of serious commercial operation, or until the onset of rearmament.[39] Throughout the 1920s and 1930s the infrastructure of commercial air operations and air routes spread all over the world. Every ocean was crossed and every continent. Airmen, and women, caught the popular imagination, pioneers of a new and remarkable modernity. No major state lacked the development of what was called 'air mindedness'. The response to the aircraft and its rapid and general application matched that to the motor vehicle. It served similar propaganda purposes in linking politics and the machine age. Stalin basked in the reflected glory of Soviet air exploits: 'Aviation is the highest expression of our achievements.' Hitler toured Germany electioneering in an aeroplane, carefully uniting fascist mystique with technological progress.[40]

Yet the aircraft was a two-edged sword, building bridges of communication, broadening horizons and narrowing distances, but bearing the menace of destruction. The view memorably stated by the British Prime Minister Stanley Baldwin that 'the bomber will always get through' was widely shared. The theory of the 'knock-out blow' popularized by the Italian strategist General Douhet made the aircraft the weapon of the machine age *par excellence*.[41] War was perceived as a war against civilians and civilian morale, as much as a war between armies. The home front, attacked in a sporadic and ineffective way by bombers in the First World War, became a legitimate target of war. The aircraft, attacking suddenly and in mass, might paralyse the economy, administration and communications of the victim state and bring about capitulation in a matter of days. Harold Macmillan later wrote that 'we thought of air warfare in 1938 rather as people think of nuclear warfare today'.[42] In practice the aircraft posed much less of a threat than had been supposed. No power was operationally capable of mounting a knock-out blow in 1939; but British, and then American, fears that Germany might defeat them from the air pushed both powers to produce their own strategic bombing campaign whose results vindicated the worst fears of the interwar strategists. Some three-quarters of a million German civilians died and 80 per cent of Germany's major industrial cities were destroyed or damaged. Japan was brought to the point of surrender by the systematic destruction by fire-bombing of its major cities. The home populations were involved with air power in other ways too: the mobilization of the population for anti-aircraft

Table 4.3 *Aircraft Production in the Second World War*

Country	1939	1940	1941	1942	1943	1944	1945
USA	5,856	12,804	26,277	47,836	85,898	96,318	49,761
USSR	10,382	10,565	15,735	25,436	34,900	40,300	20,900
Britain and British Commonwealth	8,190	16,694	22,694	28,247	30,963	31,036	14,145
Germany and Occupied Europe	8,295	10,247	11,776	15,409	24,807	39,807	7,540
Japan	4,467	4,768	5,088	8,861	16,693	28,180	11,066
Italy	1,800	1,800	2,400	1,600	—	—	

Source: R. J. Overy, *The Air War 1939–1945* (London, 1980), p. 150.

and civil defence, for work in the aircraft industry (which took almost 40 per cent of all the labour and resources of the war effort), and in servicing the great air fleets. The effort in the air turned warfare in a very real sense into total war.[43]

Air power represented a more fundamental break with the warfare of the past than did the motor vehicle, not only on the home front but on the battlefield and its supply lines. During the First World War motor vehicles played a very limited part. Even the primitive tanks which first appeared in 1917 were not available in sufficient quantity and were not technically advanced enough to revolutionize the fighting. During the Second World War the tank, jeep and lorry were much more in evidence, but only the American army was fully motorized, and not until the last two years of the war were tanks of high quality deployed in any real numbers. Though the cavalry was made redundant by motor vehicles, it was the aircraft that actually brought cavalry reconnaissance to an end. During the Second World War the German and Soviet armies, unlike the Western armies, still depended for much of their transport on horses and railways.[44] It was the aircraft rather than the motor vehicle that made the Second World War, more than the First, the fulfilment of the concept of modern industrialized warfare. Indeed, many car firms were converted to produce aero-engines and aircraft parts instead of vehicles. The mass production of aircraft was an organized industrial effort without parallel. In five years annual world production of aircraft rose from 38,000 to over 255,000. In all, the major combatant powers produced over 840,000 aircraft, each one a complex and expensive piece of engineering, requiring the mobilization of almost half the productive capacity devoted to war production (See table 4.3).[45] The ability to mobilize resources effectively to meet these demands was a major component of the exercise of air power; and it is striking that some of the earliest enthusiasts for strategic bombing were drawn not from aviators but from industrialists – William Weir in Britain,

Table 4.4 *The number of horses in selected countries 1913–70 (000s)*

Country	1913	1925	1930	1938	1950	1960	1970
USA	23,015	16,400	13,511	10,800	5,402	2,953	2,238
Canada	2,866	3,554	3,295	2,820	1,796	571	354
Britain	1,735	1,447	1,221	1,100	494	157	—
Germany[a]	3,806	3,916	3,521	3,442	2,293	1,157	370
France	3,334	2,880	2,924	2,692	2,397	1,729	629
Italy	955	989	942	791	798	430	296
Australia	2,521	2,250	1,792	1,741	999	640	—
USSR[b]	21,900	25,200	31,000	17,700	12,700	11,000	7,500

Notes: [a]From 1950 figure for East and West Germany.
   [b]Figures for Russia are for 1910, 1925, 1930, 1940, 1950, 1960, 1970.
Sources: Mitchell, *Statistics*, p. 150; *International Yearbook of Agricultural Statistics*
(annually, Rome, 1921–46); United Nations, Food and Agriculture Organization, *World
Census of Agriculture*, 1950, 1960, 1970; *The Canada Year Book 1961* (Ottawa, 1961), p. 444;
Pocket Compendium of Australian Statistics (no. 46, Canberra, 1961), p. 192.

Michelin in France and Caproni in Italy.[46] Organizing air power on this scale
took an important element of the military effort out of the hands of the armed
forces and into the hands of civilians – officials, engineers and businessmen.
The technical and productive demands of both world wars were vital in the
development of modern aviation. After 1945 the wartime evolution of radar
and modern radio communication, of jet engines and pressurized cabins,
transformed the technical possibilities of aircraft development and air
transport, and created the conditions for the spread of mass air communication and for the conquest of space itself.

THE SOCIAL AND ECONOMIC IMPACT

The coming of mass motorization and mass aviation represents a significant
and identifiable discontinuity. The effects of both have been wide-ranging,
both direct and indirect. The most visible impact was the effect on traditional
forms of transport, first horses, then shipping, then finally the railway. The
motor vehicle ended man's long dependence on the horse. The number of
horses has declined almost continuously since the First World War (see table
4.4), and with it the significance of the horse not only for short-range travel,
but in agriculture and war.[47] Few Europeans or Americans have direct contact
with horses after half a century of mass motoring; the geography, and the
smells, of the city have changed. The shipping industry was undermined by air
travel more slowly after 1945, except for the transport of bulk goods; the
major ports have shrunk in size and number and the culture of shipping and
ship travel has been replaced with 'air mindedness'. In 1920 there were 35
airlines, by 1960 there were 260; the number of passenger miles increased from

1,300 million in 1935 to 70,000 million in 1960. Though the railway has also survived, its goods traffic has been diverted to road transport wherever possible, and its significance in passenger traffic has dwindled.[48] Many places in the developed world are no longer linked by railway, and the peculiar social impact of the rail era has likewise evaporated.

Instead the motor car and aircraft have revolutionized individual mobility. They have ended geographical isolation – the airship and aeroplane cartographers completed the charting of the world's surface in the 1920s and 1930s – and have contributed, particularly in the more developed world, to literally speeding up the pace of daily life. These are not simple extensions of the possibilities open to people in the nineteenth century, but represent a qualitative change in the nature of social life, economic opportunities and personal freedom. They have raised expectations, improved standards of service and made possible the extension of services of all kinds over whole populations. Of course some of these changes were the product of other developments as well, but in most cases efficient motorized transport is the permissive factor, highlighting the extent to which poor mobility, isolation and long travelling times inhibited the work practices, services and leisure time of nineteenth-century societies. Motor transport has also obtrusively transformed the environment, through road-building, the dispersal of urban populations, the increases in noise and pollution, and the very visible infrastructure of services and street furniture designed for the motor vehicle. Coping with the environmental consequences of mass motorization has led to a great increase in government services, and the growth of direct state regulation.[49]

The motor vehicle and aircraft have also contributed in a number of complementary ways to the development of the modern industrial economy. Though it is arguable that a cluster of different products might have led to the same growth effects, the motor and aviation industries have both contributed to sustaining high levels of economic growth and technical change at a vital period in economic development, when the technical and market possibilities of the first industrial revolution were reaching a climactic point. They made possible the next leap forward. If this seems an exaggerated view, it must be measured against the scale of the industries they sustained and the impact of faster and cheaper transport on other industries. The motor and aircraft industry both grew to be the largest heavy manufacturing sectors, with very high levels of employment, paying relatively high wages, and enjoying a complex set of linkages both backwards into the supply and component industries, and forwards into marketing, distribution and services. By 1960 businesses that serviced or used motor vehicles in the United States employed fourteen times the number employed in making vehicles.[50] Motorization was, and is, a major consumer of oil, petrol, steel and high-quality metals. The employment created by sectors related to motor traffic and aviation (the road haulage industry, the air transport network, public motor transport systems, etc.), though it has to be offset against the loss of jobs in declining sectors, has also greatly expanded. The motor car has also made necessary the construction world-wide of a new system of high-quality roads, producing, in the road-building booms in Europe and America, an effort not very different from the railway boom of the nineteenth century, and with the same economic effects. In America, where less than 150 miles (240 km) of roads in 1905 had a tarmac or brick surface, the construction of improved roads capable of supporting motor traffic was a vast project, reaching a total of 1.2 million miles (1.9m km) by 1925, 2.5 million (4m km) by 1960.[51] Air transport required the building and maintenance of airports, each a large employer of labour, each with its own network of specialized and ancillary services. All this shows that the economic effect of the motor vehicle and aircraft was not confined simply to its transport effect, but also its impact as a source of employment, productive investment and demand throughout the industrial and service sectors.

The motor-transport industries have contributed in another important way to the development of the modern industrial economy. Car firms have been, in a great number of cases, among the leading businesses to evolve into the modern business corporation organized along multinational lines. This has been a direct result of the nature of car production in the era of mass motoring, which has required the organization of very great numbers of workers and the production and distribution of large and expensive products. It has been the result, too, of the need to safeguard supplies of components or raw materials, or to secure particular market advantages. By the 1920s Ford had moved from assembling other people's components to producing more of the car in his own factories, buying up the suppliers of other specialized components, and even supplies of coal and iron; 'From Mine to Finished Car: One Organization' ran the slogan.[52] This pattern of corporation building was common to most major producers, setting new standards of management and planning for other businesses, and encouraging the wider spread of 'rational' production. The old 'heroic' car makers have been replaced by corporate officials and managers. Both industries, but particularly aviation, needed a highly skilled scientific and engineering workforce. This contributed in more general ways to raising the technical skills of the labour force and the threshold of technology.

HERALDS OF MODERNITY

The relative importance of both sectors has declined since the 1960s with the rise of a range of new industries and services, and with the de-industrialization of weaker economies. But their impact in sustaining levels of economic growth after the two world wars, even during the slump of the 1930s, mark both industries out as unique contributors to the establishment of an economic and social system demonstrably different from the world of small-scale capitalism, with its low wages and poor mobility, its limited social opportunities and narrow culture, characteristic of most of the industrialized world in 1900, to say nothing of the areas where modernization was only just beginning. Is this perhaps too large a claim? We return to that question of what the modern world would have been like without cars and aircraft. Both succeeded from the outset in being popularly perceived as the heralds of modernity, of something distinctively different from the inventive era which produced them.

There are wider issues here about the transformation that technology wrought in European society. Mechanical invention was an important part of the bourgeois-liberal world-view; it signalled the rational ordering of things, the conquest and appropriation of nature. Yet the same bourgeois idealism that gave rise to the striving for order encouraged a progressive scientific and technical culture which threatened disorder. Though the inventors themselves were uninhibited by this challenge, they found that the popular attitude to the development of both planes and cars could be discouraging and often overtly hostile. For sections of the educated and commercial middle classes there were clearly boundaries to the technical imagination and the willingness to innovate and experiment. Of course no serious brakes were placed on technical development, since it was inherently difficult to do so. But in a world of increasing uncertainty, the disintegrative impact of radical invention was all the greater. In that famous Edwardian fable of the *fin de siècle*, *Wind in the Willows*, published in 1908, it is the motor car that overturns innocent stability, the golden age; aboard a car Toad becomes 'the terror, the traffic-queller, before whom all must give way or be smitten into nothingness and everlasting night . . . fulfilling his instincts, living his hour, reckless of what might come to him'.[53] The most powerful image of all was the threat from aircraft, which might destroy the European order entirely: a positively millenarian vision of ruin from the heavens. This relationship between air power and the *fin de siècle* was vividly drawn by H. G. Wells in another novel of 1908, *The War in the Air*. In the following passage Wells drafts an epitaph for the 'age of progress':

And now the whole fabric of civilisation was bending and giving, and dropping to pieces and melting in the furnace of the war. The stages of the swift and universal collapse of the financial and scientific civilisation with which the twentieth century opened followed each other very swiftly . . . Up to the very eve of the War in the Air one sees a spacious spectacle of incessant advance, a world-wide security, enormous areas with highly-organised industry and settled populations, gigantic cities spreading gigantically, the seas and oceans dotted with shipping, the land netted with rails and open ways. Then suddenly the German air-fleets sweep across the scene, and we are in the beginning of the end.[54]

The fears of technical revolution opened up by cars and planes had more mundane features too. Motorization immediately offered the prospect of greater mobility, particularly in the countryside; it broke down the isolation and fragmentation of a large section of Europe's population and challenged the monopoly of horse-based mobility enjoyed by the upper and middle classes. Liberating peasants or even workers from restrictions of space carried threat as well as promise. Motorized transport and aviation also required a whole army of skilled workers to service and operate the new machines. This raised the status and demand for scientific and technical expertise, contributing to social mobility and a changing relationship of dependence between classes as the horse-servants departed from the households of the well-to-do. This problem raised itself most acutely in the armed forces, where the officer corps found it difficult to adjust without resentment to the social and technical demands of their new armament. As late as 1922 Field Marshal Haig argued that the tank and the aeroplane 'were only accessories to the man and the horse' and 'as time went on they would find just as much use for the horse – the well-bred horse – as they had ever done in the past'. The French general Weygand expressed his view of motorization in class terms: 'What a hotbed of Communism, this troop of mechanics.' Even in the 1930s a British officer could write contemptuously of the 'Garage Army'.[55]

Yet in many ways the social and cultural reordering which accompanied the rise of mass motoring and air power opened the way to new kinds of integration. The broadening of opportunities and the lifting of restrictions on mobility were just as likely to create new kinds of solidarity and identity, even linked to the existing order, as they were to transcend it entirely. And the optimism engendered by motorization, of a better life for ordinary people through mass consumption, mass travel, 'mass' society, eroded class differences and class antagonisms as much as it hastened the decline of bourgeois or aristocratic exclusiveness. Significantly the fears we have described were not American fears, for in the United States the relationship between technology and society was different. America's own self-image embraced easy social and spatial mobility and energetic technical advance. The much more rapid spread of motorization and aviation in America which resulted, contributed substantially to the 'Americanization' of European culture that began in the 1920s. While traditionalists bemoaned the European *fin de siècle*, many others welcomed the social vigour and flamboyant consumerism which they found in American culture. Driving cars and flying planes endorsed the rejection of a decaying Europe and asserted commitment to a constructive modernity that was specific to neither class nor nation, but had dimensions that were ultimately global.

NOTES

1 C. Gibbs-Smith, *The Invention of the Aeroplane 1799–1909* (London, 1966); H. Perkin, *The Age of the Automobile* (London, 1976), pp. 31–7; L. A. Everett, *The Shape of the Motor Car* (London, 1958), pp. 15–29; A. Bird, *The Motor Car 1765–1914* (London, 1960), pp. 1–24.

2 O. Lilienthal, *Birdflight as the Basis of Aviation* (London, 1911), p. 94.

3 H. Lörr, *Osterreichische Pioniere der Luftfahrt* (Vienna, 1953), pp. 21–31, 107–9.

4 E. Cressy, *A Hundred Years of Mechanical Engineering* (London, 1937), pp. 104–6; W. H. G. Armytage, *A Social History of Engineering* (London, 1961), pp. 220–2; Everett, *Shape of the Motor Car*, pp. 30–2.

5 Cressy, *Hundred Years*, pp. 117–18; St J. Nixon, *The Invention of the Automobile. Karl Benz and Gottlieb Daimler* (London, 1936); D. Scott-Moncrieff, *Three Pointed Star. The Story of Mercedes-Benz Cars* (London, 1955), pp. 4–37; Bird, *Motor Car*, pp. 25–48.

6 J. M. Laux, *In First Gear. The French Automobile Industry to 1914* (Liverpool, 1976), pp. 68–132; Bird, *Motor Car*, chs. 3–5.

7 R. W. Brewer, *The Art of Aviation: A Handbook upon Aeroplanes and Their Engines* (London, 1910); A. Berget, *The Conquest of the Air* (London, 1911), pp. 155–67.

8 S. B. Saul, 'The motor industry in Britain to 1914', *Business History*, 5 (1962), 22–44; H. H. von Fersen, *German High-Performance Cars* (London, 1965), ch. 1 (Opel began making sewing machines, then bicycles, finally cars); J. M. Laux, 'Rochet-Schneider and the French motor industry to 1914', *Business History*, 8 (1966), 77–85; J. Rae, *The American Automobile: A Brief History* (Chicago, 1965), ch. 1.

9 On Britain see D. Thoms and T. Donnelly, *The Motor Car Industry in Coventry since the 1890s* (London, 1985), pp. 14–66; H. Kerr Thomas, 'The effect of the automobile industry on the Midlands', *Proceedings of the Institution of Mechanical Engineers*, 1927, pp. 618–27; on France, Laux, *In First Gear*, pp. 52–4, 81–97.

10 J. Rae, *The Road and Car in American Life* (Cambridge, Mass., 1971), ch. 3; Rae, *Automobile*, pp. 54–60; J. Wolff, 'Entrepreneurs et firmes; Ford et Renault de leurs débuts à 1914', *Revue Economique*, 67 (1957); G. V. Thompson, 'Inter-company technical standardisation in the Early American automobile industry', *Journal of Economic History*, 14 (1954), 1–11; D. G. Rhys, *The Motor Industry: An Economic Survey* (London, 1972), pp. 4–9.

11 Von Fersen, *German Cars*, chs. 2, 3; Moncrieff, *Three Pointed Star*, pp. 96–114, 135–7; R. Hough, *A History of the World's Sports Cars* (London, 1961), pp. 15–30; K. Kavslake and J. Pomeroy, *From Veteran to Vintage. A History of Motoring and Motor Cars* (London, 1956).

12 K. Hopfinger, *Beyond Expectation: The Volkswagen Story* (London, 1954), pp. 15–58.

13 Rae, *Automobile*, pp. 11–26; M. Wilkins, *American Business Abroad: Ford in Six Continents* (Detroit, Mich., 1964), pp. 35–59.

14 Lörr, *Pioniere*, p. 209. Of all the records held up to 1912 France had 76, Austria–Hungary 23, Italy 11, USA 9, Britain 6, Germany 5, Belgium 1.

15 *Ibid.*, pp. 121–2; J. H. Morrow, *Building German Airpower, 1909–14* (Knoxville, Tenn., 1976), pp. 74–7; E. S. Gorrell, *The Measure of America's World War Aeronautical Effort* (Norwich University, Vermont, Publication No. 6, 1940), pp. 2–7. America had only twenty-six fully qualified military pilots in 1917, and no regular front-line aircraft.

16 Perkin, *Age of the Automobile*, pp. 54–5; von Fersen, *German Cars*, p. 18; Rae, *Automobile*, p. 17. Petrol in Britain increased in price from 8d. (3p) in the 1880s to 1s. 9d. (9p) in 1914.

17 R. Garrett, *Motoring and the Mighty* (London, 1970), pp. 3–4, 19, 37, 60–7.

18 On Britain see J. Hibbs, *The History of British Bus Services* (London, 1968), pp. 42–59.

19 P. A. Wright, *Old Farm Tractors* (London, 1962), pp. 2–4, 24–9; G. W. Grupp, *Economics of Motor Transportation* (London, 1924), ch. 2 on the growth of commercial motor transport. Lorry production in the United States rose from 411 in 1904 to 322,000 in 1920, and total tonnage carried from 600,000 to 1,200 million tons.

20 Perkin, *Age of the Automobile*, pp. 35, 40, 47; A. Bird, *Roads and Vehicles* (London, 1969), pp. 203–12; W. Plowden, *The Motor Car and Politics in Britain* (London, 1971), pp. 3–46.

21 F. L. Paxson, 'The highway movement 1916–1935', *American Historical Review*, 51 (1946), 238–49; K. Kaftan, *Der Kampf um die Autobahnen 1907–1935* (Berlin, 1935).

22 See for example P. S. Bagwell, *The Transport Revolution from 1770* (London, 1974), pp. 202–8. Out of 393 car firms in Britain before 1914 only 113 were still trading in that year.

23 A. Bird, *Early Motor Cars* (London, 1967), p. 157; Rae, *Automobile*, pp. 58–9.

24 W. R. Morris, 'The motor industry', in H. Schonfield (ed.), *The Book of British Industries* (London, 1933), pp. 252–3; the car-maker W. O. Bentley thought Morris had the appearance 'of a legal clerk dedicated to his calling and determined to do well in it': *The Cars in My Life* (London, 1961), pp. 68–9. On Renault see A. Rhodes, *Louis Renault: A Biography* (London, 1969), pp. 14–17, 24–5, 53–5; on Porsche, Hopfinger, *Beyond Expectation*, pp. 30–2; on Herbert Austin, designer of Britain's most successful small mass car in the 1920s, Z. E. Lambert and R. J. Wyatt, *Lord Austin: The Man* (London, 1968), pp. 31–5, 123–6; on Ford, A. Nevins, *Ford: The Times, the Man, the Company* (New York, 1954), pp. 36–53; A Jardim, *The First Henry Ford* (Cambridge, Mass., 1970), pp. 35–8.

25 C. Maier, 'Between Taylorism and technocracy: European ideologies and the vision of industrial productivity in the 1920s', *Journal of Contemporary History*, 5 (1970), 27–61; Rhodes, *Louis Renault*, pp. 66–75 for Ford's reception in France. See too H. Ford, *Today and Tomorrow* (London, 1926), pp. 5–6: 'Efficiency is merely the doing of work in the best way you know rather than in the worst way. It is the taking of a trunk up a hill on a truck rather than on one's back. It is the training of

the worker and the giving to him of power so that he may earn more and have more and live more comfortably. The Chinese coolie working through long hours for a few cents a day is not happier than the American workman with his own home and automobile. This one is a slave, the other is a free man.'

26 Garrett, *Motoring and the Mighty*, pp. 66–8; M. Dobb, *U.S.S.R.: Her Life and her People* (London, 1943), pp. 69–70; Wilkins, *American Business Abroad*, pp. 215–25.

27 O. Mosley, *My Life* (London, 1968), pp. 344–6; on Ford's anti-Semitism and alleged financial support for the Nazis see J. Pool and S. Pool, *Who Financed Hitler? The Secret Funding of Hitler's Rise to Power* (London, 1978), pp. 85–130. Ford was the first American to be awarded the Grand Cross of the Supreme Order of the German Eagle (the highest decoration for non-Germans) by Hitler in 1938. Renault was also suspected of collaborating with the radical Right in the 1930s and with the Nazi occupiers during the war, and his business was nationalized in October 1944; see Rhodes, *Louis Renault*, pp. 175–82.

28 P. Berg, *Deutschland und Amerika* (Lübeck, 1963), pp. 98–107 on the impact of Ford in Germany. There were plenty of opponents of Fordism as well, who saw the machine age as threat rather than promise. On the ambiguous attitude to technology see J. Herf, *Reactionary Modernism: Technology, Culture and Politics in Weimar and the Third Reich* (Cambridge, 1984).

29 Hopfinger, *Beyond Expectation*, pp. 68–73.

30 Generalinspektor für das deutsche Strassenwesen, *Drei Jahre Arbeit an der Strassen Adolf Hitlers* (Berlin, 1937), p. 7; Hopfinger, *Beyond Expectation*, pp. 100–21; R. J. Overy 'Transportation and rearmament in the Third Reich', *Historical Journal*, 16 (1973), 400–5.

31 D. Aldcroft and H. Dyos, *British Transport* (London, 1969), pp. 338–71; J. A. Davis, 'Motor vehicle legislation', in J. Labatut and W. Lane (eds.), *Highways and Our National Life: A Symposium* (Princeton, N.J., 1950), pp. 431–40. Major legislation controlling road haulage was passed in Britain in 1933 and the United States in 1935.

32 Rae, *Automobile*, pp. 58–61, 65–7.

33 R. J. Overy, *William Morris, Viscount Nuffield* (London, 1976), pp. 16–26; Society of Motor Manufacturers and Traders, *The Motor Industry of Great Britain 1939* (London, 1939), p. 47; H. G. Castle, *Britain's Motor Industry* (London, 1951), pp. 153–72.

34 Rae, *Automobile*, pp. 57–61; F. G. Woollard, *Principles of Mass and Flow Production* (London, 1954), pp. 15–33; *idem*, 'Some notes on British methods of continuous production', *Proceedings of the Institute of Automobile Engineers*, 19 (1924/5), pp. 419–41.

35 C. C. Edmonds, 'Tendencies in the automobile industry', *American Economic Review*, 13 (1923), 422–39; Thompson, 'Inter-company standardisation', pp. 12–13. By 1925 the top ten American companies controlled 89 per cent of the market, by 1939 three companies produced 88 per cent. See L. Rostas, *Comparative Productivity in British and American Industry* (Cambridge, 1948), pp. 58–63. On Britain see R. Church and M. Miller, 'The big three: competition, management and marketing in the British motor industry 1922–1939', in B. Supple (ed.), *Essays*

in British Business History (Oxford, 1977), pp. 163–83. By 1938 the top three companies in Britain produced 62 per cent of private cars, the top six 93 per cent.

36 Society of Motor Manufacturers and Traders, *Motor Industry*, pts IX, XI.

37 L. J. White, *The Automobile Industry since 1945* (Cambridge, Mass., 1971); P. Dunnett, *The Decline of the British Motor Industry 1945–1979* (London, 1980).

38 M. Maurer, *The U.S. Air Service in World War I* (Office of Air Force History, Washington, D. C., 1978), vol. II, pp. 135–6, 227–8; P. Christienne, *Histoire de l'aviation militaire française* (Paris, 1980), pp. 185–6; K. W. Förster, *Verkehrswirtschaft und Krieg* (Hamburg, 1937), p. 32.

39 P. Fearon, 'The British airframe industry and the state, 1918–1935', *Economic History Review*, 2nd ser., 27 (1977), 236–51; G. Simonson, 'The demand for aircraft and the aircraft industry 1907–1958', *Journal of Economic History*, 20 (1960), 361–82; E. Homze, *Arming the Luftwaffe: the Reich Air Ministry and the German Aircraft Industry 1919–1939* (Nebraska, 1976).

40 K. E. Bailes, *Technology and Society under Lenin and Stalin* (Princeton, N.J., 1978), p. 393. On the growth of international air traffic see W. E. Wynn, *Civil Air Transport* (London, 1946). In 1936 American airlines flew 73.3 million aircraft miles, France 7.07 million, Holland 4.56 million and Britain 4.78 million.

41 G. Douhet, *The Command of the Air* (London, 1943), pp. 14–24.

42 U. Bialer, 'Elite opinion and defence policy; air power advocacy and British rearmament during the 1930s', *British Journal of International Studies*, 6 (1980), 37; see too M. Smith, *British Air Strategy between the Wars* (Oxford, 1984), ch. 2.

43 R. J. Overy, *The Air War 1939–1945* (London, 1980); E. Beck, *Under the Bombs: The German Home Front 1942–1945* (Lexington, Ky, 1986).

44 For the general background on army motorization see D. Orgill, *The Tank: Studies in the Development and Use of a Weapon* (London, 1970); R. M. Orgorkiewicz, *Armoured Forces: A History of Armoured Forces and Their Vehicles* (London, 1970).

45 J. Rae, *Climb to Greatness* (Cambridge, Mass., 1968), pp. 143–57; Overy, *Air War*, pp. 149–84; G. Hartcup, *The Challenge of War: Scientific and Engineering Contributions to World War II* (Newton Abbot, 1970), pp. 89–158.

46 W. J. Reader, *Architect of Air Power: The Life of the First Viscount Weir of Eastwood 1877–1959* (London, 1968), pp. 73–5; on Caproni, C. G. Segrè, 'Douhet in Italy: prophet without honour?', *Aerospace Historian*, 26 (1979), 70–1.

47 F. M. L. Thompson, 'Nineteenth-century horse sense', *Economic History Review*, 2nd ser., 29 (1976), 60–79.

48 R. E. G. Davies, *A History of the World's Airlines* (London, 1964), p. 497. On the railway see D. Aldcroft, *British Railways in Transition* (London, 1968), pp. 55–8; J. H. Parmelee and E. Feldman, 'The relation of the highway to rail transportation', in Labatut and Lane (eds.), *Highways*, pp. 227–37; J. F. Storer, *The Life and Decline of the American Railroad* (New York, 1970), pp. 223–33, 235–42. High-revenue freight on the American railways declined from 53 million tons in 1920 to 15 million in 1940 and only 3 million in 1960.

49 K. M. Gwilliam, *Transport and Public Policy* (London, 1964), pp. 79–93, 107–47; C. D. Buchanan, *Mixed Blessing: The Motor in Britain* (London, 1958), esp. ch. 4; Plowden, *Motor Car*, chs. 16–20.

50 Rae, *Road and Car*, pp. 46 8.

51 *Ibid.*, pp. 63–70; S. Miller, 'The History of the modern highway in the United States', in Labatut and Lane (eds.), *Highways*, pp. 88–107; G. Hindley, *A History of Roads* (London, 1971), pp. 97–123.

52 Thompson, 'Inter company technical standardisation', p. 11; Edmonds, 'Tendencies in the automobile industry', pp. 431–2.

53 K. Graham, *The Wind in the Willows* (London, 1908), p. 123.

54 H. G. Wells, *The War in the Air* (London, 1908), pp. 352–4.

55 P. C. Groves, *Behind the Smoke Screen* (London, 1934), p. 138; A. Horne, *The French Army and Politics 1870–1970* (London, 1984), p. 55; 'The garage school of thought', *Army Quarterly*, 21 (1930/1), p. 380. This last article concluded that the next war 'will be principally fought and won by men on their feet'!

☙

FIVE

NATIONALISM, ANTI-SEMITISM, SOCIALISM AND POLITICAL CATHOLICISM AS EXPRESSIONS OF MASS POLITICS IN THE TWENTIETH CENTURY

ENZO COLLOTTI

Towards the end of the last century the basic structure of politics changed. This change was closely related to the rise of 'mass society'. There is no doubt that the evolution of politics has to be seen as connected with the developing industrialization and urbanization of both Europe and America. The resulting concentration of people in large groups imposes new forms on social life, engendering public and private services for the satisfaction of new needs in politics, society, culture and everyday life. A second essential factor in the reforging of political organization was a tendency towards the formation of nation states. While on the one hand the Dual Monarchy of Austria–Hungary represented the most important attempt to form a multinational state, on the other hand one sees a clear tendency towards the formation of nation states in important areas of Europe – principally Germany and Italy – following in the footsteps of countries like France, the instigator of Grand Revolution, in which the unity of state and nation had found a new synthesis in the ideas of egalitarianism and democracy spawned by the Revolution.

The coincidence of the great changes in economy and society and the trend towards the formation of unitary nation states signalled the end of a way of life which was archaic, individualistic, dominated by the few who possessed land or wealth, to the frustration of the majority who had no rights and were generally forced to engage in alienated work. The ideal expressed in the ethics and laws of classical liberalism – equality of opportunity – was never achieved, nor could it have been in European society prior to 1848. Paradoxically, one could say that the only time these ideals were approached was much more recently, in the achievement of the Welfare State by socialist movements, by Labour in Britain, and by social democracy in central and northern Europe. These movements were advocating ideals of collectivism opposed to liberal individualism, the latter being indissolubly linked to the idea of a non-interventionist state.

The organization of labour in factories nurtured the conception of radical social change and of socialism, at the very time when the necessity to expand production and trade, which brought national markets into being, encouraged a drift towards nationalism in the very contractors and tradesmen who would naturally have tended to identify with liberal individualism. 'Nation and liberty' – the slogan of 1848 – was not realized in practice in any country. In the German Empire the separation of the two concepts was made evident after the unification of 1871 by the manner in which Bismarck politically humiliated the emergent bourgeoisie by permitting freedom of action only on the economic plane. In the Dual Monarchy of Austria–Hungary, the conflict between liberty and the nation was never to be solved. The Germans and the Magyars remained the dominant nationalities, in a hierarchy which was not only political but also social.

The fledgeling organizations for the protection of the rights of working people, and the simultaneous tendency towards constitutionalizing the exercise of political power (recalling the division of power envisaged in the French Revolution), proposed a dialectical relationship between the rulers and the governed, which in embryo represented a model for supplanting the power of the absolute monarch, and approaching in different ways in different countries, forms of constitutional or even liberal-democratic government. In this climate more or less everywhere the problem arose of enlarging the range of participation, or as one might say nowadays of 'consensus'. The necessity of establishing a new and fairer balance between the political establishment and the people, and between the ruling classes and the masses marked the beginnings of universal suffrage, though this was often limited to voters with property qualification or just to the male population. The processes of national unification presented in their turn the further problem of the formation and consolidation of a concept of national consciousness. This was especially true for such social groups, generally belonging to the various strata of the middle class, whose cultural identity was not shaped as in the case of the working classes by their identity in the process of production, but by a compound set of values which were identified with national values, thus providing a means of socially collective integration.

NATIONALISM

In simply postulating the existence of nation states, the concept of 'nation' as forged by both the Enlightenment and Romanticism did not necessarily imply the existence of a concept of *nationalism*. That idea changed its meaning for historically determined cultural and social reasons, and either appeared as an anti-rationalist and anti-Enlightenment view, or as a replacement for the values of democracy and liberty. It was mainly the change from the mere history of political thought to the actual praxis of political action that gave strength and political status to nationalism. As seen in a historical perspective, this extension of the political process to the level of the masses – a process defined by George Mosse as the 'nationalization of the masses' – is at the same time a prerequisite and a consequence of universal franchise.

The second half of the nineteenth century was seen by many historians as the apotheosis of the bourgeoisie and of liberalism, especially if considered from the deceptive angle of the *belle époque*. In fact it was characterized by a number of nationalist currents. Sometimes, as in the case of Disraeli's Britain, they were triggered by great power imperialism, which was already accustomed to colonialism and the idea of world domination. In other cases, as in Bismarck's Reich, they were part of a delayed national unification and its authoritarian realization – here the attempt to 'confuse' rather than 'fuse' nation with state was especially clear, calculated not only in reaction to socialist internationalism, but also to weld together with the state a society which had little autonomy, either in political or civil matters. The nationalist reaction in France after the Commune and the Dreyfus affair was of a yet different kind.

France witnessed a confluence of Catholicism and nationalism (*Action française* was from its birth in 1908 until the mid-twenties one of the main foci for the traditional right wing), which represented the search for a national identity based on traditional and conservative values capable of holding in check the subversion threatened by the extreme Left. The problem of nationalism is more complex in Imperial Russia. Here there was no attempt to create a balance in the manner of the Austro-Hungarian model; instead the plurality of nationalities and the survival of a social structure, still predominantly agricultural and feudal, tended to encourage Panslavism, thus representing not only Tsarist imperialism but also religious and cultural hegemonism. Finally, Italian nationalism can only be interpreted in part as the result of irredentism concerning the Italian territories belonging to the Habsburg Empire. It was, rather, the political result of protests against both the process of democratization of Italian society attempted by Giolitti's liberalism, and of the industrialization which, being late, was even more aggressive in its feverish search for markets (whence the Libyan War, in fact fought against the Turkish Empire for supremacy in the Balkans), and territorial conquests.

Spawned by the nation states, nationalism was the expression of a struggle for power but also the expression of a profound modification in the basic structures of politics. The explosive growth of nationalism manifested itself without restraint at the beginning of the First World War in 1914, but in fact it had already permeated European society as one of the great political currents in the last decades of the nineteenth century. As a mass phenomenon nationalism was used to build up a consensus not based on class values or around the validation of democracy or social class. Everywhere nationalism was identified with the myth of the Nation and the strong State. Italian nationalism elaborated a theory of the state which was to become part of the view of the state held by fascism: namely, the view of a strong state based on corporatist structures, above class, against social conflict, and capable of guaranteeing appeasement between Capital and Labour within political and economic structures dominated by Capital. This strong state would guarantee social peace as a prerequisite of the unity of the nation not only against internal enemies (democracy and socialism) but especially against external enemies: the state is thus seen as a function of foreign policy, and nationalism as the internal and ideological support for imperialism.

By overemphasizing the idea of the nation and the primacy of one nation over the others, nationalism was deeply anti-egalitarian. It therefore was inherently anti-democratic, and supported authoritarian and anti-parliamentary tendencies in all countries. By denying democratic pluralism it also tended to support those modes of political struggle which rejected democratic contrast. Although nationalism cannot be systematically identified with racism, the oligarchic principle which was a typical characteristic of nationalist movements (the charismatic leader in the authoritarian and fascist regimes was a direct derivation from that aristocratic principle) provided also a cultural path towards racism. At first sight there would seem to be a contradiction between the oligarchic principle and the importance given to the masses – but this is so only superficially. The weight of numbers ('numbers mean power', Mussolini was later to say), in the sense of the weight of demographic power, was one of the war-horses of nationalists who, at the same time, would reject its interpretation according to the spirit of democracy and of the sovereignty of the people. Gustave Le Bon, undoubtedly one of the founders of nationalist sociology, in his fundamental *Psychologie des foules* (1895), was among the first to theorize the presence of the masses as a factor of political conflict. The crowd of which he writes is a depersonalized mass, far removed from that process of politicization which was at the time mainly associated with socialism. This crowd was consolidated beyond the principle of class, and unified through the concepts of nation and national power. The phenomenon of Bonapartism, to use Marx's example from the history of the Second Empire, foreshadowed the relationship between leaders and masses in the twentieth century – with the addition in fascist regimes of elements of Sorel's syndicalism. George Mosse has vividly described how the masses were disciplined by the creation of a political liturgy and ritual which exploited the resources of political symbology to an extreme: now, the political use made of the masses by both nationalism and socialism was fundamentally at the heart of the refusal by both conservative philosophers and exponents of liberal thought to countenance the participation of the masses in political life. In his over-pessimistic *Untergang des Abendlandes* (1918) Oswald Spengler celebrated aristocratic Caesarism. But even Ortega y Gasset, a liberal thinker, in his *La rebelion de las masas* (1930) separated democracy from liberalism and thus unwittingly placed himself against the great movements of democratization which occurred after the First World War, and favoured authoritarian solutions to the crisis of the liberal regimes.

Nationalism was certainly responsible for the degeneration of national causes into the explosion of the First World War. It also contributed to the formation of fascist and authoritarian regimes in both western and eastern Europe which supported revanchism even in such smaller countries as Bulgaria, Hungary and in some measure Poland, that had either been defeated in the war or had arisen from the dissolution of the Habsburg Empire.

RACISM AND ANTI-SEMITISM

In a way, nationalism facilitated the penetration of racism into the European political world even if one cannot claim that it necessarily led to racism. In its late nineteenth-century form, racism was not the expression of the generic sense of superiority of single national groups as seen in the phenomenon of European colonialism. Especially in its anti-Semitic version, which was the form by far prevailing and historically more important, racism was the result of a complex set of cultural and socio-economic elements with roots in anthropology and the biological sciences. The development of anti-Semitism is on the one hand indissolubly linked to the socio-economic role played by Jews in modern society, especially in the less advanced areas of eastern Europe and in the more advanced ones of western Europe; on the other to those reactionary movements which spread all over Europe in opposition to the achievements of the French Revolution, one of which was Jewish emancipation. Jewish integration was easier in France and Italy, perhaps partly because of the small size of those communities, than it was in such countries as Germany, Austria, Russia and other territories of eastern Europe, including Poland and Romania, where the 'Jewish question' was part of a broader context of complex national and social conflicts. The second half of the nineteenth century not only witnessed anti-Semitic ideology but even the formation of actual anti-Semitic political movements: they had no common political platform, since they were following different tendencies and their motives were different in different countries. However, there was a common origin to the upsurge of anti-Semitism, namely the economic crisis of 1873. That crisis caused reaction against those capitalists, financiers and businessmen who ran the economy, including the Jewish groups who were generally identified as owners of means of production. At this stage, anti-Semitism did not have specifically racist connotations, but was rather a retroaction to the dominant position of Jews in some sections of economic and social life – a circumstance with cultural and historical causes, including the religious ostracism declared against them by the Catholic Church. No doubt this was a salient element in the origins of anti-Semitism, especially in central Europe (Germany and Austria).

Elsewhere, the problem of Jewish integration into national societies became confused with the fight between authoritarianism and liberalism. This was especially true in Imperial Russia where in the nineteenth century and the first years of the twentieth the notorious pogroms – the most radical forms of anti-Semitic violence – took place, especially following the accession of Alexander III. In Imperial Russia particularly, the Jewish question was demagogically used to deflect towards the Jews the dissatisfaction of those who were oppressed and starved of freedom – as if the Jews should really be the scapegoats for national calamities and disasters, this being a process which the Nazi regime was to take to its extreme consequences in the twentieth century. It is no accident that the most notorious anti-Semitic pamphlet, the 'Protocols of the Elders of Zion', appeared in Russia, later to be widely utilized in Nazi propaganda.

In the nineteenth century Jewish emancipation had considerably progressed, mainly in Germany and Austria. In 1878 the great powers who assembled at the Berlin Congress to consider the 'Eastern question' had guaranteed religious equality for Jews in south-eastern Europe (especially Romania). But at the same time as this progress in integration was taking place, an anti-Semitic ideology was developing whose motivations were totally different from the traditional anti-Semitism of the Catholic Church. It was now that, due to the influence of irrational and vitalist trends which were present in both positivism and social Darwinism, the first doctrine to exalt the superiority of the Aryan–Nordic races was outlined in the works of the Frenchman Arthur de Gobineau, author of the *Essai sur l'inégalité des races humaines* (1853–55), and especially Houston Chamberlain, Wagner's English son-in-law, whose work *Die Grundlagen des XIX Jahrhunderts* (1899) can be considered the most direct source material for the theoreticians of Nazi anti-Semitism. Chamberlain's work, by exalting the role of the Aryan race and the necessity of preserving its purity, upheld a view of life based on the struggle amongst races in which the weakest ones were destined to succumb, and thus outlined for the first time an ideal of racial hierarchy strictly conceived on biological grounds and later deployed by Nazism. Imperial Russia, Germany and Austria were the main centres of anti-Semitism until 1914, although grave episodes of racial intolerance occurred in other places – for example, in France during the trumped-up Dreyfus affair of 1894. In Russia anti-Semitism was brought to an end by the 1917 Revolution. In Germany and Austria, anti-Semitism asserted itself also against the fledgeling Jewish nationalist movement (Zionism). In Germany, prior to the accession of Kaiser Wilhelm II, and with support from nationalist and academic circles, the Protestant court preacher Adolf Stoecker was the first to endeavour to create a mass political movement based on anti-Semitic views when in 1878 he founded the workers' Christian Social Party whose fortunes reached their zenith in 1893 when sixteen anti-Semitic members of parliament were elected to the Reichstag. In the same year with the foundation of the Pan-German League, anti-Semitism, a concept scientifically meaningless but as attractive as all myths, was officially included amongst the goals of German imperialism, with the theoretical support later provided by Chamberlain's work. Anti-Semitism, particularly in Austria, ceased to be just propaganda or a merely religious or cultural phenomenon (like the anti-Semitism of the social-Catholic school and its main representative, Karl Vogelsang) and became a real political movement. It derived from the reactionary Pan-Germanic and atheistic tendency of Georg Ritter von Schönerer (1842–1921) and the extremist wing of the Catholic movement, whose most authoritative representative was the Viennese burgomaster Karl Lueger. During his administration (1897–1910), Lueger turned the Austrian capital, which had the strongest Jewish community, into the centre of anti-Semitic struggle. It was from this climate in Vienna that the young Adolf Hitler absorbed the germs of his violent and fanatical anti-Semitism.

Anti-Semitism, which did not disappear in Kaiser Wilhelm's Germany, flourished again in the climate of defeat following the First World War, culminating under the Nazi regime in its extreme biological form – the physical destruction of the European Jewish communities. Nazi racism not only pushed the anti-Semitic tradition to an extreme, on the basis of the pseudo-scientific theories of A. Rosenberg, W. Darré, H. K. F. Günther (the Jew as a 'foreign body' to the German people, a parasite endangering its racial purity), but also extended such views to everybody who was different in a vast project of eugenics. There were strong anti-Slav undertones, and projects of euthanasia and biological purification were carried out within the German population itself.

In spite of the lessons of the Nuremberg Trials (1945–6) which classified Nazi genocide amongst crimes against humanity, racial prejudice has not disappeared from contemporary political phenomena and practices. Just as it played an important role in the colonialist and nationalist traditions, it continues to be a major element both in unresolved circumstances inherited from the old relations of colonial domination and in societies characterized by strong ethnic contrasts – and indeed in the relations between the new Israeli state (founded in response to the Nazi genocide) and the Arab world. While in the USA the fight for civil rights has greatly ameliorated the political and social integration of Blacks, there is no doubt that the American intervention in Vietnam had a racist component: ferocity applied with the most sophisticated technologies of destruction against a population considered culturally and biologically inferior. Also, the French attempt to retain Algeria as the last outpost of her colonial empire was characterized by outbreaks of racist violence comparable to the last convulsions of Portuguese colonialism. Nowadays, the South African regime of apartheid is perhaps the most striking case of the institutionalization of racism, and is universally known. But latent racism survives more or less everywhere. Even where there are no direct national frictions, social problems have arisen which have reproduced many of the stereotypes of traditional racism, based on objective conditions or demagogical imperatives. In the world-wide conflict between north and south, the plague of racism has found new breeding-grounds in the identification between skin colour and social status. Racial tensions have become stronger during phases of recession or of great change in the world economy which reduce employment. The trend towards the liberalization of the international labour market and the related new migrations from less developed countries thus clash with the defence of employment and rekindle the flames of racism.

SOCIALISM

The rise of socialism, both as an ideology and as a political movement, was certainly one of the major elements in framing the new mass politics towards the end of the nineteenth century. In fact the political movements involved in the Second International (1889–1914) cannot be attributed to a single ideological origin. Often the aims were the same but the ideological and cultural backgrounds were different. The process of industrialization, and consequently the birth of the new proletariat – the working classes in the modern sense – had taken place at very different times in the different countries of Europe and America: the result of this was the formation of a highly differentiated labour movement, greatly influenced by the stage and form of capitalist development in the different countries. It would be totally wrong to assume that socialism and Marxism were the same thing. When Marxism became the overriding, though not homogeneous, trend in the Second International, there were already several working-class movements whose roots were not Marxist. This is especially true for Britain, where the organizations fighting for better social justice – the common platform of all movements which were broadly speaking 'socialist' – had their roots in the liberal tradition (Chartism) and a kind of utopian reformism. Traditionally, British socialism did not advocate a revolutionary change in social organization by opposing a specifically socialist model to the capitalist one. However, this does not mean that, though supporting gradualism, it was less radical in its defence of working-class interests than the continental revolutionary movements. It was a different view of socialism, more based on trade union work than political ideology. British labourers were not less belligerent than the continental working classes, or their strikes less tough, but for them what mattered was a strong spirit of solidarity and the fight for practical achievements. This did not only derive from the fact that the development of the labour movement in Britain preceded that of Marxism. The emphasis on trade unionism derived also from the fact that the British working classes had already obtained the franchise. Thus they did not have to fight for the franchise, a fact which was to be decisive for the politicization of the continental working-class movement. Because of these peculiarities, the British working-class movement, unlike the continental one, tended to appear quite neatly separated from the rest of national culture, thus overemphasizing its trade unionist character and its own unique cultural models.

French socialism before the Paris Commune had also been heavily influenced by the views of various utopian schools of thought and forms of social solidarity not based on class struggle. In a social structure for so long dominated by a kind of industrialism largely based on craftsmanship, the late eighteenth-century utopian movement and Proudhon's non-class-based socialism were able to strike a sympathetic chord. France was also fertile ground for the preaching of anarchism, which gave rise to the anarcho–syndicalist current violently opposed to the idea of a political party. French socialism, which became united at the beginning of the twentieth century, was thus the result of elements of different cultural provenance; Marxism was not the unifying character, this function being fulfilled by the democratic and republican tradition of the great Revolution, the secular spirit which opposed the powerful sectarian Catholicism which increasingly supported the conservative camp after the fear caused by the Commune. The humanitarian aspect of French socialism was often both the strength and the weakness of its internationalism. In fact French socialism also had deep national roots outside the ideals of the Second International. Jacobin tradition was undoubtedly stronger than Marxist influence; moreover syndicalism, even in Sorel's version, was strongly national and scarcely or not at all internationalist.

Historians agree that the socialist movement in the German Reich was the leading socialist movement towards the end of the nineteenth century. The workers' movement in Germany, which had arisen in the context of delayed and therefore accelerated industrialization, was characterized by a strong trade unionism at the same time as a strict political organization – this even going back beyond the historical dates of 1863 (foundation of Lassalle's party), 1875 (the Marxist unification at Gotha) and 1891 (the Erfurt programme).

The German socialist movement – later considered as a party, and as the point of departure for studies of its theoretical contradictions, and of difficulties in the relation between broadly Kautskyan revolutionary tendencies and the reformist praxis of the Second International – was the first to experience direct confrontation between a great movement of working-class emancipation and the strength of an authoritarian state. Bismarck's antisocialist legislation in the end helped the quantitative growth of the movement even though it influenced its orientation for ever. It was the most striking of the reactionary moves by the conservative ruling class against the ascent of a strong popular movement which disputed the monopoly of politics maintained by a small aristocratic and bureaucratic oligarchy. That legislation was also an attempt to affirm the authority of the state as the only valid political agency in dealing with social unrest. The concept of civil and political society as autonomous and distinct from the state was alien both to the Prussian political tradition and to the manner of formation and unification of the German Reich. The antisocialist legislation, which tried to deny participation to the popular movement which promised to expand and transform society in the second half of the nineteenth century, was in a certain sense a continuation of the defeat of liberalism in 1848–9. It was an attempt to prevent the development of mass politics or at least to confine its possibilities. Bismarck was the first to understand the character of modern political and social conflict, but he was unable to give an equally modern answer so far as the structures of the state were concerned. He did not try to manage and mediate conflict, but endeavoured to pre-empt it and to extirpate its roots. In that programme he sought to establish in German political life and culture a horror of conflict, diversity and the free negotiation of social pacts, and this contributed to the weakening of all instances of social and political autonomy. Thus a strongly corporatist society was being built in the Second Reich; the result was more a kind of fragmentation of the state and its diffusion within society, than the articulation of autonomous forces and agencies. The latter better describes what was happening in Italy and France, under different political traditions and cultural influences (the weakness of both the central state and of a state tradition in Italy was amongst the factors which contributed to the fragmentation of the political and social spectrum). In that society the identification of the interests of classes and groups with the interests of the state was one of the unwritten rules of the political system. If social action was a function of the state's interests, then political mediation was excluded. This on the one hand explains the radicalization of the socialist movement, at least in those sectors more directly influenced by Marx's views and by a global project of social transformation; on the other hand, it also explains the intention and repressive power of a state which underwent a process of national and social militarization in the process of industrialization. Nowhere so much as in Germany did discipline in factories tend to reproduce a kind of military discipline. Nowhere so much as in Germany was the consensus of the masses – as a passive consensus – built on the symbols of military glory. It is true that the Second Empire and the Third Republic in France were full of pompous patriotic rhetoric. The existence of a national tradition prior to the Revolution meant that the socialist movement did not have to respect the categories imposed by the middle classes for the definition of their national identity. For the German socialist movement everything was more difficult. In explaining these difficulties, it is only partly true to maintain that socialism there withdrew into a kind of sub-culture in spite of its revolutionary phraseology and the theoretical strength of which some of its major intellectuals were capable. This view would in fact mislead us by ignoring the threat posed to the working-class movement by both nationalist fervour and the antisocialist legislation, even after the Reichstag had voted to repeal it.

The expansion of the socialist movement from Britain into continental Europe – and to a lesser extent into countries outside Europe, including the USA where it was brought by immigrating European labourers – was a major factor in the dissemination of the most diverse socialist views. The strength of the movement was first of all its capacity to fuse together political initiative with a set of ideological values. It matters little that, as many recent studies have shown, the great mass of the late nineteenth-century proletariat, gathered in consensus around a strong and learned nucleus of intellectuals, knew very little of the so-called scientific socialism, and had read little of the theoretical literature of Marxism or of any other socialist tendencies. But the strength of the ideal was by no means an abstraction. All socialist programmes were reacting to conditions of real exploitation, of real attempts to isolate the masses, of real opposition between classes, even when conflicts were spirited away or denied outright. Socialism, intended not only as the utopian vision of a new society based on the transformation of capitalism, but also as the ideological unification of the many diverse and diffuse forms of working-class resistance and solidarity, is the most general creation of a 'counter-culture' ever known in contemporary European society.

The history of the Second International provides remarkable evidence as to how mass politics can change the modes of political conduct, and the socialist movement was unified beyond national boundaries. Mass politics did not only mean the transformation of politics beyond narrowly circumscribed parliamentary constituencies and electoral colleges, but also the envisioning of the external phenomena of politics. It is important for the socialist movement to be able to count its members and to have a quantitative conception of its numerical strength. The most important aspect of the change in the modes of political conduct is not in the mere ritual of processions, demonstrations and rallies. Politics is taken out of closed rooms, becomes public, speaks to large masses, opposes restrictions on representation and on membership of the political classes by affirming the necessity to enlarge the franchise and extend representation to those who feel excluded. This is generally an urban phenomenon because the proletariat is a function of the industrialized city, and because it is the urban landscape which represents the visualization of politics. The struggle for universal suffrage, even though it tends to forget about women, is an essential stage in the process of the aggregation of the masses, who recognize their identity in the great ideals of socialism. It also represents a fundamental stage in the process whereby the existing political system and the monopoly of conservative groups were rendered ideologically illegitimate.

The capacity to organize and mobilize large masses of labourers was not only the new character of the mass politics which developed with the socialist movement. It is fundamentally important that the movement tended to arise simultaneously in the most diverse places. The speed of transmission of information (a result not only of organization but also of the new development of a mass-circulation press) is not only an element of success, it is also an essential foundation of the new way of doing politics. Gathering behind red flags or behind political and cultural slogans (for example, the slogan 'knowledge is power', which underpins the development of all mass culture) expresses the need of the masses to discover moments of self-identification in supreme unifying values, different from the traditional bourgeois values.

The struggle for universal suffrage represented in the highest degree the desire to be reckoned with, to become part of the recognized institutions, to become the ruling class at all levels of government and local administration. There the new socialist representatives began to speak a different language supporting through parliamentary representation the needs of hitherto neglected classes. The May Day demonstration was not only part of a ritual: it expressed the needs and the reality of a non-corporatist working-class solidarity, which went beyond national borders and coalitions established in instances of the defence of employment (which were not as such purely defensive). There are many elements which represent the new presence, the new type of representation and the new era of politics: the combative spirit of the May Day demonstrations; iconography in which symbols of work and emancipation coalesced; the usage of urban space in ways which challenged the rigid social topography of the separation of the residential city from the working city and even more so from the suburbs of the poor. May Day more than any other day represents the synchronization and therefore the

amplification of countless voices everywhere in the world. May Day provides
a photo-fit picture of a movement of protest and by sheer weight of numbers
amplifies the sense of power of a whole class. What happened in 1914 was to
show how illusory that unification was across national borders. However, it
would be difficult to deny or even reductively interpret the tendency towards
solidarity and emancipation. Of course the fact that the May Day celebration
has survived as the memory of a tradition accentuates its ritual aspect.
However, it would be totally wrong to fail to interpret the profound meaning
of aggregation according to the criteria of those days, rather than our own.
That movement was not only the result of organized action, but also of a wide
circulation of ideas and the widespread identity of human and social
conditions.

Socialism implied the escalation of political battle from the purely parliamentary field to mass struggle. The unification of mass struggle with
parliamentary politics was typical of the period of the Second International,
when socialist parties were forces of opposition even when they were
parliamentary parties. The extra-parliamentary dimension of mass struggle –
only exceptionally anti-parliamentary in the traditional democracies – validated trade unionism, the struggle for suffrage and social protest in general. It
was also the main means pursued by the strong anti-militarist tendencies of
the socialist Left (above all Karl Liebknecht in Germany), and the anti-
imperialist tendencies (the Bolsheviks and Rosa Luxemburg). The dialectical
relationship between the parliamentary and the mass struggle was also highly
representative of a long period in the history of the working-class movement
in which class and party tended to be seen as identical. The First World War
caused a crisis in many of the values expressed by socialism, such as
internationalism and the identity of party and class. The collapse of the
Second International in the face of the war and the alignment of the various
parties according to the stance taken by national governments, especially in
Germany and France, lay at the root of the wartime problems. However,
through the left-wing minorities and the Zimmerwald antiwar movement,
those problems also lay behind the origin of the Communist International
founded in 1919 following the secession of the socialist Left from the
traditional parties.

From then onwards the unity of the international working-class movement
was broken for ever. As a consequence of this, communist parties had to
develop basically as revolutionary minorities with the aim of building
socialism in one country – the Soviet Union. On the other hand, after the brief
episode of the Union of Vienna (1921–3), characterized by the 'Austro-
Marxism' of the Austrian Social Democratic Party, the traditional Social
Democratic parties after 1918 became the main vehicles of the Western
working classes, and evolved in a gradualist and reformist manner. In
western, northern and central Europe they nearly always became government

parties, losing many of the characteristics they shared at the time of the Second International, and have become deeply integrated into national societies (hence the end of internationalism), and reverted to entirely parliamentary action. The reformism of the 1920s and 1930s can be seen as at the root of the most recent Welfare State. It is however more difficult to trace any historical continuity in the communist parties which came together in the Third International and the so-called 'real socialism' of the eastern European socialist countries, beyond the way those regimes represent themselves.

POLITICAL CATHOLICISM

The long march of international socialism obviously encountered the resurgence of Catholicism as a political movement and the foundation of social movements inspired by Catholic doctrine in many places in the second half of the nineteenth century, especially in such traditionally Catholic European countries as France, Austria, Italy and Belgium, but also in countries with strong components of other religions, such as Germany, Switzerland and the Netherlands. Often sociologically opposed to the socialist movement because of the dominance of the clergy in the countryside, the Catholic movement eventually gathered the masses together. The Catholic Church radically revised its attitude to its presence in society and (at the end of the century) its view of industrialism. This followed its reaction to the French Revolution, the crisis of the Romantic opposition to the Industrial Revolution, when the economic and cultural privileges of the Catholic Church were attacked through the secularization of church possessions and the ending of the religious monopoly over education. Pius IX's complete exclusion of the modern world and reaction to the loss of temporal power caused by Italian unification, left Leo XIII with the task of fixing a new framework for the relationship between the church and the process of secularization undertaken by the new nation states. The aim of Leo XIII's policy was twofold: to preserve the autonomy of the Catholic Church within the new nations vis-à-vis the political power of the bourgeoisie, without losing the privileges which still survived in some special situations (e.g. in the Habsburg monarchy); and to attempt to counteract the growing strength of the socialist movement through the development of a Catholic social movement, prompted by fear of the Paris Commune, which renewed the fear of the French Revolution. Leo XIII realized that capitalism and industrialism were historically irreversible phenomena – this was his 'modernity'. The diffusion of the socialist movement in all urban areas caused the Catholic Church to attend to the necessity of opposing the concept of class struggle with a Christian social solidarity. The encyclical *Rerum novarum* (1891) tried to provide universal foundations for Catholic social doctrine by outlining a kind of social ethic based on the moral responsibility of property and the employer, thus totally rejecting class struggle. The alternative view this supported was collaboration amongst the classes based on collaboration between Capital and Labour. At the practical level, the Catholic Church was demanding recognition of the autonomous organization of a Catholic social movement based on ideals of social peace. This would be an organization including labourers and employers (i.e. corporatist), which a few decades later was to converge with the corporatism of nationalist movements and fascist regimes, their different provenance notwithstanding. Appeals to autonomy of the Catholic organization were especially strong where the Catholic Church was in conflict with the liberal state. This was so in Italy until the first decade of the twentieth century. The same happened in the Protestant Reich. There Bismarck's *Kulturkampf* appeared in one sense to be a strict political and religious conflict between Protestantism and Catholicism, but in another was also determined by Catholic demands for autonomy within the Reich, notwithstanding the truth of Bismarck's accusation that the German Catholic clergy were the subalterns of the Church in Rome.

To quote two extreme cases, the *rapprochement* between church and state followed similar paths in Italy and in the German Reich, in spite of the two different religious contexts. The 'social question' provided the field for mediation and reconciliation with the state. Whilst jealously guarding its autonomy from the state, in both these cases social and political Catholicism realized how necessary it was not to isolate itself from society, and then gradually endeavoured to settle its conflict with the state. It is symptomatic that in the Reich, after its persecution in the *Kulturkampf*, German Catholicism contributed in turn to antisocialist persecution. This shows that German Catholicism was not involved in the struggle for freedom, but was only concerned to protect the values of the Catholic Church and the Catholic social ethic, thus competing with the socialist movement. Furthermore, one cannot accept the generalization that the strong development of social Catholic associations in Germany contributed to the democratization of that country.

In Italy, the first sensational expression of reconciliation with the liberal state was the so-called 'Gentiloni pact' of the 1913 election; and its equally sensational outcome was the appeasement of the Lateran Pacts of 1929 between the church and the fascist regime. This reconciliation was cleverly facilitated by Giolitti. He had pursued the aim of integrating the moderate Catholic masses into the pre-fascist political system in order to counterbalance the socialist movement. Giolitti's plan agreed with the Catholic Church's interest in retaining its presence in Italian society. The tacit agreement on the 'social question' was the first stage of a process that induced Catholicism to abandon the abstentionist policy outlined in Pius IX's time. The Catholic presence in national society (during the Libyan War one could speak of a real 'Catholic nationalism') was the second stage in the ending of political abstinence, when the Catholic Church was to provide the authoritarian fascist regime with a consensus it had previously denied to the liberal state.

The First World War was a watershed for the Catholic movement as well, both in Italy where for the first time a mass Catholic party was created in Luigi Sturzo's Partito Popolare, and in the Reich where the Zentrum party converted its initial strong support for the monarchy into support for the Weimar Republic. In Austria the Christian Social Party accepted a marriage of convenience with the republic after the demise of the Habsburg monarchy. In their total opposition to socialism, the Catholics represented the forces of conservatism and reaction, and ended up forming alliances with the pro-fascist *Heimwehr* and playing a major role in the clerical-fascist dictatorship of Dollfuss and the antisocialist military repression of 1934.

Universal suffrage, extended to women in Germany and Austria after the First World War, and in Italy after the fall of fascism, strengthened the militancy of political parties deriving from Catholicism, in circumstances which were particularly favourable. The division of Germany after 1945 changed religious geography, thus permitting the success of the Catholic component in the German Federal Republic embodied in the Christian Democratic Parties of CDU and CSU. In Italy the new Christian Democratic Party inherited the mantle of the Catholic mass organizations, which were the only organizations legally tolerated under the fascist regime and permitted to be neither fascist nor anti-fascist.

ESSENTIAL REFERENCES

For the general socio-political development of the second half of the nineteenth century, see
Hobsbawm, E. J. *The Age of Capital, 1848–1875* (London, 1975)
Schorske, C. E. *Fin-de-siècle, Vienna: Politics and Culture* (New York, 1981).

For the development of political thought, see
Bracher, K. D. *Zeit der Ideologien* (Stuttgart, 1982)
De Ruggiero, G. *Storia del liberalismo europeo* (Milan, 1962; reprint of 1st edn of 1925)
Hobsbawm, E. J. *et al.* (eds.). *Storia del marxismo* (Torino, 1978 *et seq.*)
Stuart Hughes, H. *Consciousness and Society* (New York, 1958).

On the subject of nationalism in the history of individual nations, see
Gaeta, F. *Il nazionalismo italiano* (Bari, 1981)
Gentile, E. *Il mito dello stato nuovo dall'antigiolittismo al fascismo* (Bari, 1982)
Gentile, E. *Le origini dell'ideologia fascista* (Bari, 1975)
Hobsbawm, E. J. *Industry and Empire: An Economic History of Britain since 1750* (Harmondsworth, 1968)
Mayeur, J. M. *Les Débuts de la troisième république (1871–1898)* (Paris, 1974)
Rebérioux, M. *La République radicale? 1898–1914* (Paris, 1975).

For a stimulating investigation of a particular case (from which one should extrapolate only with caution to other situations), see

Mosse, G. L. *The Nationalization of the Masses: Political Symbolism and Mass Movements in Germany from the Napoleonic Wars through the Third Reich* (New York, 1974).

For racism, in its anti-Semitic version, see in the first instance the following general works

Claussen, D. *Vom Judenhass zum Antisemitismus* (Darmstadt–Neuwied, 1987)

Massing, P. *Vorgeschichte des politischen Antisemitismus* (Frankfurt-on-Main, 1959)

Mosse, G. L. *Masses and Man. Nationalist and Fascist Perception of Reality* (New York, 1984)

Mosse, G. L. *The Crisis of German Ideology: Intellectual Origins of the Third Reich* (New York, 1964)

Mosse, G. L. *The Culture of Western Europe* (London, 1963)

Mosse, G. L. *Towards the Final Solution: A History of European Racism* (New York, 1978)

Poliakov, L. *Histoire de l'antisémitisme* (4 vols., Paris, 1955 et seq.)

Pulzer, P. G. J. *Die Entstehung des politischen Antisemitismus in Deutschland und Oesterreich 1867–1914* (Gütersloh, 1966).

For a particular case, see

Cohn, N. *Die Protokolle der Weisen von Zion: der Mythos von der judischen Weltverschwörung* (Cologne, 1969).

On the development of Hitler's anti-Semitism, see

Jenks, W. A. *Vienna of the Young Hitler* (New York, 1960).

On the subject of Nazi anti-Semitism, see

Cecil, R. *The Myth of the Master Race: Alfred Rosenberg and Nazi Ideology* (London, 1972)

Neurohr, J. F. *Der Mythos vom Dritten Reich* (Stuttgart, 1957)

Saller, K. *Die Rassenlehre des Nationalsozialismus in Wissenschaft und Propaganda* (Darmstadt, 1961)

Vermeil, E. *Doctrinaires de la révolution allemande 1918–1938* (Paris, 1939).

For an original reconceptualization of the historical and political phenomenon of nationalism (and racism) and their relationship with industrialization, which treats some themes touched on in my text, see

Gellner, E. *Nations and Nationalism* (London, 1983).

Among the many histories of socialism, the best is undoubtedly

Cole, G. D. H. *A History of Socialist Thought* (London, 1953 et seq.) (the Italian edition of this work contains a substantial updated bibliography, lacking only the works of the last decade).

For other histories, apart from works already cited, see
Abendroth, W. *Sozialgeschichte der europäischen Arbeiterbewegung* (Frankfurt, 1965)
Haupt, G. *La II internazionale* (Florence, 1973).

For an introduction to the histories of the socialist movements of individual nations, see
Groh, D. *Negative Integration und revolutionärer Attentismus: die deutsche Sozialdemokratie am Vorabend des I. Weltkrieges* (Frankfurt, Berlin and Vienna, 1975)
Lefranc, G. *Le Mouvement socialiste sous la troisième république* (2 vols., Paris, 1977)
Manacorda, G. *Il socialismo nella storia d'Italia* (Bari, 1966)
Pelling, H. *Origins of the Labour Party 1880–1900* (London, 1965)
Roth, G. *The Social Democrats in Imperial Germany: A Study in Working Class Isolation and National Integration* (Totowa, N.J., 1963)
Steinberg, H.-J. *Sozialismus und deutsche Sozialdemokratie* (Bonn, Bad Godesberg, 1973).

On the general questions concerning the connection between the social life and the cultural institutions of the working classes, see the many valuable essays collected in
Hobsbawm, E. J. *Worlds of Labour* (London, 1984).

Concerning the crisis in the Second International at the outbreak of the First World War, it is impossible to do justice to the substantial bibliography available: but see in the first instance the discussions generated by
Haupt, G. *Le Congrès manqué: l'Internationale à la veille de la première guerre mondiale: étude et documents* (Paris, 1965).

For the schism in the international workers' movement and the foundation of the communist movement, see in the first instance the extensive bibliography in
Agosti, A. 'L'Historiographie de la troisième internationale', in *Cahiers d'histoire de l'Institut de recherches marxistes*, 36 (1980), 7–61
Agosti, A. *La terza internationale: storia documentaria* (3 vols., Rome 1974 et seq.)
Cole, G. D. H. *A History of Socialist Thought* (cit.), vol. IV, *Communism and Social Democracy*
Hájek, M. *Storia dell'internazionale comunista (1921–1935)* (Rome, 1969).

On socialism between the wars, see
Collotti, E. (ed.). *L'Internazionale operaia e socialista tra le due guerre* (Milan, 1985) (a monograph in the 'Annali Feltrinelli' series).

For the history of political Catholicism, see the bibliography contained in the comparative study
Lönne, K. E. *Politischer Katholizismus im 19. und 20. Jahrhundert* (Frankfurt-on-Main, 1986).

❧

SIX

MASS MEDIA AND CULTURE IN
FIN-DE-SIÈCLE EUROPE

PATRICK BRANTLINGER

> Here comes the New Man, demoralizing himself with a halfpenny newspaper.
> George Bernard Shaw

In one of their brief, pre-1900 films, Louis Lumière and his brother Auguste 'showed a sausage machine; a pig was put in at one end and the sausages came out at the other, and vice versa. My brother and I had great fun making this fictitious machine.'[1] Several features of 'Charcuterie Américaine' suggest the promise and the threat of a variety of mass cultural phenomena near the turn of the century. One is the association with mass production and technological innovation. Like some other Lumière films, this one depicts, albeit in parody form, an industrial process; it also depicts a fantasy machine roughly analogous to motion picture cameras and projectors. And a second is the traditional association between swinishness and consumption – self-indulgence, gluttony, materialism.

In the burst of new techniques and inventions that characterized the 'Second Industrial Revolution', developments in communications and transportation were powerful shapers of cultural productions of all sorts, from music to sports, poetry to advertising. Responses to new cultural patterns ranged from a facile technological optimism to diagnoses of 'degeneration' and 'the dusk of nations'. For conservatives, mass culture threatened traditional forms of cultural authority and social control, including religion. For the Left, it threatened indigenous forms of popular culture, which contained at least the potential for true class-consciousness and radical change. The new 'age of the masses' was also the era of the Decadent movement and the first *l'art pour l'art* modernisms. Mass culture and its apparent opposite, the artistic avant-garde, were the symbiotic corollaries of advanced capitalism between the 1880s and 1914. The same period witnessed the development of sociology, which like the artistic avant-garde can be seen as a response to modern mass society and its culture. Durkheim, Weber,

Simmel and Pareto all felt it urgent to establish a scientific understanding of urbanization and mass behaviour; they shared a general cultural pessimism with avant-garde artists that might be summed up by Simmel's thesis of the tragic nature of social experience as such. Both groups of intellectuals tended to read social rationalization and technological progress not as progress, but the reverse – as symptoms or causes of social disease. 'Nothing avails', wrote Nietzsche in 1888; 'one *must* go forward – step by step further into decadence (that is *my* definition of modern "progress").'[2]

I

The cinema was the most spectacular of the new communications media; through the entrepreneurship of the Lumières and others it rapidly became a new type of mass entertainment, which by 1914 was 'the most widely distributed cultural form that there had ever been'.[3] According to René Doumic, 'the age of cinema' had dawned, and the 'new cult', having penetrated all Europe, was conquering the world (writing in 1913, Doumic cites the existence of 'picture palaces' in such faraway places as Rangoon and Shanghai).[4] The success of 'kinetoscopic' exhibitions from 1895 forward led to the opening of the first cinemas in many cities in the early 1900s. London had approximately 500 cinemas in 1912, while Manchester had 111; by that date, British attendance may have reached 350 million annually, drawn from a total population of about 40 million.[5] Similar figures from the other European countries and America testify to the rapid spread and mass nature of cinema: there were, for example, 270 cinemas in Hungary by 1912, 92 in Budapest, while in Germany Berlin alone had about 300 'Kinos'.[6]

Other communications devices – the transoceanic cablegram, the type-writer, the telephone, the phonograph, the wireless, inexpensive photo-graphic equipment and new methods of printing were almost as spectacular as cinema. Bell invented the telephone in 1876; a year later Edison invented the phonograph. Typewriters came on the market in the late 1870s, and the first 'Kodaks' in the next decade, giving rise to a new popular hobby. Marconi received his first patent in 1897, and in 1906 came the first voiced radio broadcast. The mass propaganda and entertainment uses of radio did not develop until the 1920s, but were forecast by some observers in the 1890s. On the other hand, by then the telephone was already revolutionizing communications. About 8 million telephone calls were made in Germany in 1883; by 1900 the figure had soared to nearly 700 million per year.[7]

Each of these communications devices made the instant transmission and sometimes mass reproduction of messages possible, although it was a matter of debate as to whether messages thus transmitted gained or lost in accuracy, value, truth or beauty. Speed and in some cases massification were also the most obvious effects of new vehicles: the automobile, the bicycle, the electric tram, the subway, the aeroplane. Not all of these new forms of travel immediately affected the masses, but several did. Thus the 'cyclomania' of the 1890s was a mass though mainly middle-class phenomenon, while the new forms of mass transport benefited workers almost immediately.[8]

The term 'masses' evokes the question of who they were. The population explosion coupled with immigration to the cities made urban growth rates tremendous. Between 1880 and 1910, while many British cities nearly doubled in size, Brussels mushroomed from 314,000 to 720,000, Hamburg from 290,000 to 931,000, and Vienna from 834,000 to over 2 million.[9] This, despite massive emigration from Europe. The rise of labour parties, starting with the German Social Democratic Party in the 1870s, sharpened the Marxist identification of the masses with the industrial proletariat. But this definition was blurred by another – the masses as the anonymous, apparently classless 'crowd', the indiscriminate urban conglomeration. The masses in the first sense threatened upper-class hegemony through revolution. The masses in the second, perhaps equally frightening sense, threatened class distinctions through entropy and apathy, overwhelming social boundaries by sheer numbers and blunting the weapons of socialism in the process. Besides the population explosion, the factors that made this second meaning significant are summed up in the phrase 'consumer society', characterized by a sharpening separation between the spheres of production and consumption.

The proletarian masses of the Marxist tradition were identified even in hostility with work or production. But the masses of modern consumer society were large numbers of people on holiday or after work, crowding the stadiums, the new retail outlets, the tourist resorts. Increased leisure and rising expectations about living standards, the proliferation of consumer goods, large-scale advertising campaigns, widespread dependence on credit and the appearance of the first department stores formed the context for an apparent 'democratization of luxury'. Of course that phrase meant little to the masses of urban and rural poor. Ironically, the new consumer society emerged during the 'Great Depression' between 1873 and 1896, buoyed by rising real incomes in much of western Europe. In Britain, according to Eric Hobsbawm, the period of greatest improvement in working-class living standards was probably 1880 to 1895, despite increased unemployment. 'This is because falling living-costs benefit the poorest as well as the rest, indeed proportionately more than the rest, and the "Depression" was . . . primarily a period of falling prices – but they fell largely because an entire new world of cheap, imported foodstuffs opened before the British people.' Hobsbawm names a variety of once expensive foods such as jam and fresh fruits, as well as new 'multiple' groceries, butcher shops, and the fish-and-chips shops characteristic of the modern 'British proletarian scene'.[10]

New foodstuffs were not the only items in the 'democratization of luxury', which included everything from clothing to tourism. That phrase 'stood for a market that was now prepared to turn practically any retail article into a mass-consumer good. And thus . . . it stood for the realization that bourgeois culture was coming more and more to mean a consumer culture.'[11] Subject of Zola's *Au bonheur des dames* (1883), the department store typified an age of what Veblen called 'conspicuous consumption'. And commercial advertising typified the new consumer culture (advertising is, indeed, the underlying form of all mass culture). Between 1880 and 1914, the advertising business boomed: national and international campaigns promoted everything from corsets to imperial power and glory. Though advertising agencies had existed on a small scale in Europe since the late 1700s, only with the expansion of markets and consumer goods from the 1870s forward did they emerge as primary shapers of culture. By the turn of the century, there were several hundred advertising agencies in London alone, conducting a far larger volume of business than fifty years earlier.[12]

The new forms of communication and transportation were also rapidly developed as commercial goods and services. It was an era of incessant commodification, when big business, catering to masses of consumers, exploited both new technologies and traditional popular leisure activities. Two of the more familiar transformations occurred in sports and popular music. In Britain before the 1850s, football was the preserve of upper-class amateurs, notably public school students. From about mid-century on, however, 'football developed a plebeian and commercial tone, with its encroaching professionalisation, heavy capital investment in new stadiums, and armies of fiercely partisan supporters . . . By the late 1880s, professionalism . . . had become a *fait accompli*.'[13] Other sports followed a similar path, including cricket, rugby and tennis. And large-scale commercialization was the fate also of music hall in Britain, France, Germany and elsewhere. By the 1880s, music hall entertainment was 'a capitalist operation, with an increasingly monopolistic thrust'.[14] The commercialization of music hall was, in turn, a precondition for the rapid commercial exploitation of cinema.[15]

Each cultural and technological innovation evoked controversy about its uses and effects. The very shift in emphasis from production to consumption, although indicating increased leisure and prosperity for many, called forth feelings of guilt and decadence. To the puritanical (whether religious or political), time off and fun could never be goals of work. To many observers, pubs, music halls and cinemas were dens of iniquity, while to some even bicycles seemed licentious, at least when the cyclists were female.[16] Even the telephone inspired protest from those who worried that it threatened privacy or was no substitute for face-to-face dialogue.[17] Greater concern was sometimes expressed about wireless and cablegrams, echoing James Russell

Lowell's fear that the telegraph, 'by making public opinion simultaneous, is also making it liable to those delusions, panics, and gregarious impulses which transform otherwise reasonable men into a mob'. Quoting this opinion in *The Psychology of Jingoism* (1901), John Hobson declared that cablegrams were 'the ideal mode of suggestion' for influencing 'the general mind' by playing upon 'the common pulse of passion which sways them as members of a crowd. The terse, dogmatic, unqualified, and unverifiable cablegram is [a] potent . . . emotional explosive.'[18]

If mass 'suggestion' could be an effect of the cablegram, it could even more clearly be an effect of film, which seemed to many critics a threat to literacy. Robert Donald told the British Institute of Journalists in 1913 that the cinema and phonograph would make people 'too lazy to read, and news will be laid on to the house or office just as gas or water now is'.[19] Similarly, in his 1916 analysis of film, Hugo Münsterberg declared that 'the masses of today prefer to be taught by pictures rather than by words'.[20] But for Münsterberg the substitution of pictures for words (exaggerated by the silence of early film) was not threatening. He saw film as a new art form which, rightly used, might greatly benefit society. Through it, the theatre could be democratized, brought to the masses for the first time; film could also 'supplement the schoolroom and the newspaper . . . by spreading information and knowledge'. Münsterberg, however, thought education secondary to the task of bringing 'entertainment and amusement to the masses'(p. 12), and contended that 'the greatest mission which the photoplay may have in our community is that of esthetic cultivation' (p. 99).

Münsterberg's moderate approach conflicts with those of more extreme theorists who might be labelled cinematic utopians and dystopians. The utopians included Edison, who declared, 'I intend to do away with books in the school . . . When we get the moving-pictures in the school, the child will be so interested that he will hurry to get there before the bell rings, because it's the natural way to teach, through the eye.'[21] Even more extravagantly, Henry Hopwood ended his book *Living Pictures* (1899) by assimilating the celluloid gaze to an omniscient gaze, God as the supreme viewer of the ultimate motion picture: 'So a . . . record of the earth's history in its slightest details is continually streaming off into the eternal void, and, granted an eye capable . . . one universal perception extending through the infinity would embrace . . . an eternal and universal living picture of all past events.'[22]

Opposed to such technological euphoria, many critics claimed that, even if it didn't spell the demise of literacy, at the very least cinema compromised any hope for the true enlightenment of the masses. Louis Haugmard declared in 1913 that '"the masses" are like a grown-up child who demands a picture album to leaf through in order to forget his miseries'. Cinema was a 'circus' or day-dream world which gave only the illusion of putting the masses in direct touch with reality. 'Through it the charmed masses will learn not to think anymore, to resist all desire to reason and to construct, to open their large and empty eyes, only to look, look, look . . . Will cinematography comprise, perhaps, the elegant solution to the social question, if the modern cry is formulated: "Bread and cinemas"?'[23] Haugmard accuses film of distracting the mass mind after the manner of Roman bread and circuses. Although right-wing, he thus offers a variant of the Marxist theme of ideological manipulation by the capitalist media. But other critics worried more about an apparently contrary phenomenon, the politicization of the masses: trade unionism, labour parties, socialism, anarchism on the Left; imperialism, racism, militarism on the Right. Evidently the masses had more than one mind.

II

Ironically, the 'age of cinema' saw the approach of nearly universal literacy in most industrialized nations. In 1900 about half the population of Italy and well over two-thirds of the Russian Empire were illiterate, but even these figures were rapidly shrinking. By that date, too, national systems of education were the rule throughout western Europe. 'The standards of education were extremely high', declares Norman Stone. 'There was a great appetite for serious literature of all kinds, and this age produced scholars who could write, without condescension, for a general public, and a general public which could read learned works without mystification.'[24] The entry of the working and lower middle classes into the political arena sharpened perennial questions about what the masses were either reading or not reading. When they did read, many critics held, then they were imbibing dangerous political and religious doctrines, literary trash, sensational journalism, sex and violence, the 'sporting news'.[25]

Like his friend Nietzsche, Jakob Burckhardt saw no solution to the problems of modern history through mass education: 'The greatest innovation in the world is the demand for education as a right of man; it is [merely] a disguised demand for comfort.'[26] For both Burckhardt and Nietzsche, genuine culture and the masses were mutually exclusive; they attributed German decadence in part to the democratization of education, as did the other exponents of 'the politics of cultural despair'.[27] In *The Communist Manifesto*, Marx and Engels had denounced the bourgeois emphasis on culture or education as a social panacea: 'That culture . . . is, for the enormous majority, a mere training to act as a machine.' If that was all the education of the masses under capitalism could effect, then dystopian visions like Burckhardt's were understandable. Meditating on the Paris Commune, Burckhardt wrote: 'I have a premonition [that] the military state must become one great factory. Those hordes of men in the great industrial centers may not be left indefinitely to their greed and want. What must logically come is a definite and supervised stint of misery, with promotions and in uniform, daily begun and ended to the sound of drums' (p. 36).

Similarly, in Gissing's *New Grub Street*, the paper manufacturer John Yule declares that 'your Board schools, your popular press, your spread of education' are 'machinery for ruining the country'. According to Yule, echoing Carlyle, 'there's no such way of civilising the masses of people as by fixed military service'.[28] Gissing agrees at least with the idea that mass literacy, instead of civilizing the masses, is just machinery for undermining traditional values. And Henry Adams saw a connection between mass education and new, dangerous forms of collectivist politics: 'All State education is a sort of dynamo machine for polarizing the popular mind; for turning and holding its lines of force in the direction supposed to be most effective for State purposes. The German machine was terribly efficient.'[29]

At the heart of many of the paradoxical complaints about mass literacy as a new social problem rather than solution lies a concern with the allegedly nefarious effects of the 'sensational' press. The warmongering 'yellow journalism' of the United States was matched by the imperialistic 'new journalism' of Britain, and similar developments characterized the history of the press in France and Germany. 'American' techniques – bold headlines, shorter articles, human interest stories, interviews with the rich and famous, puzzles and contests, and photographic illustrations – helped boost the circulations of the new dailies and weeklies 'for the masses'. Along with the immense increase of people able to read, the two chief stimulants to mass journalism were technological innovation and soaring advertising revenues. In Britain, Alfred Harmsworth was the first to recognize that advertising could provide a new financial basis for newspapers. 'He published his own sales figures, challenged his rivals to do the same, and in effect created the modern structure of the press as an industry and an expression of market relationships with the "mass reading public".'[30]

The series of inventions that made press expansion possible began with the rotary press in 1846, and included the linotype machine, automatic paper feeders and cutters, cheap newsprint, and the halftone process for reproducing photographs. Using a rotary press, the Parisian paper *La Patrie* increased its circulation from 3,140 a day in 1846 to 24,500 twelve years later, but these figures are minuscule compared to the enormous circulations achieved by the major dailies in the 1890s.[31] The circulation of the Paris dailies increased two-and-a-half times between 1880 and 1914. Although the circulation of *Le Petit Journal* had been huge from its outset in 1863 and had reached the enormous figure of 580,000 by 1880, it climbed even higher in the next decade, soaring beyond the million mark by 1890. Competition from *Le Petit Parisien* cut into its circulation after that, but it still sold about 835,000 copies a day in 1910, while its chief rival reached the million mark in 1902.[32]

The British newspapers associated with what Arnold in 1887 dubbed the 'New Journalism' and attacked as 'feather brained' achieved comparable circulations.[33] The first issue of Harmsworth's *Daily Mail*, 4 May 1896, sold 397,215 copies. Its circulation reached 700,000 four years later, and at the height of the Boer War it sometimes topped a million.[34] The circulations of such German newspapers as *Berliner Tageblatt* were less spectacular, but still enormous. Between 1885 and 1913, newspaper circulation in Germany doubled, from about 8 to 16 million.[35]

Such statistics, indicating that vast numbers of new readers were consuming vast numbers of newspapers, journals and books, did not allay fears that the masses and genuine enlightenment were farther apart than ever. To many critics, the political influence of the mass press seemed mainly deleterious. 'Yellow journalism' in the USA was widely held to have sparked the Spanish-American War. With the Boer War in mind, Hobson declared that 'a biased, enslaved, and poisoned press has been the chief engine for manufacturing Jingoism'.[36] And in France, the Dreyfus affair seemed partly manufactured by the press, eager to sell regardless of social costs. 'The French press has fallen into deplorable disrepute', wrote Gabriel Monod in 1898; 'it has become almost impotent as a force for good, and is now little more than an agent of moral disintegration, a fomenter of hatred and of future civil wars.'[37] At the end of the First World War, Bertrand Russell concluded that one of its causes had been the press, by stimulating racism and nationalism among the masses. By then, the perception was widespread that newspapers represented 'the mob spirit, a vast, impersonal, delirious, anarchic, degenerating, and disintegrating force'.[38]

With yet another political crisis in mind, the Boxer Rebellion in China in 1900, G. M. Trevelyan denied that the 'yellow peril' was as much a threat to European civilization as the 'white peril', consisting of 'the uniform modern man', creature of 'the great cities'. 'By modern machinery . . . moulded for good or for evil with a rapidity of change unknown at any previous epoch', the 'white peril' was also moulded by what it read:

Journals, magazines, and the continued spawn of bad novels, constitute our national culture, for it is on these that the vast majority of all classes employ their power of reading. How does it concern our culture that Shakespeare, Milton, Ruskin, in times gone by wrote in our language, if for all the countless weary ages to come the hordes that we breed and send out to swamp the world shall browse with ever-increasing appetite on the thin swollen stuff that commerce has now learnt to supply for England's spiritual and mental food?[39]

Nothing seemed more nightmarish to Trevelyan than the 'uprooting of taste and reason by the printing press' (p. 1050), except the image of its readers swamping the world. Foreshadowing Ortega's 'revolt of the masses', the 'white peril' of 1900 was already on the march, a barbarian invasion from the heart of civilization, manufacturing and consuming enormous quantities of journalistic 'nonsense' and 'vulgarity' to spur itself on.

III

The connections between the artistic avant-garde and mass culture have often been noted. Artistic modernism declares its implacable hostility to mass culture; it also frequently adopts mass cultural themes, forms and processes, as in surrealist film-making and Bauhaus design. From the opposite direction, the mass communications industries perpetually co-opt the latest, most experimental art, reproducing it as 'kitsch'. Both the avant-garde and mass culture are marked by the fetishization of the new, and both therefore, as Renato Poggioli remarks, share in the phenomenon of fashion: 'Hence the profound truth of Baudelaire's paradox, which gives to genius the task of creating stereotypes. And from that follows . . . that the avant-garde is condemned to conquer, through the influence of fashion, that very popularity it once disdained – and this is the beginning of its end.'[40] Crudely put, the avant-garde aspires to the condition of mass culture (Theodor Adorno remarks that 'industrialization is the vanishing point towards which art moves').[41] The opposition between the avant-garde and mass culture, characterizing modern cultural history, thus acquires a dialectical tension at once contestatory and symbiotic.

Instances in which avant-garde writers and artists reproduce mass cultural forms – whether as parody or celebration – are just as numerous as expressions of uncompromising rejection. Though neither avant-garde nor mass cultural, *New Grub Street* is instructive for its failure to be one or the other. Gissing understood that his brand of social realism was no longer avant-garde; neither was it popular. His novelist characters – Reardon, Biffen and the rest – yearn for a popularity they despise, while also yearning for a literary originality they cannot achieve. The novels they imagine and write – Biffen's 'Mr. Bailey, Grocer', for example – merely reproduce the exhaustion of *New Grub Street* itself, marking the slide of realism from critical form to mass cultural formula. For Gissing, every conceivable form of writing falls under the sign of journalism, another name for the commercial prostitution of art. It was therefore easy for Max Nordau, in his 1893 bestseller *Degeneration*, to include Zola and novelistic realism among the various tendencies he condemned as decadent. Indeed, late nineteenth-century realism and the Decadent movement share a sense of failure: both oppose mass cultural tendencies, yet seem able to do little more than envy and parody those very tendencies.

Just as commercial journalism appears to be devouring literature in *New Grub Street*, so Oscar Wilde remarks that the old notion that journalism was 'the fourth estate' is no longer true: 'at the present moment it . . . is the only estate. It has eaten up the other three . . . We are dominated by Journalism.'[42] Given that situation, it was inevitable that decadent writing should take the form of the very thing it deplored. Thus Wilde's poses and self-promotions both mocked and sought to capitalize upon the practices of sensational journalism and advertising. The Aestheticism of the 1890s was rooted in 'the beginnings of modern spectacular and mass society and depended upon image and advertising', writes Regenia Gagnier. 'With *The Importance of Being Earnest*, first produced one year before [Alfred] Jarry's revolutionary insult to bourgeois audiences in *Ubu Roi* (*King Turd*, which began with Firmin Gemier strolling to the footlights to yell "Shit!" at the audience), the "society of the spectacle" – of image over substance – emerges.'[43] The obverse of Wilde's and Jarry's *épater le bourgeois* stance is the aesthete's adoption of the glitter of high fashion and a rarefied consumerism. Huysman's decadent hero Des Esseintes vehemently rejects the bourgeois life-style of materialist consumption, yet his very aestheticism is an 'attempt to create an authentic style in consumption uncontaminated by the marketplace'.[44] A 'final aristocrat' like Dracula, Des Esseintes too is an exemplary consumer, in the avant-garde of perpetually new and therefore perpetually jaded tastes, fashions, sensations: the new is never new enough.

If the decadent artist simultaneously rejected and adopted mass cultural tendencies through pose and parody, other avant-garde movements offered explicit celebrations of technological change. The automobile, blazing the trails of tomorrow, was the special symbol of modernity in Shaw's *Man and Superman* (1903) and also in Marinetti's Futurist Manifesto of 1909: 'A roaring motor car which seems to run on machine-gun fire is more beautiful than the Victory of Samothrace.'[45] More significant than the Futurists' love affair with the automobile and speed are the countless assimilations between the avant-garde and cinema. Pirandello's 1915 novel *Shoot: The Notebooks of Serafino Gubbio, Cinematograph Operator* both satirizes and draws inspiration from the new film culture. Apollinaire's Baron d'Ormesan is also a film maker whose skill with montage allows him to exist in many places at once and to die in 820 different locations around the world.[46] Similarly, as Raymond Williams remarks, Strindberg's *The Road to Damascus* (1898), *A Dream Play* (1902) and *Ghost Sonata* (1907) 'are in effect screenplays'.[47] And Joyce's *Ulysses* shows the influence of cinematic techniques; Joyce was fascinated by film and in 1909 was responsible for establishing the first cinema in Ireland.[48]

One theme shared by many *fin-de-siècle* commentaries about society and culture is that of technological innovation itself displacing, for better or worse, older, individualized forms of creativity and cultural expression. Benjamin's thesis of the destruction of the 'aura' of 'the work of art in the age of mechanical reproduction' is a later, more complex formulation of this theme. The long, convoluted tradition of opposition to machinery and machine-made goods formed a basis for modern intellectual and artistic resistance to mass culture. Inspired by Ruskin and Morris, the arts and crafts movement was an expression of that opposition. Veblen pointed out that the very advantages of industrialized consumer goods – cheapness, standardization, utility – were strikes against them in terms of traditional cultural values. For his part, Veblen preferred the 'perfection of workmanship' of machine-made products to the merely 'honorific' superiority of 'hand-wrought goods'. He wrote caustically about Ruskin's and Morris's 'exaltation of the defective', and was even more caustic towards those who rejected mass-produced articles because of their 'commonness'.[49]

Despite the distaste felt by those who wished to consume only 'honorific' products, 'common' industrial goods were becoming universal. Sometimes the inventor (Marinetti preferred the racing-car driver) seemed to be displacing the artist as culture hero. If Dante, Michelangelo and Beethoven were the creative geniuses of past ages, Edison was 'the wizard of Menlo Park' and of the modern age. Material as opposed to spiritual or artistic illumination was his special gift – the light bulb, the kinetoscope – though he was also the democratic-heroic inventor of waxed paper, the alkaline battery, the mimeograph, and so forth (one new invention every ten days was the goal of his research team). Sometimes machinery itself seemed to be taking charge of the world, as in much science fiction. In *Anticipations of the Reaction of Mechanical and Scientific Progress upon Human Life and Thought* (1902), H. G. Wells declared: 'Invention runs free and our state is under its dominion.'[50]

A similar theme appears in treatments of modernization by the great turn-of-the-century sociologists. The flourishing of sociological theory between 1880 and 1914 was obviously dependent on its subject matter, the stuff of modern history: division of labour, urbanization, bureaucracy, secularization, social class, 'crowd psychology'. Tönnies's analysis of *Gemeinschaft* and *Gesellschaft*, Durkheim's of 'anomie' and suicide, Simmel's of big city life, Pareto's of elites versus masses all suggest that sociology is the science of mass society and its culture. Although the best sociology transcends the irrationality of its subject, like Aestheticism it was in part a product of the ever-accelerating division of labour which Durkheim saw as a main driving force of modernization. In its approach to social themes and evidence – its positivistic reifications, its disciplinary specialization, its recourse to large numbers – sociological discourse reproduces even as it analyzes the structures of mass society.

Sociology also had its popular practitioners, who themselves transformed social theory into intellectual kitsch, as in the many applications of social Darwinism to class, race and empire. In *The Great Society* (1914), Graham Wallas noted that an analysis of the mass mind had been 'widely popularised, especially by [Gustave] Le Bon . . . so that the "Psychology of the Crowd" now enjoys in the social philosophy of the newspapers some of the old authority of the Laws of Political Economy'.[51] Published in 1895, Le Bon's *The Crowd: A Study of the Popular Mind* painted a dire picture of the dangers posed by the intrusion of the masses into politics: 'To-day the claims of the masses . . . amount to nothing less than a determination to destroy utterly society as it now exists.'[52] Like Nordau's *Degeneration*, Le Bon's essay offers an exaggerated patching together of the pessimistic themes in more sophisticated sociology. Thus, there is little in his account of 'the substitution of the unconscious action of crowds for the conscious activity of individuals [as] one of the principal characteristics of the present age' (p. 3) which cannot be found in Gabriel Tarde's and Robert Park's taxonomies of 'publics' versus 'crowds', or in Simmel's classic essay, 'The Metropolis and Mental Life'.

For Simmel, 'the sociological tragedy' arises from the fact that 'the more refined, highly developed, articulated the qualities of an individual are, the more unlikely are they to make him similar to other individuals and to form a unit with corresponding qualities in others'. The 'mass' – indeed, all social formations – involves a transformation of quality into quantity. 'Individuals, in all their divergencies, [contribute] only the lowest parts of their personalities to form a common denominator.'[53] This is precisely the tragedy of mass culture, and therefore of modern social experience. It is also the tragedy which Max Weber had in mind when he wrote of the 'iron cage' of modern capitalist society as one we are all destined to live within – masses and elites, artists and scientists, capitalists and workers alike (because we live within the cage we are necessarily members of the masses).

No one knows who will live in this cage in the future, or whether at the end of this tremendous development entirely new prophets will arise, or there will be a great rebirth of old ideas and ideals, or, if neither, mechanized petrification, embellished with a sort of convulsive self-importance. For of the last stage of this cultural development, it might well be truly said: 'Specialists without spirit, sensualists without heart; this nullity imagines that it has attained a level of civilization never before achieved.'[54]

Though Weber seems to have thought of the future in terms either of more of the same or of some 'rebirth' of religion or tradition, it is possible to envisage a different development of authentic freedom and equality, based on a democratically planned prosperity for all. But one can also imagine that Weber's 'last stage of . . . cultural development' is the first of a 'postmodern' condition, doomed to be forever new, forever productive of spectacles, fashions, illusions, ideological mirrors – the apotheosis of the commercialized mass culture that all of the great early sociologists and avant-garde artists often deplored, occasionally celebrated, and inevitably lived and worked within.

As Andreas Huyssen contends in *After the Great Divide: Modernism, Mass Culture, Postmodernism*:

Ever since the mid-19th century, the culture of modernity has been characterized by a volatile relationship between high art and mass culture. Indeed, the emergence of early modernism in writers such as Flaubert and Baudelaire cannot be adequately understood on the basis of an assumed logic of 'high' literary evolution alone. Modernism constituted itself through a conscious strategy of exclusion, an anxiety of contamination by its other: an increasingly consuming and engulfing mass culture.[55]

The 'great divide' lies between high and mass culture, but another 'divide', according to Huyssen, has opened since the Second World War, between the era of modernism and that of a postmodernity characterized above all by a collapsing of the distinction between high and mass culture. Huyssen's thesis about the emergence of postmodernity is, as he is well aware, highly debatable, but not the facts that the period from about the time of Baudelaire down to the Second World War was profoundly shaped by mass literacy and journalism and by the emergence of new mass communications technologies, and that high literary and artistic modernism can only be understood in relation to these developments.

Whether or not we have now moved beyond the modern era into postmodernity, the terms of the mass culture debate evident among *fin-de-siècle* writers, artists and sociologists are still current. The 'revolt of the masses', whether leading to one brand of totalitarianism or another, or merely to a rampant consumerism and materialism ending in some ultimate 'culture of narcissism' based on the extreme privatization and fragmentation of experience coupled with the reified worship of 'celebrities' and 'stars', remains the concern of many social critics. The extent to which journalism, film, radio and television can or cannot promote social intelligence and democracy is perhaps the central unanswered question of modern history. All cultural processes and productions, whether mass or high, modern or postmodern, folk or academic, capitalist or socialist, are sites of struggle in which this central question is being answered in specific, contradictory, 'micropolitical' ways. As the American novelist James T. Farrell declared in regard to 'the language of Hollywood', 'The contradictions between the film as merchandise and the film as art are . . . not general, formal, abstract. They appear as contradictions concretely, individually, in the making of films; in the give-and-take; in the conflicts among producers, directors, and writers that often occur when a film is being made: in general, the results constitute some form of compromise . . . weighted on the side of merchandise.'[56] That is why criticism of particular mass cultural productions often also declares itself to be a form of 'radical' political practice, a significant mode of intervention in the cultural politics of modern and now, perhaps, 'postmodern' times.[57]

In another of their motion pictures, the brothers Lumière filmed workers leaving their factory. 'The film begins with the large doors of the factory opening inward. Men and women, on foot and on bicycles, stream through the open doorway and move to the left and right along the sidewalk. Finally, as the last of the workers – a man in a suit and straw hat – emerges from within, the left-hand door is swung shut.'[58] Because of its documentary simplicity and brevity, 'Sortie d'usine Lumière' seems to defy interpretation; 'Charcuterie Américaine', after all, had its pig, its fantastic machine, its sausages. But for that very reason the factory film may leave the viewer with an impression of mystery: who are the workers and where are they going? Home? To the nearest cafés, shops, theatres? Are they workers still, once they leave the factory? Are they also 'the masses'? If so, are they masses only inside the factory, the site of mass production? As they disperse and disappear, they seem to reacquire the marks of individual identity, taking separate routes towards distinct though unknown destinations. Neither their lives outside the factory nor their work within it are visible: only their dispersal and the closing of the door.

Of course these individuals are also images: both as anonymous members of the masses and as cinematic representations they seem infinitely fragile and expendable because infinitely reproducible. As cinematic images, they lack aura. And yet even in this simple film there is an ironic aura or, perhaps, counter-aura, of the sort that Benjamin detected in the earliest daguerreotypes:

In photography . . . one encounters a new and strange phenomenon: in that fishwife from Newhaven, who casts her eyes down with such casual, seductive shame, there remains something that does not merely testify to the art of . . . the photographer, but something that cannot be silenced, that impudently demands the name of the person who lived at the time and who, remaining real even now, will never yield herself up entirely into *art*.[59]

And one might add, will never yield herself up entirely into the masses either. So it is with the Lumières' anonymous workers, streaming out of the factory towards their separate, inscrutable lives beyond work – members of the masses, yes, but also film stars of sorts, 'remaining real even now' through the ephemeral immortality of mass culture.

NOTES

1 Louis Lumière quoted in H. M. Geduld (ed.), *Film Makers on Film Making* (Bloomington, Ind., 1967), p. 25.
2 F. Nietzsche, *The Portable Nietzsche*, ed. W. Kaufmann (New York, 1976), p. 547.

3 R. Williams, 'British film history: new perspectives', in J. Curran and V. Porter (eds.), *British Cinema History* (Totowa, N.J., 1983), p. 14.

4 R. Doumic, 'L'Age du cinema', *Revue des deux mondes*, 16 (15 August 1913), 919–20.

5 P. Corrigan, 'Film entertainment as ideology and pleasure: a preliminary approach to a history of audiences', in Curran and Porter (eds.), *British Cinema History*, p. 27.

6 I. Nemeskürty, 'In the beginning, 1896–1911', in J. L. Fell (ed.), *Film before Griffith* (Berkeley, Calif., 1983), p. 79.

7 B. R. Mitchell, *European Historical Statistics 1750–1970* (London, 1975), p. 653.

8 E. Weber, *France, Fin de Siècle* (Cambridge, Mass., 1986), pp. 70–1, 195–206.

9 Mitchell, *European Historical Statistics*, pp. 76–8.

10 E. J. Hobsbawm, *Industry and Empire* (Harmondsworth, 1969), p. 162.

11 M. Miller, *The Bon Marché: Bourgeois Culture and the Department Store, 1869–1920* (Princeton, N.J., 1981), p. 165.

12 W. Fraser, *The Coming of the Mass Market, 1850–1914* (Hamden, Conn., 1981), p. 138. For a contemporary account of these developments in France, see G. D'Avenel, *Le Mécanisme de la vie moderne* (4 vols., Paris, 1922).

13 J. Walvin, *Leisure and Society, 1830–1950* (London, 1978), pp. 88–9.

14 P. Bailey, 'Custom, capital and culture in the Victorian music hall', in R. D. Storch (ed.), *Popular Culture and Custom in Nineteenth-Century England* (London, 1982), p. 187.

15 M. Channan, *The Dream That Kicks: The Prehistory and Early Years of Cinema in Britain* (London, 1980), pp. 130–70.

16 Walvin, *Leisure and Society, 1830–1950*, p. 93.

17 J. Brooks, 'Telephone literature', in I. de Sola Pool (ed.), *The Social Impact of the Telephone* (Cambridge, Mass., 1977), pp. 209–11.

18 J. A. Hobson, *The Psychology of Jingoism* (London, 1901), p. 11.

19 Quoted by A. J. Lee, *The Origins of the Popular Press in England, 1855–1914* (London, 1976), pp. 216–17.

20 H. Münsterberg, *The Film: A Psychological Study* (New York, 1970), p. 11.

21 Edison quoted by C. B. Brewer, 'The widening field of the moving-picture', *Century Magazine*, 86 (May 1913), 72. See also R. W. Clark, *Edison: The Man Who Made the Future* (New York, 1977), p. 178.

22 H. V. Hopwood, *Living Pictures, Their History, Photo-Production and Practical Working* (New York, 1970), p. 234.

23 Haugmard quoted in R. Williams, *Dream Worlds: Mass Consumption in Late Nineteenth-Century France* (Berkeley, Calif., 1982), pp. 80–3.

24 N. Stone, *Europe Transformed, 1878–1919* (Cambridge, Mass., 1984), p. 33. For turn-of-the-century literacy statistics, see C. M. Cipolla, *Literacy and Development in the West* (Baltimore, Md, 1969), pp. 113–30.

25 See, for example, J. G. Leigh, 'What do the masses read?', *Economic Review*, 14 (April 1904), 166–77.

26 J. Burckhardt, *Force and Freedom* (New York, 1955), p. 135.

27 Compare the opinions of Paul Lagarde and the other figures in F. Stern, *The*

Politics of Cultural Despair: A Study in the Rise of the Germanic Ideology (Garden City, N.Y. 1965).

28 G. Gissing, *New Grub Street* (Boston, Mass., 1962), p. 21.

29 H. Adams, *The Education of Henry Adams* (Boston, Mass., 1961), p. 78.

30 R. Williams, *The Long Revolution* (Harmondsworth, 1965), p. 224.

31 Lee, *Origins of the Popular Press*, p. 56.

32 P. Albert, 'La Presse française de 1871 à 1940', in C. Bellanger *et al.* (eds.), *Histoire générale de la presse française* (5 vols., Paris, 1972), vol. III, pp. 296, 305.

33 M. Arnold, 'Up to Easter', *Nineteenth Century*, 21 (May 1887), 638.

34 H. Herd, *The March of Journalism: The Story of the British Press from 1622 to the Present Day* (London, 1952), pp. 239–43.

35 O. J. Hale, *The Great Illusion, 1900–1914* (New York, 1971), p. 141.

36 Hobson, *The Psychology of Jingoism*, p. 125.

37 Gabriel Monod quoted in Albert, 'La Presse française de 1871 à 1940', p. 244; my translation.

38 F. Peterson, 'The newspaper peril', *Collier's Weekly*, 37 (1 September 1906), 12–13. See also B. Russell, *Roads to Freedom: Socialism, Anarchism, and Syndicalism* (London, 1918).

39 G. M. Trevelyan, 'The white peril', *Nineteenth Century*, 50 (December 1901), 1049–50.

40 R. Poggioli, *The Theory of the Avant-Garde* (New York, 1971), p. 82.

41 T. Adorno, *Aesthetic Theory* (London, 1984), p. 309.

42 O. Wilde, *The Artist as Critic: Critical Writings of Oscar Wilde*, ed. R. Ellmann (New York, 1969), p. 276.

43 R. Gagnier, *Idylls of the Marketplace: Oscar Wilde and the Victorian Public* (Stanford, Calif., 1986), p. 8.

44 Williams, *Dream Worlds*, p. 133.

45 F. T. Marinetti, 'The Futurist Manifesto', in A. Lyttleton (ed.), *Italian Fascisms from Pareto to Gentile* (New York, 1973), p. 211.

46 S. Kern, *The Culture of Time and Space, 1880–1918* (Cambridge, Mass., 1983), p. 74.

47 Williams, 'British film history', pp. 19–20.

48 R. Ellmann, *James Joyce* (New York, 1965), pp. 310–13.

49 T. Veblen, *The Portable Veblen*, ed. M. Lerner (New York, 1948), pp. 191–2.

50 H. G. Wells, *Anticipations of the Reaction of Mechanical and Scientific Progress upon Human Life and Thought* (New York, 1902), p. 87.

51 G. Wallas, *The Great Society: A Psychological Analysis* (Lincoln, Neb., 1967), p. 121.

52 G. Le Bon, *The Crowd: A Study of the Popular Mind* (New York, 1960), p. 16.

53 G. Simmel, *The Sociology of Georg Simmel*, ed. K. H. Wolff (Glencoe, Ill., 1950), p. 32.

54 M. Weber, *The Protestant Ethic and the Spirit of Capitalism* (New York, 1958), p. 182.

55 A. Huyssen, *After the Great Divide: Modernism, Mass Culture, Postmodernism* (Bloomington, Ind., 1986), p. vii.

56 J. T. Farrell, *The League of Frightened Philistines* (New York, 1945), p. 169.

57 See, for example, T. Eagleton, *Walter Benjamin, or Towards a Revolutionary Criticism* (London, 1981).

58 M. Deutelbaum, 'Structural patterning in the Lumière films', in Fell (ed.), *Film before Griffith*, p. 301.

59 W. Benjamin, 'A short history of photography', *Screen*, 12, no. 1 (Spring 1972–3), 7.

☙

SEVEN

FORWARD RACE AND THE LAUGHTER
OF PYGMIES: ON OLYMPIC SPORT

HENNING EICHBERG

As the 19th century now fades away, there is the keen activity which so often occurs at the end of a long era, as if there were a need to catch up on lost time and to clear the way in a dignified manner for the new, rising era. A feature of our age, dominated by the speed of the bicycle, is the rush and frantic advance in all cultural areas; and, praise God, the movement is mostly in a forward direction. (Wickenhagen 1898)

These words, written two years before the turn of the century by a German teacher who was co-publisher of *Zeitschrift für Turnen und Jugendspiele*, reflect the prevailing atmosphere of the time. He echoed the dichotomy which had been felt during that era: tensions between dignity and haste, fall and rise, catching up and advancing. This refers neither exclusively to a fading mood of the *fin de siècle* nor to the enthusiasm of futurism (in its twentieth-century meaning); – what did it express?

It is perhaps helpful that the metaphors of that time often lend themselves to images from the culture of sport, of the body, and movement. As the cited text says: race and chase, movement and the speed of the bicycle. This can be an incentive for a closer examination of the actual basis of such rhetoric. What was the social language of sport expressed here in figurative terms?

The first modern Olympic games had taken place two years earlier in Athens. Did they represent a revival of classical antiquity or rather a mass spectacle for twentieth-century media? Do the games provide an answer to the question of the relationship between the mood at the end of the era and future 'legacy'? How did they contribute to the epoch-making structure of the 1900 'watershed'?

CHANGES IN THE CHAIN OF PROGRESS

The Olympic games of 1896 began a series of events which is still continuing (with Barcelona planned to be the next venue in 1992) and which has been interrupted only by the two world wars. From the point of view of Olympic self-understanding, of Western media and of west European states sports ideology, the chain is continuous. It is a continuity characterized by performance, youth and health, accord between the masses and the elite, between patriotism and internationalism, the meeting of the peoples, peace and understanding beyond borders, organized progress and humanism (Berlioux 1984; Diem 1965 and 1917; Schulke 1976; Umminger 1962 and 1971). This 'progressive' picture is underlined by the chain of records: the recorded data lend themselves 'objectively' and without gaps to a tabulated history, which begins in 1896 and which leads forwards and upwards (Kamper 1983).

A closer look at the history of the individual events reveals a much less unified picture (Mandell 1984, pp. 203–17, 237–61; also Mandell 1967, 1971, 1976). The 1896 games in Athens were predominantly a Greek national festival. The games were given an international flavour only by the few tourists who were allowed to compete, together with two distinct groups of German gymnasts and American track athletes. The Greek people were celebrating themselves. Later, in Paris, 1900 and in St Louis, 1904, the games became events at the periphery of world exhibitions. Baron Pierre de Coubertin, the founder of the modern games, turned away in disgust. In London, 1908, the games became a forum for rising international animosity, being combined with a British–French exhibition (against Germany, the future enemy). They provoked discussions about cheating amongst the British judges and were marked by tensions between the English and the Americans over the Irish problem.

It was not until Stockholm, 1912 that the Coubertin ideals were realized – possibly because fundamentally these games were affected by quite different Scandinavian gymnastics. The sequence continued in Antwerp (1920), Paris (1924), Amsterdam (1928) and Los Angeles in 1932 when sportification and the production of records, women's sport and internationalization, media coverage and the Olympic ceremonial gradually began to take shape.

This structure reached a climax and, at the same time, a turning point in Berlin (1936): the games now became a showcase of the political-economic-military systems. First of all it was the fascist states (Nazi Germany, Italy and Japan) whose athletes dominated the medals. There was formed a new festival model: with an Olympic village and a monumental stadium, with an Olympic fire relay race and theatrical mass games. Leni Riefenstahl filmed the event, and for the first time television cameras produced 'live pictures'. The Olympic games had reached 'maturity'.

When the games recommenced in London (1948), followed by Helsinki (1952), this model was continued until the rivalry between East and West brought a new dynamic to the system. The games were now characterized by state amateurism with training camps, high financial input by the host nations and cold war – Melbourne (1956), Rome (1960) and Tokyo (1964). During this time, however, increasing numbers of athletes from the non-industrialized states were making an impact. Mexico City (1968), with a murderous use of armed forces against demonstrators, showed the possibilities of a new Olympic model – one beyond the western or eastern European type of social control. In Munich (1972) the attempt was made to create an alternative 'cheerful scenario'. This failed in the fire of a terrorist attack on Israeli sportsmen. The building of completely new Olympic suburbs and the introduction of new brighter colours, the design of the logo and the perfecting of Olympic computers, the transmission to between 500 and 1,000 million television viewers and the investment of between 600 and 1,000 million dollars (much more than had originally been envisaged) did not alter the fact that – in Munich – a tragic climax had been reached. There followed massive, unexpected overspending at Montreal in 1976, an American boycott of the Moscow games in 1980, and the Soviet boycott of Los Angeles in 1984. But the more dominant the trends of gigantism, especially in combination with media-technological and commercial exploitation, the clearer the limits of such a model became. The Third World, the majority of countries in the world, cannot compete under such conditions. The games in Seoul (1988) have resulted in open questions about who 'owns' the Olympic Games.

FIRSTLY: THE SYNCHRONOUS DEVELOPMENT OF 'INDUSTRIAL' SPORT

Closer examination reveals that the linear Olympic story dissolves into an intermittent sequence of different models; a national patriotic festival (1896), a side-show of a world exhibition (1900), a festival of sport (1912), a political-economic-military showpiece (1936), a commercial spectacle (1972), the appearance of the Third World . . . the Olympic festival speaks many languages. Its answer to the question about the structure at the *fin de siècle* – 'forward' or 'backward' – is not as clear as it might have seemed in the beginning. Is that all that can be said about it?

A closer look shows that it may be possible to find a physical basis of Olympism underneath the superstructure of political, ideological, military and economic exploitation. Olympism is based on the competing body. The Olympic competition reflects what is happening on the industrial front. Is the body language of Olympic sport perhaps of that kind of clarity for which we are asking here?

Again, at first glance, it would appear to be so. *Citius, altius, fortius* – faster, higher, stronger – that is the configuration of modernity. Performance, tension, speed – this pattern had been developing since the eighteenth century in close parallel with the Industrial Revolution (Eichberg 1973, 1978, 1986;

Guttmann 1978; Elias and Dunning 1986). At the end of the nineteenth century it reached an organised shape – the world championships and the world federations of the different sport disciplines. They formed the peak of a hierarchical system within which the championship was fought for at every step, from the top of the world down to the level of town and suburb, school and club, the aim being victory at tournaments and the production of records. Records: this meant the production of quantitative data, the representation of performance in centimetre, gramme, second and point.

A good illustration is the history of track events. During the early modern period peasants and townspeople traditionally held their running competitions (Schaufelberger 1972). This has usually been referred to as a sort of forerunner of the modern movement. More precise analysis shows, however, that the folk competitions of the early modern period had little to do with modern sport. Then, neither speed nor time mattered as such, let alone establishing results. It would have been possible to measure the performance, but this was not the aim of the competition. The aim of the race was something else: to find a winner and to delight in a bizarre presentation of the body. Timing was not necessary to find a winner – only the comparing of what was happening at the moment.

The race winner was for the rest a marginal figure, there was less interest in the 'fast man' than in the 'strong man': winners in such games as shot-put, tossing the caber, wrestling or finger-pulling. In the attempt to win a foot-race, moreover, obstruction by competitors was tolerated and even desired. This seems incomprehensible to people who are only interested in the results. Yet there was a certain logic about it. Everyone took pleasure in the playful qualities of the race, the tripping and tumbling, the holding and escaping. Special variations were staged in the form of sack-races, racing with water-jugs on the head, egg-races, three-legged races or hopping. In this way the race became part of a folk carnival – a culture of laughter that staged the grotesque body, a topsy-turvy world, the crooked line of stumbling (Bakhtin 1968; Burke 1978).

The sporting race which became the standard in Athens, 1896, was not just a further development of this pattern: it represented a structural change. First steps in this direction were made by the English 'pedestrianism' of the seventeenth century, becoming now a 'match against time'. Later it appeared in the practice of pedagogues like J. C. F. Guts-Muths, acolyte of Rousseau who from the end of the eighteenth century developed the new pattern of racing against the clock, with a special running track, with results measured in seconds and entered into tables. Only now did running take on the shape which was to become the 'norm' from 1896: a race of performance, results, time.

The significance of this structural change can be seen in that the pattern of the running races (with such time-oriented variations as walking, hurdles, marathons, etc.) was imposed analogously on other forms of activity. Swimming, which had been practised for thousands of years, now became a sport dominated by time and speed. Likewise rowing and sailing took on a new look with streamlining and emphasis on time. Riding sports – formerly dressage and jousting – also became exercises against the clock. No matter what the sport, be it roller- or ice-skating, skiing, sledging, or even the more modern inventions like cycling, motor-car, motorbike or motor-boat racing, all were henceforth dominated by one aim – to achieve ever faster times.

Progress, career, futurism

It was not mere chance that the formation of the new type of sport occurred in the early nineteenth century at the same moment as two concepts originating in 'speed sport' took on special significance for the public and the individual: 'progress' and 'career'. In itself the term 'progress', which began to be used after the 1830s in titles of newspapers and political parties, ideologies and fighting songs (*Avanti, Fortschritt, Vorwärts, Progress*), did not have any special significance. But it indicated the new mode of moving forward by way of sportive striding and running. Arguments could be made concerning the political character and content of 'progress', but there was agreement concerning the quasi-natural character of the desire to get ahead. Evolutionists of both the Left and Right were at one in their description of the Race of Peoples, soon theoreticized in Social Darwinism.

In the life of the individual, progress was the 'career'. Originally this term indicated the quick pace of the horse or the track for horse-racing; it now became the race-track of man competing in his professional life for advancement and social achievement. Collective and individual self-understanding was thus transformed into 'dromocracy', i.e. the domination of the bodily-real myth of speed (Virilio 1977 and 1978).

In view of this development, Olympic competition represented a climax. A picture of Athens in 1896 shows the start of the 100 metre final (Kamper 1983, fig. 2). The runners, instead of being allowed to push and shove, are strictly separated from each other by line markings. The straight line of the cinder track replaced the bunching and tripping. An American athlete, Thomas Burke, was the first and only competitor to crouch in deep-start. His body thus took on the shape of a bullet, and he won the race in 12.0 seconds.

However, as has been mentioned, the new approach resulted not only in gains, but the structural changes implicated losses as well. Seconds were not to be laughed at. The relationship of earlier times between running and popular carnival was broken. Sport and the culture of laughter were divorced.

The new Olympic sport was thus shown to be up-to-date and deeply synchronous. It was a reflection (or prototype) of industrial culture, serving as a model to the latter's construction of 'progress', 'career' and intensified use of time. The parallel development in sport and society manifested itself at the turn of the century. Frederick Winslow Taylor, an American who was born in 1856, is reported to have taken part in the sport of climbing in Switzerland at the age of eleven or twelve and to have invented suitable equipment for it. Later, when he was sixteen, he thought up further innovations to shorten the amount of 'standing still or no-play' in ball games; in addition he developed a new tennis racket which made it easier for him to win. This was in fact a foretaste of what was to become at the turn of the century the central theme of this engineer and philosopher of industrialism: performance, increased productivity and efficiency. *The Principles of Scientific Management* (1911), and the stopwatch used for time and motion studies, transferred the body techniques of sport into work rationalization. Taylorism came to represent the myth of streamlining in the industrial society (Witte 1928).

Futurism was another movement at the turn of the century to which sport served as a guide. The futurist manifestos glorified the racing-car and the beauty of speed (1909). And in 1913 it was said: 'A Futurist is a person who loves life, energy, joy, freedom, progress, courage, the new functionality, and speed . . . Anyone who loves the open air life, sport and gymnastics and who daily looks after his own body to keep it supple and strong . . .' (Baumgarth 1966, pp. 26, 155).

This was saying: Away with the cult of the past, the 'passatism'! Destroy the museums! Replace them with sports grounds! Competition and cars are the pointers for the future! Here was another avant-garde on the move to Olympism. Fascism, especially in the Romance countries, would later draw part of its sports-aesthetic dynamic from this view (Guttmann 1983; Hobermann 1984).

The question then arises as to the limitations of an analysis seeing in sport only the aspect of synchronism. Certainly Taylorism, Olympism and Futurism depict sport from one side which is paradigmatically modern and intrinsic to industrial culture: performance, excitement, speed – racing forwards and producing results. But is that all?

SECONDLY: THE CULT OF ANTIQUITY AND NATURAL ENERGY

Avery Brundage, who later became President of the International Olympic Committee, declared that his experience of the Games in 1912 had 'converted' him to the Olympic 'religion'. Underlying such concepts are hidden pictures which are not just those of the sportlike rushing forwards: *Convertere* – turning and rotating (in a circle); *religio* – binding or going back to the origins;

and finally: Olympia – a place in antiquity. Thus Olympic sport represented simultaneously a quite different thing: nostalgia, turning back to (pre-) history, to save the present by taking inspiration from the past.

'Ancient Olympia was a city of athletics, art and prayer. It is a mistake to reverse the order of these three terms, as is sometimes done. The sacred and aesthetic character of Olympia were consequences of its muscular role. The city of athletics was intermittent; the city of art and prayer permanent. It will be the same with the modern Olympia.' As here with Coubertin in 1910 (1967, p. 22), the discourse on the Olympic idea took its point of departure from antiquity and in the end returned to it again and again. Olympic officials, when giving speeches, often said that Olympism had its origins in archaeology. In 1875 Ernst Curtius started the excavation work in Olympia. The festival of 1896 took place in the stadium of Herodes Atticus (AD 101–177).

This was not only a subject for the speeches, discourses and *mise-en-scène*. From the depths of fear and instinct, forces of history and 'naturalness' were having an effect. Coubertin had been deeply affected by the defeat of France in 1871, which he considered to be the result of an excess of Prussian-German historical energy. He saw similar forces at work in England, a country whose colonial expansion he admired – forces which he related to sport in the public schools. French society, in contrast, was sick; it needed a 'renaissance' which would draw on the virility of the past and of 'naturalness'. Back to nature, and: *Bronzer la France*.

So, in spite of all his republicanism and internationalism, Coubertin was not so very far remote from the philosophy of nostalgia and anti-decadence, prevalent in French nationalism at the turn of the century, and from such men as Maurice Barrès and Charles Maurras. But while their 'integral nationalism' developed early pre-fascist traits, it was only later in the thirties that Coubertin followed to a lesser extent. Meanwhile, frustrated and isolated, he observed German fascism with measured fascination (Boulongne 1975; Teichler 1982; MacAloon 1984). The Nazi state coincided with him to some extent when it developed its own 'Olympic-Aryan' spirit of looking back: whether in the form of neo-classicism or racial naturalism, of the boxing pedagogy in the Nazi *Ordensburgen* or Leni Riefenstahl's Olympic film and the resumption of archaeological excavations in Olympia.

Almost every aspect of the historical assumptions of Olympism have been undermined in the meantime by critical historical research. Hardly anything was left uncriticized, not even the unique position of the agones in ancient Greece; nor did antiquity confirm the 'amateur spirit', the 'taking part is everything', the fair play, the 'Olympic peace', and the postulated internationality. Nor can the modern pattern of movement and performance, with the accent on results, the stopwatch and the primacy of speed, be traced back to antiquity.

But when considering the part played by 'the return to the past' on the pattern which emerged around 1900, historical 'accuracy' is not the primary concern. The 'future' of Futurism was just as much a fiction as was that of Taylorism with the stopwatch. Yet they became material violence.

Thereby the dichotomous picture of sport and its body language deepens at the turn of the century. Their language contains both the increasing production of quantified records by engineer-athletes and the return of the archaic-naturalism of the strong body. Sport simultaneously resonates with the efficient industrial society and with the opposite image of physical excess and religiosity. It has within it the speed on the finishing straight and the hope for a renaissance, taking inspiration from times long past; the burning of museums and the cult of history; synchronism and non-synchronism with the industrial process.

THIRDLY: LEISURE CULTURE AND THE ENTERTAINMENTS INDUSTRY

The dichotomy, however, does not yet provide a sufficient characterization of the picture. There is at least a third dimension. What were those people really like who laid the foundations for Olympic sport? They were neither prevailingly engineers nor athletic 'naturalists'. They were second-rank intellectuals, academicians and bureaucrats, gentlemen and members of the upper bourgeoisie. They lived well, paid no income tax and enjoyed banquets which lasted for many hours. Coubertin flattered them by bestowing titles on them, gave receptions and other social events, impressed them with members of the nobility, and a succession of yet more banquets (Mandell 1976, pp. x–xi).

It is here that a third aspect of Olympic sport emerges fitting neither the 'progressive' nor the 'archaic' model. Coubertin himself portrayed a critical picture of this life-style in an article written in 1898 entitled 'Does cosmopolitan life lead to international friendliness?':

Cosmopolitan life is no longer an insignificant fact, an eccentricity of a few elegant women . . . Nowadays the whole aristocracy of Europe leads that sort of life. It scales the mountains of Switzerland or of the Tyrol, makes yachting trips to the fiords of Norway, shoots grouse in the highlands of Scotland, goes to Bayreuth to hear Wagner's operas and to Monte Carlo to lose its money; it spends Holy Week in Seville and the Carnival in Nice, ascends the Nile in a dahabeah, and coasts down the frozen slopes of St Moritz on toboggans in winter . . . Men of letters and artists have followed the footsteps of the leisured classes. (Quoted from MacAloon 1984, pp. 263–4)

Coubertin kept a critical distance from the neo-colonial attitudes of this social type, but in part his own image of 'true internationalism' was just an extension and spiritualization of cosmopolitanism, and in part he himself directly and consciously used the dynamics of cosmopolitanism. His International Olympic Committee (IOC) was precisely a club for the wealthy and dignitaries. For example, just before the First World War its German members consisted of a prince, five counts, a baron and just one commoner.

Seeing things from the point of view of a technocratic-progressive evolutionism, Thorstein Veblen had at that time (1899) discussed the relationship of sport and the leisured class in a somewhat similar way, but with opposite evaluation. For him, the sporting life-style represented the gradual expropriation of the producing class by an unproductive elite, which legitimized its existence through conspicuous consumption. A central feature of this idleness was sport in which, according to Veblen, were mixed absolute senselessness, the remnants of an archaic robber mentality, refined self-dramatization and naturalistic nostalgia.

But as well as being a brilliantly fitting description, this was at the same time a typical misunderstanding of the basic social nature of sport. Veblen has over-emphasized the 'parasitic' traits and reconstructed something redolent of late feudal aristocratic culture, a picture of non-productive activity, of non-synchronism. Sport, however, was also something quite different. Not even the cosmopolitanism depicted by Coubertin was as specifically 'noble' as might appear at first sight. Coubertin stressed that 'the railroad and telegraph' made this life-style suitable for the businessman as well.

The leisure culture not only survived the demise of the nobility, but took on a new impetus in the twentieth century. This went in two directions. The new media and means of public information turned sport into a centrepiece of the new *entertainments industry*. The Olympic Games and television culture were interconnected from the beginning: the location of the first live television camera was in an Olympic stadium (Berlin 1936). The other direction further developed the oligarchic *structure of notabilities*. The leadership of the international Olympism today appears as neo-monarchic and neo-feudal. 'The President' awards orders and jets from one congress to another, from one diplomatic reception to the next. Profiles of high-ranking Olympic representatives in colour, together with their pathetic utterances, are distributed in representative volumes throughout the world (Berlioux 1984). The merry-go-round of conventions in sport moves faster than in almost any other arena, repetitions of events at which the same faces, discussing the same topics, meet – in castles, in air-conditioned luxury hotels and in academic environments – again and again.

However, this self-staged vanity is put to purposeful use by sponsors, producers of sports equipment and the advertising industry. Adidas in particular is well known for providing free hotel visits, sumptuous receptions and luxury cars placed at the disposal of international sports officials in return for favourable business deals. The way for this was paved by the ad hoc committees and congresses organized by Coubertin at the turn of the century.

The patterns of leisure culture and of the entertainments industry are neither identical with that of progressive, forward-looking, futuristic sport, nor with that of nostalgic-naturalistic Olympism. In a sense, all three aspects partly contradict one another. Sport is more than a dichotomy, it is a trichotomy. And yet all three relate together and support one another. Indeed, the total picture of sport at the turn of the century can only be completed by their relationship, by the 'impurity' of synchronous and non-synchronous developments.

'ANTHROPOLOGICAL' GAMES AND WORLD CONQUEST

The 'impurity' of Olympic sport does not mean that it did not have a clear impact. The way in which the contradictory elements actually work together is shown in its neo-colonial dynamic.

The preliminary result worries even top officials of Western sport. Willi Weyer, President of the German Sports Federation (Deutsche Sportbund), warned his colleagues in 1986:

World sport must not remain a one-way street . . . Let us not forget the traditional sports in our own countries lest we have the same experience as the Solomon Islands Sports Council. The Secretary General, Mr. Davidson Nwaeramo, wrote to us that he had been talking with some of the islands' elders about traditional games on the Solomons and goes on to say: . . . It was evident that there were traditional games played on our islands. However, when in the 1950s modern sports like soccer and cricket were introduced, the traditional games ceased to exist. (Baumann 1986, p. 25)

The Olympics of 1896 represented a dynamic entry into this one-way street.

Coubertin's model was English sport. As an Anglophile, he repeatedly pointed to British-colonial expansion as proof of sporting vitality. But the public school sport of the upper classes could be seen not only as the qualification and impetus for conquering the world. It was also true that colonization of foreign people resulted in the imperial export of sport. Cricket and football were played in the best clubs in the Sudan, India, Canada and tropical Africa, even in the remote Trobriand Islands (Mangan 1986; Leach 1976). At the same time Theodore Roosevelt, in America, was portrayed simultaneously as a representative of imperialism and an excellent sportsman.

The colonial quality of Olympic sport was particularly evident at the games held in St Louis in 1904. They were furnished with a special annex: 'Anthropology Days' (Stanaland 1981). Newspaper headlines announced 'Barbarians meet in Athletic Games'. The Games were at that time a side-show of the World Exhibition, and at this event, African pygmies, Argentinian Patagonians, Japanese Ainu, Red Indians from Vancouver Island,

Manguinans and Eskimos were all 'displayed'. Especially groups of Red Indian tribes from the USA were presented to the public – Pawnees, Wichita, Kickapoo, Maricopa, Nez Perce, Chiricahua, Apache, Sioux, Kiowa, Zuni, Moquai, Navajo, Arapaho and Chippewa, as well as nationals from the recently conquered Philippines, Igorots, Moros, Bogobos, Visayans and Negritos. Thirteen of these tribes were to compete in races under the aegis of the Olympic games.

Competitions were held over two days in eighteen different sports. There were seven running events, two types of jumping, some forms of throwing – javelin, baseball, shotput, 56 lb weight, bolo – as well as archery, tug-of-war, pole climbing and mud fights. Some of these 'indigenous' competitions (i.e. mud fight and bolo) consisted of one single 'anthropological' group only, with no rivals at all.

The measured results were shameful – but for whom? The official Olympic report used this event as proof of the inferiority of the natives and held them up to ridicule. It was pointed out that some of the 'records' in throwing events could easily be beaten by schoolchildren, or that a result in running long jump could be bettered by top American athletes doing standing long jump. The myth of the 'noble savage' as a natural sportsman was shattered; it was unmasked as a Romantic vision.

Newspapers took great delight in the 'anthropological' games – they saw them as a spectacle of curiosities. This had more to do with entertainment than with sporting 'progress' (or naturalistic nostalgia). Almost by chance something positive emerged in this conflict of cultures. A pygmy suddenly interrupted pole-climbing to chase away photographers. Another wanted to take his clothes off for the competition and was dissuaded only by much effort by the puritanical organizers. But the pygmy participants distinguished themselves in particular by their laughter and readiness to view the situation as great fun. False starts, or seeing a participant stumble, struck them as being especially humorous. That which the media of the entertainment industry saw as charming curiosities actually illustrated something else: a conflict of cultures and the fact that Olympic sport had lost the quality of laughter and popular carnival.

SPORT: FROM COLONIALITY TO TOTALIZATION

Coubertin found all this vulgar. It contradicted his ideal of elitist games with Anglo-Saxon sport as its basis, whether it was basque pelota (as had been planned for Paris in 1900) or tobacco-spitting (which he had feared might happen in St Louis in 1904). And it was the English model which endured. The 'Anthropology Days' were never repeated.

Instead, the colonial sport expanded without integration of the contrasting indigenous competitions. Carl Diem, the Olympic historian of the Coubertin mould, expressed the dominant perspective of colonial expansion:

The American continent originally took its sport from Europe and is today more or less fully integrated into world sport. Asia too began to develop in this way in 1900 and has been almost completely assimilated . . . Australia, with England, was there from the beginning, as was the major part of the Oceanic Islands. Now Africa is in the midst of sporting expansion, where once Egypt and then the Union of South Africa led the way, connected as she was with the West . . . The total conquest of Africa is therefore a process soon to be rapidly accomplished. (Diem 1971, p. 1104)

But the conquest did not progress as smoothly as indicated here. In Stockholm in 1912 the Olympic winner in the Pentathlon and Decathlon was the Sac and Fox Indian, Was-tho-huck (Bright Path). He became known to the world under his colonial name of Jim Thorpe and was famous for his short, friendly answer to the King of Sweden, when the latter named him the greatest athlete in the world – 'Thanks, King'. But the following year saw him stripped of his medals. This was against the rules and was questionably founded in Thorpe's alleged infringement of the principle of amateurism. By 1932, the year of the Los Angeles games, he was too poor to buy an entrance ticket. However, he was rediscovered in 1951, and became the subject of a film starring Burt Lancaster: *Jim Thorpe – All American*. Even in failure he rendered service to the cause of Western sport and of the white state. To quote film posters: 'Everyone's hero – and a woman's idol! – An entertainment glorious as the grand guy it glorifies. – He wore America's heart over his!' (Wheeler 1983).

The expansionist tendencies of neo-colonial sport have, however, experienced change. There have been new developments over the last ten or twenty years which are, perhaps, the real base for the critical view – here indicated – of the history of Olympism. Three of these are: the totalization of sport; the discussion of a 'new world order of sport'; and the exoticism of Western sporting culture.

Firstly, it had been the claim of Olympic sport that the best athletes would stand a chance of winning, each according to his individual performance. Since at least the 1950s, with the arrival of state amateurism, there has been a quite different development. The performance of an individual athlete became the product of a system. Training schedules and special schools, preparation camps and institutionalized scientific sport research, the technology of chemical aids and new materials, wind tunnels and sport engineering, top management and organized mass sport, financial support and the systematic search for talent – all these became prerequisites for Olympic success. Gradually, even among the 'active' Olympic participants, the athletes became a minority: they were outnumbered by trainers and sports doctors, advertising men and spies, managers and sports psychologists, etc. Increasingly, therefore, top medalists came from the superpowers while athletes from African, Asian and Indo-American countries less able to provide the necessary support stood even less chance. This was quite clear by the 1970s and has since been described as the 'totalization of sport' (Heinilä 1982).

The situation was, however, not entirely new. As the 'Anthropology Days' of 1904 showed, the concept of 'individual performance' had been based on an ethnocentric illusion from the beginning. It was the myth, albeit a powerful one, of liberal colonialism at the turn of the century. When participants raced along the cinder track, at no time were they racing as mere individuals. Rather, they represented a competition between cultures.

'NEW WORLD ORDER' AND 'EXOTICISM' OF WESTERN SPORT

Secondly, while the totalization of sport was being discussed, new tensions came to mark the Olympic 'world politics'. From about 1976 there had been conflicts between the (Western oligarchic) International Olympic Committee and UNESCO, where representatives from the Third World had a majority. Sports politicians of the non-aligned nations began to press for a 'New World Order of Sport' (Hietanen 1982; Eichberg 1984). In 1983 UNESCO decided on a major programme of education which would give particular attention to 'traditional games and dances' and the 'national heritage'.

These conflicts never came to open confrontation. Probably the 'neofeudal' hotel- and consensus-culture of the international Leisure Class and the industries behind – the sponsors, the media and the sports accessories – made their influence felt. Instead battles arose in the 1980s over Olympic money *within* Western sport. These quarrels – between the IOC, national Olympic committees and national sports federations – resulted in a critical look at the neo-colonial theme of Olympic sport. Who is doing the most to promote 'Sport for All' and traditional physical exercise became a main argument of all against all. By this time it was discovered that world sport did not consist solely of the stopwatch-dominated Olympic events as established around 1900, but also of Chinese Wushu and Ta Chi, of Eskimo dance festivals and walrus-skin-jumping, of Indonesian war dances and Nigerian dances, of Scottish hammer-throwing and tossing the caber, of *Bosseln* and *Klootscheeten* in Friesland and the Netherlands, of French *boule* and Italian *bocchia* . . . (Baumann 1986, pp. 20–32, M5–23).

Thirdly, the new reasoning in world sports politics had a real basis in Western sporting culture. Since the 1960s and 1970s a transformation could be perceived which appeared as a form of 'exoticism' (Satyarthi 1979–81,

Nitschke and Wieland 1981, Kleinman 1986). Taekwon-Do and Karate, Tai Chi Chuan and Kung Fu, Aikido and Judo have all become popular in Western societies. The USA and western Europe have seen the advent of the Afro-Brasilian martial art Capoeira. The Soviet authorities experienced problems with unlicensed Karate clubs. The cries of Japanese Kendo can be heard in German sports halls, and in Austria in 1986 there was the first world championship in the Indonesian martial sport Pencak silat to be held outside Asia. Centres for Thai boxing are springing up in western European cities.

Boundaries have become less defined between the more spiritual East Asian martial arts and the novel practice of meditation and health pedagogy, yoga, physical therapies, healing gymnastics (Pa Tuan Chin) and acupuncture, acupressure and massage, including spiritual and neo-religious movements. Even the top Western sport could now be described as yoga, crossing the line between motion and meditation, between sport of performance and peak experience (Murphy and White 1978). Increasingly, Oriental psychotechniques were introduced into everyday sports training. In addition, and to an extent overlapping, the carnival and the samba developed while the dance of the youth culture was influenced by Afro-American patterns. Thus it can be seen how widely within society these changes were received – from youth sub-culture to evening classes in yoga for housewives, and to meditation techniques against the professional stresses of the managerial class.

However, despite the dramatic emergence of these phenomena in the 1960s, they are not completely new either. The first innovations of this type could already be experienced shortly after the turn of the century. It was then that the Afro-American jazz dance and the Afro-Cuban tango first arrived in Europe and caused disquiet amongst cultural critics as being 'shake dances'. People took an interest in Indian yoga and Islamic Sufi dances. The victory of the Japanese over the Russian fleet in 1905 marked the arrival of a wide wave of ju-jitsu in the West. However, at that time the basic structure of Olympic sports was in no way questioned by the reception of activities originating in foreign cultures. This is, however, the case today.

Bearing in mind the opening words of this essay, the end of the nineteenth century approached with the pace of a bicycle taking part in a sports race. The course of Olympic history illuminates the di- or, to be more precise, the trichotomy of this 'race'. It was swinging between historical, naturalist nostalgia, an industrial-futuristic urge to get ahead, and an entertainment-oriented leisure culture. Far from being arbitrary and blurred, the glitter and the taint were of significance in a historical context. The Olympic competition was no longer an event of popular carnival and laughter, as was the case for hundreds of years in earlier times in Europe. It had become a colonial 'one-way street'. Most of the non-European motion cultures fell victim to it.

The ambiguity of the process was reflected on the cinder tracks in Athens in

1896 by the physical bodies themselves. Clearly the races were future-orientated, directed forward to one aim. They were the climax of a development of top performances which had already been going on for a century; and they were the starting point for the chain of records, following in the twentieth century, for high industrial dynamics and mobility. Thus 'progress'. And yet it also represented a novel immobilization. For since then the nature of the Olympics sport has undergone scarcely any structural changes. Now, as then, the deep-start, the separation of the lanes, the finishing straight, the clock, determine the Olympic set-up. There have been only minor technical accommodations in order to intensify the proceedings – the cinder track has been replaced by artificial track, the stopwatch has given way to electronic time-keeping. Otherwise there has been no 'progress', only stagnation – the end of an historic line?

The century started off with full energy into a one-way street. Is the end of the road visible? Be that as it may, it feels good, even today, to hear the laughter of the pygmies in 1904.

BIBLIOGRAPHY

Bakhtin, M. *Rabelais and His World* (Cambridge, Mass. and London, 1968).
Baumann, W. (ed.). *Fundamentals of Sport for All. International Congress* (Frankfurt-on-Main, 1986).
Baumgarth, C. *Geschichte des Futurismus* (Reinbeck, 1966).
Berlioux, M. (ed.). *Le Mouvement olympique/The Olympic Movement*, Edition IOC (Lausanne, 1984).
Blödorn, M. (ed.). *Sport und Olympische Spiele* (Reinbek 1984).
Boulongne, Y.-P. *La Vie et l'oeuvre pédagogique de Pierre de Coubertin (1863–1937)* (Montreal 1975).
Burke, P. *Popular Culture in Early Modern Europe* (London, 1978).
Coubertin, P. de. 'Does cosmopolitan life lead to international friendliness?', *American Monthly Review of Reviews*, 17 (1898), 429–34.
   Mémoires olympiques (Lausanne, 1931).
   The Olympic Idea (Schorndorf, 1967).
Diem, C. *Gedanken zur Sportgeschichte* (Schorndorf, 1965).
   Weltgeschichte des Sports, 2 vols. (3rd edn, Stuttgart, 1971).
   Ausgewählte Schriften, 3 vols. (Sankt Augustin, 1982).
Eichberg, H. *Der Weg des Sports in die industrielle Zivilisation* (Baden-Baden, 1973).
   Leistung, Spannung, Geschwindigkeit (Stuttgart, 1978).
   'Sport im 19. Jahrhundert', in H. Ueberhorst (ed.), *Geschichte der Leibesübungen*, vol. III/1 (Berlin, 1980), pp. 350–412.
   'Olympic sport – neocolonization and alternatives', *International Review for the Sociology of Sport*, 19, no. 1 (1984), 97–106.
   Die Veränderung des Sports ist gesellschaftlich (Münster, 1986).
Elias, N. and E. Dunning. *Quest for Excitement* (Oxford, 1986).

Enquist, P. O. *Katedralen i München* (Copenhagen, 1973).

Esman, K. *Foråret, der døde* (Aarhus, 1972).

Espy, R. *The Politics of the Olympic Games* (Berkeley, Calif., 1979).

Fendrich, A. *Der Sport, der Mensch und der Sportsmensch* (2nd edn, Stuttgart, 1914).

Graham, P. J. and H. Ueberhorst (eds.). *The Modern Olympics* (West Point, Conn., 1976).

Guttmann, A. *From Ritual to Record* (New York, 1978).

'Le Plaisir du sport. French writers of the 1920s', *Arete*, 1, no. 1 (1983), 113–24.

The Games Must Go On. Avery Brundage and the Olympic Movement (New York, 1984).

Heinilä, K. 'The totalization process in international sport', *Sportwissenschaft*, 12 (1982), 235–54.

Heitanen, A. 'Towards a new international sports order?', *Current Research on Peace and Violence*, 5 (1982), 159–75.

Hobermann, J. *Sport and Political Ideology* (Austin, Tex., 1984).

The Olympic Crisis (New Rochelle, 1986).

Hopf, W. *Soziale Zeit und Körperkultur* (Münster, 1981).

Kamper, E. *Lexikon der Olympischen Winterspiele*, (2nd edn, Stuttgart, 1964).

Die Enzyklopädie der Olympischen Spiele (Stuttgart, 1972).

Lexikon der 14000 Olympioniken (Graz, 1983).

Kleinman, S. (ed.). *Mind and Body. East Meets West* (Champaign, Ill., 1986).

Kloeren, M. *Sport und Rekord. Kultursoziologische Untersuchungen zum England des 16. bis 18. Jahrhunderts* (Leipzig, 1935;, repr. Münster, 1985).

Kluth, H. 'Amtsgedanke und Pflichtethos in der Industriegesellschaft', in G. Hartfiel (ed.), *Das Leistungsprinzip* (Opladen, 1977).

Lämmer, M., 'Die Zukunft der Olympischen Spiele liegt nicht in ihrer Vergangenheit, in *Bulletin des 11. Olympischen Kongresses* no. 6 (Munich, 1981), pp. 12–15, 42–8.

'Der sogenannte olympische Friede in der griechischen Antike', *Stadion*, 8/9 (1982/3), 47–83.

Leach, J. W. (dir.). *Trobriand Cricket* (film) (Berkeley, University of California, 1976).

MacAloon, J. J. *This Great Symbol. Pierre de Coubertin and the Origins of the Modern Olympic Games* (Chicago, 1984).

Mandell, R. D. *Paris 1900: The Great World's Fair* (Toronto, 1967).

The Nazi Olympics (New York, 1971).

The First Modern Olympics (Berkeley, Calif., 1976).

Sport – A Cultural History (New York, 1984).

Mangan, J. A. *The Games Ethic and Imperialism* (Harmondsworth, 1986).

Mevert, F. *Internationale und europäische Sportorganisationen* (Wiesbaden, 1981).

Murphy, M. and R. A. White. *The Psychic Side of Sports* (Reading, Mass., 1978).

Nitschke, A. and H. Wieland, (eds.). *Die Faszination und Wirkung aussereuropäischer Tanz- und Sportformen* (Ahrensburg, 1981).

Oettermann, S. *Läufer und Vorläufer. Zu einer Kulturgeschichte des Laufsports* (Frankfurt-on-Main, 1984).

Pauker, E. T. *Ganefo I: Sports and Politics in Djakarta* (Santa Monica, Calif., 1964).

Prokop, U. *Soziologie der Olympischen Spiele* (Munich, 1971).

Satyarthi, S. D. *Kroppens veje*, 2 vols. (Copenhagen, 1979–81).

Schaufelberger, W. *Der Wettkampf in der alten Eidgenossenschaft*, 2 vols. (Berne, 1972).

Schulke, H.-J. (ed.). *Die Zukunft der Olympischen Spiele* (Cologne, 1976).

Segrave, J. and D. Chu (eds.). *Olympism* (Champaign, Ill., 1981).

Sie, S. 'Sports and politics: the case of the Asian games and the Ganefo', in B. Lowe *et al.* (eds.), *Sport and International Relations*, (Champaign, Ill., 1978), pp. 279–96.

Stadion 6 (1980). *Beiträge zur Geschichte der Olympischen Spiele.*

Stanaland, P. 'Pre-Olympic "Anthropology Days", 1904' in A. Taylor Cheska (ed.), *Play as Context*, (West Point, Conn., 1981), pp. 101–6.

Teichler, H. J. 'Coubertin und das Dritte Reich', *Sportwissenschaft*, 12 (1982), 18–55.

Ullrich, K. *Olympia von Athen bis Moskau* (Berlin, GDR, 1977).

   Coubertin (Berlin, GDR, 1982).

Umminger, W. *Helden – Götter – Übermenschen. Eine Kulturgeschichte menschlicher Höchstleistungen* (Düsseldorf and Vienna, 1962).

   (ed.). *Olympisches Lesebuch* (2nd edn, Hanover, 1971).

Veblen, T. *The Theory of the Leisure Class* (New York, 1899).

Virilio, P. *Vitesse et politique* (Paris, 1977).

   Fahren, fahren, fahren . . . (Berlin, 1978).

Weiler, I. *Der Agon im Mythos* (Darmstadt, 1974).

   Der Sport bei den Völkern der Alten Welt (Darmstadt, 1981).

Wheeler, R. W. *Jim Thorpe* (Oklahoma, 1983).

Wickenhagen, H. *Turnen und Jugendspiele* (Munich, 1898).

Witte, I. M. *F. W. Taylor* (Stuttgart, 1928).

❧

EIGHT

PHOTOGRAPHY, CINEMATOGRAPHY AND THE THEATRE: A HISTORY OF A RELATIONSHIP

BARBARA LESÁK

THE FIGURE OF THE 'PHOTOGRAPHER' ON THE STAGE

In accordance with the country's pioneer role in the development of photography, the parts and personalities of drawing-room comedies in France – or to be more exact, the theatre of Paris – were infiltrated by a new character role in the years following the middle of the nineteenth century. In line with the dynamic development of capitalist society taking place at that time, drawing-room comedies sought constantly to expand the dramatic personnel on the stage and, as necessary, to restructure their personnel register. On the other hand, the dramaturgical structure of the story, as well as the dramatic sequence of events in which these figures are embedded, was able to adhere to the conventional i.e. the customary, framework. The intruder into the illusory world of the schematized drawing-room play with its prefabricated comedy, predictable plot and happy ending, is the figure of the 'photographer' who wields a technical invention which consequently proved to be a dangerous competitor for the theatre. However, it was not until photography extended its photo-chemical picture techniques to achieve the reproduction of movement that it presented a serious challenge to the theatre. Only the advent of moving photography, i.e. cinematography, was to drive the theatre into a deep crisis from which, once the necessary stage and structure reforms had been implemented, it emerged with new vigour. At the beginning of the 1860s, photography presented no danger to the position of the theatre. Accordingly, this potential traitor – the photographer – was invited to appear on the stage.

Another reason why the figure of the 'photographer' is so interesting is that it marks the arrival of the theatre at a watershed where theatrical means were still just sufficient to reproduce the characteristic technical and professional image of the photographer on the stage. On a more general plane, however, the theatre also experienced problems in presenting the changing way of life caused by the technical as well as the industrial revolution.

Published in 1865, *Le Photographe*[1] is the unambiguous title of a comedy by Henri Meilhac and Ludovic Halévy, a French writing team who also penned the librettos for Jacques Offenbach's most successful operettas. Paradoxically, they had rationalized their writing technique and, with a view to their individual talents, specialized to such an extent that their work is reminiscent of the mechanism of a machine. It was with the aid of this rationalized and accelerated writing technique as employed in the so-called 'writing factories'[2] of the nineteenth century that the dramatists were able to meet the growing need of their audiences for entertainingly packaged information about the dazzling, rapidly changing phenomena of modern life in the big city and the world at large, which, thanks to the possibilities offered by the new communication techniques, had suddenly come to the attention of a public which was not only hungry for knowledge but which also craved sensation. At that time, the traditional means at the disposal of the theatre still appeared adequate for depicting – indeed reproducing – the highly complex realities of modern life. Ultimately condemned to failure, material taken from life was formed in a dramaturgical *tour de force* and presented on a stage which was constantly being re-equipped and modernized in accordance with general technical inventions. However, it was the invention of cinematography – which is generally considered to have been born on 28 December 1895, the date of the first public showing in Paris of a film by the Lumière brothers from Lyon – that was to put the theatre in its place and jeopardize its extremely exaggerated principle of illusion.

The dramatic technique used by Meilhac and Halévy to create the professional image of the 'photographer' before the eyes of their audience not only had didactic qualities but is also the source of comedy. Their vehicle is an 'imposter' who pretends to be a photographer in order to seduce a society lady. However, the imposter does not know how to use the various photographic materials (which are brought on to the stage in the course of the first scene by a series of suppliers). In this way, the medium photography is presented and explained in a most amusing reversal process, without having to resort to a dull, pontificating tone. The comedy arises from the differences between the knowledge of photography which could be assumed of audiences in 1865 and the ignorance of the hero. At the same time, those members of the audience who still knew too little about photography could learn from the hero's mistakes.

No matter how shallow this one-act comedy may be, it nevertheless offers an amazing amount of information about the social standing of the photographer and the prestige he enjoyed in French society – or better, in the enlightened, urbane society of the cosmopolitan city of Paris. And there can be no doubt about the correctness of this assessment of the social role of the photographer because the trivial play does not form any opinions itself but only operates with the more or less stereotyped or socially sanctioned mental images, behaviour patterns and standards of its mostly bourgeois audience who, in the theatre, only wanted to see themselves reflected within the framework of their perspectives. That the photographer had become acceptable to the theatre-going public and that a respectable man-about-town could slip into this role for a time without losing any social standing, is the result of an opinion-forming process during which the social, commercial and artistic significance of the medium 'photography' was recognized and acknowledged.

Before leaving the comedy *Le Photographe* – which was selected from the enormous bequest of the nineteenth century as an authentic piece of evidence for the social acceptability of photography, we should recapitulate on its message for the modern reader who, beneath the ageing varnish of this amorous comedy, will find a well-kept and fresh narrative about the formative years of photography. The reader learns that, in 1865, it was not possible to take photographs without technical knowledge and expertise – the typical amateur photographer is a phenomenon of the twentieth century – so that photography was regarded by painters as an independent branch of art which did not poach on their traditional preserves. However, as cameras became increasingly easy for laymen to use, this opinion was temporarily revised. It is not difficult to imagine that, as a result of the influence exercised by photography as early as the 1860s, visual expectations changed and that this also left its mark on classic areas of art such as the theatre. Accordingly, the reader is likely to be confirmed in the opinion that photography – and only photography – could have been the 'billeting officer' for film, or, as it was called then, cinematography.

THE SOCIETY OF THE LATE NINETEENTH CENTURY
PREPARES FOR THE INVENTION OF FILM

The science-fiction stories of the nineteenth century – especially the adventure stories of the French technological visionary Jules Verne – anticipate many inventions which, in the form of technically developed products, came to determine – indeed, dictate – the pattern of civilized life in the twentieth century. Gifted with an extremely fertile imagination, Jules Verne only had to listen to the rumours coming out of the scientific and experimental laboratories of his time to be able to invent fabulous technical equipment for his heroes. By paying attention to interesting technical inventions being patented, he was able to build the amazing machines which soon thereafter became reality.

However, the technical inventions of Jules Verne were still surrounded by an air of magic and mystery, reflecting the anxiety and dread of the nineteenth-century reader in the face of the demon machine. It was not until the following century that his inventions lost this air for good when they became secularized utilities and consumer goods. Presenting in all its old-fashioned and dated eccentricity that superstitious mistrust which a part of the figures – characterized by Verne as backward, uneducated and primitive – held towards machinery, technical devices or scientific discoveries, was part of the pedagogic strategy of the positivist Jules Verne who strove above all to convince his readers of the benefits of technology. To this end, and to avoid producing a monotonous song of praise in favour of technology, he employed an ironic description of the fearful amazement at the technical progress of his century as a complementary aspect of the story with the function of giving an extra gloss to the technical apotheosis. By identifying with Verne's heroes – who were naturally ideal representatives of his positivistic, scientific way of thought, the reader was obliged to accept, apply and further develop the technology of the time in real life, too.

In his novel *The Carpathian Castle*[3] Jules Verne combined two inventions – the phonograph developed by Thomas Alva Edison in 1879 and the *laterna magica*, a well-known optical trick device – and thereby took up an idea of the American inventor Edison who tried to combine motion pictures (film) with sound in 1889. However, in view of the great technical difficulties associated with the combination of pictures and sound,[4] efforts were once again concentrated on perfecting silent film techniques. Set in contemporary times, the hero of Jules Verne's story, a lovesick Romanian count who has apparently seen all kinds of technical equipment on his travels abroad, projects a painted likeness of a deceased Italian singer on to the pitch-black Transylvanian sky and simultaneously plays recordings of her voice. Although, given the absence of essential features such as movement and a photo-mechanically produced sequence of pictures, the combination of sound and projection described by Verne admittedly has little to do with the cinematography of 1895, it nevertheless caused a shock typical of the new reproduction media. After all, people at the close of the nineteenth century first had to get used to the idea that the amazingly exact images of objects and people which could be created using the new reproduction techniques went hand-in-hand with a loss of their material, haptic and vital existence. To increase the impact, Verne had his hero reproduce the voice and the image of a dead person, thereby drawing attention more pointedly to the immaterial character of this new type of sound/picture conservation. Described by Verne as primitive and backward Carpathian peasants, the terror of the Transylvanian population at the mechanical reproduction of a voice and the projection of a human form which, despite the perfect illusion of presence, was not really there at all, was no different from that experienced by many city dwellers in so-called civilized countries. There are numerous similar reports of the devastating effect of film illusions on a naïve public during the early days of cinematography. For example, it is quite well known that members of the audience at the first Lumière films fled in panic as a locomotive pulling into a station appeared on the screen, thinking that it was really bearing down on them and would crush everybody in its way. Those audience members who, in the early days of cinematography, were overwhelmed by the illusory power of moving pictures had no repertoire or reactions with which they could have seen through and mastered the situation.

LIVING PHOTOGRAPHY – CINEMATOGRAPHY – FILM

Before cinematography emerged from the factory of the brothers Auguste and Louis Lumière as a genuine film product – in principle no different from the product still in use today – its precursor, living or motion photography, was a scientific/technological problem in the skilled, not always profit-orientated hands of scientists, amateur inventors, engineers and technicians. Even at that time (around 1890), the presentations of their electrotachyscopes, or *Elektrischer Schnellseher*[5] as the apparatus was known in German-speaking countries, for the purpose of showing sequences of movements of people and animals which had been researched and recorded with the aid of instantaneous photography, were a cross between science and entertainment. The seriousness of the results of the research was undermined by the narrative mode of presentation of the various sequences of movement, which had been studied using live models. In principle, the instantaneous photographs of movement brought together as a continuous sequence of movement in the *Elektrischer Schnellseher* – in which one picture followed the other at intervals of one-thirtieth of a second – represented a kind of entertainment. Regardless of the scientific purpose behind it, the sensory pleasure experienced by the viewer when watching the fascinating illusion of movement soon predominated. That this is not a mere assumption is shown by an eyewitness report on the first *Elektrischer Schnellseher* demonstrated in Vienna in 1890. The writer broke out into aesthetic raptures about the sequence of pictures he had watched: '. . . [one] sees . . . movement created by the series of pictures, in the finest detail and delightful completeness'.[6] During this performance, a group of Austrian experts were shown six different motion pictures: a running dog, marching soldiers, people jumping and horses.

In actual fact, it was not long before these demonstrations of movement, all of which were based on the principle of the well-known but technically improved stroboscope, left the field of scholarly experiment, known as the science of chronophotography, and moved into the arena of mere entertainment and pleasure.[7] From the moment it became possible to construct a coin-operated automatic machine able to offer the viewer lively and entertaining moving stories, the originally vacillating area of application for this invention became clear cut: from that point on, it was to be firmly in the hands of the still very primitive fun-fair art before developing into an independent branch of art – with aesthetics derived from its new type of technology and differing significantly from traditional art forms. However, until the first real film presentation as we know it today took place – in other words, the projection of a film on to a screen in front of a large audience – the city fun-fairs of the early 1890s were the home of Edison's Kinetoscope[8] – that primitive automatic viewing device the main fault of which was that, as in the case of the older automatic peepshow machines, only one viewer at a time could enjoy the photographed sequence of movement.

In the very early days of cinematography (the somewhat long-winded name given to film at that time), i.e. in 1895, the various processes involved in the production of a film, as well as the complex operations required for its practical application, were still in the hands of a single entrepreneurial pair of inventors, the brothers Louis and Auguste Lumière,[9] who possessed their own industrial workshop for manufacturing still cameras and photographic plate, where they were able to transform their photographic inventions into reality. Beginning in 1896, the Société Anonyme de Plaque et Papiers Photographiques S. Lumière et ses Fils of Lyon produced the world's first practical film camera, the 'Cinématographe', which was not only a camera and projector in one but also included all accessories. The company produced the raw film material and – in a symbiosis of manufacturing and simultaneous application which was still possible during this pioneer age of film – they used their raw film material to record simple scenes and then sell the resulting films throughout the world. Although the manufacture, production and distribution were separated in the course of later specialization, the initial centralization of all working processes in one place, the Lyon factory, was important for the economic success of cinematography which, thanks to the professional manufacturing and sales methods of the 'Lumière et ses Fils' company, was able to commence its triumphal march throughout the world.

In next to no time, Europe was covered with a network of dealers who swarmed out into the cities to sell the 'Cinématographe'. Thanks to the almost amateurish handiness of the design, it was a great success. In Vienna, for example, one of the Lumières' representatives arranged the first public performance of the 'Cinématographe'[10] as early as 22 March 1896. The exact date and place of this performance has been handed down to us by a witness of the event who was aware of its historical significance and, indeed, even mentioned the name of the first operator of this performance.[11] Only 15 metres long and lasting just one minute each, the famous repertoire of these first film strips included nine typical sequences of movement which, although they stemmed from everyday French life, could fairly claim to be generally understandable. However, the primary objective of these early film performances was not to present the films. Instead, the organizers were mainly concerned with showing what a splendid piece of equipment the 'Cinématographe' was. Looking at the contents of these first films – 'a gate of the Lumières' factory in Lyon with hundreds of workers leaving the premises – cyclists coming into view – a wagon drawn by white horses approaching the audience and then turning a corner – a carnival procession in Nice – a train entering the station – the arrival of a steam liner – a beach scene at a seaside resort – children playing – a game of cards'[12] – it is astonishing that the Lumières, who worked anonymously for the most part, had such a good nose for themes which were not only cinematically of interest but which also contained a narrative sufficient to satisfy the need of the audiences for a story, no matter how brief.

For whom and for what purpose was this cinematographic process good? After reaching the market in 1895 as a more or less non-utility invention, it had to hold its own against a host of other new technical products. Given that the area of application and the economic benefits of cinematography had yet to be defined exactly, it was left to the buyer, the user to make the decision. It was up to him to do with it what he wanted, i.e. to use it to his own advantage, and to produce another article, namely the exposed roll of film, which was equally reproducible and could itself be sold. For the dilettanti, parvenus and fortune hunters of the late nineteenth century, cinematography represented the ideal foundation for meteoric careers, profiteering and the fulfilment of artistic dreams. In contrast to this, in the hands of scientists, physicians and ethnographers, it was a practical instrument for their scientific inquiries. Using the new medium, the former group broke new artistic ground, marked out – often unconsciously – the creative boundaries of film and developed the feature film. In other words, they give cinematography its aim and object: its primary purpose from which a whole branch of industry – the film industry with its national centres of production – was to develop after the turn of the century. Others, those in the latter group, used the ability of film to reproduce reality exactly to help solve their research problems. In 1909, for example, the French physician Dr Commadon employed micro-cinematography to demonstrate the destructive effect of microbes. Above all, his film showed the dramatic way a microbe carrying sleeping sickness attacks a healthy, resistant cell.[13] The military also experimented with cinematographic recordings, in connection with ballistic tests. Shortly before the First World War, the Austrian Imperial Army tried to film artillery shells in flight with the aim of gathering data which could be used to improve the design of the projectiles.[14]

Despite the sensation created by cinematography in the year of its invention, 1895, and a year later when it was introduced to other countries, the new media nevertheless required a certain starting-up period – roughly a decade – before becoming an economic giant, the most marvellous product of which was cinematic art in all its multifarious variations, from pure entertainment to art. During this latent time, it hardly competed with the established theatre. The bastions of high culture had yet to be taken by storm. Although this technical process for reproducing the moving world had the creative and interpretative potential to shatter the boundaries of theatrical illusion, the technical standards were still too primitive to record more complicated sequences on film. However, it was hardly necessary to possess prophetic abilities to be able to forecast a great future for cinematography. Everybody could see that this technological age, as the twentieth century proudly promised to be, had been given an adequate technological means for making recordings, which, given both greater technical perfection and artistic creativity, promised to be able to produce an unparalleled realistic image of the world and store it for eternity. In addition, as was to be expected, cinematography also mobilized mass audiences, which meant it could become the mass article of culture which it had already promised to become in 1895.

The proud success of cinematography after the turn of the century is evidenced by quantitative information, statistics and data from commemorative publications of the photographic industry, which had not only become extremely powerful in the intervening years but also supplied the accessories required for filming. In Germany, AGFA (Aktien-Gesellschaft für Anilin-fabrikation) began the production of raw cinematographic film. At the time, the technical production of film was a great challenge for inventors and industrialists. However, as AGFA pointed out in 1920 in a *Handbuch für Kinematographie*, 'only a few companies had the combination of energy, capital, inventiveness and experience necessary for success in this branch of industry which was still relatively untouched by scientific and technological research'.[15]

In 1909, after the great increase in demand for cinematic film which had taken place in 1906, film began 'to exchange its wretched nomadic existence at fun-fairs for a more permanent residence in the cities',[16] and AGFA's production of film climbed to some 10 million metres per year. By 1916, a cinema film – which, for just a little money, could transport its audience into a fairy-tale world, take them to the Swiss mountains, the Italian lakes or distant and exotic cities, make them laugh or cry – measured several kilometres in length. The fact that cinematography would soon – barely twenty years after its first public performance – be considered of eminent political significance is shown by the ban on the export of cinematographic accessories imposed by the German government during the First World War. Just how significant this industry was for the national interest is revealed by a newspaper article published in 1916 in the country responsible for the outbreak of war: 'The necessary expedients are also supplied by our allies to Austria's film photographers, who have made some outstanding productions, while exports have now been stopped.'[17]

Born in the last decade of the nineteenth century in an atmosphere vacillating between decadence and upheaval, it was only after crossing the threshold into the twentieth century that this extremely future-orientated invention – a kind of dowry for the new century – could fully develop into a mighty branch of industry. The prospect of enormous economic success which, with the triumph of the medium in the form of full-length feature films, became reality from 1906 on was almost unexpected, and the industry noted with amazement that 'with the undreamt of spread of the cinemato-graphic theatre, the bearer of the cinematographic picture, the cinefilm, became an extraordinarily popular commodity, the demand for which was soon to exceed the expectations of all experts by an enormous degree'.[18]

THE THEATRE AT THE TURN OF THE CENTURY

A large part of society – above all the members of the educated classes – was particularly inclined to attach special significance to the turn of the century. Even in the theatre, direct allusions to the term itself in certain plays gave expression to the feeling that an era was drawing to a close. For example, Ferdinand Bronner, a long and rightly forgotten Austrian dramatist, gave the name *Turn of the Century (Jahrhundertwende)* to his cycle of dramas published in Germany between 1900 and 1902. And it is certainly no coincidence that Martin Langen, another forgotten author of the early twentieth century, added the subtitle *A Drama from the End of This Century (Drama aus dem Ende dieses Jahrhunderts)* to his work *Edith* (1895), as if the oft-evoked spirit of the turn of the century was sufficient to have a fateful impact on a life.

Because it was still young and primitive, cinematography took the hurdle of the turn of the century without hesitation. Unencumbered by intellectual problems and self-doubt, this new art form was able to move forward parallel with technical progress. The theatre, on the other hand, proved to be infected with that real or imagined fear of crossing thresholds which caused people to regard the closing years of the nineteenth century pensively, critically and anxiously. As a result of its 2,000-year history, as well as its long period of development which had given rise to numerous different theatrical forms, the theatre seemed particularly susceptible to ideas involving a loss of strength and originality and to be choking on conventionalism and petrification. Resisting these restrictive theatrical conventions, however, led to an accumu-lation of the explosive material which made it possible to blast away the non-theatrical ballast gathered over the centuries and to achieve a new form.

The production of drama at the beginning of the twentieth century was the subject of lively reflection, of conflict and of the categorizing presentation of theatre critique, which was promoted by a liberal newspaper culture and was, above all, a criticism of drama itself. Critics observed drama productions with a highly perceptive eye. By 1900, the theatrical review had developed into an art form which, equipped with the finest sensorium, paved the audience's way to the new, difficult plays. Audiences had become competent, in some respects professional observers who carried, accompanied, praised, reinforced, explained, criticized, expounded and helped the theatre to develop into a powerful institution. Generally speaking, the European theatre at the turn of the century was anchored firmly in the cultural life of society and its cultural and political programme. At that time, the theatre still dealt with all important contemporary issues – from social questions to sounding the depths of the unknown human psyche – and produced exemplary productions on these themes. Equally, it satisfied the need of city dwellers for diversion and distraction with an almost unlimited range of sensational and sentimental plays. In the shadow of cinematic art – which was not only new but also perfectly in tune with modern life – the theatre developed eschatological blooms of great beauty.

Up to the turn of the century, the theatre was dominated by the massive influence of the naturalistic drama which took up and realistically depicted many of the topical problems faced by bourgeois society at the end of the nineteenth century. In this connection, the naturalistic dramatists worked in accordance with the new positivistic methods employed in the natural sciences, in order to present reality as it was: full of sham morality and social injustice when idealizing exaltation and palliation were dispensed with. As in social drama, the presentation of indefensible social conditions was often based on knowledge to be found in studies by the followers of so-called scientific socialism. On the programmes of the big theatres were the major figures and pioneers of naturalistic drama: the Scandinavians Ibsen, Bjørnson and Strindberg. Also to be seen were works by the naturalists born around 1860, some of whom were more critical of society, others less so. Not all of them, however, were to remain true to their naturalistic creed. In Germany, this group was represented by Gerhart Hauptmann and his school, as well as by the satirist and moralist Frank Wedekind; in England, it was Bernard Shaw and Oscar Wilde; in Austria, Arthur Schnitzler and Hermann Bahr; in Russia, Maxim Gorki, in Holland, Herman Heijermans, in Italy, Giovanni Verga, to mention but a few well-known dramatists who relentlessly diagnosed the social diseases of their time. A consequence of this topical dramatic art was the 'metropolitan drama' (*Grossstadtdrama*) – a specific genre which introduced a new dramatic character, modern man, the product of the multifarious sensual and intellectual impulses of urban life around 1900. Even during his lifetime, the Austrian author Arthur Schnitzler was regarded as a 'metropolitan poet' who described the complicated forces and ideas which drive and motivate people living in the scintillating, kaleidoscopic atmosphere of the city.

Firmly established in the entertainment sector, the theatre ignored no topical aspect of civil life. For example, cars could well become the subject of a comedy, as in the case of the *Automobil* published by the German comic playwright Ludwig Bauer in 1905. However, the fascination of this technical discovery – in other words, the fetishism associated with the commodity 'car' – was something that only the film could adequately convey.

With the establishment of the naturalistic theatre between 1890 and 1900 came the first criticism of its method of 'meticulous portrayal with photographic attention to detail', as Erich Urban put it in his *Welttheater* published in 1912. The competition for the theatre heralded by photography in 1865 had at last materialized. Photography set new standards for the reproduction of reality. And it was against these standards that the theatre was judged. For reproducing reality, photography – and later cinematography – had better means at its disposal. This competitive pressure led to the theatre taking an anti-realistic turn which manifested itself in proposals by Adolphe Appia, Gordon Craig and Georg Fuchs for the radical renewal of the scenery, the form of the stage and of the play itself. These reforms, which ushered in abstract tendencies into the theatre, were orientated on the new secessionistic and symbolic forms of painting, in which the subject lost much of its significance. On the other hand, a so-called neo-Romantic movement formed in opposition to naturalistic drama, the main spokesmen of which were Maurice Maeterlinck, Gabriele D'Annunzio and Hugo von Hofmannsthal. They consciously regarded themselves as symbols of the decay of the century as it – not just literally – advanced towards the end, i.e. the *fin de siècle*. Hence, they preferred to look back to past cultures and epochs, to cultivate their melancholic knowledge of their own decadence and to discover neo-Nazarene and Romantic tones. Despite their inclination to look to the past, with their predilection for introspection and dreams, they gave the theatre access to the Freudian 'id', to the subconscious. One could say that as a – still unconscious – reaction to film, which was to assume responsibility for the external sphere of reality, they created the 'drama of the soul'. Twenty years later, in 1921, as the European debate on the differences and similarities of theatre and film was in full swing, the Austrian feuilletonist Felix Salten ascribed the 'drama of the soul' unequivocally to the theatre and the 'drama of events' to film.[19] In this respect, neo-Romantic drama not only possessed a hidden restorative but also a future-orientated tendency which indicated a way for the theatre to leave the course of extreme reality aimed for in naturalistic drama but which could only be achieved in film. Parallel to the struggle to free the stage from the grip of illusionism and shallow imitations of reality, a non-European influence became apparent, which served as an example for the European reform movement. For the first time in the history of the Western theatre, an exotic, Asian culture – namely the Japanese theatre – provided important impulses in the direction of stylization, symbolism and less complicated theatrical forms. Something which had long had an effi-cacious influence on art – for example, the influence of stylistic elements from Japanese wood carving on the art nouveau era – started to have a similar effect on the theatre, too. Consequent on the imperialistic world policy, the world economy and the new transport opportunities, Europe was directly confronted with foreign cultures: for instance, in 1900 a Japanese theatre group appeared in Berlin and captivated audiences with its performances. In a German theatre almanac dated 1902, a Japanese guest production was analyzed and conclusions drawn about its influence on domestic theatrical reforms.[20] In Japanese theatre, the theatrical reformers found a complete version of the anti-illusory decoration and stagecraft principles they were still searching for and, from this point on, twentieth-century theatre became a part of artistic world communication before being pushed aside by the inter-national film industry at a later date.

That the 'turn of the century' threatened to become a dangerous obstacle for the theatre as an institution, and it was an extremely powerful institution at that time, is shown by the illuminating minutes of a theatre congress[21] which was part of the 1900 World Exhibition in Paris. Held in July of the first year of the twentieth century, this five-day conference tackled several topics which – as a result of concern that it would not be possible to meet the demands of the time, which could be of a practical as well as cultural or aesthetic nature – presented the theatre with great difficulties. The compo-sition of the participants at this conference, the majority of whom came from the conservative, bourgeois camp, was symptomatic of the general situation of the theatre at the turn of the century. It represented the bourgeois theatrical establishment which influenced the theatre in the whole of Europe and was at most interested in gradual reform. However, as this composition was similar to that of the mass of theatre goers, who also tended to be conservative, it is also necessary to take this establishment into account in any analysis of the theatre at the turn of the century. The congress was dominated by the leading theatre and opera directors, conductors, senior stage designers, theatre critics, writers and stage engineers in Paris who debated about the gradual adaption of the theatre to modern times. As the most important topics, they discussed fire-protection regulations, the modernization of props and equip-ment and the 'people's theatre movement', new urban-planning consider-ations regarding the location of the theatre, as well as copyright questions in relation to the use of phonographs or cinematography in the theatre.

The 1880s and 1890s were a time of calamitous, tragic theatre fires, the consequences of which were so disastrous that a continuation of the theatre appeared to be endangered. Accordingly, the participants of the congress put together a catalogue of the most important fire-protection measures. Incidentally, the problem of fire protection was something the theatre had in common with the young 'cinematography' of the time: in order to ensure film presentations without danger to the audience, the photographic industry was working feverishly on the development of a non-inflammable 'safety film'.

At the congress, consensus was also reached on the introduction of the 'circular horizon' as the most important technical innovation for the stage. With the replacement of the old, cumbersome scenery by a modern, more flexible mechanized system of decoration – i.e. by the 'circular horizon' – which would have permitted a less restricted, more abstract set design, it was hoped that the theatre could be pushed further in the direction of a regeneration and revival of its artistic means. For, given the fact that cinematographic reproduction techniques exposed the painted settings of the theatre for what they were, theatrical realism produced with the aid of illusionistic scenery appeared completely outdated. The theatre's chance for the future – where it would continue to exist as a partner of equal standing alongside the motion-picture industry – was considered to lie in the creation of an ideal stage. In a letter to the theatre congress, foresighted people from the theatre world – among them the French stage reformer Lugné-Poe, who had introduced abstract symbolic decoration to the stage – pleaded for the foundation of a training school for theatre technicians. For Lugné-Poe, it was evident that the new stage decoration with its immaterial, abstract atmosphere could only be effective with the aid of fully mechanized stage technology. Insulated from the reality of the outside world, the stage was to become the counterpart of cinematography as it spread across the globe.

Naturally, the theatre of the turn of the century was not immune to the social changes and upheavals taking place at that time: the looming social revolution of oppressed workers which would shake the foundations of capitalist society. By 1900, it was already apparent that the theatre could not remain the preserve of the ruling classes. Accordingly, an urgent demand was made at the congress for a 'people's theatre' which would unify all classes. As a certain M. Eugène Morel put it: '[Il] constate le mouvement qui se produit actuellement autour de l'idée du théâtre populaire et démontre que la réalisation de cette idée est devenue une nécessité sociale.'[22] In contrast to the theatre, cinematography was, in principle, designed as a form of art and entertainment for mass audiences. Thanks to its mechanical reproduction process, it was much better equipped to cater for the impending mass society of the twentieth century and the onslaught of a mass audience.

Another suggestion for adapting the theatre to modern times and the new urban audiences was made by a German participant at the congress. In his opinion, it was necessary to give consideration to ways in which the theatre could be linked to the mechanized and electrified transport networks. For, he argued, in conjunction with so-called democratic means of transport, such as trams, underground railways and automobiles, the theatre would be easy to get to and, therefore, attract mass audiences.

The theatre was also seeking a way to employ modern technology for its own ends, whereby its partner was to be the new technical methods for reproducing audio-visual reality. Barely five years after the invention of cinematography, the theatre saw an opportunity for co-operation instead of competition. The phonograph could record voices while cinematography made it possible to capture the best performances of an actor for posterity. This chance to preserve an otherwise ephemeral theatrical performance was also to benefit the theatre. Accordingly, a study on copyright problems associated with the economic utilization of cinematographic recordings of theatrical performances was also presented to the congress.

Taking a last look back at the turn of the century and at the young film industry in comparison with the established theatre, it is evident that a contemporary would have to have been very perceptive to detect any sign of rivalry between the two media. After its highly promising start in 1895, motion pictures in the first decade of the twentieth century were modelled more and more on the theatre and threatened to become a substitute for it. Nevertheless, the position of imitator was a weak one and film could hardly become a real competitor of the theatre on such a basis. It was not until later, in the 1920s, that circumstances changed and the film industry became aware of its special potential. This enabled it to break away from the tutelage of the established medium and develop into an independent genre. However, having undergone a permanent process of change since 1900, the theatre was prepared for this and better equipped to face the competitive situation which developed thereafter.

NOTES

1 H. Meilhac and L. Halévy, *Le Photographe, Comédie en un acte* (Paris, 1865).
2 The founder of these writing factories was the French dramatist Eugène Scribe (1791–1861) who, together with other authors, produced several hundred plays.
3 J. Verne, *Le Château des Carpathes* (Paris, 1892).
4 Edison had to drop his 'optical phonograph' project (developed between 1888 and 1889) owing to the weak volume of the phonograph.
5 Constructed by Ottomar Anschütz (1846–1907) in 1885, the *Elektrischer Schnellseher* was a device for recording and reproducing a series of pictures. Cf. J. M. Eder's description, 'Der elektrische Schnellseher', in *Neues Wiener Abendblatt*, 21 April 1890, p. 4.

6 Eder, 'Der elektrische Schnellseher', p. 40.
7 This 'crime' perpetrated by scientifically motivated moving photographers was noted with disapproval by A. L. Donnadieu, a contemporary observer, in his pamphlet on 'Photographie animée' (Paris, 1897): 'la science chronophotographique a été vulgarisée' (p. 23).
8 Towards the end of 1894, cinetoscopes could be seen in shops along the Boulevard Poissonnière. The automatic viewing device was started by inserting a ten-centime coin. Cf. Donnadieu, *Photographie animée*, p. 12.
9 Louis Lumière (1864–1948) and Auguste Lumière (1862–1954), French photographic engineers and proprietors of a factory for photographic products founded by their father Antoine Lumière. The inventions of Louis Lumière include the first technically usable still camera.
10 Cf. pamphlet by Eugène Dupont, 'Die lebende Photographie dargestellt durch den "Cinématographe" der Herren August und Louis Lumière aus Lyon' (Vienna, n.d.). A resident of Vienna, the trade representative describes the construction of the 'Cinématographe' and explains the principles of cinematography.
11 In a review, 'Die Anfänge der Kinematographie in Wien', in *Neue Freie Presse* (offprint, 2 April 1916), J. M. Eder, former director of the k.k. Graphische Versuchs- und Lehranstalt in Vienna, recalls the exact circumstances of the legendary arrival of film in Vienna.
12 *Ibid.*
13 Cf. L. Tranchant, *La Cinématographie pour tous* (Paris, c. 1912), p. 13.
14 Cf. H. Freiherr von Cles, 'Kinematographische Aufnahme fliegender Artilleriegeschosse bei Tageslicht oder bei künstlicher Beleuchtung', offprint from *Mitteilungen über Gegenstände des Artillerie- und Geniewesens*, pt 12 (Vienna, 1914).
15 *AGFA: Handbuch für Kinematographie* (Berlin, n.d.), p. 3.
16 *Ibid.*, p. 4.
17 Eder, 'Die Anfänge'.
18 *AGFA: Handbuch*, p. 3.
19 F. Salten, *Schauen und Spielen*, Studien zur Kritik des modernen Theaters (Vienna, 1921), p. 130.
20 *Deutsche Thalia*, Jahrbuch für das gesamte Bühnenwesen, vol. I (Vienna and Leipzig, 1902), pp. 105 and 107.
21 'Congrès International de l'Art Théâtral tenu à Paris du 27 au 31 juillet 1900', *Procès-Verbaux Sommaires*.
22 *Ibid.*, p. 22.

NINE

ॐ

FIN-DE-SIÈCLE PAINTING

JENNIFER BIRKETT

Writing in *The Studio*, in 1893, C. W. Furse described the confusion of the contemporary art scene: 'The unfortunate student . . . anxious for guidance, has fallen on troublous times: for no sooner has he emancipated himself from the Academy, than he finds himself tossed hither and thither in a whirlpool of mushroom schools, who are vibrists today, rosicrucians tomorrow, and Turkey-carpet-cum-Jap the day after'.[1] The new painters, he added, had nothing in common but their inability to use oil paint; they always laid it on too thin or too thick.

Impressionists, decadents, symbolists, aesthetes, practitioners of art nouveau – the artistic whirlpool of the last two decades of the nineteenth century reproduces the turmoil of the period's politics. The shock of the new – innovatory subjects and techniques, defying the limiting conventions of the Academy – prevented many contemporaries from perceiving fundamental differences between schools. Not many, for example, of the Parisians who flocked to Le Barc de Boutteville's First Exhibition of Impressionist and Symbolist Painting, in 1891, seem to have thought the combination odd. A few, however, could make distinctions. As early as 1876, Stéphane Mallarmé described the politics of Impressionist style as an attempt to demystify the world, reproducing it not as the object of an authoritative vision but as the collective property of the newly important proletariat:

[T]he transition from the old imaginative artist and dreamer to the energetic modern worker is found in Impressionism.

The participation of a hitherto ignored people in the political life of France is a social fact that will honour the whole of the close of the nineteenth century. A parallel is found in artistic matters . . . The noble visionaries of other times, whose works are the semblance of worldly things seen by unworldly eyes (not the actual representations of real objects) appear as kings and gods in the far dream-ages of mankind; recluses to whom were given the genius of a dominion over an ignorant multitude. But today the multitude demands to see with its own eyes; and if our latter-day art is less glorious, intense, and rich, it is not without the compensation of truth, simplicity, and child-like charm.[2]

The aristocratic 'visionary' tradition was not as far in the past as Mallarmé's tenses suggest. It is with the Idealists, to whom the term *fin de siècle* is usually applied, that this essay is concerned – in particular, the French artists, Gustave Moreau, Odilon Redon, Félicien Rops and their followers – whose painting attempts to seize back control of the world from the multitude, freezing the narrative of a history on the brink of change. In 1876 the Naturalist Emile Zola recognized Moreau's challenge:

He paints his dreams – not the simple, innocent dreams that we all have, but sophisticated, complex, enigmatic dreams, where you can't immediately get your bearings . . . I see in this a simple reaction against the modern world.[3]

Fin-de-siècle painting was certainly disorienting for its bourgeois subjects, but it also exercised a fascination over them, not excepting Zola himself. It evoked their double situation: still holding on to the levers of power, but increasingly conscious of the threat of displacement. The main challenge was perceived to lie in the socialist and feminist movements, which were temporarily checked by the repression of the Commune in 1871, but gathered strength again in the eighties and nineties. James Ensor's crowd scenes point dramatically the fear of the liberated mob, the terror of political and personal supersession. 'L'Entrée du Christ à Bruxelles' (1888) presents the vibrant, jostling colour of a carnival crowd. At first sight, this picture provides the same pleasure in sampling – at a distance – the coarse gaiety of the proletariat that makes the charm of Chéret's or Toulouse-Lautrec's posters for the circus or music-hall, and was one of the preferred pleasures of J.-K. Huysmans's decadent hero, Des Esseintes (*A rebours*, 1884). But the grotesque masks with their blank eyes and fixed grins, almost indistinguishable from the unmasked faces, generate a threatening unease; Christ is lost in a crowd of monsters; the Toytown band carries a cynical placard ('Fanfares doctrinaires: Toujours réussi'); and the banner dominating the crowd ('Vive la Sociale') is enigmatic. Ensor shares his contemporaries' perceptions of the double face of Demos. This is not a celebration of collectivity, but a foregrounding of the violent, anarchic potential of the mob. The title confirms this: the Entry into Jerusalem. The carnival of the oppressed leads straight to Calvary. The crowd was not, however, the only threat to the bourgeois's security. Even greater problems had emerged from within his own world. Changes in the structures of capitalism – the rise of the big corporations – meant that the market that had formed the dominant and domineering bourgeois 'individual' now cast him in a more marginal role. The stockmarket crash of 1882, inaugurating the economic slump of 1882–95, destroyed countless small

2 'L'Entrée du Christ à Bruxelles' by James Ensor (detail)

shareholders, as did the Panama Canal Company scandal in 1888. Zola's *Germinal* (1885) not only shows the rise of organized labour but also describes how small shareholders and managers in small mining companies are pushed aside by national and international monopolies. *L'Argent* (1891) charts the downfall of the last speculator-hero, crushed by the international (Jewish) banking ring. At the same time, the perceived relationship of the 'individual' to his state was under revision. Octave Mirbeau's decadent novel *Le Jardin des supplices* (1899) bemoans the rise of the faceless institutions of the state (judiciary, army, universities) of which the individual, to his horror, suddenly discovers himself the puppet.

Fin-de-siècle art, glamorizing this sense of impotence, has a clear political function, diverting and checking disruptive frustrations within the middle class. Sacher-Masoch, who took the Paris establishment by storm in 1886, is its presiding genius. Gilles Deleuze's analysis of Sacher-Masoch's work isolates points which are as visible in the painting of the period as in the literature: the fetishistic displacement of anguish; the aestheticization and containment of rebellious violence; and the focus on a threefold figuration of Woman, the architect of decline.[4] Woman appears as Aphrodite, seducer of the innocent, or sadistic Oedipal Mother, stand-in for a cruel patriarchy, or both together, 'the oral mother . . . who nurtures and brings death' (p. 49). According to Deleuze, 'Disavowal, suspense, waiting, fetishism and phantasy together make up the specific constellation of masochism' (p. 63). All these are characteristics of decadent art.

Fin-de-siècle painting is aware of the more vigorous versions of self and society emerging in socialism and feminism. But an artist interested in making a living had little incentive to change allegiances. Selling the values of the wealthy to the developing mass market was a profitable business. The middle classes, as Baudelaire indicated, controlled the museums and galleries.[5] Until late in the century, painters in France could only exhibit at the annual Salon, and were dependent on public commissions. Public interest in painting expanded tremendously in the seventies. The number of paying visitors to the 1878 Salon de l'Exposition universelle tripled from 58,102 in 1867 to 185,000 in 1876, while the introduction of free entry on Sundays and Thursdays meant that all classes were gaining access.[6] But what was seen was still the choice of the few. Similarly, the plethora of new little salons and galleries that appeared from the late seventies set art free from the Academy, but not from the rich. (London was first, with the Grosvenor Gallery, 1877, later supplanted by the New Gallery, Regent Street; Brussels offered the Salon des XX, founded in 1884 by Octave Maus, which in 1894 became La Libre Esthétique; in Paris, belatedly, the Salon du Champ de Mars appeared in 1890, followed by the Salons de la Rose + Croix, 1892–7, and accompanied by the galleries of Durand-Ruel, Le Barc de Boutteville, Ambroise Vollard and Samuel Bing.) During the last decade of the nineteenth century, improved techniques in printing and photography made reproduction and distribution easier. Magazines such as *L'Estampe originale*, *La Revue blanche*, *L'Album des peintres-graveurs*, like the English *The Studio*, provided cheap reproductions of new works for a wide market. But all these things still required significant finance. An artist had to sell to the wealthy before he reached the masses.

The features that recur throughout the painting of the period are those that sell submissiveness. The prevailing mood is one of dream and evasion, rather than action and intervention. The authority of the artist is always visible, reshaping the world by effects of style (colour, line, perspective and frame) and imposing his vision on the spectator, flattering the 'infantile desire to be deceived'.[7] The canvas becomes another kind of theatre, where the spectator learns the charm of masks and poses. The expressive use of colour – from Moreau's bright, violent contrasts to the pastels of the Symbolists, or Redon's black and whites – manipulates emotional and moral responses. Rich, detailed ornament distracts eye and mind from the meaning of the whole. The players on this painted stage are enveloped in stillness, even in their wildest motions, freezing change at the moment of inception. There are occasional disturbances: mirrors reflecting a carefully composed image may crack, as in Holman Hunt's 'The Lady of Shallot' (1887–1905). Fragments of writing, intruding from another order of representation, can ripple the harmony. Rops's whore stands under the price-list in a café doorway ('La Dèche', 1882); the lithographs in Redon's album *A Edgar Poë* (1882) are deliberately made more enigmatic by their titles. The logical terminus of this deconstruction of homogeneous, realistic surfaces lies in Braque and Picasso. Redon's experiments with colour, or the abstraction of Moreau's later work, adumbrate more radical revisions of conventional perception. But the unease generated in these paintings is carefully moderated. *Fin-de-siècle* art succeeds by self-censorship, simultaneously noting and circumscribing its own progressive tendencies.

A handful of subjects and motifs return obsessively, charged with ideological value. Chief among these is Woman, the figure of hostile, rebellious nature, whom the patriarchal subject is required to defeat. She appears on the canvas already constructed into a tamed erotic object, in the familiar masks of Western classical and Christian culture: mother-goddess, demon, Virgin, whore. The business of living is drawn as a heroic struggle between male and female, body and spirit, embodied in narratives and landscapes from ancient and biblical history, myth, legend and fantasy. The exotic décor, like the Woman who inhabits it, is a specious promise of novelty and change. In fact, it enshrines the past, and permanently pre-empts innovation.

Few of the *fin-de-siècle* painters provided explicit statements of their political sympathies. When they theorized their work, their language was aesthetic or philosophical. But the body of their painting made its allegiance clear enough, and where ambiguity might have arisen, the pens of contemporary authors quickly intervened. For us, as for their contemporary audience, it is hard to separate our own vision of Moreau, Rops and Ensor from the polemic versions offered by J.-K. Huysmans, Joséphin Péladan or Jean Lorrain. It is their writing that has fixed the painters as the standard-bearers of decadent ideology, crystallizing the aspirations and anxieties of a nervous bourgeoisie, enclosing gestures of rebellion in the consoling embrace of authority and order. In what follows, it will often be necessary to link the images on the canvas to their imaginary mirror in the printed page.[8]

THE ORIGINS OF *FIN DE SIÈCLE*: MOREAU, REDON, ROPS

The movement that centres on *fin-de-siècle* Paris began in the English Pre-Raphaelite school, formed in the revolutionary year of 1848 and first seen in Paris at the International Exhibition in 1855. Edward Burne-Jones (1833–98) and Dante Gabriel Rossetti (1828–82) offered a new iconography of female types: the languid Blessed Damozel, suffering Ophelia and, most important, the *femme fatale* (Lady Lilith, Helen, Circe). By the end of the 1890s, their emblems – the sunflower, the lily and the peacock's feather – and the red-gold hair and flowing garments of their women had passed into fashionable French style, and their preference for artistic dream over simple reality had gripped the French imagination.

In France itself, Gustave Moreau (1826–98) and Pierre Puvis de Chavannes (1824–98) were already themselves adapting the Quattrocento masters who influenced their English colleagues. Puvis, a painter's painter, was a major influence on Symbolist art, with his static, pale-lit compositions of simplified figures placed in bizarre relation to the landscape. But it was Moreau, who studied not only the old masters but also the illuminated manuscripts, Japanese prints and Persian and Indian miniatures in the Bibliothèque Impériale, who caught the imagination of contemporary critics, poets and novelists and now stands inscribed in the history of art as the doyen of the *fin de siècle*.

Moreau provided, according to Jean Lorrain, a mysticism of cruelty, power and sexual excess, an ideology expressly conceived for modern capitalism.[9] His blend of old ideas and novel forms responded exactly to the needs of the moment. Though his work breaks with many of the traditions of the Academy, he remained throughout his career a man of the establishment, gathering in medals, honours and offices. In Paris during the short reign of the Commune, he was implacably opposed to the Communard ideal. Hostility to the usurping mob and desire for strong leadership to contain it are the determining context of his work. A sketchbook note of 1876, commenting on three studies of Jacob and the Angel, King David, and the young Moses he was to show at the Paris World's Fair in 1878, deplores the decline of order, authority and tradition:

Jacob may be taken as the angel of France checking the country in its foolish race towards material things. Moses, as hope in a new law represented by this dear innocent child prompted by God. David, as the sombre melancholy of the past age of tradition so dear to great minds bewailing the sad modern decay, the angel at his feet ready to restore inspiration if only some willingness to listen to God may be shown.[10]

Moreau offered his bourgeois contemporaries a mirror of their own fantasy relationship to power that definitively focused the decadent imagination. He draws power, always, in a glamorous association with violence, terror and death. He shows it as precarious, residing in perpetual conflict. Man's eternal struggle against matter to forge his ideal (the mystified version of the human condition, on which *fin-de-siècle* art is centred) is the theme that Moreau obsessively extracts from pagan and biblical myth. In 'Oedipe et le Sphinx' (1864), the hero is matched with his natural enemy, the eternal feminine: 'the earthly chimera, as base as matter and as alluring, represented by this charming head of a woman, with wings presaging the ideal, but the body of a monster, a flesh-eater that rends and annihilates'.[11] In 'Orphée' (1865), the still central figure of a woman holds Orpheus' head, moulded into the frame of a lyre. At first sight, this seems an image of the victory of matter over the artistic spirit. But the line of the painting reasserts the persistence of man's creative powers, sweeping down to a pair of tortoises, waiting only for a new maker to transform them (like Hermes in the Homeric Hymn) into new instruments, and then up to the hills, and a group of piping shepherds.

Male power is both thwarted and sustained by the female. The woman in this picture, the 'oral mother' of whom Deleuze writes, who both kills and mourns her victim, on this occasion bears the consoling message of the indestructibility of the artist's powers which is at the heart of the Orphic myth. More often, however, Moreau splits the female role. The fatal Beauty – Helen, Salome, Messalina – glorifies death and failure. Princess or priestess, her beauty is cause and justification of man's repeated falls from grace. She appears as the natural enemy of man's desire for perfection – substitute, as Deleuze suggests, for the destroying Father whom the *fin de siècle* seldom had the stomach to attack directly. By contrast, Europa, Deianeira, Leda appear as victims, testimonials to the omnipotence of the male.

In Moreau's iconography, the perfect image of man in complete possession of his powers is the androgyne, who has transcended the disabling divisions of matter and spirit and resolves in his single figure the antagonism of the sexes. Moreau transforms the image of the hero, casting Hercules and Jason in the same mould as his poets ('Un Chanteur indien', 1884; 'Le Poète arabe', 1886). This is not a denial of patriarchy but its reassertion. The feminine features and trailing robe of the Arabian poet are countermanded by the phallic upthrust of his right arm, his wand and the stem of his lyre; while the mast and prow of the Argonauts' ship ('Le Retour des Argonautes', 1897) are decorated with ram's horns, winged horses and a bull's head.

Whatever resistances the world may offer him, man is always the directing subject of Moreau's work, the confident artist-creator: 'After seeing paintings by Gustave Moreau, one acquires a taste for sumptuous garments, for things diverted from their natural grace to become symbols . . . one enjoys seeing as intellectual forms the beings through whom the mind of the poet, their only artificer, passes.'[12]

These powers of transformation can serve a political purpose. Moreau manipulates frames and perspective (temporal and spatial) to replace the uncertainties of present and future with a self-confident past. History and legend are invoked to restore religious fear to landscape. Perspective encloses a space where man's fantasies of power can run free. In 'Galatée' (1880), the all-powerful eye of the Cyclops encompasses the nymph and her grotto, a microcosm of the universe. In 'Œdipe et le Sphinx', the illusions of perspec-

3　‘Œdipe et le Sphinx’ by Gustave Moreau

tive, coupled with a clever double framing, transform the balance of power, allowing the hero to dwarf and dominate the monster.

In other paintings, as the surrealists recognized, Moreau's transformations of conventional perspective and rationalist categories push the decadent vision to the point of liberation. Objects torn from their original contexts are placed on the single field of the canvas in new relationships. 'Les Licornes' (*c*. 1885) is still a well-organized dream of wishes fulfilled, where the authority of religion domesticates the erotic. In contrast, the unfinished 'Les Chimères' (begun 1884) is an exercise in transgression, the foreground crammed with the perverse dreams of the crowded city seen through a cleft in the rocky background. The picture offers a startling and disruptive vision of the cruel fantasies contained by the starched shirt and black frock-coat of the respectable nineties' citizen.

Moreau's influence made itself felt in various ways among his admirers and pupils in the nineties.

In Joséphin Péladan's Salons de la Rose + Croix catholique (1892–7), the political direction of *fin-de-siècle* painting is made explicit. In his earliest art criticism, Péladan attacked the democratization of art and presented his alternative creed: 'I believe in Ideal, Tradition and Hierarchy', best expressed, he thought, in the images of woman and sinful flesh offered by Moreau, Rops and Puvis de Chavannes.[13] The order of the Rose + Croix Esthétique which he founded in 1891 invoked occultism, Catholicism and art, in the effort to restore vanished hierarchy: 'There must be an inventory of the treasures bequeathed by the past and of our modern conquests; above all, there must be action in a mode capable of civilising the Barbarians who will come after us. Where mysticism has failed, only Art can act on the collective soul.'[14] And in his novel *Le Dernier Bourbon* (1895), Péladan wrote of his Wagnerian dream of an international 'freemasonry of high culture', through which the power of the Catholic Right could be restored.

The first and highly successful annual Salon was held at the Durand-Ruel Gallery and was preceded by processions and Mass on the Champ de Mars. The Statutes called for works based on legend, myth and allegory, on subjects taken from Catholic dogma or oriental theogonies (but not those of the 'yellow races'), or the 'idealized nude'. Patriotic (i.e. Republican), military and modern themes were excluded, and work by women artists was banned. In Péladan's metaphysics, man – the Magus – is ordained to be the sole creator and woman – the Fairy – to be his inspiration and support, and all political and social disorder can be traced back to the refusal of this fundamental hierarchy. Péladan's novels invite women to model themselves on the serene, passive images of femininity offered by Leonardo and Botticelli; the model for men is the artist-prophet.[15] Péladan was not alone in his eagerness to limit female creativity. The Ecole des Beaux-Arts refused to admit women until

1897, and the entry of the first cohort triggered a riot.[16] Not surprisingly, the decadence in France produced few women artists.

Many of the French avant-garde considered laughter the only appropriate response to Péladan's campaign to restore the sense of the mysterious. But there was still an avid public for painters eager to press Moreau's morbid eroticism to new extremes, while evacuating it of its morality and its metaphysics. (The same public were also enjoying the erotic in other forms in such works as Georges Rochegrosse's 'Les Derniers Jours de Babylone' (1891), exercises in Oriental epic which shaped the imagination of such early Hollywood directors as Cecil B. De Mille.)[17] The work of Edgar Allan Poe, recently translated by Baudelaire, provided fresh motifs to convey the masochistic pleasures of futility and decay. The picture acts as a narcotic, generating a thrill of terror or perverse excitement, or an uneasy ache of suspense. Blocks of colour and simplified lines evoke a limited, stylized range of moods. William Degouve de Nuncques's pastel 'Le Cygne noir' (1896) draws nature congealing into the patterns of art. The heavy black bird, motionless on the lake, and the bizarre ivy embossed on the lakeside tree produce a sense of trapped foreboding. Jeanne Jacquemin's 'Rêverie' (c. 1892–4?) is a less intimidating version of the cult of quiet despair: a simple, melancholy female profile, hair wreathed with forget-me-nots. In sharp contrast to Jacquemin's meek canvas, 'Ill Omen' (1893), by Frances Mac-donald, one of the Glasgow Four, turns the patient waiting of the passive victim into the intense anticipation of revenge. A tall draped woman stands still and straight among trees, long hair blown out in a stiff horizontal line, parallel to the flying arrow of five ominously stiff-winged birds.

In other paintings, immobility is not a trap for the spirit but a cage for the black energy of instinct. In Jean Delville's 'Les Trésors de Satan' (1895), a crowded seascape and a blasted landscape are linked by a stream of human bodies, crowned by the flaming hair of a Miltonic Satan. The straddling left leg of the devil stills the energy of the writhing flesh. Georges de Feure's 'La Course à l'abîme' (1894) depicts a riot of exotic flowers, sharp-clawed birds poised to tear each other to pieces, and a pair of naked, long-nailed lesbians. Nature's violence is circumscribed by a phallic frame of windmills and peaks: an oblique celebration of the patriarchal authority invoked by the decadents to hold their own excesses in check.

The peacock image – the cruel fascination of devouring beauty – appears to better effect in William Degouve de Nuncques's pastel 'Les Paons' (1898), where the dream effect comes not from crude symbols but from striking juxtapositions of colour (bright blue peacocks, spruce green trees, aquamarine grass) and from line (the sweeping tails of the peacocks and the trailing branches). With the turn of the century, morbid and melodramatic images and themes become less a focus of interest than the experiments in stylization

4 'Ill Omen' (or 'Girl in the East Wind with Ravens passing the
Moon') by Frances Macdonald

to which they give rise (in the work, for example, of Eugène Grasset, or of the
Glasgow Four), which feed directly into the decorative arts movement.

A very different version of the macabre appears in Odilon Redon (1840–
1916), who copied many of Moreau's themes but in his own manner,
eschewing realism, colour and rich detail for simple lines, sparse images and
shadow play. Huysmans, who tended to simplify, overstressed the similarities

between Redon and Moreau. In his *Croquis parisiens* (1880), he characterized
the engraver's images as nightmare distortions of reality (impossible flowers,
with metal leaves and human heads, embryonic creatures), reservoirs of
silence, filled with fear, irony and cruelty ('Cauchemar', in *Dans le rêve*). In
'Le Monstre' (*Certains*, 1889), he foregrounded the eroticism of Redon's
illustrations for Flaubert's *La Tentation de Saint Antoine*. Jean Lorrain also
seized on Redon's macabre, 'ghouls, ghosts and monsters' ('Un étrange
jongleur', *Echo de Paris*, 10 April 1894), though he noted also his sentimental
idealism, in his exquisite female profiles, pale-faced Byzantine princesses and
Wagnerian divinities, magical Celtic and mediaeval atmospheres.

Both writers travestied Redon in the light of their own obsessions. Though
inspired by Baudelaire, Poe and Flaubert, his interest was not in the simple
thrills to be derived from their subject matter. Albums such as *Dans le rêve*
(1879), dedicated to Poe, *A Edgar Poë* (1882), *La Tentation de Saint Antoine*
(1888), *A Gustave Flaubert* (1889), exploit affinities of a different quality:
idealism, the cult of mystery and the cult of suffering, and most of all, the cult
of form and its transformations.

Redon described his art as an investigation, following da Vinci, into the
expressive powers of light and shadow and abstract lines, and into expansive
forms.[18] His technical innovations foster dream to liberate creativity: 'Decadence or not, that's how it is. But better to call it a development or evolution of
art for the supreme flight of one's life, an expansion of life . . .' (*A soi-même*,
p. 26). He learned how to draw shadows cast on solids, so that 'I found it
easier to bring together the real and the unreal, and could give visual logic to
elements glimpsed by my imagination' (p. 21). His art is an exercise in
ambiguity. 'My drawings . . . place us, like music, in the ambiguous world of
the indeterminate' (pp. 26–7). In 'Femme et serpent', for example (*c.* 1885–
90), both serpent and woman merge with the pillared arch of the doorway,
while the woman's head echoes the shape of the serpent's. Unusually for the
period, these are images of expansion, not closure. The serpent-door
surrounds light, not shadow, and cascades of flowers.

Redon's idealism did not lead him to wholesale rejections of the modern
world. He played creatively with the discoveries of evolutionary science (the
album *Les Origines* appeared in 1883). His 'monsters' were extrapolations of
natural structures, not just, as Huysmans claimed, simple copies from under a
microscope (p. 28). The botanist Armand Clavaud certainly introduced
Redon to microscopic forms, but he also initiated him into the metamor-
phoses of evolution: the newly discovered interface creatures that are animals
in daylight, plants in dark. 'All my originality consists in giving human life to
creatures that are realistically impossible, and as far as I can, putting the logic
of the visible at the service of the invisible' (p. 28).

Redon is the liberating impulse of the *fin de siècle*, a break with tradition and an original adaptation of contemporary conventions that frees the symbols of mystery from their constraining contexts and suggests new ones. Critics have pointed connections between his art and Chagall's (in its exploitation of detached symbols, and also, as in 'L'Arbre rouge', 1905, its unconventional, expressive use of colour). 'Orphée' (after 1903) is a light, semi-transparent head emerging from the lyre, not, as in Moreau's version, modelled into it; and the landscape in which it exists is not the densely referential landscape of Moreau's version, only a mountain peak, a few flowers and vast shadow, hinting at new space. Eyes, detached from human heads, are disturbing, but no longer dead and ghoulish. They focus in fresh directions, like the flowers with eyes in *Les Origines*: 'Il y eut peut-être une première vision esquissée dans la fleur' (No. 2). The grotesque need not intimidate: 'L'Araignée souriante' (1887) is a jolly grinning spider with ten legs and upturned eyes, casting an inverted shadow of light over the bottom half of the sketch.

There is more comedy in the art of Félicien-Joseph-Victor Rops (1833–98), showing the double face of decadence. On the one hand, Rops parades its fascination with its own neuroses, obsessions and eroticized fears of supersession; on the other, he satirizes its pretensions. The Belgian artist provided illustrations for some of the key texts in which the decadent sensibility took shape: Baudelaire's *Les Epaves* (1866), Barbey d'Aurevilly's *Les Diaboliques* (1879), Joséphin Péladan's pornographic version of *Femmes honnêtes* (1885), and several of the early volumes of Péladan's epic *La Décadence latine*.

Contemporaries appreciated the modernity of Rops's vision, fixed on the streets of Paris. Like Baudelaire, he refused to veil contemporary ugliness with classical form: 'We shouldn't be drawing the breasts of Venus de Milo; we have to draw Tata's breasts, which may be less lovely but are the breasts of the day.'[19] He drew with equal realism the values by which his city lived: seduction, perversion, hypocrisy, masking and greed, writing in 1863: 'Love of brutal pleasures, obsession with money, petty self-interest have fixed on most of our contemporaries a sinister mask where Edgar Poe's "instinct of perversity" is written in capital letters.'[20] Like his fellow Belgian, James Ensor (1860–1949), Rops turned the mask into an icon of the perverse delight of modern man – and woman – in evil.

Sexuality is the main preoccupation of his world, founded on brutal pleasures, paid for with cash. 'La Prostitution et la folie dominant le monde' is the theme of a pencil drawing of 1879. In his work, the most natural of human functions is irremediably corrupted by civilization. Hence (as in Moreau) his fetishization of female ornament, particularly clothing, providing an iconography which has shaped twentieth-century erotic art. In Joséphin Péladan's words: '[Rops] has lodged the seven deadly sins in a fold of cloth, not animating but animalizing the gown . . . he is the inventor, in art, of those long gloves and long black stockings which lose none of the curves of the flesh but introduce an extraordinary, perverse note.'[21]

His art suggests the sources of corruption: bourgeois society and its institutions ('Le Scandale'); a repressive Catholic Church ('La Tentation de Saint Antoine', 1878); man's fantasies of his own potency, feeding on centuries of erotic tradition ('L'Incantation', *c.* 1878). Most of all, however – and in this lay its charm for the decadents, and for the Catholic Right – it sets the blame for modern decay firmly on the shoulders of woman. In 'La Femme au pantin' (1877) a domineering female figure plays with a male puppet, whose slit stomach drops gold coins into a waiting chalice. Woman, leagued with the devil to drive modern man to impotence, comes hung around with all the negative symbols of biblical, occult and pagan traditions, crucifying man with her insatiable worship of his phallic power (*Les Sataniques*, 1882). In 'L'Initiation sentimentale' (1887), frontispiece for Joséphin Péladan's book, woman – the Flesh – is the executioner and man – the Spirit – her helpless victim. In the frontispiece for Péladan's *Le Vice suprême* (1884), the consequences of the betrayal of Spirit for flesh are taken beyond the personal into the political, as in Péladan's right-wing mysticism: Woman is made responsible for the death of the nation.

APPLYING ART TO LIFE

The applied arts movement inaugurated by William Morris flourished in England from the 1880s, aiming to produce everyday objects that were both functional and beautiful, an alternative to the uniform artefacts churned out for the mass market. The elitist implications of Morris's work were obvious from the beginning, despite his socialist professions, and the movement in France was similarly ambivalent. Initially, the applied arts appeared in France in a left-wing context. Thadée Natanson's introductory article on 'Art nouveau' (in the anarcho-socialist *La Revue blanche*, vol. 10, 1896) came out while the *Revue* was running its series on 'Les Socialistes anglais'. Natanson explained that there was a bigger demand for luxury living, from a poorer clientele, so that things needed to be simpler, made of cheaper material and easier to look after. He noted a generation gap: the applied arts were increasingly preferred by the younger artists. Applied art was first exhibited in its own right at the Champ de Mars, Paris, 1891.

The Nabis (from the Hebrew, meaning 'prophets') first found their way into the Salons by this route. Formed in 1889, the group included Paul Sérusier (1864–1927), Maurice Denis (1870–1943), Pierre Bonnard (1867–1947) and Edouard Vuillard (1876–1940). Members made no secret of their aesthetic and political antipathy to Péladan's Rosicrucians. Their work appeared frequently in *La Revue blanche*. Many of them later – like the *Revue* – became

Dreyfusards, and suffered a consequent loss of popularity. Gauguin was a crucial influence, inspiring their determination to paint the world as they saw it, but in intensified and idealized colours. From the Japanese, they borrowed the free-flowing arabesque, which Denis, particularly, used to join subjects into new relationships. They sought to bring fresh perspective to the familiar: '[to transform] common sensations – and natural objects – into sacred, hermeneutic, imposing icons'.[22] Their work in theatre (non-illusionist décors for the Théâtre de l'Art and the Théâtre de l'Oeuvre, including the set for Alfred Jarry's anti-bourgeois satire, *Ubu roi*, 1896) led them to an interest in public and domestic interiors: tapestries, embroideries, murals, wallpapers, panels and stained glass, with which, as one critic wrote in 1895, they brightened the humdrum of everyday existence, 'bringing into the monotony of everyday life their exuberant gaiety, a glittering fairyland'.[23]

They were also interested in book illustrations and posters, which in the nineties became a new and major art form (its development facilitated by the law of 1881 establishing liberty of the press, which 'changed the aspect of the street in France and made the illustrated placard first a commonplace and then a major craft').[24] In 1894, *La Plume* began to advertise and sell posters by subscription, and Claude Roger-Marx produced his book on *Les Maîtres de l'affiche*. The first volume of the London monthly, *The Studio*, founded in 1893, contains an illustrated essay on 'The Collecting of Posters. A New Field for Connoisseurs', stimulated by Edouard Sagot's new illustrated catalogue. Using a new critical criterion especially appropriate to consumer art – does it work? – and concluding that English posters don't, because they aren't arresting enough, the author points to French models: Jules Chéret, with his gay, exuberant colours, Eugène Grasset, adapting heroic mediaeval subjects, and Adolphe Willette, modern, bitter and grotesque. The illustrations include Willette's poster for his own anti-Semitic candidacy in the legislative elections of September 1889.

The colours of the French artists form a striking contrast to the severe black and whites of Aubrey Beardsley, who also appears in the first volumes of *The Studio*. Beardsley is lauded by his critics as the first genuine artist to turn to book illustration, as well as the first to make full use of the new photo-mechanical method of line blocks, started in the 1870s, and established by the 1880s as the cheapest and easiest method of facsimile reproduction.[25] Brian Reade argues that Beardsley's importance is especially formal:

His unique way of embodying Pater's, and Bacon's, maxims on the beauty of strangeness, the style of certain of his slow-moving lines and rigidly conventionalised trees and roses and peacock feathers, the manner in which he gave decoration and substance equal weight, all became set in the repertoire of art-nouveau from Glasgow to Milan, and from Germany to the United States; while the short cuts taken by Beardsley, his occasionally near-abstract forms, his concentration on what was

A POSTER BY WILLETTE

5   Poster by Willette from *The Studio*, 1893

essential to the dramatic presentation of the subject – which seemed to be cantilevered on to the page without any of the old and erudite supports – were liberating forces in the development of avant-garde artists like Kandinsky and Klee, and even Picasso within the next dozen years.[26]

But his subjects and his tone – Pre-Raphaelite mediaevalism overlaid with macabre modern satire, reminiscent of Rops and Ensor in its emphasis on masking, violence and the erotic – must be considered equally liberating and influential.

A similar connection between *fin-de-siècle* formal innovations and subsequent developments in avant-garde art is suggested by Werner Haftmann, writing about Gustav Klimt (1862–1918) and the Secession style, 'a strange mixture of Jugendstil, Naturlyrismus, and English decadence, combined with the distant influence of French Neo-Impressionism and Symbolism', which is said to lead straight to Kandinsky's abstract painting and the new architecture of the Bauhaus.[27] Whatever open forms it may have led to, Klimt's art was not in its original context always a liberating force. In technique, it draws close to the art of Moreau, with its cult of sexuality and death, its portraits of women drawn from erotic mythology, exquisite and deadly, its golden visions, and its artistic transformation of persons and landscapes.

The Secession movement, which held its first (government-subsidized) exhibition in 1898, would seem to have functioned in the Vienna of the first decade of the twentieth century, under the aged Emperor Franz Joseph I, much as Joséphin Péladan had hoped his own Catholic art movement would function in end-of-century France. Werner Hofmann draws on Adolf Loos's analysis of 1908, 'Ornament and Crime':

Loos believed that by clinging to archaic methods of production, the cult of ornamentation wastes and cripples the forces of productivity. It acts as a layer of whitewash over what should in fact be completely changed, and is thus essentially in collusion with a reactionary order of state . . . Gustav Klimt will therefore be seen as the most notable exponent of a concept of art and culture which the bourgeoisie used in a last effort to arrange the way of life of a democratic society on an elite basis.[28]

Klimt, like Péladan, was inspired by a sense of cultural mission, to provide art for all, and to make the arts interact with everyday life – shaping minds by shaping their environment. Not all social groups, of course, could experience their art in the same way. The Secession emphasized artistic craftsmanship; it was hostile to new technologies; and it styled its products for the affluent elite, rather than the multitude of Viennese paupers. Street pageants were organized, in which all citizens were invited to forget their social differences in the promiscuity of carnival (not unlike the art students' processions and balls that were a feature of the nineties in France). But basically, the less affluent were encouraged to play an onlooker's role. Secession exhibitions offered the complete décor for an ideal bourgeois consumerist life-style: 'A shop-window reproduction of reality'.[29]

SURREALIST INFLECTIONS

The diversity of innovation in *fin-de-siècle* art makes it difficult to limit the discussion of its equally varied inheritors. At the furthest remove, there is a connection with the movement which concerns itself with pure form. Moreau's pupils included Matisse, Marquet and Rouault, early participants in Fauvism, concerned with the exploitation of pure colour and (Rouault excepted) violently anti-symbolist.[30] But in general, *fin-de-siècle* art is rather the source of that other major twentieth-century current: art applied to the construction of a magical counter-reality, through the symbolic use of colour and line. A number of individual affiliates of this tradition have already been noted. The largest single group to adopt – and adapt – it are the surrealists, through whom it persists into the present day. The rediscovery of Moreau by the twenties and thirties is echoed by the revivals of the sixties (greatly assisted by the critical work of Philippe Jullian). As at the earlier period, violent, erotic fantasies, images of frustrated potential, develop in response to the situation of the individual, subject to the power of the mass market.

André Breton's Surrealist Manifestos use the vocabulary of his decadent precursors, speaking of 'imagination', 'dream', the 'marvellous' and 'myth', just as surrealist practice invokes obsessively the same symbols (women, eyes, flowers, birds). But surrealism, which also traces back its heritage to Marx and Freud, is not a reactionary but a revolutionary movement: 'Everything has to be done, and all methods are acceptable to destroy the notions of family, country and religion.'[31] In *Les Vases communicants* (1932), Breton distinguishes the surrealist dream from dream with a metaphysical, religious element: surrealism is a human, progressive enterprise, because its 'beyond' is 'within'.[32] It seeks to transform relationships between human subjects, objects and landscapes, breaking the links that bind and subordinate men and women to the things of their own creation, liberating the object and, in consequence, the human subject. The decadent canvas frames dream-chaos into harmonious order. Surrealist art multiplies confusion and rejoices in the uncalculated. Artistic control over subject matter is no longer a virtue. Breton's *First Manifesto* (1924) lists those artists, Moreau among them, whose work has surrealist elements but is too consciously organized.

Some aspects of *fin-de-siècle* painting led Breton to important insights. The vision of frustrated desire drawn by 'the great visionary and Magician' Gustave Moreau,[33] in all its obscene beauty, is the vision shaped by inherited culture which must be confronted and comprehended, since it is the raw material from which all new dreams must come. Moreau's work, according to Breton, is crucial for its focus on lust and its disclosure of the fundamental sadism of twentieth-century erotic dream: his abandoned works 'skirted the abyss, touched the realm of the forbidden'.[34] Breton is fascinated by Moreau's hieratic style, his *femmes fatales*, and his luxurious ornament, especially his Baudelairean blends of jewels and naked flesh. The surrealist acknowledges the seductions of reaction: the ambivalence of his inheritance persists.

Elsewhere, analysing his pleasure in the 'fascinating' eyes of Moreau's Delilah ('Samson et Dalila', 1882), Breton rediscovers the radical moment in decadent style.[35] He speaks of the thrill of perceiving in those eyes an icon of potentiality, energy frozen on the brink of being. This perception of the powers frozen in decadence, which surrealism tries to release, appears again as an element in his definition of that key surrealist concept, 'convulsive beauty', in *L'Amour fou* (1937).

In general, surrealist painting brings an ironic and critical edge to its decadent borrowings. Salvador Dali's androgyne Narcissus ('Les Métamorphoses de Narcisse', 1934) exposes the sterility of a vision that reconstructs the world in its own mirror-image. The dream world of Dali, Max Ernst, Yves Tanguy, in its 'magical realism', brings together incompatible objects in fantastic perspectives, echoing Moreau's illusionary realism. But it makes no attempt to substitute one set of mystifications for another; rather, it underlines the absurdity of human constructions. The isolated elements on the canvas are drawn with a heightened realism, but with unexpected distortions of form or colour, or are placed in unconventional relationships, so that the ultimate effect is of discrepancy and fragmentation. A closer look at the work of the Belgian Paul Delvaux (b. 1897) and that of Giorgio de Chirico (1888–1978), born in Greece, Italian and French by adoption, will indicate the diversity of surrealism's adaptations. These two have been chosen to indicate the continuing internationalism of *fin-de-siècle* influence, which accompanies the growing internationalism of the market, and also to show its persisting ambivalence. Delvaux's work conveys a sense of liberation. De Chirico, co-inventor with Carlo Carrà in Ferrara, in 1917, of Metaphysical Art, was disowned by the surrealists when he changed styles and developed fascist sympathies. Like his *fin-de-siècle* precursors, he turns his perceptions of the ferment of modern life into a despairing call for order.

The best of Giorgio de Chirico's work uses the forms of the past to recreate mystery within the landscape of modern life. His serene, hallucinatory settings, with their classical towers, arcades and squares, are influenced by the still landscapes of Arnold Boecklin, the frozen townscapes of Alfred Kubin, and by his Italian inheritance: Giotto, Uccello, and the exponents of ideal architecture (the fifteenth-century architect Luciano Laurana, for example, whose 'View of an Ideal City' in the Ducal Palace, Urbino, presents a silent, empty square, with deep, vanishing perspective, centred on a round building with half-open door, evoking suspense and expectancy). But in many of de Chirico's versions (for example, 'Mistero e malinconia di una strada', 1914), the mystery stays locked in the landscape.

De Chirico's blend of myth with the modern produces radical dislocations of temporal and spatial perspective, which cruelly expose contemporary humanity's pretensions to grandeur. Moreau's painting had claimed that images and values of the past were still relevant for the modern world. De Chirico shows them grotesquely out of place ('La battaglia tra Opliti e Centauri', 1909; or his lithographs for Jean Cocteau's *Mythologie*, 1934). In his version of Odysseus' Return (1973), that favourite of modernist myths is resituated within the confines of a bourgeois drawing room, with a temple on the left wall, a sofa on the back wall, a boat in the middle of the carpet and the sea outside, seen through the window. The contrast with Moreau's 'Les Prétendants' is striking. The patterns of legend are repeated in the modern world, not as tragedy but as farce.

The modern landscape evacuates the human from its space, leaving only functional traces, in the form of isolated objects ('Canto d'amore', 1914), or else turns men into manikins. De Chirico's collapsing of rationalist categories, confusing organic and inorganic, produces forms that are more, not less, rigid, commenting on the mechanization of modern life. His human figures are tailor's dummies, crueller versions of Rops's puppets (though not as cruel, it must be said, as the dolls of Hans Bellmer), or collocations of bits of machinery.

When Paul Delvaux gives a contemporary setting to the favourite myths of the *fin de siècle*, he too exposes the weakness of modern man. But he sets optimistically against it, in a reversal of the inherited prejudice, the vital challenge of nature, figured by female sensuality. Delvaux's female nudes, wreathed in flowers and vines, invade the world of suits, science and business, often ignored, but ever-insistent. Galatea, Penelope, Venus, Leda, reappear in ancient ruins disrupted by intimations of modernity. 'Vénus endormie' (1944), a nude with fathomless eyes, reclining on a sofa in the centre of an antique square, is the focus of a dream-world of familiar images of sexuality and death shot through with a redeeming humour that promises the possible liberation of desire. The creative conflict of sexuality is Delvaux's constant theme – and the fate of his timid bourgeois, confined and defined by his suit, elbowed out of the picture by the sensuous female, an object lesson for the spectator.

THE CINEMATIC INHERITANCE

With the transfer of its dream images from canvas to the screen (Paris saw the first public showing of motion pictures in December 1895), decadent ideology made an indelible mark on the modern imagination. The first experiments in fantastic cinema came from Georges Méliès (1861–1938), another of Moreau's pupils, who made a total of seventy-five films in the period 1896–1912, with such titles as 'La Tentation de Saint Antoine' (1898), 'Barbe-Bleue', 'Le Palais des mille et une nuits' (1905), 'Le Rêve d'un fumeur d'opium' (1907).[36] Méliès took full advantage of the film's ability to subvert time and collapse space, creating an alternative and self-sustaining world of dream. At the same time, paradoxically, his films foreground the procedures of their own construction, making the spectator aware of the directing presence of the artist. (In this context, John Frazer has suggested – very tentatively – that Méliès's films may have been influential on Picasso.) Méliès appears to have been a radical; in 1899, he made a pro-Dreyfus documentary.

Philippe Jullian includes F. W. Murnau's 'Nosferatu' (1921) in the decadent tradition,[37] for its imaginative use of special effects to conjure up the pleasurable terror of the vampire, along with the fantastic décors of Fritz Lang, the symbolism of Cocteau and the *femmes fatales* of Eric von Stroheim. The surrealist films of Salvador Dali and Luis Bunuel ('Un Chien andalou', 1929, for example, or 'L'Age d'or', 1931) show objects freed from conventional restraints merging, interpenetrating, 'to make the dissolution of visible reality fascinatingly and tormentingly plausible'.[38] These films, like those of Fellini and Robbe-Grillet, are aimed at an elite audience. Roger Vadim's 'Barbarella' (1968), however, a camp erotic adventure set in a futuristic decadence complete with androgynous angel, lesbian sadists, flesh-eating dolls, bridges the avant-garde and popular markets. In the latter, particularly with the eighties vogue for science fiction and fantasy (Ridley Scott's 'Blade Runner', or the ornate epic 'Dune'), the commercial future of *fin de siècle* remains assured.

NOTES

1 C. W. Furse, 'The Grafton Gallery. A summary', *The Studio. An Illustrated Magazine of Fine and Applied Art*, 1, no. 1 (April 1893), 33.

2 S. Mallarmé, 'The Impressionists and Edouard Manet', *The Art Monthly Review* (September 1876), quoted by P. Florence, *Mallarmé, Manet and Redon* (Cambridge, 1986), p. 18.

3 E. Zola, 'Deux Expositions d'art au mois de mai', *Le Messager de l'Europe*, June 1876, collected in E. Zola, *Le Bon Combat*, Collection Savoir (Paris, 1974), p. 181.

4 G. Deleuze, *Sacher-Masoch: An Interpretation*, tr. J. McNeil (London, 1971), pp. 48–9.

5 C. Baudelaire, *Salon de 1846*, in *Œuvres complètes*, vol. II, Bibliothèque de la Pléiade (Paris, 1976), pp. 415–17.

6 Zola, 'Deux Expositions', p. 201.

7 P. Hamerton, *Thoughts about Art*, 1889, quoted by B. Denvir, *The Late*

Victorians: Art, Design and Society 1852–1910, (London and New York, 1986), p. 191.

8 The attempt to place *fin-de-siècle* art in France as part of a total cultural and political moment is a major preoccupation in a number of recent studies, with varying specialist focuses (J. Pierrot, *L'Imaginaire décadent*, Paris, 1977; Jean-Luc Daval's *Modern Art: The Decisive Years 1884–1914*, London, 1979; my own *The Sins of the Fathers: Decadence in France 1870–1914*, London, 1986; B. Dijkstra, *Idols of Perversity: Fantasies of Feminine Evil in Fin-de-siècle Culture*, New York and Oxford, 1986; E. Weber's *France, Fin de Siècle*, Cambridge, Mass. and London, 1986). Bernard Denvir's excellent in-depth survey of the institutional framework in which English art operated (see n. 7) still lacks its French counterpart.

9 J. Lorrain, *Monsieur de Phocas. Astarté* (Paris, 1901), p. 350.

10 Gustave Moreau, quoted by P. L. Mathieu, *Gustave Moreau*, tr. James Emmons (Oxford, 1977), p. 130.

11 Moreau, quoted by Mathieu, *Gustave Moreau*, p. 84.

12 M. Proust, *Contre Sainte-Beuve*, Bibliothèque de la Pléiade (Paris, 1971), p. 419.

13 J. Péladan, *L'Art ochlocratique* (Paris, 1888), p. 45.

14 J. Péladan, *La Gynandre* (Paris, 1891), p. 349.

15 See for example J. Péladan, *Le Vice suprême* (Paris, 1884), *Comment on devient mage: Ethique* (Paris, 1892), *Comment on devient fée: Erotique* (Paris, 1893).

16 Weber, *France, Fin de Siècle*, p. 95.

17 Dijkstra, *Idols of Perversity*, p. 113.

18 O. Redon, *A soi-même, Journal 1867–1915* (Paris, 1961). S. Sandström, *Le Monde imaginaire d'Odilon Redon* (Lund, Sweden, 1955) and J. Seznec, 'Odilon Redon and literature', in U. Finke (ed.), *French Nineteenth-Century Painting and Literature* (Manchester, 1972) have also been useful in the preparation of this section.

19 Félicien Rops, August 1878, quoted by G. Lascault, 'Petit Dictionnaire autour de Félicien Rops', in *Félicien Rops 1833–1898* (Paris, 1985), p. 54.

20 Lascault, 'Petit Dictionnaire', p. 56.

21 Joséphin Péladan, 1885, quoted by Lascault, 'Petit Dictionnaire', p. 48. Lascault gives an excellent account of some of Péladan's twentieth-century heirs, pp. 47–8.

22 Maurice Denis, quoted by G. L. Mauner, *The Nabis: Their History and Their Art 1888–1896* (New York and London, 1978), p. 42.

23 Quoted by Mauner, *The Nabis*, p. 160.

24 Weber, *France, Fin de Siècle*, p.155.

25 See Brian Reade, *Aubrey Beardsley*, Aubrey Beardsley Exhibition held at the Victoria and Albert Museum, May–September 1966 (London, 1966).

26 *Ibid.*, p. 7.

27 W. Haftmann, *Painting in the Twentieth Century* (2 vols., New York, 1976), vol. I, p.56.

28 W. Hofmann, *Gustav Klimt*, repr. (London, 1974), pp. 9–10.

29 *Ibid.*, p. 15.

30 R. von Holten, *L'Art fantastique de Gustave Moreau* (Paris, 1960), p. 54.

31 A. Breton, *Seconde Manifeste du surréalisme*, 1930, repr. Collection Idées (Paris, 1972), p. 82.

32 A. Breton, *Les Vases communicants*, 1932, repr. Collection Idées (Paris, 1955), pp. 65–6.

33 A. Breton, *Le Surréalisme et la peinture*, 3rd edn rev. and corr. (Paris, 1965), p. 361.

34 *Ibid.*, p. 266.

35 Breton, *Les Vases communicants*, p. 91.

36 See *Méliès et la naissance du spectacle cinématographique*, Colloques de Cérisy (Paris, 1984), especially the papers by Hélène Puiseux, 'Une lecture sociale des films de Méliès' and John Frazer, 'Le Cubisme et le cinéma de Georges Méliès'.

37 P. Jullian, *Esthetès et magiciens* (Paris, 1969), pp. 271–3.

38 Haftmann, *Painting in the Twentieth Century*, p. 273.

❦

TEN

PERSONALITIES AND PRINCIPLES: ASPECTS OF LITERATURE AND LIFE IN *FIN-DE-SIÈCLE* ENGLAND

ALISON HENNEGAN

During the first half of 1883 W. P. Frith, one of mid-Victorian England's most popular and successful painters, planned and executed an elaborate insult. His target was twofold: a movement, Aestheticism; and a man, Oscar Wilde. His medium was a painting. Earlier in the century Frith had proved himself a master of crowd scenes. He had made his name, and a very substantial fortune, with large and vigorous canvases whose densely populated, minutely observed surfaces recorded mid-Victorian life at its busiest and most vital. *Ramsgate Sands* (1854) had been followed by *Derby Day* (1858) and *The Railway Station* (1862). Much admired by Queen Victoria (who bought *Ramsgate Sands* for the Royal Collection where it remains today), he had laboured, at Victoria's command, for two years on *The Marriage of the Prince of Wales* (1865), the picture which jeopardized his health and, some claimed, all but destroyed his talent, even though it indubitably consolidated his reputation.[1] But that was almost twenty years ago and there were those who said that although Frith remained a superb technician, he was now creatively played out, overtaken by newer, more modern developments.

How better for Frith to woo fashion than by attacking the fashion which had rejected him? Resentment and fear, thinly disguised as the artist's lofty amusement, underlay Frith's new painting, *The Private View at the Royal Academy, 1881*. It, too, was a crowd scene. In it the late Victorian worlds of High Art and High Fashion mingle as Academicians, writers, intellectuals and the comfortably leisured come together for one of the ritual occasions of the social calendar – the Private View of the Royal Academy's annual exhibition.

Beyond the desire of recording for posterity the aesthetic craze as regards dress [wrote Frith], I wished to hit the folly of listening to self-elected critics in matters of taste ... I therefore planned a group, consisting of a well-known apostle of the beautiful, with a herd of eager worshippers surrounding him. He is supposed to be explaining his theories to willing ears, taking some pictures on the Academy walls for his text ... On the left of the composition is a family of pure aesthetes absorbed in affected study of the pictures.[2]

The 'apostle' was Wilde. In Frith's painting he is immaculately attired, his top hat flawlessly burnished, but his luxuriant and glossy hair is long and in his buttonhole he wears a lily.

There was nothing novel about attacks on either Wilde or Aestheticism. For the past few years, Frith's close friends at *Punch* had mocked the fashions of aesthetes in décor and dress, had guyed their intense pursuit of The Beautiful in both artefacts and emotions, and had echoed the extremely 'unEnglish' enthusiasms of language and gesture in which they expressed their response to beauty.

Week after week, in his elegantly vicious cartoons, Du Maurier, *Punch*'s leading artist, created a gallery of aesthetic types: the patroness of the arts, Mrs. Cimabue Brown; the poet, Jellaby; the critic Maudle (who, such is the curious relation of Art to Life, bore an uncanny physical resemblance to the man Wilde would become, and whom Lautrec and Beerbohm would caricature, a dozen years hence).[3] Du Maurier set his characters in drawing rooms and studios freed from the period's massive mahogany furniture – impeccable in materials and craftsmanship, often deplorable in design, yet still so loved in unaesthetic households – and filled them with the paraphernalia of the new movement. Here was the old blue and white china which the London-based American artist, James McNeill Whistler, had instructed them to love. Japanese fans adorned the walls, partly in modest homage to the newly discovered, passionately admired Japanese artists of earlier centuries, partly in sheer defence against the ubiquitous Benares brassware so fondly and proprietorially imported by home coming Anglo-Indians. Bowls of living lilies complemented the painted ones which gleamed from Pre-Raphaelite canvases, and vases of real peacock feathers were mirrored in the patterns of wallpapers and fabrics designed by William Morris and retailed by Liberty.

Du Maurier clad his women in the softly flowing, purely coloured 'mediaeval' gowns adopted in revolt against the grotesquely ugly lines and harsh, mass-produced aniline dies of prevailing female fashion. He caves-dropped as his characters discussed the tenets of the new Rational Dress movement, dedicated to the overthrow of obsessional tight-lacing (which deformed women's spines, all but bisected their livers, inverted their nipples and contributed to a host of difficulties and dangers in pregnancy and childbirth). In real life both Wilde and his wife, Constance, were prominent amongst those urging the adoption of looser, lighter, healthier garments which acknowledged rather than travestied the needs and form of the human body.[4]

And, pleasurably shocked, Du Maurier portrayed men and women urging

each other simply 'To *be* – but to be *beautifully*.' For what Du Maurier
mocked most were the words and body language his aesthetes used. Theirs
was a diction generously garnished with heavily emphatic adverbs – 'utterly',
'divinely', 'consummately' – which, in England, are usually held to be the
mark of 'female' language, just as the clasped hands, rapturous sighs, soulful
gazes and upturned eyes displayed impartially by Du Maurier's male and
female aesthetes alike are, in a 'properly' constituted world, the prerogative of
women only. Already, in the late 1870s, Du Maurier was saying, codedly but
quite clearly – and in a mass-readership, family magazine – that Aestheticism
was not only 'unEnglish': it was also, even more worryingly, 'unmanly'. Or
was it 'unEnglish' *because* it was 'unmanly'? That question, hinted but not yet
clearly articulated by Du Maurier, would come to dominate intellectual,
artistic and political life in the last two decades of the century.

Certainly, if the anti-aesthetes were looking for wicked foreigners to blame,
there was a whole nation of them just across the Channel. From France, a
notoriously immoral country as every good Englishman knew, had come an
insistence on 'l'art pour l'art', art for art's sake, an attempt to free art and
artists from the burden of a naïvely didactic moral teaching. The new
movement brought an emphasis on the prime importance of style and form,
and the beginnings of an aesthetic philosophy which taught that the
boundaries separating the arts – music, painting, sculpture, dancing, poetry
and prose – are sometimes more apparent than real. Sounds may have
colours, words may be music, movement may speak, visual line may be
poetry. Poets such as Gautier, Baudelaire, Mallarmé and, later, Verlaine and
Rimbaud, explored the new possibilities in their work. Poets and prose
writers alike questioned a whole host of time-honoured assumptions: about
'suitable' and 'unsuitable' subjects for art; about the nature of morality and
immorality; about the nature of gender and human sexual response; about the
characteristics of 'good' and 'bad' art and the connections, or not, between
the morality of art and the morality of the artist who creates it.

In novels such as *Seraphitus-Seraphita* (1834) Balzac had paid wary
homage to the androgyne, a creature who was consequently to haunt painting
and literature on both sides of the Channel. In *La Fille aux Yeux d'Or* (1835)
he took the first step in that long, tortuous love–hate relationship which male
European authors were to conduct throughout the century with The Lesbian
– and a curiously unreal creature she proved to be, as manufactured in the
fearful brains of Swinburne, Zola, Maupassant, Strindberg and Henry
James.[5] Gautier's *Mademoiselle de Maupin* (first published in 1835 with a
Preface which contains one of the earliest formulations of 'l'art pour l'art')
offered a tantalizingly ambiguous hero/ine whose irresistible attractions force
other characters to recognize their own bisexuality. (Swinburne, Pater and

Wilde all admired the book deeply and Aubrey Beardsley, when already dying, produced six illustrations for it.)[6] In 1856 Flaubert (whom Pater would not hear criticized in his presence and whom Wilde acknowledged as 'my master')[7] published *Madame Bovary* in serial form in the *Revue de Paris*. His coolly objective study of a provincial adulteress and the tightly constricting community which stifles her, resulted in his arrest for 'offences against public morals'. He was acquitted after a trial which became one of nineteenth-century France's greatest *causes célèbres*. The issues raised became wearisomely familiar to English authors: they also were to know a series of censorship trials and vetoes later in the century. In 1880 Guy de Maupassant (Flaubert's devoted pupil) began that astonishing decade in which he poured out more than three hundred short stories. Their formal perfection carried the genre to new heights whilst their author's seemingly objective, actually loving portrayal of those rejected by society made from the 'unspeakable' a thing of great beauty. For the rest of the century, in England as in France, the short story was to be one of the most important literary forms and Maupassant its undisputed master, with disciples in unexpected places. Max Beerbohm, for example, that most delicate of humorists, acknowledged his debt in 'A Relic', which he wrote in 1918 after rediscovering the manuscript of 'A Fan', his very first essay in fiction, inspired by Maupassant's example.[8] After Maupassant's collapse into madness, the result of syphilitic infection, Wilde would be the first to send to England news that the Frenchman was dying.[9]

A new poetic school, 'Symbolism', developed round the figures of Mallarmé and Verlaine. The symbolists extolled the virtues of the fluid rather than the fixed. Poetry's true subject matter should be the poets themselves, or, rather, a world experienced and expressed through poets' emotions, moods, intuitions and impressions. Small groups of writers, mainly café-based, discussed each others' work and formulated aesthetic theories which they then embodied in poems, essays and literary polemic. Their writing often bristled with a basic contradiction: fiercest intellectual and artistic energies spiritedly devoted to an elaboration of the world-weariness, *ennui* and *langeur* which assailed the dying century, a century which was gradually falling away, decaying in both a literal and metaphorical sense. Theirs was *un esprit décadent*, spirit of a world where jaded palates required strong spices – of sensations, excitements and novelty. It was a spirit impatient of received wisdom, sceptical of or downright hostile to conventional definitions of the Good, the Beautiful and the Natural. Painters, too, found themselves aligned with the new movement. Older artists, such as Puvis de Chavannes, Gustave Moreau and Odilon Redon, found their work eagerly acclaimed by a younger generation of writers, who responded excitedly to the fusion of the biblical, allegorical, supernatural and diabolic to be found in their paintings.

Gradually 'decadence' and 'symbolism' merged into each other, and the worlds became virtually interchangeable, in England as in France. Later, 'aesthete' joined them, to make, in the eyes of adversaries, an unholy Trinity. Subsequent critics have laboured to distinguish carefully between the three. The writers and artists who lived through those last two decades of the nineteenth century were very much less precise. And when, at the century's end, Arthur Symons, the period's most consistently impressive critic, came to write the book which so influenced Yeats and Eliot, *The Symbolist Movement in Literature* (1899), he almost called it *The Decadent Movement*, instead.[10]

From the mid-seventies on, self-appointed ambassadors brought British artists news of the cultural ferment across the Channel. Arthur O'Shaughnessy, a poet and close friend of the first Pre-Raphaelites; Edmund Gosse, already in training for his favourite role of mandarin of English letters; Charles Whibley, protégé, friend and general dogsbody to W. E. Henley, the irascible radical-reactionary editor of *The National Observer*: men as diverse as these brought the news that was eagerly awaited.[11]

During the last quarter of the century English writers not only devoured French books; they also journeyed to meet their authors. Memoirs and correspondence of the day make it seem as though Paris was eternally filled with visitors from Albion: from Hibernia, too. The Irishman, George Moore, was already there by 1873, reading voraciously, visiting eagerly, listening, discussing and observing, always observing this endlessly fascinating and exhilarating world, so different from the provincial Ireland he had loathed and left. His *Confessions of a Young Man* (1883), which recalled those earlier days, in itself inspired other young men and women to experience France at first hand. Irish, English and American visitors, including Wilde, Havelock Ellis, Edmund Gosse and Arthur Symons, paid their respects to Mallarmé, in the little flat at 89 rue de Rome where, from 1880 until the mid-nineties, he was 'At Home' on Tuesday evenings.[12]

Unexpectedly, perhaps, French authors returned the compliment to their British *confrères*. London's sulphurous yellow fogs acquired for French eyes a glamour as potent as any Englishman's wistful fantasies of sinful Paris. And, indeed, was not England the home of the Dandies, those curiously anarchistic narcissists who so fascinated Baudelaire with their strict adherence to sartorial conventions of their own creation, allied with a fundamental social iconoclasm? The model also exerted a powerful influence over Whistler, Wilde and Beerbohm. Moreover, Whistler's impressionistic studies of London's landscape, especially of the Thames at night, had taught the French to see new beauties there. Mallarmé himself knew England well and lived there for a number of years. He loved it deeply and constantly urged younger French writers and artists to visit and learn to love it, too. In 1875 Verlaine, who had just served a two-year prison sentence for shooting at and wounding his ex-lover, Rimbaud, sought solace and refuge in the Lincolnshire village of

Stickney, where he taught the local children and even managed to find the English winters charming. Shortly afterwards he moved to Bournemouth and taught there, too. (Almost thirty years later Max Beerbohm produced one of his funniest cartoons, depicting a crocodile of schoolboys accompanied by this most unlikely of masters.)[13] Later, in 1893, billed as 'The Convict Poet' and supervised by a fussily anxious Arthur Symons in the stressful role of impresario, Verlaine lectured to enthusiastic, largely female, audiences in London, then went on to Oxford and Manchester.[14]

Artists as well as writers made the journey to and fro across the Channel. Whistler and Beardsley were amongst Mallarmé's visitors. Walter Sickert kept an eye on French developments, as did Will Rothenstein, the precocious young Jewish artist from Bradford who was constantly in Paris. (It was at his instigation that Verlaine undertook his English lecture tour.)[15] When in England, Rothenstein sought to inspire his compatriots with a love of things French. He was, said Max Beerbohm, 'Paris in Oxford',[16] and Rothenstein's innumerable lithographs of the painters, poets, sculptors and novelists of contemporary France and England are the perfect complement to Beerbohm's caricatures.

Not only were British artists and writers experiencing one of their rare periods of cosmopolitanism: the English capital itself was vibrant with new influences from a multitude of nations. The British policy, implemented throughout the second half of the century, of extending hospitality to political dissidents 'wanted' by other countries' secret police had filled the city with refugees and exiles, some of whom sought merely to forget, others of whom continued the struggle for causes and revolt begun at home. European refugees – from Germany, Italy and France – had arrived after 1848, the Year of Revolutions.[17] Much of the planning for Italian unification was done in London. Later, during the 1880s and 1890s, anti-Tsarist refugees began to arrive from Russian territories. Some, both Jews and gentiles, were politically active opponents of the Tsarist regime, but there were also many thousands of poor Jews from central and eastern Europe seeking simple respite from a daily grinding economic assault and the savagery of pogroms.[18] London's population was swollen by foreign socialists, communists, nationalists and anarchists, many of them writers and intellectuals. Although the new immigrant arrivals often gravitated towards particular parts of the city which gradually became their own, they also contributed to the larger community. Excellent cheap French restaurants in Soho and electrifying Yiddish performances of Shakespeare in Whitechapel's Jewish theatres were just two very different examples of the cultural diversity available in London. Many British writers ate in the former and paid homage to the latter.[19]

There were also immigrants of a less overtly exotic kind: a small American invasion, for instance. Whistler had been in England since the 1860s but his fellow painter, John Singer Sargent, and the novelist Henry James were also permanent residents. Henry Harland, soon to be the editor of *The Yellow Book*, the quarterly forever identified, however wrongly, as the quintessentially 'nineties' publication, had also settled in England, as had Frank Harris, charlatan, liar, editor of genius who transformed *The Fortnightly* and *The Saturday Review*, and author of an utterly unreliable, utterly readable autobiography, *My Life and Loves*, which contains gems and paste in equal measure. He also wrote a biography of Wilde, which has been variously described as the finest and the worst.[20] More elevatedly, the Eton and Cambridge educated Howard Sturgis (cousin of George Santayana) was settled in Windsor, where he wrote a wistfully homoerotic school novel, *Tim* (1891)[21] and the more substantial *Belchamber* (1904) which won the admiration of E. M. Forster and Virginia Woolf but caused anxiety to the always rather easily anxious Henry James. And, down in Sussex, another American exile, the ardently Anglophile Edward Perry Warren, was conducting an idiosyncratic experiment in living which involved poetry, austerity, fiercely controlled homoeroticism and a passionate recreation of ancient Athens.[22]

As if the Russian-Jews and the Germans and the French and the Italians and the Americans weren't enough to be getting on with, there were also those visitors from a nearer nation which technically was, yet spiritually most definitely was not, British: the Irish. Wilde was not the only unignorable Irishman in London; there was also his contemporary, George Bernard Shaw. George Moore had returned to England from Paris in 1880. Their junior, W. B. Yeats, had received much of his schooling in West London.

All in all, anyone anxious to blame the 'unhealthy' state of contemporary British art and letters on unwholesome foreign influences had some remarkably varied ammunition.

Yet, despite the unlovely English tendency to dismiss all unwelcome ideas by labelling them 'foreign' (a form of xenophobia which, in other contexts, Du Maurier was swift to mock), Aestheticism was, in certain aspects, very much a home-grown product.

Its origins lay in that sweeping mid-nineteenth-century reappraisal of 'the mediaeval', perceived less as an historical reality than as a potent symbol of values which materialism, secularism and industrialization seemed likely to obliterate. The painters and poets who formed the Pre-Raphaelite Brotherhood – Rossetti, Burne-Jones, Holman Hunt and Morris – initially sought to fuse beauty, truth and morality. Their early paintings combined the physical truthfulness of perfectly observed, faithfully rendered natural detail and the moral truthfulness of subject matter chosen for its power to inspire and to concentrate attention upon spiritual rather than worldly values. It was, in part, a reworking on canvas of the Keatsian dictum that 'Beauty is truth, truth beauty'. It was also a conscious revolt against the increasing and seemingly wilful ugliness, moral and physical, which had accompanied England's rise to industrial pre-eminence and for which many of her people and so much of her landscape paid so high a price. Beauty, the Pre-Raphaelites insisted, was not a luxury but the pre-condition of a fully human life. It was needed everywhere: in housing, furniture and clothing which must combine usefulness and beauty; in relations between employer and employed, ideally rooted in mutual respect and justice; in decent physical working conditions which recognized the bodily and psychological needs of those who worked in them; in humanity's relations with the natural world, which was to be cherished, not violated. The subjects which the Pre-Raphaelites chose to paint might, at first sight, appear to be purely escapist – Arthurian legends, pastoral idylls, reworkings of classical mythology – but always the moral impulse behind the painters' choice and treatment was strong. Even 'escapism' might be an act of resistance: as Burne-Jones said defiantly, the more locomotives *they* created the more *he* would paint pictures of angels.[23]

There were those who failed to find the Brotherhood's morality moral. Millais's painting of 'Christ in the House of His Parents' (1850) drew from Dickens an outraged howl, in print, against the 'hideous, wry-necked, blubbering red-haired boy in a night-gown' (the child Christ). As for the Virgin, she 'would stand out from the rest of the company as a monster in the vilest cabaret in France or the lowest gin-shop in England'.[24] To attempt the depiction of biblical characters in any but the most anodyne colours was to court disaster for the whole of the century and their representation on the public stage was utterly forbidden. Permission to perform Wilde's *Salomé* was refused in 1892. Nevertheless, the possibilities of a fully human Christ would draw many of the later 'decadent' authors, especially those who were homosexual.

Fifteen years after Dickens's outburst the controversy aroused by the Pre-Raphaelites continued, directed this time at their poetry as well as their painting. Under the name 'Thomas Maitland', Robert Buchanan launched a full-scale attack against 'The Fleshly School of Poetry', a diatribe against D. G. Rossetti who was arraigned for poor draughtsmanship, limited range, an obsession with a 'morbid deviation from healthy forms of life', and a 'weary, wasting, yet exquisite sensuality; nothing virile, nothing tender, nothing completely sane'.[25] Deviation; effeminacy; lack of proper feeling; insanity: here, already, is the roll-call of charges which will be levied, ever more loudly, later in the century against the writers and artists of Aestheticism. Rossetti's self-defence, published two months later in *The Athenaeum*, was neatly titled 'The Stealthy School of Criticism'.[26] He urged his critics to read the whole of his works, not to wrench lines and phrases out of context, and to distinguish between the sentiments of fictional personae and the writer himself. Wilde would find himself fighting the same battles some twenty years later. (And, most unexpectedly, amongst his fiercest and most outspoken supporters would be that same Robert Buchanan, who, in a letter to *The Star* of 23 April 1895, deplored 'the rarity of Christian charity under the sun', and argued that 'Whatever [Mr. Wilde] is, whatever he may be assumed to be, he is a man of letters, a brother artist, and no criminal prosecution whatever will be able to erase his name from the record of English literature.')[27]

Meanwhile, until his death in 1896, William Morris strove to make explicit the essential connections between artistic beauty, social justice, and private and public morality. For over forty years he worked devotedly for the labour movement, engaged in practical experiments to create ideal workers' communities, attempted to re-educate a nation's aesthetic taste, and warned, in a series of utopian and futuristic writings, of the dangers inherent in an arrogantly callous society which valued technological advance more than human happiness.

Other champions and advocates of the Pre-Raphaelites added their own distinctive emphases as they transmitted, elaborated and transmuted the Brotherhood's ideas. The support of some brought scandal rather than esteem: Simeon Solomon, for example, and the poet who so much admired him, Swinburne. Solomon, the young Jewish painter, revered Rossetti's work, and his own delicate, often allegorical, pictures ('Love dying at the breath of Lust') won praise from his most eminent contemporaries. Thackeray, assessing the Royal Academy Exhibition of 1860, reserved his highest praise for Solomon's 'Moses', and Burne-Jones said 'he was the greatest artist of us all'.[28] But in the early 1870s Solomon was convicted for soliciting in a public urinal, served a term of imprisonment and afterwards slid gently into alcoholism, poverty and a seemingly enjoyable squalor which, as dutiful friends intent on rescue were to discover, he was loath to leave.[29] For young aesthetes later in the century Solomon's work, his homosexuality, his imprisonment and his cheerfully determined adherence to the disreputable made him a potent symbol of martyrdom and revolt.[30] (When, at last, in 1895, the bailiffs were sent into the bankrupt Wilde's house and its contents sold, for derisory sums, at public auction, pictures by Solomon were amongst the possessions whose loss Wilde most mourned.)[31] Swinburne, one of Solomon's most enthusiastic admirers until his conviction when the poet promptly dropped him, was himself a powerful influence upon the aesthetes. His defiant rejection of Christianity, his ambivalent attitude to Christ himself, his perfervid adoration of an Ancient Greece no more real than the Pre-Raphaelites' Middle Ages, his rhapsodic eulogies of sins and vices more dreamed of than performed, his masochistic hymning of intensely pleasurable pain, and the technical mastery of the irresistibly sensuous metres in which he expressed it, all left their mark on later artists and writers.

Amongst critics, John Ruskin was an ardent supporter of the Pre-Raphaelites. His partnership would eventually bring him into public conflict with Whistler. Whistler, initially an admirer and close friend of Rossetti, quarrelled violently with him (as he did with all his friends) and moved from Pre-Raphaelitism towards Impressionism, becoming eventually one of its finest exponents. When Ruskin, in an article, accused him of 'flinging a pot of paint in the public's face', Whistler sued. The resulting court case, in which Whistler was awarded a mocking farthing's damages, was to be one of the most famous trials of the century.[32] Ruskin reserved some of his warmest praise for a young artist called Kate Greenaway. Her first published work appeared in 1867, her last seven years after her death in 1901. Her most successful work took the hitherto lowly form of book illustration and greetings cards, a domestic mode which carried her work into many homes. In her illustrations were combined two elements which were to become particularly characteristic of the later century: an idealization of childhood, allied with a fondness for settings and costumes which appear to refer to specific historical periods (especially the late eighteenth century) yet neverthe-less manage to suggest a curious timelessness. Greenaway's was one of the most influential of the many 'lost worlds' which later nineteenth-century artists and writers invented, celebrated and mourned.[33]

Ruskin's long sequence of widely read books – studies of European architecture and painting, open letters to The Working Men of England (sometimes illustrated by Greenaway), treatises on the nature and function of art, disquisitions on the education of girls and women – brought him to Oxford, where, as Slade Professor of Fine Art, he was able to exert direct influence over new generations of undergraduates. (The young Wilde, or so he claimed, was one of those who went to learn the dignity of manual labour by, briefly, working on Ruskin's ill-fated exercise in road building.) Also at Oxford was Walter Pater, the physically nondescript, intellectually exciting Fellow of Brasenose. His likeness was captured in a fine drawing by Simeon Solomon, whom Pater much admired.[34] Pater's influence was to be rather greater than he sometimes wished. Wilde, in Oxford at the same time as Pater but never formally taught by him, declared his Studies in the History of the Renaissance (1873) to be the 'holy writ of beauty'.[35] More sombrely, it was to be amongst the first books he asked for in prison.[36] The book's Conclusion, influenced partly by the Pre-Raphaelite emphasis upon emotional intensity, but also suffused by that heady mixture of the aesthetic, religious, emotional and sexual which was entirely Pater's own, became notorious: so much so that Pater withdrew it from the second 1877 edition. With a blend of defiance and apology, he restored it, slightly altered, for the third edition of 1888, but explained he had originally suppressed it 'as I conceived it might mislead some of the young men into whose hands it might fall'.[37] The Conclusion, which declared 'To burn always with this hard, gemlike flame, to maintain this ecstasy, is success in life', was to be much quoted, parodied, vilified and cherished for the next few decades.

Parody, indeed, was one of the most helpful indications of Aestheticism's increasing hold. Pater had already been parodied as 'Mr. Rose', in *The New Republic*. This *roman-à-clef*, published in 1877 and written by W. H. Mallock, borrowed a little from Plato's Dialogues, a little from Peacock's novels, and added a lot of spirited malice from Mallock himself who exposed and mocked a fractiously debating cast of disputants clearly modelled on Matthew Arnold, Benjamin Jowett of Balliol, Ruskin, Thomas Huxley and Herbert Spencer. Violet Paget, a formidable art historian and aesthetician who also wrote some remarkably fine ghost stories, made waspish notes during the late seventies and used them as the basis of her novel, *Miss Brown*, published under her pen name 'Vernon Lee'. This vicious attack on 'fleshly school' aesthetes was published in 1884, with the active encouragement of Henry James, who later came to regret it.[38]

Vernon Lee was one of many who, prematurely, declared Aestheticism dead. As early as 1881 she told her mother that it was already dying fast in London.[39]

She couldn't have been more wrong. In art and life Aestheticism continued to flourish. Popular songs, such as Herbert Harraden's 'The High Art Maiden' (1887), continued to appear, with lampooning covers.[40] The young Molly Hughes, going to Cambridge to begin a teacher-training course in the mid-eighties, found that one of her fellow students was known quite simply as 'the Aesthete'.[41] Aestheticism even became part of the subject matter of juvenile fiction. Mrs Molesworth, that extremely popular and very good children's author, made her ten-year-old male narrator of *The Girls and I* (1892) a connoisseur of blue and white china, a child so knowledgeable about women's clothing that his mother calls him her 'little man milliner', and an observant critic of pictures, jewellery and interior décor. Interestingly, Mrs Molesworth also endows him with considerable anxieties about his own gender identity.[42] Clarice March, in *Doris's High School Days*, includes two 'aesthetic' sixth formers '. . . who were not overburdened with intelligence' and 'devoted themselves chiefly to clothing themselves in fearful and wonderful ways, after which they fondly but erroneously imagined that they strongly resembled the pictures of Sir Edward Burne-Jones!'[43] The novel was published in a series intended 'for younger boys and girls' (that is, eight- to eleven-year-olds). In 1898 Robert Hichens, an author well aware of the literary market-place, could still feel it worth his while to write a short story about the social rehabilitation of a young male aesthete successfully reclaimed for normal, healthy English manhood. (It was only three years since Wilde's conviction so, for safety's sake, reclamation was the only possible ending.)[44]

And, in the last year of the century, E. W. Hornung gave A. J. Raffles, his amateur cracksman and gentleman burglar, a set of rooms in Albany whose walls carried 'reproductions of such works as "Love and Death" and "The Blessed Damozel"' and whose general appearance revealed 'a fine streak of aestheticism in his complex composition'. The rooms, in fact, of one 'who might have been a minor poet instead of an athlete of the first water'.[45]

Nevertheless, despite the plethora of general parodies, when, in 1883, Frith came to make his own pictorial comment on Aestheticism and the cult of the Beautiful, Wilde was the obvious target. In Beerbohm's words '. . . Beauty had existed long before 1880', but 'It was Mr. Oscar Wilde who managed her *début.*' By the summer of 1881 the young Irishman had been in London for about two years. He had arrived in triumph from Oxford where he had won the Newdigate Prize for poetry (with *Ravenna*) and had taken First Class Honours in Greats. He was intent on being known as quickly and as widely as possible. He had brains, persistence, florid if slightly fleshy good looks and, most important of all, conversational powers touched with genius, enhanced by a speaking voice of great beauty. Social gifts, allied with social determination, took him into some of the grandest houses in London and his flamboyance, wit, attentive courtesy and very considerable charm rapidly made him a welcome visitor. It did not, however, make him a social equal: he was a performer, not a peer, a middle-class Irishman, not an English aristocrat. His father, an internationally renowned doctor, had been knighted, it's true, and his mother, Speranza, was well known throughout Ireland for her patriotic songs and poems demanding freedom from England.[46] But an Irish knight cut little ice with the English aristocracy. Wilde was in Society but not of it, a fact that would be particularly painfully demonstrated when Society abandoned him after his conviction.

But, in 1881, the future looked promising. His first book, *Poems*, had been published that June and would go through four editions before the end of the next year. Ellen Terry, England's leading actress; Sarah Bernhardt, France's greatest tragedienne; Lillie Langtry, 'the Jersey Lily' who was a favourite of the Prince of Wales: all these were his friends. His apparently effortlessly produced epigrams were quoted everywhere (although some people, such as Whistler, claimed crossly to have uttered them first). No one quite knew now whether Wilde was copying Mr Du Maurier's cartoons or whether Mr Du Maurier was copying him, but it hardly mattered: either way the publicity was fine for Wilde. And although W. S. Gilbert had originally intended Swinburne to be the model for Bunthorne in the D'Oyly Carte Opera, *Patience* (first produced in the spring of 1881), that didn't matter either. Everyone assumed it was Wilde who ranked 'as an apostle in the high aesthetic band', who walked 'down Piccadilly with a poppy or a lily in [his] mediaeval hand'.[47] Both Wilde and D'Oyly Carte were happy to encourage confusion. When Wilde set off on his American lecture tour later that autumn, with a velvet jacket, knee breeches, silk stockings and pumps, very long hair and an air of ineffable superiority, he did so with the joyous approval of Colonel D'Oyly Carte who had sent him on ahead as advance publicity for the American production of *Patience*. Who was mocking whom?

Wilde, it seems, had the last laugh. So too with Frith's painting. Viewed today Frith's carefully planned insult, like so many of those offered to Wilde, proves a failure. Our eyes cannot distinguish so clearly now the once vital differences between the garments worn by the despised Aesthetes and the respectable Others. Missing the visual clues which tell us whom to mock and whom to admire, we can see only that Wilde dominates the picture. He does so partly by virtue of sheer size – in Life as in Art: he was well over six foot –, partly by sheer beauty. The neighbouring Academicians, who may to contemporary spectators have seemed reassuringly bluff, splendidly hearty and handsome, look merely red-faced and bull-necked. The women who surround Wilde, Frith's 'herd of eager worshippers', appear neither bovine nor mindlessly sycophantic. Rather, their faces suggest intelligence and sensitivity. One bears more than a passing resemblance to Ellen Terry, that friend for whom Wilde wrote three sonnets.[48] Two other celebrities pictured in the crowd, the novelist Anthony Trollope and Henry Irving (soon to be the first English actor ever knighted), were intended to represent the acceptable face of fame but, although alertly interested in Wilde, neither of them looks censorious or surprised. As is so often the case with artists, Frith has, unwillingly and unwittingly, found beauty in the thing he sought to vilify and has enhanced the dignity and stature of a man he meant to belittle.

For the next twelve years, until his imprisonment in 1895, Wilde would be continually caricatured, photographed, parodied, lampooned and quoted. He made the transition from blatant young self-publicist, who made lots of noise but didn't actually *do* much (or not, at least, on paper), to a serious, hard working and remarkably fruitful writer who produced critical, philosophical and political essays, short stories, fairy tales, a novel and seven plays, of which *The Importance of Being Earnest* ranks as one of the very greatest comedies in the English language. But, until the end, Wilde was always 'good copy'. He took good care to be. And when, sometime during the mid- to late eighties, 'aesthetes' gave way to 'decadents', who ushered in their own English *fin de siècle*, Wilde would, for most of his contemporaries, be the man most closely associated with the *new* new movement. So long a period of public odium transforms a vendetta into a relationship. Clearly, the society that mocked him so obsessively for so long needed him at least as much as he needed it.

An aesthete could become front-page news in the eighties because aesthetics themselves were, to a degree unknown before or since in England, part of daily popular concern. And, ironically, industrialization and technological advance, seen by many artists, philosophers and intellectuals as The Enemy, were largely responsible for that.

Prince Albert's brainchild, the Great Exhibition of 1851, had been conceived as a celebration of the marriage between Industry and Art. Thousands upon thousands of exhibits poured in from all over Britain, Europe and North America. They ranged from domestic utensils, furniture and fabrics to agricultural implements, statuary, architectural designs for workmen's cottages and elaborately executed, newly invented musical instruments. Some contemporary critics, deploring the taste or lack of it which they saw revealed by the Exhibition, held aloof and poured a steady stream of condescending abuse upon this enormous middle-class festival. Nevertheless, the Exhibition itself, the crowds who flocked to it, the excitement it generated, the column inches of newsprint devoted to it and the lavishly illustrated catalogues of exhibits which found their way into homes throughout the country all combined to give discussions of beauty, utility, craft, materials and taste a central place in everyday thought and conversation.

Those catalogues and newspapers were themselves part of a small industrial revolution. Improvements in printing techniques enabled more papers of higher quality to be produced in greater numbers more quickly – and for a smaller cost. Reprographic advances brought illustrations to their pages, first via engraving, later via photography. Developments in engraving, etching and lithography made it possible for even the poorest homes to boast one or two reproductions of original works by either old masters or contemporary artists. Sales of prints, Frith's amongst them, were enormous. Victorian painters could carry the values they espoused into hundreds of thousands of very different homes. They had the power to create and disseminate iconographically potent images: of family life; mothers and children; English landscape; idealized villages and cottagers; 'lost pasts' – of ancient Greece and Rome, mediaeval chivalry, conflicts between Roundheads and Cavaliers; a particular version of the eighteenth century and the Birth of the English Gentleman; great moments from Shakespeare; key episodes in imperial history. Cumulatively these artists helped to create pervasive versions of Britishness and, more particularly, Englishness, which played their part in unifying (or restricting and falsifying, depending on your point of view) conceptions of the country, its people, their past and their destiny.[49]

Books benefited, too, from reprographic innovations. During the last quarter of the century lavishly illustrated volumes brought to readers reproductions of works of art from all over the world – monochrome, usually, it's true, but of a quality too rarely found today. And many of those books were comparatively inexpensive. Improvements in cheaper, mechanized binding saw to that. New possibilities in book illustration, design and decoration provided fresh outlets for artists. Kate Greenaway was just one of a bevy of fine illustrators who were to include Walter Crane, Arthur Rackham, Edmund Dulac, Charles Ricketts, Clemence Housman (sister of A. E. and Laurence) and that wayward genius, Aubrey Beardsley. In the last decade of the century the physical beauty of books was to be as important as their contents, and that was as true of the cheap popular series, such as J. M. Dent's Temple Classics, as it was of fine volumes produced by small presses and the books emanating from the vastly influential John Lane at the Bodley Head.

The Elementary Education Acts of 1870 and 1880, which made full-time education compulsory for young children, marked the beginnings of the growth of a whole new reading public. At the lower end of the adult market publishers catered for them with magazines and newspapers busy in design, frenetic in their jumble of news items, gossip, poems, jokes, court cases, helpful hints, letters and serial stories. More ambitiously publishers embarked upon series of one-volume novels. Producing them in one volume mattered: up until now the private, commercial circulating libraries took care to insist that publishers continue to print novels in three volumes: that way, libraries could lend the same novel to three separate readers simultaneously and pocket a triple fee. Henry Vizetelly, that much wronged man who translated many of the great nineteenth-century French novelists – Flaubert, Zola, Maupassant – and introduced them to English readers, a man who fought incessantly against literary censorship and was eventually so battered by the judicial system that he died as the result of a most monstrous prison sentence, was the first to break the tyranny of the circulating libraries. With a translation in 1884 of Georges Ohnet's *The Ironmaster; or, Love and Pride*, he and his son launched their one-volume series. And, for that substantial core of politically engaged, intellectually vigorous working-class readers, there were cheap series of historical, philosophical, scientific, biographical and political volumes: Owen, Huxley, Spencer, Macaulay, Gibbon, Carlyle, Ruskin and many others, all available for a few pennies.

Easier, cheaper printing; new readers; and, for the women of the middle classes, much greater leisure, most of it spent in their homes: all three factors led, in the last three decades of the century, to a tremendous proliferation of periodical publications, covering literary, political, religious, artistic and domestic concerns. Women and children were recognized as, and encouraged to become, distinct readerships. Both groups were carefully targeted and efficiently marketed to. For advertising, also, was growing up, or declining into hopeless vulgarity, depending on your point of view. George Gissing, that sombrely realist writer, was one of the first to suggest the more pernicious dangers of the admen's world in his 1894 novel, *In the Year of Jubilee*, a work set in 1887, Victoria's Golden Jubilee. American promotional methods had crossed the Atlantic and were gradually adopted by English businessmen, including publishers and periodical proprietors.

So many periodicals, catering for brows of every height, and all of them hungry for copy. For young aspiring writers the new publications offered innumerable outlets in which to serve an apprenticeship to letters. Journalism's relentless demands – for copy of the right length and tone, punctually produced to meet intractable deadlines – forced upon the learners lessons of concision, lucidity and discipline. Many of the period's leading writers, including stylists as diverse as Richard Jeffries, Jerome K. Jerome, Alice Meynell, Robert Louis Stevenson, Arthur Symons, G. B. Shaw and Wilde himself, studied in that exigent, not over-refined school. It is in this period that commercial schools of journalism begin to emerge. Robert Hichens gives in his autobiography an entertaining account of the one in which he began to learn his trade, taught by a man whom some might call a fraud but whom others revered as an inspired teacher.[50] This is also the period of a new, and eventually very important figure: the literary agent. A. P. Watt founded his now celebrated firm at some time in the mid-seventies. James Pinker did not officially open his agency until 1896 but had been performing an agent's services for authors such as H. G. Wells, Stephen Crane and Wilde before that time. Later, with his agency established, he would include amongst his grateful clients Henry James, Ford Madox Ford and Arnold Bennett.[51]

Artefacts and ideas were not the only things promoted by new commercial practices and technological advance: people were, too. This was the first age of The Personality, the Celebrity whose words were swiftly communicated via the personality interview, whose face became familiar to thousands through the photographs reproduced in papers and on the postcards sold in shops and advertised at the back of magazines. Statesmen, athletes, actors, singers, musicians, authors, national heroes, all were available, pocket-sized in pasteboard. And, with the increasing cosmopolitanism and loosening up of England's 'Second Court' – Marlborough House, the London home of the Prince and Princess of Wales – even aristocratic ladies consented to be 'sold' as 'postcard beauties' (although, in the eyes of their more rigorous peers, they declassed themselves by doing so).

Already, in the sixties, photographers such as Nadar of Paris were producing magnificent portraits of French celebrities: the novelist, Victor Hugo, for example, and the young Sarah Bernhardt at the start of her career. In England Julia Margaret Cameron, a remarkable self-taught photographer who didn't handle a camera until middle age, created some of the finest photographs of her own or of any time, in a series which included studies of Tennyson, Browning and Ellen Terry, together with recreations of some of the period's most famous paintings and poems.[52] Cameron combined artistic excellence with commercial astuteness, paying punctilious attention to details of retailing, distribution and exhibition.[53] Oscar Rejlander, a Swede who settled in England, combined ceaseless technical innovation and experiment with a passionate attempt to make photography the artistic equal of great painting. A friend of Prince Albert and Lewis Carroll, he too produced outstanding portraits.[54] Downey of London collaborated enthusiastically with Bernhardt in her incessant moulding of her own image. Earlier, in the seventies, Bernhardt had organized a photo-session of herself in her coffin. The resulting pictures were supposedly for private distribution but they seemed to circulate remarkably far remarkably fast.[55] Sarony of New York already had an enviable reputation as *the* celebrities' photographer long before the remarkable sequence taken of Wilde during his 1881–2 lecture tour.[56]

There was, of course, nothing new about portraiture itself. But the ability to reproduce the same image thousands of times over, the means of distributing it swiftly across enormous geographical areas, the capacity to 'capture' the human model and then offer it for sale to another human being who thereafter 'had' the sitter in permanent, possessible form – all these were different indeed. With them begins that curious and often frightening process whereby, over the years, the 'image' of public people has become almost more important, because more 'real' and available than the person.[57] Later, in the twentieth century, political movements would explore and exploit the power of mass-produced visual images – of leaders, symbols, scapegoats – to enlist the allegiance of whole populations. The Third Reich is the most obvious and horrific example, although the Edwardian British suffragette movement can justifiably claim to be the first.[58]

But in the last two decades of the nineteenth century the focus is still on the single human being whose constantly replicated image begins to create in the beholder an entirely specious sense of knowing the person depicted. In the 1870s novels such as *The New Republic* presented recognizable portraits of celebrated people to a still small, tightly knit readership who, as often as not, did actually *know* the people portrayed. By the nineties *romans-à-clef* could be offered to a much larger readership who merely *felt* as though they knew people made superficially familiar to them via newspapers and magazine items. E. F. Benson's 1893 novel, *Dodo* (with its central portrait of Margot Tennant, later Asquith), became a runaway bestseller as did Robert Hichens's 1894 *jeu d'esprit*, *The Green Carnation*, a spoof of Wilde and his circle which both Wilde and his lover, Lord Alfred Douglas ('Bosie'), greatly enjoyed.[59] Just a year later, with Wilde facing his first battle in the law courts, Hichens and his publisher, William Heinemann, withdrew the book. Both men saw with horrid and prophetic clarity how easily the book could be used against Wilde.[60]

In part the book gained its power to harm from a threefold confusion: between Hichens's fictional characters, the living originals on whom they were based, *and* the ideas and characters those living authors in their turn created in their own real works. Boundaries between writers, their work and other people's perceptions of them became hopelessly entangled. What *is* the true relation between the artist and the artist's creation? What responsibility, if any, must artists take for the utterances and actions of their characters? Has art any responsibility to be moral? And, if it has, does that mean the artist who creates it must be moral in private life? And who or what is to be the arbiter of morality? Tradition? Organized religion? The law of the land? Cultural 'experts' who deliberate and then hand down their rulings to lesser breeds, incapable – by virtue of belonging to the wrong class, the wrong faith, the wrong age group, the wrong race, the wrong gender, or even the wrong political party – of exercising their own judgement? Questions such as these Flaubert had already faced in mid-century France. In England they gained particular force during the last quarter of the century and dominated its last decade. Here again, Wilde became the focus – and, this time, the victim – of society's intensifying fears.

Technically Wilde was sentenced for a clear breach of the law. Since 1885 homosexual acts between men had been ruled illegal, even if performed with full consent, in private, between men who had attained the age of majority.[61] But, in effect, his trials became a very public debate on the nature of the morality of art, the relations between art and life, the social obligations of artists and the nature of society's claims upon them. The really crucial battle came in the first trial when the Marquess of Queensberry, rather than Wilde, was in the dock. Outraged by Wilde's relationship with Lord Alfred Douglas, the Marquess's son, Queensberry had, after taking legal advice, sent an intentionally insulting card to Wilde, 'posing as a somdomite'. (Whether the misspelling reflects rage or illiteracy remains open to question.) Wilde, against his better judgement but urged to it by Douglas, had sued for libel.[62]

Wilde, as plaintiff, found himself cross-examined by the Marquess's counsel, the formidable Edward Carson, himself an Irishman and one of Wilde's fellow collegians from their student days at Trinity College, Dublin. The examination, surely one of the most remarkable of the many remarkable passages of arms witnessed at the Old Bailey, in effect put Wilde on trial for aesthetic, philosophical and moral ideas painfully elaborated over half a century by artists and writers on both sides of the Channel. Because Queensberry's solicitor had advised him to insert the all-important word 'posing' on his insulting card, the 'impressions' and 'appearances' which Wilde created, in his works and in his life, were deemed admissible evidence. The utterances of Dorian Gray and Lord Henry Wotton were as relevant as the utterances of Oscar Wilde.[63] Unacceptable sentiments expressed in university magazines written by undergraduates known to admire Wilde became evidence that he had corrupted the authors.

The trial transcript makes agonizing reading, not just because, with hindsight, we know that this was the first stage of a process that would end in a sentence which those who imposed it knew was, quite literally, the equivalent of a death sentence to a man of Wilde's class and background.[64] Equally agonizing is the growing realization that Wilde was being forced to conduct his case within the framework of an externally imposed moral universe whose authority and value he utterly repudiated. The key words – beauty, morality, art, goodness – which Carson hammers home time and again, menacingly, sneeringly, incredulously, mean utterly different things to the two men and, despite brilliant parries as dramatic as anything the London stage could offer, Wilde was slowly and relentlessly cornered in a setting where only Carson's reading of those words was permitted. Wilde, riding so high that year with two of his plays being simultaneously performed in the West End, found himself here a subordinate actor in a legal system as heavily ritualized and consciously theatrical as any classic drama. And, ultimately, the most important words in the script could not be of his writing.

Those last few sentences, with their heavy use of theatrical metaphor, may sound overstrained. Yet when we read of Wilde's fellow prisoner who, during the dreary daily hour of compulsory silent walking in the prison exercise yard, told him that he had been at every single one of Wilde's First Nights – *and* at all his trials, the point is reinforced.[65] At one level the meaning is simple enough: here is an ardent supporter of Wilde, probably himself homosexual, wanting the author to know that he shared Wilde's triumphs and his defeats. But, at another level, it acknowledges that both the plays and the trials were 'performances' and, equally important, both the appearances in court and in the theatre were 'trials'. Wilde, in the theatre, had 'tried' and frequently found guilty a society which he longed to conquer, yet basically despised. Wilde, in court, was tried and found guilty by that same society which had for fifteen years found him both fascinating and fearful. What made him fascinating is clear enough. What made him frightening was the fact that he seemed to embody some of the age's most pressing anxieties about itself. What were they?

The idea that arbitrarily determined measures of time, such as centuries or decades, have their own organic life is irrational but pervasive. Metaphorical figures of speech which refer to centuries as 'new', 'middle-aged' and, ultimately, 'dead', not only reflect thought: they also help to shape it, to establish self-fulfilling prophecies. The belief that the nineteenth century, and with it much of European civilization, was 'dying', rather than simply ending, was widespread among many thinkers and writers. And, since death is frequently the result of disease, with 'dying' came the concepts of 'decay', 'decadence', 'disintegration' and 'degeneration'. *Degeneration* was indeed the translated title of an influential book by Max Nordau (*Die Entartung*,

1893) which first appeared in England in 1895. This impassioned jeremiad painted a lurid picture of a century engulfed in a tidal wave of neurasthenia, indecency, female erotomania, diabolism and some ill-defined but much feared 'unnaturalness'. Constantly lurching between metaphor and supposedly empirical data, the book made a series of dangerous assumptions about the connections between 'degenerate' ideas and physical human decay. Degenerate, once solely an adjective, had become a noun: people could be 'degenerates'. This change (in which a grammatical shift accurately reflects a considerable movement in thought) is important for the period. Other adjectives – socialist, communist, anarchist, homosexual and criminal, for example – gained an additional resonance when used as nouns. 'Criminals' are those whose total human identity is deemed to consist of their criminality. It is a way of thinking tailored for those who seek scapegoats, who require always to be allowed to believe that danger can be kept out, 'over there', outside and beyond one's own self or circle. First identify accurately the enemy, then isolate, eject, eradicate it, and all will be well. The body politic is purged of its canker.

Nordau could call on an array of embryo and pseudo-sciences to support his case, chief amongst them the thoroughly dubious though often enticing study of Eugenics and the early efforts of psychologists, psychiatrists and criminologists. Symbolists, socialists, feminists, Ibsen – all Nordau's pet hates, objects of his deepest fears, were condemned with the full authority of 'Science'. Nordau reserved much of his fiercest condemnation for Wilde who was for him the archetype of the man who corrupts by virtue of his supremely powerful personality.[66] An inevitable reading, perhaps, in a century which hitherto had based a whole school of hero-worshipping historiography upon Great Men, reducing history to little more than the record of their lives and deeds. For Nordau and others like him Wilde represented a man who had betrayed his high calling of Artist as Teacher and had exchanged it for the baser role of Artist as Seducer. Moreover, in Nordau's eyes, Wilde had gathered about him acolytes and disciples whom he first corrupted, then sent out into the world to continue the work of corruption.

Degeneration offered one man's passionately expressed prejudices *and* a popularizing digest of currently fashionable theories. The combination was attractive to readers who shared his anxieties about a rapidly changing world and who wanted to know where to lay the blame. Fears of invasion, literal and metaphorical, were in the air. The British and French watched Germany's growing military power with apprehension. Germany herself, in the person of the Kaiser, conducted a tormented love–hate relationship with England, Victoria and the Prince of Wales. Britain's, and especially London's, rapidly growing immigrant population raised anxieties about cultural 'invasion', fears that native-born Britons would become aliens in their own land. Pockets

of virulent anti-Semitism appeared in the last decade of the century and
various efforts were made to introduce legislation to prevent or curb further
Jewish immigration (although not until 1905 and the passing of the Aliens Act
would Britain finally forfeit her right to be regarded as a haven for Europe's
exiles).[67] Fears were growing that 'good British stock' was being adulterated,
unless the adulteration came from American millionairesses marrying impoverished British peers when, on the whole, the threat somehow seemed less
terrifying. There was also the enemy within – growing agitation from
working-class activists demanding decent wages and conditions. Conflicts
between demonstrators and police had eventually culminated in the particularly ugly riot in Trafalgar Square in 1887, put down with considerable police
brutality. There was plenty to worry the anxious.

Underlying everything was a fear that 'Britishness' itself, that painstakingly
constructed but essentially fragile phenomenon, repository of so many myths
and hopes and dreams, was under attack. For much of the second half of the
century 'British' belonged with 'Empire' as inevitably as 'bread' belonged
with 'butter', or, at least, for those who could afford butter. Until the end of
the century large chunks of other people's land were still being grabbed for
Britain: Cecil Rhodes 'secured' a swathe of Africa and renamed it Rhodesia as
late as 1889. The imperial theme was sounded everywhere, from press, pulpit,
music hall songs, boys' papers, fine art canvases, novels such as Rider
Haggard's and school syllabuses. The young, of all classes and both genders,
were instructed, somewhat partially, in the Empire's history and fired with
enthusiasm for its service. Institutions as diverse as the public schools' Officer
Training Corps, the Boys' Brigade, the Boy Scouts and the Girls' Friendly
Society reinforced the message with meetings, uniforms, rallies, street
processions and oaths of allegiance, all often undertaken with the formal
support of organized religion.[68] Even – or perhaps particularly – the Salvation
Army used the language of Empire in its prayers, its hymnology, its hierarchy
and its intractably military model of the ceaseless war against sin.

Throughout the second half of the century, following hard on the heels of
the Imperial dream, came an intensifying emphasis upon the concepts of
British Manhood and British Womanhood. Each was an essential element in
the securing and consolidating of Empire. For Him, the initial task of
conquest, often military, sometimes mercantile, followed by an equally
important period of administrative consolidation. For Her, the no less
important task of wifely support and matronly rearing of the next generation
of empire makers and colonial administrators. Despite the odd female
maverick who joyously broke bounds – all those formidable Victorian lady
travellers, missionaries, artists and doctors, for instance, such as Mary
Kingsley, Isabella Bishop and Marianne North – the roles were in the main
rigidly polarized. That polarization both reflected and reinforced the period's

changing interpretation of the meaning of 'maleness' and 'femaleness', 'man' and 'woman'. In the early part of the century, the opposite of 'manliness' was deemed to be 'childishness' and it was a man's adult qualities rather than his masculine ones which made him 'manly'. By the end of the century 'manliness' is constantly defined in opposition to 'womanliness': to be 'a real man' is to avoid the appalling stigma of effeminacy rather than the shame of immaturity.[69] One of the things which made the aesthetes in general, and Wilde in particular, so very frightening was that they created confusion about both the value and the definition of the new, crude masculinity. And, because it was still so comparatively new, it was vulnerable. Social behaviour which was perfectly 'manly' when judged by the criteria of the old dispensation was suspect under the new. In the all-male societies of the public schools and Oxford and Cambridge, men earlier in the century had walked unselfconsciously arm in arm through public streets and in their letters to each other had given expression to passionate attachments in language which, by the 1890s, might have put them in the dock. Already, by 1850, some reviewers declared that *In Memoriam*, Tennyson's grief-stricken lament for Arthur Hallam, struck an unwholesome note, and Dean Farrar's *Eric, or Little by Little*, a moral tale with a public school setting (1858), was condemned for the unacceptable amount of 'osculation' indulged in by its schoolboy heroes. (Farrar, Head Boy of an evangelical school in the Isle of Man during the 1840s, had been an adolescent in sexually less anxious days.)[70]

Aesthetes and decadents were not, of course, the only people challenging or refuting essentialist concepts of masculinity and femininity. Organized feminism, growing rapidly during the second half of the century, both contributed to existing debates and gave rise to further ones. Two divergent strands of feminist thought developed, one committed to the concept of essential, eternal differences between men's and women's 'mission' in life, the other arguing that the bulk of perceived intellectual and psychological differences between the sexes were culturally induced and perpetuated. But, whether arguing for nature or nurture, feminism itself was a crucial element in the intellectual and social ferment aroused by considerations of gender. Tremendous improvements in girls' education and the growth of good secondary schools (not to mention the battle for women's university education, inaugurated by the founding of Girton College, Cambridge, in 1869) provided one of the period's many new readerships, and feminist authors paid particular attention to the younger female readers from whose ranks must come the next generation of feminists. And, since fiction is often more palatable and easily digested than polemic, the novel proved a particularly useful vehicle. It was used to create attractive portraits of professions newly available to women – medicine and journalism, for example. It could dramatize conflicts between rebellious young 'New Women' and their parents or brothers whilst also suggesting strategies by which family harmony and female emancipation might both eventually be attained. Even an ostensibly conservative author such as the best-selling Rosa Nouchette Carey, whose ambition had always been to try 'to write books which any mother can give a girl to read',[71] was capable, as early as 1884, of publishing a work which explicitly argued that suddenly impoverished young women need not forfeit their claim to the status of 'lady' merely because they must now earn their livings as dressmakers (*Not Like Other Girls*).

During the eighties and throughout the nineties female authors explored and exposed the injustices suffered by girls and women in the name of 'womanliness': daughters ill educated because their brothers' school and university fees were so high; married women, venereally infected by promis-cuous husbands and doomed to miscarry or produce sickly children, although the family doctor never explained why (his silence protected the husband's reputation, the wife's 'modesty'); seduced women carrying the full burden of society's rejection while the man went free; women condemned to squander health and strength in the production of the annual baby, either because of false *pudeur* surrounding the fact and use of contraception, or because of a punitive belief in the sinfulness of contraception *per se*. All these ills and others were discussed fictionally – and not always by women authors. Thomas Hardy caused scandal in 1891 when he subtitled *Tess of the d'Urbervilles* as '*a pure woman faithfully presented*'. George Gissing returned again and again to analyses of the changing position of women, in novels which included *The Emancipated* (1890), *The Odd Women* (1893), *In the Year of Jubilee* (1894) and *The Whirlpool* (1897). George Moore produced, in 1894, the very unexpected *Esther Waters* which told of a young woman's struggle to keep her illegitimate child. It shocked for many reasons, including its account of a lying-in ward. Dramatists, too, amongst them Pinero (*The Second Mrs. Tanqueray*, 1893), Wilde (*A Woman of No Importance*, 1894) and Shaw (*Mrs. Warren's Profession*, 1898), explored the sexual double standard by means of plays centred upon women 'with a past'. Most shattering of all was the impact of a foreign dramatist whose works Edmund Gosse had been urging upon English readers since the early seventies: Ibsen's treatment of cruelty within marriage and eventual revolt against it (*A Doll's House*), of venereal disease (*Ghosts*), and of the lethal destructiveness of ill-matched marriages (*Hedda Gabler*) all received their first English perfor-mances between 1889 and 1893. Critical response ranged from awed acclaim to hysterical denunciation. 'Ibsenite' joined aesthete and decadent as a term of abuse. It was an insult which many wore proudly, including Wilde who awarded the highest praise he knew to *Hedda Gabler*: 'I felt pity and terror, as though the play had been Greek.'[72] Later, in prison, he would ask Robert Ross to send him copies of *Little Eyolf* and *John Gabriel Borkman*.[73]

There were those who argued that this upsurge of male interest in female emancipation had less to do with altruism and more to do with commercialism or self-interest. Ibsen had merely climbed on a band wagon; Gissing's own misogyny made him obsessively attentive to what The Enemy was doing; H. G. Wells and Grant Allen, author of a tremendously successful 1895 novel about the double standard, *The Woman Who Did*, were both backing emancipation because they thought liberated women would offer increased sexual opportunities for heterosexual men. So said the cynics.

Certainly 'The New Woman' was a commercially sound proposition for publishers and authors during the nineties. As was Aestheticism, Decadence and the *fin de siècle* itself. Enemies might see British Civilization threatened by the joint assault of Decadents and Feminists: better informed observers sometimes saw little more than an enormous publishers' and publicists' jamboree. Foes, such as Clement Scott, theatre critic for *The Daily Telegraph*, and friends, such as Maurice Baring, novelist and *Yellow Book* contributor, could at least see eye to eye on *that*. Aestheticism and Wilde, claimed Scott in 1891, had triumphed 'merely through the misguided efforts of [Wilde's] journalistic friends. It would all have died out [sic] a natural death, had it been consistently snubbed instead of persistently puffed.'[74] Maurice Baring, writing thirty years after the end of the century, maintained that the recent spate of critical and autobiographical writing recalling the nineties presented a world unrecognizable to him: 'they seem to me to weave a baseless legend and to create a fantastic world of their own creations'. For Baring, 'The 'nineties were, from the point of view of art and literature, much like any other period', and the main difference between *The Yellow Book* and any other contemporary periodical 'was chiefly in the colour of the cover'. 'There are', maintains Baring, 'only a certain number of writers available in London', and most of them will go where work is offered.'[75]

At first sight Baring's judgements seem startling and more than a trifle perverse. So many people, then and now, seem so convinced that the writers and works of 'the yellow Nineties' had their own inalienable quality and, furthermore, that it was one at odds with the day's mainstream. If we take one of the period's most 'characteristic' volumes – *Verses* (1896), by Ernest Dowson, he who was faithful to Cynara in his fashion[76] – the titles alone suggest much of that quality: villanelles, reflecting the emphasis upon revived poetic forms; poems about madness, renunciation, sexual frustration, guilt, remorse and despair; a concern with the conflict between flesh and spirit, often expressed as a conflict between 'Pagan' (usually Greek) and Christian values; heavy use of classical Latin titles and verse forms, with an occasional hint of mediaeval Latin, cherished for its entrancing mixture of linguistic 'decadence' and emotional freshness; poems in which present-day women and mediaeval heroines merge their identities; versions of Verlaine; titles chosen in conscious echo of Baudelaire; an emphasis upon transitional times – twilight, autumn, the death of desire, dying; an ambivalence towards the language of the Christian mysteries, used sometimes in apparent and self-conscious blasphemy, used sometimes with an anxious near-belief; the not unpleasurable terror of souls in search of punishment; and, brooding over all, a sense of loss.

Themes and motives such as those appear time and again in the work of the English decadents. All in all a heady but 'unwholesome' brew, in the eyes of their adversaries. Some, such as W. E. Henley, the often repellent, frequently inspired editor of *The National Observer*, set themselves up as conscious Opposition. Henley led a 'counter-decadence', and cast himself as the Commanding Officer of a spiritual army made up of his much younger contributors (who included Kipling, Yeats, H. G. Wells, Joseph Conrad, J. M. Barrie and Kenneth Grahame). Somewhat deflatingly Beerbohm dubbed them 'the Henley Regatta'.[77]

Yet, on closer examination, much of Baring's claim is justified. There was a constant overlap between Decadents and Counter-decadents. Not only were the members of these opposing armies frequently found writing in 'enemy' publications. They also shared common preoccupations and concerns which informed their work. The myths which each side promulgated about themselves and each other helped to conceal the connections. On the whole, Decadents worked hard to make themselves Exotic; Counter-decadents proclaimed their daunting Normality. Arthur Symons, for example, created a legendary Dowson who was, in Symons's account, a hopeless drug addict,[78] and in his own poems and recollections carefully presented himself as a rather tiresomely Great Lover. Nevertheless, the shadow of the Welsh Nonconformist chapels of his childhood hangs heavily over all.[79] Henley, on the other hand, made a full-time job of his blustering masculinity and took particular pleasure in his collaboration with John Farmer, chief editor of a monumental dictionary, *Slang and Its Analogues* (1890).[80] Henley himself contributed a large number of the many hundreds of synonyms for the female genitals.[81] Henley's aggressive normality was, however, far from unassailable. He came to hate Wilde, persecuting him privately and editorially, yet once admitted to the young W. B. Yeats, in language heavy with the chivalric echoes of Knight and Squire, 'I told my lads to attack him and yet we might have fought under his banner.'[82] His ambivalence would have come as no surprise to many homosexual men of the period from whom the saga of Henley's obsessively ardent and fiercely destroyed friendship with Robert Louis Stevenson might well have drawn a weary smile of recognition.[83]

Perhaps it is *The Yellow Book* itself which makes clearest the unreal nature of the supposed pitched battle between Decadents and The Rest. *The Yellow*

Book which has gone down in popular literary history as 'Wilde's magazine' and the flagship of *fin-de-siècle* revolt was in fact neither. The property of John Lane, the publisher, and founder of The Bodley Head (or 'The Sodley Bed' as *Punch* preferred to call it), the new quarterly was, like all Lane's enterprises, shrewdly commercial. It was launched in 1894, when most of the truly innovative hard work and hard thinking about literary aesthetics had already been done by a variety of little magazines, during the late eighties and early nineties.[84] *The Yellow Book* launched itself into comparatively safe waters. Wilde himself was carefully excluded, largely at the insistence of the new magazine's art editor, Aubrey Beardsley, who had accepted the commission to illustrate Wilde's play, *Salomé*, but had incorporated no fewer than four malevolent caricatures of the author into the finished work.[85]

The Yellow Book's task was to be acceptably 'daring', a compromise already loudly hinted at in the magazine's prospectus, which stated the editor's intention: to 'seek always to preserve a delicate, decorous and reticent mien and conduct'. Delicacy, decorum and reticence: not the qualities most readily associated with scarlet sins and rapturous vice. The American, Henry Harland, was appointed editor. No stranger to the arts of self-promotion, he had begun his writing career as a novelist named Sidney Luska, supposedly an impoverished East Side Jewish immigrant, although Harland's family were gentiles settled outside New York. In the 1880s, however, Jewish immigrants made better copy than East Coast gentiles. For Harland, as for so many Americans of the day, London represented a new start. Harland and Beardsley enlisted Gosse's support for a magazine which would publish 'the oldest school and the newest side by side, with no hall-mark except that of excellence and no prejudice against anything but dullness and incapacity'. Some of the older school – Henry James, for instance – were happy to contribute. He offered a short story, 'The Death of the Lion', which underlined the dangers to a creative artist of precisely that bustling, commercial marketing of literature which was John Lane's chief characteristic. Pater expressed his gratification at being invited to contribute – and declined. The Academician, Sir Frederick Leighton, agreed and panicked later.

To read now *The Yellow Book* makes clear the gap between reputation and reality. Certainly amongst the contributors are many whom we should expect to find in any roll-call of Decadents or Aesthetes: Symons, Beerbohm, Dowson, Ella D'Arcy, Richard le Gallienne and Olive Custance (later to be the wife of Lord Alfred Douglas), amongst the writers: Beardsley, Charles Conder, Walter Crane amongst the artists. But there are also those who seem uneasy guests at any decadent gathering. Gissing, the chronicler of *The Nether World* and *New Grub Street*, contributed a short story, 'The Foolish Virgin'. Henry Nevinson, a deeply committed socialist and a much travelled war correspondent, offered poetry, as did Richard Garnett, a man of Gosse's generation and a much respected Keeper at the British Museum. (Married to Constance Garnett, the most influential of all English translators of the great Russian novelists, he and she lived for a time next door to William Rossetti, D. G.'s brother. William's daughters – Olivia, Helen and Mary – were heavily involved in publishing the anarchist paper, *The Torch*, and through them the Garnetts came to know many anarchist exiles.)[86] John Buchan, with *The Thirty-nine Steps* and *Greenmantle* still some twenty years ahead of him, published one of his earliest pieces, 'A Journey of Little Profit'. John Davidson, best known for poems and ballads in working-class or clerkly idiom such as 'Thirty Bob A Week', contributed a 'Fleet Street Eclogue'. And, most ironical of all, perhaps, Kenneth Grahame, very much one of the Henley Regatta, first published in *The Yellow Book* those vignettes of childhood which would eventually become a best-selling volume, *The Golden Age* (1895).

This promiscuous mingling of Decadents and Counter-decadents was mirrored by a shared concern for particular themes and issues. Where better to start than with the city in which so many of them lived and worked?

Throughout the century London had been becoming more ugly, noisy, dirty, crowded and big. Greatest poverty and wealth lay cheek by jowl. Vast 'clearances' of land were effected – for new roads, railways and main sewers – with no provision for the displaced populations who added their number to already overcrowded slums. London was becoming an increasingly brutal city. Writers and artists came to terms with it in different ways. Dickens had made it into a living creature whose terrors alternated with kindliness. London, indeed, became the chief 'character' in much nineteenth-century fiction. The city could be tamed by being anatomized, as the outstanding journalist, George Augustus Sala, did in *Twice Round the Clock: or The Hours of Day and Night in London* (1859),[87] or as Mayhew did in *London Labour and the London Poor* (1862). It could be antiquarianized, rendered charming, quaint and safe, by histories of the many villages which together made up London's corporate being. It could be exposed by savage gazetteers, both topographical and moral, such as James Greenwood's *The Seven Curses of London* (1869)[88] or Andrew Mearns's *The Bitter Cry of Outcast London* (1883). Its slums and poor could be regarded as a new land, desperately in need of benign conquest and colonization. The Salvation Army leader, William Booth, called his survey *In Darkest England and the Way Out* (1890), choosing a title which consciously echoed a phrase ever on the lips of missionaries, 'Darkest Africa'. Partly he wanted to point the moral that 'charity begins at home', partly he wanted to mock smug assumptions about civilized London and primitive Africa, but there was also a strong sense prevailing at the time that The Poor did indeed constitute Another Country, alien, dangerous and, therefore, to certain temperaments deeply exciting as well as deplorable.

In the last two decades of the century London's poor were to be found throughout fiction and poetry.[89] Only a tiny handful was written by genuinely working-class authors: Arthur Morrison, for example, the title of whose *Tales of Mean Streets* (1894) added a new phrase to the language and whose novel, *A Child of the Jago* (1896), blended fact and fiction in its account of Shoreditch's worst slum. Most of the work was produced by middle-class writers: often well meaning but unintentionally insulting, sometimes overtly hostile (F. Anstey's *Voces Populi*, 1890 and 1892, for instance, which first appeared in *Punch*). Others wrote with a vehement outrage informed by personal observation: the very young Somerset Maugham, when a medical student in South London, wrote his first novel, *Liza of Lambeth* (1897). Henley's poems, *London Voluntaries* (1892), were hailed by Arthur Symons as 'characteristically modern' and what made them so was their 'capacity for dealing with London'.[90]

For the self-proclaimedly world-weary and exhausted Decadents, it was the sheer vitality and colourfulness of working-class public life which drew them obsessively: to music halls (which Sickert painted and Beerbohm and Symons extolled); to People's Theatres and pubs; and afterwards, sometimes, to the rooms of prostitutes. The woes and raptures of 'bought love' are a staple of *fin-de-siècle* poetry. Arthur Symons's 'Stella Maris' caused anger when it appeared in the first number of *The Yellow Book* because it hymned 'the chance romances of the street, / The Juliet of a night'.[91] Prostitution was one of late nineteenth-century England's busiest professions – but no one was supposed to say so in poetry. And gentlemen were its most assiduous patrons, but no one was supposed to say that, either. The facts revealed at Wilde's trials shocked for two reasons. One was the gender of the male prostitutes; but the other was the exposure of the part played by prostitution itself in the life of a cultivated, celebrated gentleman. Wilde's use of prostitutes linked him with hundreds of thousands of men of his class, although those who chose female prostitutes would never find themselves in the dock at the Old Bailey for it. At one level, Wilde's homosexuality made him mercifully separate from his peers: at another, his sexual life was, in essence, theirs. It was not different enough. Hence, in part, their fury. Theirs was indeed, as Wilde had said elsewhere, 'the rage of Caliban seeing his own face in the glass'.[92]

Prostitution was only one subject which attracted hypocrisy and dissimulation. So many people had so much to conceal: social or racial origins; uncertain finances; illegitimate children; marital infidelities; fear of hereditary madness; sexual desires deemed essentially unacceptable, for instance. This was a period of great social mobility and, in England at any rate, that often entails the necessity of leaving much of one's embarrassing past behind, and of lying about the rest. Small wonder that masks become so important in the period's literature. In Beerbohm's *The Happy Hypocrite* (1897) the mask becomes the reality (a point which Symons echoed when he wrote that Pater wore a 'whole outer mask, in short, worn for protection and out of courtesy, yet moulded upon the inner truth of nature like a mask moulded upon the features which it covers'.[93] Concealment, detection, disclosure: those elements link works as diverse as R. L. Stevenson's *Dr. Jekyll and Mr. Hyde* (1886), Ibsen's *Ghosts* (first translated into English in 1885), Wilde's *The Importance of Being Earnest* (1895) and James's *The Turn of the Screw* (1898). No wonder, either, that the detective story which is primarily concerned with 'unmasking' should come to pre-eminence in this period, helped by the enormous success of Conan Doyle's creation, Sherlock Holmes, a character as morally ambiguous and subversive as any Decadent. Even the ghost story, which reached a pinnacle of popularity and achievement during the last decades of the century, shares the qualities of uncovering, unveiling. 'Beyond the veil' was indeed the stock phrase for the world beyond death. The second half of the century was increasingly preoccupied with the paranormal and supernatural. Spiritualism, yet another American import, aroused fierce passions. It had been the biggest single source of discord in the Barrett–Browning marriage: she believed, he did not, and his poem, 'Mr Sludge the Medium', is his searing denunciation of fraud perpetrated at the expense of the emotionally vulnerable. Yet many of the century's finest and most energetic minds were to devote themselves to investigation of the relations between seen and unseen worlds. The Society for Psychical Research (founded in 1882) amassed a dedicated band of investigators drawn from barristers, clergymen, medical doctors and scientists, as well as writers, artists and poets.[94] Ghost hunting was not just a drawing room sport. Spiritualism also became incorporated into certain elements of the labour movement.[95] Scientific advances were enlisted in both the perpetration and exposure of frauds. Photography found yet another use in the creation of 'spirit photographs' which purported to record ghosts and fairies, and Conan Doyle jeopardized a fortune and a reputation in his ceaseless proselytizing for the essential truth of spiritualism (and fairies). Wilde expressed his own interest, in stories such as 'The Canterville Ghost' and 'Lord Arthur Savile's Crime'. He also asked Edward Heron-Allen to cast his newborn son's horoscope and had his palm read by Mrs Robinson, a well-known and well-reputed clairvoyant.[96]

Urban slums and vice: séances and apparitions in darkened rooms. How much healthier, it might seem, to turn instead to rural life. Dedicated socialists attempted to turn the pastoral dream into reality by their creation of rural communities freed from the disease and poverty of great cities.[97] In

Yorkshire Edward Carpenter, whose book-length poem, *Towards Democracy* (1883), was to inspire so many generations of socialists, practised his own version of the Simple Life. Living openly as a homosexual, he offered hospitality to a tremendous range of visitors: local working people, visiting radical politicians, labour activists, lobbyists for sexual law reform, pacifists, writers and poets. Most of them shared, to differing degrees, his vision of a world shaped by socialism and feminism, and worked for a future in which homosexual emotions and relationships would be acknowledged and accepted. C. R. Ashbee, architect, critic, printer, designer, and, under Carpenter's influence, an increasingly open homosexual apologist, planned throughout the nineties a township of skilled artisans who would make beautiful things in beautiful surroundings. In 1902 plans materialized when Ashbee's Guild of Handicrafts, founded in Whitechapel in 1888, moved wholesale to the Cotswolds town of Chipping Campden.[98]

Yet even in the country the prevailing sense was one of loss and danger. Long before the Great War came, English country life was changing out of all recognition. Increasing mechanization, the gradual disappearance of ancient crafts, the drift to the towns, changing patterns in land ownership, the falling value of agricultural land itself: all these destabilized a way of life that had changed little over the previous three centuries. Although many fine writers – Richard Jeffries, Thomas Hardy, the young Edward Thomas, W. H. Hudson – devoted themselves almost exclusively to rural life, their work has often the hallmark of conservationism. The same is true of many of the paintings and water-colours produced during the period. 'The Country' is so popular a theme because it is already endangered. Folklorists were busy collecting traditional tales. Men such as Cecil Sharp and the young Vaughan Williams raced against time to record folk songs. Poets such as William Barnes of the West Country and T. E. Brown had, a little earlier, written defiantly in dialect and Manx, determined to extend the life of dying language. Lexicologists noted sadly that their predecessors at the beginning of the century had recorded words and syntax now no longer known. Gentleman-photographers, such as Sir Benjamin Stone, quite consciously used their cameras to record festivals, costumes, customs, crafts and rituals which they knew would soon be extinct.[99]

Theoretically Decadents and Nature had nothing to say to each other, were indeed at war. In fact it wasn't quite as simple as that. For many of the Decadents the problem was that 'Nature' had itself become perverted, unnaturally tamed and restricted so that it no longer represented truthfully the full range of its – and humanity's – needs and possibilities. Where, for example, was the virtue of a countryside which lacked fauns and satyrs, which seemed to have forgotten Pan? With tremendous thoroughness, the Decadents set about repopulating the English landscape. As did the Counter-decadents. From Wilde's cry, in 1881, to the 'goat-foot God of Arcady'[100] through to Kenneth Grahame's *Wind in the Willows* (1908) and E. M. Forster's 'The Story of a Panic' (1911), Pan and his entourage dominate the rural scene. (Henley even managed to import him into the heart of London and transformed him into the life-force of the urban masses, but that was unusual.)[101] Critics, then and since, have been extremely sniffy about this literary outbreak of Panic-ry. They have tended to dismiss it as a poetical affectation which got out of hand, a useful cliché for minor versifiers. But the goat-god was more than that. Through him writers expressed very different longings, loss and resistance. At the most basic level Pan represented part of an eternal human struggle between the animal and the divine – or, more accurately, an eternal Christian struggle. The pagans of ancient Greece, it seemed, managed these things better.

Arcady, Pan, Socrates who worshipped him,[102] and Plato who 'created' Socrates through his fictional use of him in those early Dialogues which were so insistent that the best teaching happens when male teacher and male pupil are more than a little in love with each other: for that very considerable number of late nineteenth-century authors who were both homosexual and classically educated, all those elements fused. Together they formed part of a precious vision in which male homosexual desire is at one with its setting rather than outlawed from it. Arcady became a world in the mind, a place where male beauty is acknowledged and desire is permitted. When Wilde fills his letters with descriptions of young men – in London, Paris, Italy, Algiers – who are 'fauns', 'shepherds [who] fluted on reeds for us',[103] he is not simply indulging in High Camp. He is also genuinely lauding a pre-Christian Mediterranean culture and, by implication, lamenting nineteenth-century England's frightened denial of beauty and the body's pleasures.

In an anti-pagan country, denying Pan and following him may prove equally dangerous. So, for instance, in *The Garden God*, Forrest Reid's remarkable novel of a boyhood lived almost entirely through ancient Greek literature and the dreams it fosters, pagan values bring its hero his moments of intensest self-knowledge, and destruction.[104] Too much Pan is dangerous. But too little can be fatal, as Mr. Merivale discovered in E. F. Benson's *The Angel of Pain* (1906). For too long Mr. Merivale had 'turned his head from . . . the grim side of Nature, of the country and death . . . which he called Pan'. Pan's punishment is to trample him to death.[105]

The Decadents, in fact, had every reason to be deeply interested in Nature since they were themselves so often adjudged 'unnatural'. For many of the homosexuals amongst them the paradox of their unnatural natures was a source of constant tension. Some, such as Bosie Douglas, oscillated between defiant display and grovelling abasement. Others, such as R. H. Benson and

John Gray (not the original of Dorian Gray, although everyone kept insisting he was), became Roman Catholic priests and took vows of chastity. Corvo tried to but never quite made it. A few, such as Robbie Ross, Reggie Turner (Wilde's 'dear little Jew' who nursed Wilde in his last illness) and E. F. Benson, just got on with it. Wilde himself, for most of his life, took society's judgement and turned it back upon the judges. 'Invert' was then the liberals' name for homosexuals. The term expressed the belief that homosexuals were those in whom, by some freak (of Nature, indeed), body and soul had been mismatched: homosexual men had female souls in male bodies, homosexual women had male souls in female bodies. They were 'inverted'. Wilde the Invert used a different form of inversion with which to make his most telling utterances: the paradox, in Wilde's hands a deadly weapon, is itself as 'inverted' as its user. Its point and its value lie in its power to enforce a realignment, sometimes a complete reversal, of the things we complacently think we know. It is, essentially, the utterance of one who does not see the world as the world sees itself. By the same token, it is also the utterance of one who does not see himself as the world sees him. Richard Aldington, in an essay which is, in the main, unexpectedly sympathetic to Wilde, accused him of 'a curious lack of judgement almost approximating a failure to correlate the actual world with his own private world of wish and fantasy'.[106] It is a charge many others have levelled against Wilde. But in fact much of Wilde's work is rooted in the determination to effect an alignment between the two, and he relies on his dazzling powers − of wit, charm, intelligence and persuasion − to force consent even from an initially unwilling audience.

For Wilde is essentially a performer − not 'merely' a performer: there is nothing mere about performance. Wilde revelled in the challenge of an audience to be wooed, exulted in the triumph of an audience won. (Even from the dock of the Old Bailey he drew from the packed courtroom loud applause, swiftly suppressed, for a rhapsodic speech defending love between older and younger men.) In the days before his downfall enemies might declare that his was the triumph of Personality over Principle. But it would be truer to say that he consciously enlisted the very considerable power of his personality in the struggle to induce others to question or abandon those principles he believed to be ill founded. For, as Frith saw and Nordau failed to see, Wilde was also a teacher, and many of the finest teachers are performers too.

Performers and teachers who attempt innovation, however, are engaged in a constant balancing act. They must offer a challenge big enough to be exciting, small enough to be assimilated. Overstep the mark and disaster follows. As Socrates discovered in fifth-century Athens, Teacher and Corrupter may prove to be synonymous terms if the mood of the audience changes. Paradoxically, it was Wilde's supreme good fortune and great ill luck that his teaching coincided with a period of enormous moral and intellectual upheaval expressed largely in terms of a vehement debate about the nature of personality itself. It was a debate which called into question many of the key terms and concepts fundamental to discussions of art and morality. During the second half of the nineteenth century, all over Europe, practitioners of newly developing disciplines and sciences were busily codifying humanity: Charcot in France; Krafft-Ebing in Germany; Lombroso in Italy; Tarnowsky (a woman) in Russia; Havelock Ellis in England; and even, though very few in London knew much about him yet, Freud in Vienna. They and many others were intent on identifying, describing, classifying and explaining the many variations in human physiology, psychology and sexuality.

Ostensibly their purpose was benign: arguably their impact has been unfortunate. Underlying this vast examination of human diversity was a strong belief in a human norm against which 'variations' were to be judged and found wanting. The 'variant' rapidly became the 'deviant' or 'pervert', in need of punishment, or treatment, or eradication. Forms of human behaviour hitherto deemed normal were now declared pathological. The period's frenzied outcry against masturbation and the many volumes of dangerously ill-informed rubbish on the topic, unleashed by medical science (not to mention various 'cures', including painful mechanical restraints), constitute perhaps the most notorious example. But 'the masturbator' (now, apparently, an adequate description of a whole human being) was only one in a gallery of newly categorized types. And the categorizations frequently tell us more about the categorizers' anxieties than they do about the categorized. 'Nymphomania', for example, came to describe a woman whose active sexuality disturbed too many of the period's beliefs: that 'nice' women do not feel spontaneous desire; that strong sexual emotion in women indicates animality, criminality and incipient or actual madness. The underlying fear – that heterosexual women's desire will be greater than men can satisfy – is transparent and finds both literary and artistic expression throughout Europe in many depictions of cruel, insatiable, draining devil-women.[107] The 'cure' was often brutal – surgical removal of the ovaries, in 'the best interests' of the woman – and her husband. Beneath this general rage for categorization was a determination to control, to 'manage' human beings by ordering them and ranking them, by creating hierarchies beginning with the most 'advanced' and ending with the 'least evolved'. Amongst its bitterest fruits would be the works of Alfred Rosenberg and the development of South African apartheid. For the moment all was justified in the name of 'social hygiene' and 'improving the Race'.

Three categories in particular – and the connections between them – exercised the new psychologists: The Criminal; The Genius; and The Invert. Time and again observers noted that inverts frequently possessed abilities considerably above the average and that geniuses and criminals were often curiously alike in temperament. Nowhere, they agreed, was this more clearly demonstrated than in the overwheening vanity common to both artists and convicts. In *The Criminal* (1890), Havelock Ellis spelled it out:

The vanity of criminals is at once an intellectual and an emotional fact. It witnesses at once to their false estimate of life and of themselves, and to their egotistic delight in admiration. They share this character with a large proportion of artists and literary men, though, as Lombroso remarks, they decidedly excel them in this respect. The vanity of the artist and literary man marks the abnormal elements, the tendency in them to degeneration. It reveals in them the weak point of a mental organization, which at other points is highly developed. Vanity may exist in the well-developed ordinary man, but it is unobtrusive; in its extreme form it marks the abnormal man, the man of unbalanced mental organisation, artist or criminal.[108]

Where many social commentators saw vanity as the link between criminals and artists, others might see resistance and rebellion. Certainly aesthetes and decadents believed themselves to be embattled against a stifling philistine consensus, whilst their enemies often attacked them in language more appropriate to civil war than literary exchange. In effect two concepts of the artist were in conflict. One, the older, espoused by the Counter-decadents, assumes that artists, however critical of society, nevertheless belong to it and are rooted in it. The other, newer, more disturbing vision, sees artists as essentially alienated from a society which is actively hostile to the values which artists represent and seek to further. In this vision criminals and artists are indeed linked as elements which undermine an anyway always precarious social stability. Rightly precarious, some such as Wilde would argue, because it is rooted in cruelty, stupidity, dishonesty and injustice, much of which he attempted to expose in his work. But few of the day's budding psychologists, criminologists and social anthropologists could distance themselves sufficiently from society to see the virtue of that view. One who could was Edward Carpenter, whose provocatively entitled essay, 'Civilisation – Its Cause and Cure' (1889), rejoiced in the fact that although 'Civilisation is now practically continuous over the globe, now also for the first time can we descry forming in continuous line *within its very structure* the forces which are destined to destroy it and to bring about the new order.'[109]

For Carpenter, as for so many in the period, the 'new order' was socialism, a system as fiercely feared and hated by its enemies as it was revered by its followers. Here too 'personality' (in the guise of 'individualism') was a key issue. Those who opposed socialism saw it as the end of individual freedom, the beginning of a dreary world of imposed uniformity. Those who welcomed it believed it offered the only chance of individuality in a world already hideously unfree. Wilde's discussion of the issues resulted in one of his finest

works, *The Soul of Man under Socialism* (1891), an essay still underestimated
in England, properly appreciated in Europe. Anti-Tsarist revolutionaries and
radicals in Russia even managed to print and circulate copies secretly:[110] (a
fact pleasing to a man whose very first play, *Vera: or The Nihilists*, 1880, had
foreseen the assassination in 1881 of Alexander II). To many people the idea
that Wilde – the hedonist, the aesthete, the flaunting self-publicist – should
espouse socialism may seem bizarre. In fact, this vigorous, sweeping essay –
which takes in Greek city states, English Romantic poets, rival economic
theories, Christ as Perfect Personality, the function of art, the nature of
beauty, the power of the Press, the formation of Public Opinion, the
criminality of much Justice, the growth of despotisms, the evils of slavery, and
the dangers of Sympathy divorced from Action – coheres by virtue of Wilde's
insistence that socialism, 'whether it wills it or not', cannot achieve its aims
until individual men and women achieve harmony with themselves and their
environment.[111]

The word 'personality' is central to the essay just as the fact of personality
was central to Wilde's understanding of the world. For him the term conveyed
full 'personhood', the manifestation of each human being's true self, undis-
torted by baneful influences, unshackled by false restrictions. But the very
concept of a 'true self' presents endless difficulties, depending as it does on the
assumption of an unchanging, essential selfhood. All very well for Henley to
declaim vaingloriously

> I am the master of my fate:
> I am the captain of my soul,[112]

but Materialism had questioned the soul's existence and various forms of
Determinism maintained that humanity's fate lay with biology, chemistry,
Progress or Evolution. Ironically, in this period, so pre-eminently the Age of
Personality, the self, on which personality depends, was under concerted
attack: not least from those sexologists to whom Wilde – Genius, Invert and,
eventually, Criminal – might have looked for help. In fact, the 'liberal' theory
of congenital inversion was to prove a mixed blessing. Paradoxically it
brought both freedom and constraint. To be dubbed a 'congenital invert'
freed one from the stigma of wilfully chosen perversion; but it also imposed
upon the invert a blueprint of psychological and physiological attributes
which, the sexologists declared, identified the 'truly' inverted. The moral
status of sexual actions depended on the 'real' sexuality of the actor. Actions
'natural' to the invert remained 'perverted' if performed by one who was
'really' heterosexual. Hence the importance of the concept of corruption;
'real' heterosexuals must be protected from the persuasions of 'real' homosexuals, whose actions were innocent only for as long as they were practised
with each other. To argue openly for the essential bisexuality of *all* human

beings was not yet possible and some homosexual apologists anyway rejected the idea. The concept of congenital inversion, with all its dangers, nevertheless seemed an advance on anything that had gone before.

It was a concept made familiar to lay readers in various forms: through works by Edward Carpenter such as *Homogenic Love and Its Place in a Free Society* (1894), and *Love's Coming of Age* (1896); and, for a tiny handful of readers, through John Addington Symonds's privately printed *A Problem in Modern Ethics* (1891). (The major work in which Symonds collaborated with Havelock Ellis, *Sexual Inversion*, was withdrawn in 1897, for fear of legal proceedings.) Even without the carefully annotated support of sexologists, prototypes of the idea of congenital inversion already had a long history, stretching back at least as far as the speech made by Aristophanes in Plato's *Symposium*. Lettered homosexuals now explored earlier ages carefully, uncovering their own tradition and creating their own literary canon, made up of works and authors in whom they recognized needs and desires similar to their own. Edward Carpenter collected such sources for decades and finally published *Ioläus: An Anthology of Friendship* (1902). Often the works were already familiar to the reasonably well read: but their firmly emphasized context – homoerotic love – was for many people new and shocking. To be forced to confront, for instance, Bacon's homosexuality or, more horrifyingly, Shakespeare's, caused discomfort which rapidly became anger. (In 1894 the publisher, Elkin Mathews, refused 'at any price' to publish *A Portrait of Mr. W. H.*, Wilde's essay, cast in the form of a quasi-Socratic dialogue, on Shakespeare's sonnets.)[113]

Heterosexual anger stemmed in part from the fear experienced whenever the comfortably familiar is suddenly rendered unrecognizable. But there was also the anger of dispossession, outrage that something which was 'theirs' should be claimed by others (especially when that 'something', Shakespeare, had during the course of the century become the focus of new nationalistic emotions: to 'attack' the National Poet was to attack the nation). Most important of all, perhaps, was the anxiety caused by the suggestion that a body of work so ardently cherished by so many might be the product of emotions and experiences which, in the present, were at the very least problematic and, at the worst, criminal. Did the capacity to admire works rooted in 'abnormal' emotions indicate abnormality in the admirer? Here was yet another troubling question about the relations between art, morality and the self.

Shakespeare was not the only author destabilized in that way. Sometimes it was a simple matter of insisting upon what everyone knew but preferred to forget – as with Michelangelo and Marlowe. Sometimes it was a matter of emphasizing what others preferred to push to one side – as with Winckelmann, Goethe, Byron, Da Vinci and Fitzgerald. And sometimes it was a matter of pointing out that the supposedly unassailable heterosexuality of an author should not blind readers to the fact that same-sex friendships in the lives and works of authors could assume a passion and significance supposedly found only in marriage – as with Montaigne and Tennyson. During the last quarter of the century many homosexual men of letters produced texts, editions, translations and studies of earlier authors whom they implicitly claimed for their own alternative canon: Pater's essay on Winckelmann, for example, in *The Renaissance*; John Addington Symonds's edition and translation of Michelangelo's sonnets, and his studies of Sappho, Whitman and various Renaissance figures. There were volumes in the English Men of Letters series, notably Edmund Gosse's on Sir Thomas Browne and Thomas Gray, A. C. Benson's on Pater and Edward Fitzgerald. Typifying the ambiguities of the period, this subversive work of cultural reclassification was carried out publicly by prominent members of the literary establishment.

That they could do so was possible partly because so much of late nineteenth-century English society depended upon a form of moral equivocation which consisted of never letting the right eye know what the left eye was seeing. So, for example, the study of ancient Greece enjoyed an unrivalled pre-eminence in both public school and university syllabuses, although the fact that it was a predominantly paederastic culture was largely ignored or denied. The English had become adepts in appropriating the 'acceptable' parts of earlier ages and leaving the rest. They co-opted, for example, the Glory that was Greece and the Grandeur that was Rome, then cast Britain in the role of the third, but greatest, in a trio of great civilizations. Similarly their versions of mediaeval chivalry and the Renaissance censored those elements, including homosexuality, which disturbed them. Pater, Symonds, Gosse and Benson could exploit that genius for equivocation, could make a space in which to say the 'unspeakable'. Their task was also made easier by the fact that educated English society as a whole was engaged in a new exploration of the relations between gender, love, desire and sexuality: feminism, New Women, Ibsen, Shaw, the development of psychiatry were all aspects of that.

For many it was a deeply disturbing inquiry and there were those who felt that large sections of English literary life had been shanghaied by a homosexual press-gang. As with most conspiracy theories, there was more than a grain of truth in that, although it might have been more courteously expressed. Certainly it is true that the growing self-confidence – and a strong sense of resistance – felt by many homosexual writers and artists during the last quarter of the century fired their determination to force a recognition from the majority that many of the works most valued in mainstream culture were the products of a now outlawed minority. And, true to the character of the time, such uneasy knowledge could, to a surprising degree, be accommodated because of that curious capacity to see without acknowledging what has been seen: which is what the rest of the world means by 'British hypocrisy'.

Wilde's trials put an end to that happy equivocation. That is the main reason why they aroused such hysteria, hatred and fear. Half-articulated desires, dimly perceived connections, possibilities as frightening as they were fascinating, were suddenly and ruthlessly exposed. Moreover, many widespread social fears now seemed vindicated.

The comforting barriers between Fiction and Life were broken down, as Wilde and his characters merged. Books, apparently, were truly the agents of corruption and, sometimes, things were exactly what they seemed. Queensberry had said 'to my mind to pose as a thing is as bad as to be it',[114] a view which Wilde, in a different context, had endorsed when he said that only the superficial refuse to judge by appearances. Details of Wilde's many lovers called into question the possible underlying nature of the 'romantic' affections between older and younger man which were all but institutionalized in so many parts of English society: in relations between teacher and pupil, for instance, tutor and undergraduate. The acts for which Wilde was sentenced were commonplace in English public schools, as W. T. Stead and Bosie Douglas were quick to point out in print. Did that make the flower of English boyhood criminals too? (The answer, of course, was yes.) The material generosity with which Wilde had habitually treated young men – whether they were his sexual partners or not – caused twofold anxiety: protective relationships between affluent older men and poorer young ones, with or without sexual exchanges, were also a period commonplace, as biographies of the day make clear. (The Bensons' father, later an Archbishop of Canterbury, had received such help at a crucial point in his career, as had the father of J. R. Ackerley.) How were such relationships to be viewed for the future? But, even more disturbing than that was the fact that Wilde's sexual partners were predominantly drawn from the lower classes, always a fact to freeze the blood in English veins. (As late as 1953, when Peter Wildeblood stood trial, facing the same charges as Wilde, Prosecuting Counsel and Judge were rather more appalled by the class of his lovers than they were by what he and they had done together.) In 1895 Wilde's act of 'class betrayal' aroused complex emotions. He had allowed himself to share his weakness with members of a lower caste, thereby humiliating his peers. And, by being caught, he had exposed the period's uneasy sexual commerce between two worlds supposedly distinct. That his 'procurer' was an ex-public schoolboy (Marlborough), who apparently worked as much for love as money, created further unease.

But for many of those who had admired Wilde's writings and applauded his plays, perhaps the most distressing fact was that their relationship to the man and his work was now most worryingly called into question. What does it mean when good, decent, 'normal' people have responded with pleasure and approval to the work of one now so uncompromisingly exposed as 'monstrous'? Was it to the monstrous in themselves that he had appealed? And if he was no monster why had it seemed so necessary to destroy him? Those were the last and most haunting questions the period faced in its struggle to determine the relations between Art and Life.

The panic created by Wilde's sentence lasted until the end of the century, and beyond. In England the *fin de siècle* all but ends when his imprisonment begins, on 25 May 1895. *The Yellow Book* sickened immediately: spectators had assumed that a yellow-bound French novel which Wilde carried into court was John Lane's quarterly. People and publications most associated with Wilde went quiet. Many people actually left the country, seeking more tolerant nations. Wilde's enemies crowed and fair weather friends deserted. Some, such as Shaw, continued to defend him. Robbie Ross worked to disentangle Wilde's literary estate and clear it from bankruptcy. Many of those most associated with England's *fin de siècle* did not live to see the new century. Beardsley, Dowson, Pater, Symonds were all dead by 1900. In November of that year, too, Wilde died, and Victoria herself followed him two months later. Wilde had always entertained a certain fondness for the monarch: after all, as he enjoyed pointing out in jokes, he and she were the nineteenth century's greatest queens. As he also pointed out, the new century clearly wanted nothing to do with either of them. Lionel Johnson died in 1902, Whistler, and that intractable enemy, Henley, in 1903, Harland in 1905. In 1908 Arthur Symons, who would live for a further thirty-seven years, suffered the breakdown which effectually ended his career.

    The panic was a long time dying. Slowly it became possible to republish Wilde's work and revive his plays. Studies of him and the period so closely associated with him began to appear: Holbrook Jackson's enormously influential *The Eighteen Nineties* (1913),[115] dedicated to Max Beerbohm; Osbert Burdett's *The Beardsley Period* (1925).[116] Survivors reminisced: Ross, Rothenstein, Baring, Hichens, E. F. Benson, Beerbohm. In a series of autobiographies Bosie Douglas returned obsessively to his friendship with Wilde, denouncing, adoring, blaming, forgiving. Some argued, with Baring, that 'The Nineties' were not so much a genuinely distinct phenomenon as an idea in the mind of God and John Lane. E. F. Benson went so far as to maintain that 'the revolt against Victorian conventions and reticences which is supposed to animate [the Nineties] had already taken place and had long ago been completely successful'.[117] It was a view rejected by many younger people for whom the Nineties rapidly assumed a wistful glamour they have never since lost. Poets of the 1920s, such as Betjeman, found both the form and content of *fin-de-siècle* poetry fascinating and built upon its particular vision of urban romance. Paradox and epigram, Wilde's weapons, were picked up and dextrously wielded early in the twentieth century by G. K. Chesterton, the Roman Catholic apologist. Those languid but feline young men who populated Wilde's comedies and fiction lived on in the short stories of Saki and the novels of Firbank (both men, like Wilde, homosexual) then underwent an unexpected transformation, emerging as Wodehouse's 'silly asses' and Dorothy Sayers's Lord Peter Wimsey. Other homosexual dramatists accepted Wilde's role of Outsider as Observer: Noël Coward's comedies and Joe Orton's altogether more disturbing upendings of the moral order both inherit Wilde's tradition.

Wilde himself has proved a remarkably enduring figure: of writers produced by the British Isles only Shakespeare has been more written about. His personal story, which seems to fall so satisfyingly into the ancient Greek pattern of the outstanding person ruined by a fatal tragic flaw, is part of the reason. But it is more than that. Wilde's struggle was one we recognize particularly clearly today. His contemporaries saw it in terms of the connections and conflicts between Art and Life. Many of us now would see it as a determined effort to fuse the Personal and the Political. Wilde was endlessly preoccupied with the question of loyalty and allegiance. To what or whom do we owe it? What or who merits it: class; culture; friends; lovers; Art; the Law; God; the State; our own personal sense of worth or virtue? For Wilde, as for E. M. Forster after him, the starting point had to be personal relationships: only there can we truly know and be known, and only there, if we are members of groups labelled 'undesirable' by the larger society, can we place our trust and test our own beliefs. 'The nineties', claimed Osbert Burdett, 'is not a period but a point of view.'[118] Paradoxically, for a period so often called immoral, cynical or decadent, its prevailing point of view was one which insisted that individuals take full responsibility for their own moral development. Doing so might well bring them, as it brought Wilde, into a collision with society at large. From the impact between individual and state, changes may result. Wilde said 'It is personalities, not principles, that move the age.'[119] In effect, he made personality itself into a principle and, even though he failed to move his age as far as he had wished, he shook it so hard that we feel the reverberations still.

NOTES

1 See J. Maas, *The Prince of Wales's Wedding: The Story of a Picture* (Cameron & Tayleur in association with David & Charles, London and Newton Abbot, 1977).
2 W. P. Frith, *My Autobiography and Reminiscences* (3 vols., 1887–8): cited by

Aubrey Noakes, *William Frith: Extraordinary Victorian Painter* (Jupiter, London, 1978), p. 116.

3 For Lautrec's cartoon, see R. Hart-Davis (ed.), *The Letters of Oscar Wilde* (Rupert Hart-Davis, London, 1962), opposite p.383: for Beerbohm's, see J. G. Riewald, *Beerbohm's Literary Caricatures* (Allen Lane, London, 1977), p. 159.

4 See particularly Wilde's essays, 'Slaves of Fashion', 'Woman's Dress', 'More Radical Ideas Upon Dress Reform' and 'Costume': collected in *Art and Decoration* (Methuen, London, 1920).

5 For the androgyne, see M. Praz, *The Romantic Agony* (Oxford University Press, 1933); J. Birkett, *The Sins of the Fathers: Decadence in France, 1870–1914* (Quartet, London, 1986), ch. 3. For fictional lesbians see Swinburne's *Lesbia Brandon*, Zola's *Nana* and *Pot-Bouille*, Strindberg's *A Madman's Defence* (*Le plaidoyer d'un fou*) and Henry James's *The Bostonians*.

6 S. Weintraub, *Beardsley: A Biography* (W. H. Allen, London, 1967), pp. 211, 228, 230 and 240.

7 For Pater: M. Levey, *The Case of Walter Pater* (Thames & Hudson, London, 1978), p. 76: for Wilde, *The Letters*, p. 233, in a letter to Henley.

8 M. Beerbohm, 'A Relic', collected in *And Even Now* (William Heinemann, London, 1920).

9 Wilde, *The Letters*, p. 299.

10 See D. Stanford (ed.), *Short Stories of the 'Nineties* (John Baker, London, 1968), p. 187.

11 For details of Gosse, see A. Thwaite, *Edmund Gosse: A Literary Landscape* (Secker & Warburg, London, 1984).

12 C. Mackworth, *English Interludes: Mallarmé, Verlaine, Paul Valéry, Valéry Larbaud in England, 1860–1912* (Routledge & Kegan Paul, London, 1974), p. 42.

13 Riewald, *Beerbohm's Literary Caricatures*, pp. 58–9.

14 Mackworth, *English Interludes*, pp. 100–15.

15 *Ibid.*, p. 102.

16 Beerbohm, 'Enoch Soames', in *Seven Men* (William Heinemann, London, 1919), p. 4.

17 For the German contribution to English culture, see R. Ashton, *Little Germany: Exile and Asylum in Victorian England* (Oxford University Press, 1986).

18 For late nineteenth-century Jewish immigration to England, see L. P. Gartner, *The Jewish Immigrant in England, 1870–1914* (Simon Publications, London, 1960 and 1973); for Jewish radicalism see W. J. Fishman, *East End Jewish Radicals* (Duckworth, London, 1975).

19 For information about one particular Yiddish theatre, see L. Rosenfeld, *Bright Star of Exile: Jacob Adler and the Yiddish Theatre* (Barrie & Jenkins, London, 1977). For English writers' response, see K. Beckson (ed.), *The Memoirs of Arthur Symons: Life and Art in the 1890s* (Penn State University Press, 1977), 'An Actress in Whitechapel', pp. 75–6; see also Arthur Symons's short story, 'Esther Kahn' (*Spiritual Adventures*, 1905).

20 F. Harris, *Oscar Wilde* (Constable, London, 1938).

21 H. O. Sturgis, *Tim* (Macmillan, London, 1891) and *Belchamber* (London,

Constable, 1904; World's Classics, Oxford, 1935; Leviathan Series, Duckworth, London, 1965).

22 Under the pen name, 'Arthur Lyon Raile', Warren later published two volumes of verses, *Iatmos: A Volume of Poems* (Grant Richards, London, 1903) and *The Wild Rose: A Volume of Poems* (David Nutt, London and New York, 1909), which influenced Goldsworthy Lowes Dickinson, E. M. Forster's friend and mentor. See T. d'Arch Smith, *Love in Earnest: Some Notes on the Lives and Writings of English 'Uranian' Poets* (Routledge & Kegan Paul, London, 1970), pp. 114–17.

23 D. Stanford, (ed.), *Pre-Raphaelite Writings* (J. M. Dent, London, 1973), p. xxvi.

24 *Household Words*, May 1856: cited by Stanford, in *Pre-Raphaelite Writings*, p. 29.

25 *The Contemporary Review*, October 1871: reprinted in Stanford, *Pre-Raphaelite Writings*, pp. 37–41.

26 *The Athenaeum*, 16 December 1871: reprinted in Stanford, *Pre-Raphaelite Writings*, pp. 41–5.

27 For the full text of Buchanan's letter, see J. Goodman, *The Oscar Wilde File* (Allison & Busby/W. H. Allen, London, 1988), p. 98.

28 For Thackeray's and Burne-Jones's judgements, see R. Ross, *Masques and Phases* (Arthur L. Humphreys, London, 1909), pp. 139 and 137.

29 Ross, *Masques and Phases*, p. 142.

30 For more information about Solomon, and for reproductions of some of his works, see E. Cooper, *The Sexual Perspective: Homosexuality and Art in the Last Hundred Years in the West* (Routledge & Kegan Paul, London, 1986).

31 Wilde, *The Letters*, p. 451.

32 H. Pearson, *The Man Whistler* (Methuen, London, 1952), pp. 75–87.

33 See R. Engen, *Kate Greenaway: A Biography* (MacDonald, London, 1981), for a sympathetic account of the particularly complex relationship between Ruskin and Greenaway, and for a generously illustrated record of her work.

34 He praises his work in 'A Study of Dionysus', an essay first published in *The Fortnightly Review* in 1876, later collected in the posthumously published *Greek Studies* (Macmillan, London, 1895).

35 Said by Wilde in his review of Pater's *Appreciations*, published in *The Speaker*, 22 March 1890.

36 Wilde, *The Letters*, p. 399.

37 Levey, *The Case of Walter Pater*, p. 144.

38 P. Gunn, *Vernon Lee: Violet Paget, 1856–1935* (Oxford University Press, 1964), pp. 98–107.

39 *Ibid.*, p. 98.

40 For an illustration of the cover see M. Fido, *Oscar Wilde* (Hamlyn, London, 1973), p. 114.

41 M. Hughes, *A London Girl of the Eighties* (1936); incorporated as part of *A London Family, 1870–1900* (Oxford University Press, 1946), p. 240.

42 Mrs Molesworth, *The Girls and I* (Macmillan, London, 1892).

43 C. March, *Doris's High School Days* (Blackie, London, n.d., but *c.* 1897), p. 68.

44 R. Hichens, 'A Boudoir Boy', collected in *Byeways* (Methuen, London, 1898).

45 E. W. Hornung, *The Amateur Cracksman* (London, 1899). Quotation from *The Collected Raffles* (J. M. Dent, London, 1985), p. 8.

46 For details of Wilde's parents see T. de Vere White, *The Parents of Oscar Wilde: Sir William and Lady Wilde* (Hodder & Stoughton, London, 1967).

47 W. S. Gilbert, *Patience* (1881), song from Act I.

48 N. Auerbach, *Ellen Terry: Player in Her Time* (J. M. Dent, London, W. W. Norton, New York, 1987), pp. 195–6.

49 See R. K. Engen, *Victorian Engravings* (Academy Editions, London, St Martin's, New York, 1975), for examples of these themes.

50 R. Hichens, *Yesterday* (Cassell, London, 1947), pp. 44–53.

51 See J. Hepburn, *The Author's Empty Purse and the Rise of the Literary Agent* (Oxford University Press, 1968), p. 45–66.

52 For her recreations of poems, see G. Ovenden, *Pre-Raphaelite Photography* (Academy Editions, London, St Martin's Press, New York, 1972).

53 See A. Hopkinson, *Julia Margaret Cameron* (Virago Press, London, 1986).

54 See E. Y. Jones, *Father of Art Photography: O. G. Rejlander, 1813–1875* (David & Charles, Newton Abbot, 1973).

55 See W. Emboden, *Sarah Bernhardt* (Studio Vista, London, 1974; Macmillan, New York, 1975), pp. 50–1.

56 For reproductions of some of the Sarony studies of Wilde, see R. Ellman, *Oscar Wilde* (Hamish Hamilton, London, 1987); the plates appear between pp. 210 and 211.

57 For a particularly interesting discussion of that process, examined in relation to a single 'star', see G. McCann, *Marilyn Monroe* (Polity Press, Cambridge, 1987).

58 See L. Tickner, *The Spectacle of Women: Imagery of the Suffrage Campaign, 1907–1914* (Chatto & Windus, London, 1987).

59 R. Hichens, *The Green Carnation* (William Heinemann, London, 1894; reprinted by The Unicorn Press, London, 1949, with Hichens's Introduction). For Wilde's and Douglas's reaction see Hichens's *Yesterday*, p. 72.

60 Hichens, *The Green Carnation*, 1949 edn, p. xiii.

61 As with most modern British anti-homosexual measures, the relevant section of The Criminal Law Amendment Act of 1885 was tacked on to an altogether different piece of legislation. The original purpose of the Bill was to raise the age of female sexual consent from twelve to fourteen, a measure called for when W. T. Stead, editor of *The Pall Mall Gazette*, proved, by doing it, that it was perfectly possible to buy a girl of twelve for the purposes of prostitution with full parental knowledge and consent. The anti-homosexual clauses were added at Committee Stage, after the Bill had already received its first and second readings. In just the same opportunistic way did the present (1988) Conservative government add its recent successful anti-homosexual measure, at Committee Stage, to the 1988 Local Government Bill. Section 28 forbids local councils to 'promote homosexuality', a term which lawyers have described as 'lacking any precise legal meaning'. Henry Labouchere, prime mover of the anti-homosexual clauses in 1885, was a Liberal MP, and proprietor (and sometime editor) of the 'radical' magazine,

Truth. As with many 'radicals', Labouchere's own (hetero)sexual practice was firmly rooted in the double standard.

62 For the best account of the trials see Montgomery Hyde (ed.), *The Trials of Oscar Wilde* (Notable British Trials Series, William Hodge, Edinburgh, Glasgow and London, 1948).

63 Wilde, *The Picture of Dorian Gray* (first published in *Lippincott's Monthly Magazine*, 1890; revised book form published by Ward, Lock, London, 1891).

64 In 1954 Montgomery Hyde, then an MP, was denied access by the Home Secretary to official records detailing the conditions in which Wilde served his sentence. Almost sixty years after his imprisonment, the establishment still felt guilty. See H. Montgomery Hyde, *Oscar Wilde: The Aftermath* (Methuen, London, 1963).

65 See R. Hart-Davis (ed.), *More Letters of Oscar Wilde* (John Murray, London, 1985), Appendix B, p. 199.

66 Max Nordau, *Degeneration* (London, 1895), Book Three ('Ego-Mania'), chapter 3, 'Decadents and Aesthetes'.

67 Gartner, *The Jewish Immigrant*, ch. 10. For information on growing anti-alien agitation, see W. J. Fisham, *East End 1888* (Duckworth, London, 1988), *passim*.

68 For the dissemination of aristocratic and upper-class values amongst working-class children, via Public School Missions, see P. Parker, *The Old Lie: the Great War and the Public School Ethos* (Constable, London, 1987). For individual organizations see: Donald McFarlan, *First For Boys: The Story of the Boys' Brigade* (Collins, Glasgow and London, 1982); M. Rosenthal, *The Character Factory: Baden-Powell and the Origins of the Boy Scout Movement* (Collins, London, 1986), and M. Heath-Stubbs, *Friendship's Highway: Being the History of the Girls' Friendly Society, 1875–1925* (GFS, Central Office, London, 1926).

69 This is a broad-brushed précis of an argument of considerable complexity. For one of its most elegant elaborations, see D. Newsome, *Godliness and Good Learning: Four Studies on a Victorian Ideal* (John Murray, London, 1961).

70 See P. W. Musgrave, *From Brown to Bunter* (Routledge & Kegan Paul, London, 1985), pp. 65–82.

71 See the interview with her in H. C. Black, *Notable Women Authors of the Day* (Macmillan, London, 1906), p. 154.

72 Wilde, *The Letters*, p. 293.

73 *Ibid.*, p. 522.

74 See M. Egan (ed.), *Ibsen: The Critical Heritage* (Routledge & Kegan Paul, London and Boston, Mass., 1972), p. 179.

75 Maurice Baring, *The Puppet Show of Memory* (Cassell, London, 1932; repr. London, 1987), p. 147.

76 Ernest Dowson, *Verses* (Leonard Smithers, London, 1896); the poem in which Cynara makes her appearance is 'Non Sum Qualis Eram Bonae Sub Regno Cynarae': see D. Flower (ed.), *The Potential Works of Ernest Christopher Dowson* (Cassell, London, 1934), p. 52.

77 See J. Connell, *W. E. Henley* (Constable, London, 1949), p. 216, note.

78 See Derek Stanford (ed.), *Three Poets of the Rhymers Club: Ernest Dowson,*

Lionel Johnson, John Davidson (Carcanet Press, Cheadle Hulme, 1974), p. 11.

79 See Arthur Symons, *Poems* (2 vols., William Heinemann, London, 1907, and Beckson (ed.). *The Memoirs of Arthur Symons*.

80 J. Farmer and W. E. Henley, *Slang and Its Analogues* (London, 1890; repr., as *A Dictionary of Slang*, 2 vols., Wordsworth Editions, Ware, 1987).

81 Connell, *W. E. Henley*, pp. 191 and 197.

82 W. B. Yeats, *Autobiographies: The Trembling of the Veil: Book 1: Four Years: 1887–1891* (Macmillan, London, 1955), p. 32.

83 Connell, *W. E. Henley*; the friendship with R. L. S., and its repercussions, pervade the whole book.

84 See Ian Fletcher's article, 'Decadence and the Little Magazines', in a collection he also edits, *Decadence and the 1890s* (Stratford-upon-Avon Studies 17, Edward Arnold, London, 1979), pp. 173–202.

85 They are: the Frontispiece; 'Enter Herodias'; 'The Eyes of Herod'; and 'A Platonic Lament'. See 'A Note on Salomé', by Robert Ross, printed with the Bodley Head's 1930 edition of *Salomé*.

86 See D. Garnett, *The Golden Echo* (Chatto & Windus, London, 1953), pp. 10ff; H. Oliver, *The International Anarchist Movement in Late Victorian London* (Croom Helm, London and Canberra/St Martin's Press, New York, 1983), p. 121.

87 Reprinted, with an introduction by Philip Collins, in The Victorian Library Series (Leicester University Press, 1971).

88 Reprinted, by Basil Blackwell, Oxford, 1981.

89 For a survey of relevant prose, see P. J. Keating, *The Working Classes in Victorian Fiction* (Routledge & Kegan Paul, London, 1971).

90 A. Symons, *The Fortnightly Review*, 58 (1892); cited by J. H. Buckley in *William Ernest Henley: A Study in the 'Counter-Decadence' of the 'Nineties* (Princeton University Press, Princeton and New Jersey, 1945), p. 184.

91 'Stella Maris': later collected in Arthur Symons, *London Nights* (1895). For press reaction to the poem, see F. Harrison, Introduction to *The Yellow Book: An Anthology* (1914), reprinted by Boydell Press, Woodbridge, Suffolk, 1982.

92 Preface to *The Picture of Dorian Gray*.

93 'Walter Pater', *The Monthly Review* (September 1906); reprinted in Beckson (ed.),*The Memoirs of Arthur Symons*.

94 See J. Oppenheim, *The Other World: Spiritualism and Psychical Research in England, 1850–1914* (Cambridge University Press, 1985).

95 See L. Barrow, *Independent Spirits: Spiritualism and English Plebeians* (History Workshop/Routledge & Kegan Paul, London, 1986).

96 Horoscope: Oscar Wilde, *Letters*, p. 177; clairvoyant: *More Letters of Oscar Wilde*, pp. 187, 199. A photograph of Wilde's palm, taken by Mrs Robinson, is reproduced.

97 See D. Hardy, *Alternative Communities in Nineteenth Century England* (Longman, London, 1979), and J. Marsh, *Back to the Land: The Pastoral Impulse in Victorian England from 1880–1914* (Quartet Books, London, 1982).

98 See F. MacCarthy, *The Simple Life: C. R. Ashbee in the Cotswolds* (Lund Humphries, London, 1981), and Alan Crawford's *C. R. Ashbee: Architect,*

Designer and Romantic Socialist (Yale University Press, New Haven, Conn., and London, 1985).

99 See B. Jay, *Customs and Faces; Photographs by Sir Benjamin Stone, 1838–1914* (Academy Editions, London/St Martin's Press, New York, 1972).

100 'Pan: Double Villanelle'. First published in *Poems* (1881): reprinted in *Charmides and Other Poems* (Methuen, London, 1913), pp. 131–4.

101 'London Voluntaries, Number 5: Allegro Maestoso', *The Song of the Sword and Other Verses* (London, 1892). Reissued as *London Voluntaries* (London, 1893).

102 *Phaedrus* ends with Socrates's prayer to Pan. Numbers of nineteenth-century authors harked back to that, e.g. Henry Nevinson in 'A New Pheidippides' (*The Plea of Pan*, London, 1901).

103 Wilde, *More Letters*, p. 129.

104 F. Reid, *The Garden God: A Tale of Two Boys* (David Nutt, London, 1905: reprinted by Brilliance Books, London, 1986).

105 E. F. Benson, *The Angel of Pain* (William Heinemann, London, 1906), pp. 280–4.

106 R. Aldington, *The Portable Oscar Wilde* (The Viking Press, New York, 1946), p. 6.

107 See B. Dijkstra, *Idols of Perversity: Fantasies of Feminine Evil in Fin-de-siècle Culture* (Oxford University Press, New York, 1986).

108 H. Ellis, *The Criminal* (Schribner and Welford, New York, 1890); quotation from the fourth edition (Blackwood, Scott & Co., London, 1910), p. 164.

109 E. Carpenter, *Civilisation – Its Cause and Cure* (Swan Sonnenschein, London, 1889), p. 48.

110 H. Pearson, introduction to *Oscar Wilde: Selected Essays and Poems* (Penguin Books, London, 1954), p. 15.

111 Wilde, *The Soul of Man under Socialism* (*The Fortnightly Review*, February 1891): first published in book form, as *The Soul of Man*, by Arthur Humphreys, in a private edition of fifty copies, on 30 May 1895, just five days after Wilde was sentenced to two years' hard labour.

112 Often known as 'Invictus', the poem from which the lines come is in fact 'I[n].M[emoriam]. R. T. Hamilton Bruce' (1846–1899), the fourth poem in *Echoes* (*A Book of Verses*, David Nutt, London, 1888).

113 Wilde, *The Letters*, p. 366.

114 Hyde, *The Trials of Oscar Wilde*, p. 22.

115 H. Jackson, *The Eighteen Nineties: A Review of Art and Letters at the Close of the Nineteenth Century* (Grant Richards, London, 1913); quotation from the edition of Jonathan Cape (London, 1931).

116 O. Burdett, *The Beardsley Period: An Essay in Perspective* (John Lane, The Bodley Head, London, 1925).

117 E. F. Benson, *As We Were: A Victorian Peep-Show* (Longmans, Green & Co, London, 1930), p. 312; repr. Hogarth Press, London, 1985 and 1989.

118 Burdett, *The Beardsley Period*, p. 6.

119 Jackson, *The Eighteen Nineties*, p. 86.

꙳

ELEVEN

HEROES, MEADOWS AND
MACHINERY: *FIN-DE-SIÈCLE* MUSIC

FRITZ WEBER

There is something rather peculiar about interpretations of a work of art . . . What is rational about it (that means, what may be comprehended) is almost invariably not the essence, and actually a veil that cloaks the figure . . . With these infinitely delicate and, yes, non-rational matters there is always a danger of sheer verbiage. That's why all commentaries have something so odious. (Gustav Mahler in a letter to Alma Mahler, 1909, quoted in P. Stefan, *Gustav Mahler*, Munich, 1912, p. 129–31).

Fin de siècle is usually defined as the period between 1880 and the outbreak of the First World War. Above all, the term evokes a certain atmosphere, a feeling between doomsday apprehensions and the exhilaration of setting sail for new horizons. In the following, 'classical' *fin-de-siècle* music is therefore understood as music between Romanticism and modern music (*Neue Musik*).

There was a great variety of styles, of schools and techniques, and of national features, even if we consider only the well-known composers. Who would, moreover, be able to identify opera composers such as Sigismund Bachrich (*Muzzedin*, 1883), Johannes Hager (*Marffa*, 1886), Vittorio Gnecchi (*Cassandra*, 1905) and František Neumann (*Liebelei*, after Schnitzler)?[1] Of many other composers one usually knows only the name (for example, Max von Schillings or Leo Blech or just a single opera, like Karl Goldmark's *Queen of Sheba*, 1875). To them we might add the forgotten composers of orchestral works, chamber music or songs, buried today in musical encyclopaedias: the Scot Laermont Drysdale, the Englishman Granville Bantock, Alberto Williams from Argentina, the Portuguese Francisco de Lacerda, the Norwegian Gerhard Schjelderup or the German composers Rudi Stephan (a victim of the First World War) and Theodor Gerlach, who played an important part in developing the monodrama and the spoken opera prior to Arnold Schönberg.[2]

That musicians have fallen into oblivion does not necessarily mean that they were not appreciated by their contemporaries. In Germany the average age of operas in the German repertoire was 44 years shortly before 1900 and 42 years in 1907, whereas it reached 85 years (!) in 1967. During the season 1896–7 Karl Goldmark's *Das Heimchen am Herd* ('The Cricket on the Hearth') was the most performed opera (328 times) on German stages.[3] Thus, what we consider as music of the *fin de siècle* is just a selection chosen through the filter of hindsight. (Remember the Mahler renaissance of the 1960s or the recent rediscovery of Eric Satie.)

There were, of course, earlier examples in nineteenth-century music, which pointed forward into the twentieth century: the bold dissonant chords of the first movement of the *Eroica* and Beethoven's late string quartets; Berlioz's delicate instrumentation (compare his *Nuits d'été* songs with Mahler's *Kindertotenlieder* or *Rückertlieder*); Mussorgski's operas and his 'moral' conception of art (which had to be 'true' in the same sense as used by Schönberg); and, in particular, the music of Wagner, who opened the harmonic door to our century. Yet the real and widespread breakthrough did not take place before the *fin de siècle*.

The general approach of this article is not meant to be a musicological or musical-historical one in the traditional sense, but rather a socio-historical approximation. Music is considered as an integral (though often intractable) part of social life, composing as *one* way of – explicitly or unconsciously – expressing 'social' feelings: crying, shouting, yearning, etc. The alternative to such 'subjectivism' in music was 'objectification' represented by Programme music: composers like Richard Strauss were able to depict almost anything in a truly masterful way. But Strauss composed as if there were chemical formulae for expressing emotions in music. To really touch, he had to raise the most extravagant display imaginable, as in the recognition scene between Elektra and Orestes.

The tension between the individual and society, as far as art is concerned, had already been a main issue of the German nineteenth-century philosophers. Both Schopenhauer's and Nietzsche's reflections on the 'genius' as the defiant nucleus of individual resistance against the normative pressure of industrial society focused on the composer. Not by accident, various composers of the *fin de siècle* (when Nietzsche's ideas gained their actual influence) were reading (and composing) *Also sprach Zarathustra*: Richard Strauss, Gustav Mahler, Frederick Delius and Alexander Scriabin. Even such a currently unknown representative of Kapellmeister music as Oskar Fried composed *Das trunkene Lied* after the same verses of Nietzsche that Mahler used in his Third symphony;[4] and the most important figure of Wilhelm Peterson-Berger's Swedish National Opera *Arnljot* (first performed in 1910), too, bears evident traits of the Nietzschean hero.

Classical music, however, constitutes just a small section of the musical *fin de siècle*. During those decades new manifestations of popular culture and urban civilization were taking shape: the musical revue and the musical, the 'silver' operetta, the *Schlager* or hit, and Tin Pan Alley. Many of these new elements were bound up with the technological progress of the times. The bright lights provided by electricity, for instance, were a prerequisite of the Revue. (The same is true for the Mahler–Roller performances at Vienna's Imperial Opera, which were the first to take advantage of the new lighting possibilities. Early experiments with electric stage lighting in the Viennese Opera had already taken place in 1883.)[5]

The hit, as a phenomenon affecting the masses, emphatically demanded mechanical sound reproduction; and the triumph of the gramophone, on the other hand, can hardly be imagined without Tin Pan Alley. The nineteenth century saw the emergence of a market for music; musical mass production started in the *fin de siècle*. The demands of the market also affected the composers of classical music, first of all of operas: the stories of Giuseppe Verdi and Richard Wagner concentrate on the struggle against the restraint imposed on them by the musical taste of the purveyors and consumers of operas. Here we can only touch on the consequences of market conditions on the musical attitude of composers such as Puccini or Richard Strauss, comparing it with musical monuments of the *fin de siècle*, which came into being irrespective of the wants of the market through Mahler, Schönberg and Scriabin.[6]

NINETEENTH-CENTURY MUSIC IN TRANSITION

Theodor W. Adorno once proposed that one should look at inner-musical changes as a 'mode of reacting to society'.[7] There are at least three interconnected long-term structural problems to be considered in nineteenth-century music:

the gradual liberation from the outworn corset of formal means of expression, i.e. the increasing ability of composers to express themselves more freely and individually – a process which started in the age of Philipp Emanuel Bach, Gluck and Mozart, and reached its first peak with Beethoven;
the disintegration of the classical symphonic form; and
the dissolution of the traditional major/minor harmonic system.

It was Beethoven who both accomplished and transcended the classical symphonic form, expressing (in musical terms) the humanistic optimism of his time. Beethoven's late symphonies, however, should already be seen as a response to the emerging industrial system, as a premonition that technological progress was not identical with individual liberation of *all* the people. This could help to explain the formal difficulties Beethoven soon ran into. The

Pastoral would then appear as an early Romantic symptom of escapism, the flipped-out last movement of the Seventh symphony would make more sense than being interpreted as the 'apotheosis of dancing'; we could get an idea of the reasons for the formal nostalgia of the Eighth symphony, and finally the choral effort of the Ninth symphony could convincingly be explained as necessary to make sure that Beethoven's humanistic message would be picked up by 'the world'. Undoubtedly the gradual shifting of weight to the last movement was a sign of Beethoven's change of attitude from optimistic hope to critical doubt.

According to the analysis of Paul Bekker,[8] the crucial 'problem of the fourth movement' was blithely ignored by Schumann and Mendelssohn in the further course of the nineteenth century. Franz Liszt, and later Richard Strauss, escaped into the realm of symphonic poems. Only the Austrian composers (including the Viennese-by-choice, Brahms), particularly the late Schubert and Anton Bruckner, tried to cope with the difficulties. Gustav Mahler, the 'last symphonist', undertook the final efforts in the *fin de siècle* to save the symphonic form by breaking it.

There were, of course, others than Austrians who made serious contributions to the solution of symphonic problems: César Franck tried to construct new links between the single movements in his (only) Symphony in D minor (1888). Tchaikovsky was the first to place a slow movement at the end of his *Pathétique* (in 1893, three years prior to Mahler's Third symphony). Alexander Scriabin's First symphony required vocal soloists and chorus, and the score of the *Poème du feu* (Prometheus symphony), composed in 1909–10, originally demanded a *tastiera per luce* (light keyboard): something like a colour piano of twelve notes, tuned to a colour scale of Scriabin's own, supposedly based on a musical cycle of fifths. Finally, Charles Ives's symphonies represent one of the most unorthodox answers to the symphonic problem.

The dissolution of the classical harmonic system does not require lengthy explanations:[9] just try to play a 'normal' major or minor chord after the Tristan accord. Even nineteenth-century composers, who are usually regarded as rather conservative, such as Johannes Brahms, were using highly elaborated and dissonant harmonic means at the end of their careers. Anton Bruckner, to some musicologists a dumb Upper Austrian peasant, was experimenting with the 'old' modes (i.e. the Dorian, Phrygian and Lydian scales) in order to extend the harmonic range.

During the *fin de siècle* the use of 'exotic' scales, working with overtone series, and the appearance of vague chord sets and links, which were not resolved in a traditional sense, led to a further disintegration of the classical music system: Debussy extensively used the whole-tone scale and was experimenting with hovering and pending chords. Whereas his dissonant modernism was relieved by calmness, the boldness of the new techniques emerged with Richard Strauss's *Salome* and *Elektra* (first performed in 1905 and 1907 respectively). In Strauss's music – as well as in that of the Danish Carl Nielsen – several scales were superimposed (polyharmonics), and chords were constructed of six to eight intervals without any relation in the customary harmonic sense (accordpolyphony). Another German composer, Max Reger, skimmed with abandon from scale to scale.

In the United States Charles Ives was testing the new possibilities of polytonality and polyrhythmics; and the pianist Henry Dixon Cowell shocked the audience of a San Francisco music club in 1912 by striking tone clusters with his forearms. In Vienna Schönberg and the Second Viennese school arrived at free atonality; in Russia Scriabin constructed his Prometheus chord of six intervals, developed by accumulating overtones.

All these harmonic experiments were part of the move to modern music. One of the most interesting musical alternatives was microtonality: as early as 1892, a German, G. A. Behrens-Senegaldens, patented a quarter-tone piano and published a pamphlet on quarter-tone music. The German composer Richard H. Stein started experimenting with quarter-tones in 1904 and wrote compositions for quarter-tone pianos and clarinets.

In 1898 the English composer John Herbert Foulds wrote a string quartet in quarter-tone intervals. His wife, the violinist Maud MacCarthy, could sing Hindu scales of 22 notes to the octave. There were many other musicians who used the means of microtonality: the Italian Vittorio Gnecchi composed a quarter-tone opera, *La Rosiera*, in 1910, and the Mexican Julian Carrillo wrote music based on quarter-, eighth- and sixteenth-tones. In 1907 Ferruccio Busoni published his *Entwurf einer neuen Ästhetik der Tonkunst*, a milestone in modern music, in which he suggested a system of third- and sixth-tones and a scale consisting of 18 tonal links. His own music, however, sounds less revolutionary. The most successful composer of the microtonal group was Alois Hába, who derived quarter-, third- and sixth-tones from Moravian folk music. He was said to be able to sing five divisions of the semitone, i.e. sixty to the octave. Following his design, proper instruments (pianos, trumpets, clarinets and harmoniums) for the new scales were manufactured.[10]

Folk-music was one of the most important sources of musical innovations leading to modern music: Leoš Janáček, another Moravian composer, was collecting folk songs, and experimented with the melodies and rhythms of the spoken language. In Hungary Béla Bartók and Zoltán Kodály came across new rhythms and harmonies in the course of recording folk tunes. Similar work with similar conclusions was done in England by Gustav Holst. In general, recourse to folk music was only taken by (and open to?) the national schools of the countries of the 'musical periphery'. In the core countries (i.e. Austria, Germany, France) the preference related to *exoticism*, and the folk music attitude – if present – generated mere artificialities.[11]

MR KONDRATIEFF, ESCAPISM AND THE REBIRTH OF ROMANTICISM

There could be an explanation (other than inner-musical) for the acceleration of musical progress during the last decades of the nineteenth century: the deepening of industrialization and the concentrated upsurge of new technologies. Even Egon Friedell felt convinced of an unescapable link between the rise of Impressionism and 'telegraph and telephone, steamwheel and bicycle, photography and arc light, and all the other achievements of applied natural science'.[12]

The rise of electricity (starting in the 1870s with the invention of the bulb and the telephone) led to the introduction of wireless communication by Marconi in the 1890s, thus preparing the way for broadcasting: as early as 1910 the premier broadcast of an opera performance could take place in New York. Already in 1913 there were regular weekly radio concerts in Brussels.[13] The phonograph and the gramophone were other important innovations for musical life. The moving pictures of the French Lumière brothers can only be mentioned here.[14]

During the 1880s the breakthrough occurred in experimenting with the automobile. In 1900 the production of submarines started in the USA; after the turn of the century the Zeppelin airship and the aeroplane appeared. Life in general became faster and, as many contemporaries believed, less comfortable and more dangerous. In Egon Friedell's *Kulturgeschichte*, the *Blitzzug* ('lightning' train) figures as the frightening symbol of the new style of life.[15] Sigmund Freud (and other psychologists of the *fin de siècle*) averred a close connection between telegraph, telephone and the new transport facilities: in short, between the stressful and fast 'modern' life and 'nervousness'.[16]

The rapid economic and technological change evoked reactions similar to those experienced during the First Industrial Revolution: anxiety, embarrassment, escapism and nostalgia. There had not been an unequivocal belief in progress throughout the nineteenth century: optimism about the future had always been blended with misgivings, fears and suspicions that a further growth of industry could lead to individual harm and, in the end, to general decadence and catastrophe. This ambivalent attitude seems to have been intensified considerably during the *fin de siècle*.

The rebirth of Romanticism took shape in various forms: people would dress in a *Biedermeier* manner and dance gavottes and minuets;[17] the atelier style in furnishing dwellings has been described as a 'materialistic variation of Romanticism'.[18] The German *Wandervogel* movement tried to escape from urban civilization, soon creating a music of its own, which was compiled in the famous *Zupfgeigenhansl* collection by Hans Breuer in 1908.[19] Finally, the primary motives for collecting folk songs in various countries may also serve as an indication of escapist, Romantic trends.

Flight from reality was the prevailing mood of the late nineteenth century: the middle-class salons were kept dark and dusky, stuffed with antique objects to build up the illusion of a cosy, non-industrial refugium, the real world kept outside by heavy drapery.[20] Mass-manufactured pictures and sculptures (salon art, trivial art) provided romantic paraphernalia to satisfy (and standardize) people's dreams of an arcadian (and often exotic) anti-world to capitalism. Dwellings in general are said to have looked like 'pawnshops and antique shops'.[21] Eric Satie, one of the most unorthodox and capricious musicians of the *fin de siècle*, composed sarcastic commentaries on this trend, calling his works *musique d'ameublement*.

In philosophy, the rationalism of the 1870s and 1880s was replaced by the acceptance of Nietzsche and, later, by the ideas of Henry Bergson, who became perhaps the most influential philosopher of the late *fin de siècle*. There were other (and worse) representatives of 'philosophy of life', who stood for downright reactionary tendencies: Julius Langbehn's *Rembrandt als Erzieher*, a pseudo-philosophical tract, went through dozens of reprints after 1890, and stamped the taste of generations of the German middle classes. The book was a ridiculous blend of *Deutschtümelei* (Teutonic chauvinism), anti-Semitism, irrationalism and anti-capitalistic bathos and the execration of science and technology. For Langbehn and others, like Adolf Bartels, Paul Lagarde (and in some respect also D. H. Lawrence), the city represented the incarnation of evil. Their ideal was wholesome rural life.[22]

The blood and soil mythos invaded the realm of music, too, inspiring a series of peasant operas in Germany and Austria. Music of this kind was consciously simple, quasi-archaic, constructed in the manner of woodcuts. Examples can be found in Joseph Reiter's *Der Bundschuh* or in Julius Bittner's *Bergsee* (something like the 'twilight of the peasants'), both telling stories about the Peasant Wars of the early modern times.[23] Reiter later became one of Hitler's favourite 'modern' composers.

The central European peasant operas had nothing in common with the meaty Italian *verismo* – associated with Pietro Mascagni's *Cavalleria rusticana* (1890), Ruggiero Leoncavallo's *I Pagliacci* (1892) and others. In Germany the *verismo* style was adapted by Eugene d'Albert (*Tiefland*, first performed 1903). Leoš Janáček's *Jenufa* (composed in the 1890s), too, shows some affinity to verism.

URBAN MUSIC

Flight from reality was one ingredient of the *fin de siècle*; on the other hand, the turn of the century was marked by the beginning of modern psychology and social science, associated with the names of Pavlov, Freud, Emile Durkheim, Vilfredo Pareto and Frederick W. Taylor. The latter tried to eliminate 'irrational' moral incentives, such as the workman's pride in his work, and to 'scientify' social control. Taylorism treated the worker as an appendix to the machine. Its ultimate aim was to adapt people to 'machinery'.

We do not know in detail which and how many of the new social challenges the composers of the time consciously recognized (and whether they did at all). However, we can assume that they grasped the new phenomena in society by intuition. And although music was not part of any political movement, it was – in general – 'critical': hostile to the world of money-making, of commercial, technological and scientific rationality.

In Gustav Mahler's symphonies the real world was contrasted with the composer's anti-world, and just so was the attempt of the individual to resist social pressure musically expressed.[24] In his music one is tempted to 'hear' Freud's findings as well as Marx's phrase that one has to sing reality's own melody to make it 'dance'. A similar attitude permeates some of Scriabin's works. Their affirmative counterpart was Richard Strauss (for England, Edward Elgar comes to mind). To be sure, Strauss was one of the most accomplished composers of the *fin de siècle*, a genius of instrumentation who treated the orchestra as a machinery for producing sounds, depicting an Alpine scenery, the bleating of a flock of sheep (in *Don Quixote*), the cry of a hawk (in *Frau ohne Schatten*) or the drop of a severed head (in *Salome*).

The difference between Mahler and Strauss can best be shown in their approach to Nietzsche. From Nietzsche's *Also sprach Zarathustra* Mahler selected only some verses dovetailing into his humanist universe, and integrated them in his Third symphony. Strauss undertook the delicate task of composing the highlights of the whole tract, thus printing, as Kurt Blaukopf puts it, an 'orchestral poster'.[25] The subtitle of the tone poem could serve as the headline of the poster: 'Symphonic optimism in *fin-de-siècle* manner, dedicated to the 20th century'.

The *Rosenkavalier*, composed only a few years after the revolutionary pair *Salome* and *Elektra*, already sounded the retreat from experimentation: Strauss stole away from avant-garde music with softness. The retrogressive metamorphosis and the loss of sensibility of the 'new' future Strauss demonstrate the aseptic consequence of social accommodation and musical domestication: no accident that he composed a *Sinfonia domestica*.

One of the composers who fitted well into the picture of the modern city dweller was Giacomo Puccini – a man fond of automobiles, motor boats and cigarette-smoking (one of the up-to-date symbols of 1900). Although Puccini (like Strauss) had to take care of the needs and tastes of the opera market, there is a strong affinity to Gustav Mahler: both composers set down 'critical' notes on the affliction of men (and women like Mimi, Manon or Butterfly) in the modern world. Another common urban element in the music of Mahler and Puccini consisted in giving 'voice' to the people of the cities, an attitude also to be found in Gustave Charpentier's 'cries' of Paris. Charpentier's *Louise* (1900) was (disregarding the rather exotic *Carmen*) the first factory girl on the opera stage. The 'masses' also appear in Mahler's music: he once spoke explicitly of the colourful human muddle of a popular fête as the prototype of his 'polyphony'.[26]

Puccini, Mahler and related composers were the extreme counterpart to those who began praising another side of modern life. In his *Futurist Manifesto* of 1909, Filippo Marinetti lauded the racing car, the 'beauty of tempo', the 'aggressive movement' and, in general, 'polyphonic' urban civilization.[27] The futurist composer Balilla Pratella gushed about composing the 'musical soul' of factories, trains and dreadnoughts, and expressing the 'reign of machinery' and the 'victory of electricity'.[28] In 1913, when Pratella's *Musica futurista per orchestra* was first performed, his comrade-in-arms, Luigi Russolo, used noise machines constructed by himself, the so-called *intonarumori* (howlers, crackers, thunderers, snarlers, buzzers), in his *Dawn over the City*.

Futurism, however, was a mere imperfect alternative to Romanticism and nostalgia. Adoring the world of technology was just the other side of abhorring it. The problem of finding a humanistic tonal answer to the age of industry remained to be solved later. Edgar Varese, who referred to the futurist experiments in the interwar years, may be mentioned as one example of a critical synthesis of *bruitism* ('noise music').

THE GRAMOPHONE, CHANGING INSTITUTIONS AND MUSICIANS JETTING AROUND

The scaling down of the world by railway and steamship began to revolution-ize the mobility of musicians during the *fin de siècle*. The American concert tour of the King of Waltz, Johann Strauss, in 1872 was still regarded as a sensation. The same is true for the adventurous journeys organized by Italian impresarios, who shipped singers, conductors and orchestras to Latin America.[29] But soon crossing the ocean became a normal occurrence.

In 1891 Tchaikovsky had visited western Europe and the United States; Antonín Dvořák experienced his momentous stay in New York in 1892–5.

After the turn of the century Richard Strauss, Gustav Mahler, Puccini and Scriabin followed suit. From the opposite side of the Atlantic John Philip de Sousa and his brass band set out on their triumphant European tour, and Florenz Ziegfeld came to make a study of the Folies Bergères Revues in Paris in 1906.[30]

Gustav Mahler, Enrico Caruso, Pablo Casals and particularly Arturo Toscanini represented the new type of the mobile musician: Casals's American tour in 1901 touched even desolate villages in the deserts of Texas. In 1903 he visited Brazil, in 1904 the USA again; in 1905 he travelled to Russia.[31] Toscanini shuttled across the Atlantic (between La Scala and the Metropolitan Opera House) as naturally as Beethoven had visited the outskirts of Vienna.

The next to travel, after the composers, soloists and conductors, were the orchestras: the Berlin Philharmonic started touring around in the 1880s. In 1900 the thoroughly conservative Vienna Philharmonic went to Paris for the first time; other tours followed.[32] The character of the orchestras, too, underwent a change during the *fin de siècle*. From semi-amateur bands they advanced to modern professional bodies of skilled musicians. On the other hand, the progress of the orchestra was to a great extent the merit of a new generation of conductors, who had been replacing the traditional Kapellmeister during the second half of the nineteenth century. Eventually Hans von Bülow's Meiningen system (based on an extension and elaboration of rehearsing) became the model of professionalism.[33]

The Meiningen system followed a general trend in arts: the growing importance of the element of 'work', which was perhaps best represented by the perfectly planned and performed musical shows and revues of the *fin de siècle*. To produce illusions required hard work, discipline, professionalism, training, rehearsals: the synchronized movements of the revue girl – the factory girl of the theatre – bore all the hallmarks of Taylorism.

The revues,[34] musicals[35] and 'silver' operettas of the *fin de siècle* were symptoms of the emerging entertainment industry. The songs to be heard on stage often 'hit' the taste of the people: *Das macht die Berliner Luft* (from Paul Lincke's operetta *Frau Luna*, 1899) or the songs of Irving Berlin in the USA (the creator of the Ragtime mania in 1911) became the all-pervasive hits of the day. The vogue of those hits was amplified by the invention of the gramophone: in 1877 Thomas A. Edison had built the first usable phonograph, operated by a hand-cranked, spring-driven mechanism, later to be replaced by an electric motor. The decisive onset of the 'age of the record', however, came in 1887 with Emil Berliner's invention of the gramophone. As early as 1900, the gramophone was generating a flourishing industry.[36] The production of records was part of the emerging and fast expanding 'industry of unconsciousness', which provided the masses with hits and shows, transporting the audience to an illusory anti-world, which had little in common with the musical dreams of *fin-de-siècle* composers like Gustav Mahler.

On the other hand, however, the gramophone record brought about a certain democratic progress in popularizing music life by potentially bringing classical music into every living room and to every last village. For the advantages of the gramophone were soon used by some courageous pioneers for reproducing classical music, too. Caruso became the first operatic singer who largely owed his popularity to his recordings. He, Pablo Casals and others made their premier recordings soon after 1900, when the majority of their colleagues gingerly stood aside.[37] The first complete opera to be recorded was Verdi's *Ernani* (on forty single-side records); the first complete symphony was Beethoven's Fifth by Arthur Nikisch and the Berlin Philharmonic in 1909.

At the turn of the century there were also other attempts at reform and democratization of music life. In Russia, Serge Kussevitsky conducted for peasants on a Volga vessel. In Vienna the first Workers' Symphony Concert (organized by the Social Democrats) took place as early as 1905. In London another important step towards *égalité* was taken in 1913, when women were first allowed to play in Sir Henry Wood's promenade orchestra.

NATURE AS A REFUGE

Since the inception of Romanticism, nature had been one of the favourite subjects of composing. However, with the *fin de siècle* the musical meaning of nature underwent a substantial accentuation as a symbol for the 'anti-world', 'non-industry' and calm retreat: Mahler starts his First symphony with bars sounding *Wie ein Naturlaut* ('like a tone of nature'). The whole symphony is redolent with an atmosphere of nature, wanderlust and folk tunes, before it culminates in a 'titanic' final movement.

In Mahler's later symphonies even more convincing symbols of nature and restfulness appear, particularly in the Third symphony (with the famous postillion's horn episode) and in the Seventh, with its two *Nachtmusik* movements. Night must also be considered a symbol for anti-world: natural darkness is the world of spirits, reveries and forbidden imaginings; it stands for escaping from humdrum existence. Moreover, since the Age of Absolutism, light had been identified with public control, whereas darkness had served as the symbol of individual freedom and anarchy.[38] (Wagner had used that symbolism in his opera *Tristan und Isolde*.) No surprise that (in 1918) Jean Cocteau – who was closely associated with the French *Six*, a group of anti-Romantic composers around Milhaud and Roussel – was up in arms against 'nocturnal parfumes' and demanded the creation of 'day-music'.[39]

Night = nature = absence of the world of industry, is the short formula of musical Romanticism in the *fin de siècle*, as represented by Gustav Mahler. Night and nature can also be found in the early works of Arnold Schönberg (*Transfigured Night*), Anton Webern (*Summer Wind*), Alexander Scriabin (Third piano sonata), or in Vítězslav Novák's *In the High Tatra*. In the works of Frederick Delius, nature also occupies a central place. His nature is always calm and friendly, without flash or thunderstorm. Charles Ives's *Central Park in the Dark* pictures, according to his own statement, nature and events of the pre-automobile age. Finally, we must not forget Ralph Vaughan Williams's *Pastoral Symphony*: composed during the First World War in the shadow of the bloody industrialized warfare in France, it was a nostalgic attempt musically to recreate unsullied nature.

Kindred in attitude but different in result was Claude Debussy's musical treatment of nature. His ambition was to sketch 'the psychic analogies between nature and imagination',[40] in a way which has often been compared with impressionistic and pointillist painting. The increased awareness and the general use of tone colours is a salient feature of *fin-de-siècle* music, culminating in the works of Maurice Ravel, Franz Schreker and in Schönberg's idea of the *Klangfarbenmelodie* (tone colour melody).

The folk song (already earlier blended with the Romantic enthusiasm for nature) regained an important place in the music of the *fin de siècle*, too. Many Mahler melodies that sound as if they were popular songs or folk dances are entirely imitations, integrated in Mahler's system of symbols of the 'anti-world'. At the turn of the century working at and collecting of folk music was widespread, and popular songs formed an important source of imaginative inspiration. The folk tune appears even in the works of Charles Ives.

EXOTICISM

Since Wagner's bold attack on the traditional harmonic system, the search for new means of expression had led various composers to experimenting with exotic scales. The opinion was widespread that (as Camille Saint-Saëns put it) European music had 'reached its limits' and that the major/minor system lay 'in its last agonies'. The 'old scales', he continued, were returning, 'and with them *the unlimited variety of oriental keys*'.[41] Saint-Saëns's words represent a new attitude: during the age of Baroque, Classicism and early Romanticism the use of exotic phrases or instruments, such as triangle, cymbal, and big drum (known as Turkish music) represented only an external, ornamental moment, applied even in the last movement of Beethoven's Ninth symphony (accompanying the lines *Froh wie seine Sonnen fliegen durch des Himmels prächt'gen Plan*).

In earlier centuries the world had been so far extended, that the Turkish army had to threaten the borders of European civilization before the composers in Paris or Vienna took notice of oriental music. In the railway age also musical distances scaled down; and in this respect, too, the phonograph proved a helpful innovation: previously, collectors had perceived exotic music with an 'occidental' bias, noting it in their European system of notation. Only after the invention of the phonograph did it become possible to learn knowing authentic examples of such outlandish music. In the European periphery, too, composers like Bartók and Kodály had to travel around equipped with the hand-driven phonograph, because the Hungarian villages were at that time far away from electricity. On the 'consumers'' side, Gustav Mahler was listening to phonograph recordings of Chinese music at the time when he started composing *Das Lied von der Erde*, as did Puccini after the First World War, working on *Turandot*.

Another alternative for becoming acquainted with exotic music was provided by the world exhibitions, which combined displays of industrial progress and various curiosities to attract people. No book on the history of music would omit mention of the Javanese Gamelan ensemble, which impressed Debussy at the world exhibition of Paris in 1899. But there were also a Spanish gypsy band and a Chinese theatre group accompanied by native musicians.[42]

The appearance of the Gamelan orchestra was as closely related to the transport revolution as de Sousa's European tour in 1903, which gave Debussy the opportunity to listen to cake-walk and charleston, inspiring his *Golliwogg's Cake-walk*, *Le Petit Nègre* and others. On the other hand, European composers, visiting America, were influenced by the music of the Blacks and Indians. Antonín Dvořák, who composed 'only in the spirit' of American music,[43] used the melancholic exotic tunes rather as a medium to express his own homesickness. Frederick Delius, who set out for Florida in 1884 to run an orange plantation, composed – after his return to Europe – works like the *Florida* and the *Appalachia Suite*, and his opera *Koanga*. Puccini made use of the exotic idiom, even prior to *Madame Butterfly*, *La fanciulla del West* and *Turandot*. *Fanciulla* was composed after his trip to the United States in 1906 and contains three original American folk songs.

The earliest example of exoticism in European music, however, was not related to railway and steamship, but to utopian socialism and pre-industrial adventure: the 'symphonic ode' *Le Désert*, first performed in 1844, was the result of an oriental journey, which the composer Félicien David had undertaken together with some Saint-Simonist comrades in 1833–5.[44]

The big success of David's tone poem caused a veritable avalanche of exotic music, mainly in France, with Charles Gounod's *La Reine de Saba* (1862), Bizet's *La Guzla d'Emir* (1861), *Les Pêcheurs des Perles* (1863) and *Carmen*

(1875). Saint-Saëns composed a *Suite Algérienne*; Léo Delibes, Jules Massenét and Edouard Lalo, too, paid tribute to exoticism. Add Franz Liszt's fascination with gypsy music (which he mistook for Hungarian folk music), Verdi's *Aida* and Gilbert and Sullivan's *Mikado*, and you get an impression of the colourful scenario of exoticism in the music of the time.

Exoticism was not limited to the realm of music: Japanese art influenced Europe after having been displayed at the world exhibitions of 1862 (London) and 1867 (Paris). *Japonisme* became the fashion of the 1890s, even in furnishing.[45] The fascination of Asia depended on the continuing Romantic yearning after a world different from Europe's. Not by accident did this kind of Romanticism coincide with the rise in fashion of opium as a means for escaping from the world of industry: opium and, after 1874, heroin provided poets and artists with fuel for the trip into oriental dreams.[46]

Besides Debussy, who had been composing with an exotic bias, even before he encountered the Gamelan orchestra in 1889 (*Danse bohémienne, Chanson espagnole* and *Rondel chinois*) other examples of exoticism in the *fin de siècle* can be found in Granville Bantock's Persian and Indian music scenes, in Schjedderup's *Sunrise over the Himalayas*, and in Wilhelm Kienzl's *Urvasi*, one of his early operas (after an Indian tale), which he revised in 1909, using a collection of exotic songs. Maurice Ravel's *Schéhérezade* songs of 1903, too, referred to an overture of an early oriental fairy-tale opera of his own. During the following years he composed *L'Heure espagnole* and the *Rhapsodie espagnole*. Spanish influence has to be regarded as exotic, too, since it contains a strong oriental, Hebrew–Arabic element, especially in the *cante jondo* or the *copla*.[47]

Exoticism represented an important progressive moment in the process of transition to modern music: Gustav Mahler was a different composer after the exotic *Lied von der Erde* than in his earlier works.

FIGHTING HEROES

In Gustav Mahler's work a third phenomenon is added to nature and exoticism: the musical hero fighting against death, fate, and the third impervious challenge: 'world' (= society). Although his symphonies should not be misinterpreted as Programme music, Mahler himself provided the listener with (sometimes changing) proposals for association: the Titan of the First symphony dies in the first movement of the Second; in the Sixth symphony the hero (Mahler himself) was originally smashed by the third thumb of a wooden hammer.

A similar approach can be found in some works of Scriabin. His famous Third piano sonata (composed in 1897–8) has two different hidden programmes: the first has already been cited, the second attaches fighting, deceptive lull, attempted triumph, and fall of the hero, to the single movements. A different kind of hero was introduced in Richard Strauss's tone poem *Ein Heldenleben*: the composer himself fighting against malevolent critics in a musically rather extravagant manner.

The heroes of the *fin de siècle* may be attached to Schopenhauer's and Nietzsche's philosophical 'genius'. But they also seem to reflect the search for the mystic 'leader' as he appears in the *Wandervogel* movement or in H. Hesse's novels. A touch of the new irrational spirit in music can be found in Scriabin's thinking, but also in German avant-garde circles – as a careful reading of Karl Linke's article in the famous publication in honour of Arnold Schönberg in 1912 will reveal.[48]

Even if the hero does not enter the scene evidently, there is an heroic element inherent to many musical works of the *fin de siècle*: the ever growing orchestral machinery necessary to express the composer's ideas. The world had become so filled with noise (and society so predominant) that the composer could not be sure of being heard without enormous instrumental efforts.[49] Strauss's revolutionary *Elektra* required about a hundred musicians (originally 115), the *Sinfonia domestica* even more; Schönberg prescribed 150 for the *Gurrelieder*, and at the first performance of Mahler's Eighth symphony one thousand players were engaged.

At the same time new instruments found entrance into the orchestra, extending the range of expression: harmonium, celesta, and a great variety of percussion instruments and noise machines, such as piano, gongs, rods, cow bells, wooden hammers, wind machines, and the futurist howlers and buzzers.

The megalomanic mania reached its climax with two works left behind unfinished by their composers: Scriabin's *Mystery*, designed to take place in something like an Indian Bayreuth temple, would have required a colossal orchestral apparatus, perfumes, ecstatic dancers, choruses and mass movements. At the same time Charles Ives was working on his *Universe Symphony*, for which he prescribed more than a dozen different orchestras, choruses and soloists, moving around in a hilly landscape, with one band placed on a float drifting down a river.[50]

THE EMERGENCE OF MODERN MUSIC

If musical works are considered social manifestations using a specific 'language', *fin de siècle* can be defined as the transition from one language (or grammar) to another. At its beginnings stood late Romanticism, at its end modern music, i.e. a language matching the material environment of the composers. 'Art is the cry of distress of those, who live and suffer humanity's fate . . .', Schönberg wrote, 'of those who do not, to shield their emotions, avert their eyes but open them wide to do what needs to be done.'[51]

To understand the essence of that transition, we need not go into details of the history of harmony and composition, The development in Vienna may serve as an illustration. Hugo Wolf's quasi-Impressionistic late songs as well as Alexander Zemlinsky's and Franz Schreker's colourful, sensual sound debaucheries cover part of the revolutionary innovations of *fin-de-siècle* music. The key persons, however, were Gustav Mahler and Arnold Schönberg.

In a letter to Alfredo Casella (who composed the first twelve-toned chord in 1915) Mahler himself divided his symphonic oeuvre into three periods: the first covers the symphonies 1–4, the second 5–8, and the last starts with the 'Ninth symphony' (which could also have meant *Das Lied von der Erde*).[52] Mahler was permanently in search of improvements of the musical language, and in the first movement of the Ninth he did, indeed, open the door to modern music. However, as Schönberg stated, Mahler 'hardly any longer [spoke] as a subject . . . This opus no longer expresses the voice of the Self. It offers, as it were, objective, almost passionless statements . . .'[53]

Schönberg, as well as Anton Webern and Alban Berg, started with late Romanticism and Impressionism, and soon arrived at Expressionism and free atonality. Schönberg's transitional works were the *Chamber Symphony* (1906), the *George songs* of 1908, and the six piano pieces op. 19 (composed in 1911). The main characteristics are the reduction of the orchestral apparatus, the quitting of tonality and – in *op. 19* – of another essential element of traditional music: the repetition of phrases or melodies. These short piano pieces seem like a musical answer to the monotony of the assembly-line. A similar protest against the standardization of time can be found in Debussy's flowing, 'timeless' way of composing and, perhaps, in the jerky changes of rhythms in the works of Bartók, Stravinsky and others.

During these years Schönberg was also formulating the antithesis of heroism: the monodrama (e.g. *Erwartung*, composed in 1909) was the musical equivalent of psychoanalysis and of the art of Kokoschka, who portrayed, according to his own statement, people 'in their anxiety and pain', perceptible only behind their façades.[54]

Other avenues of modern music were opened by Stravinsky's *Le Sacre du Printemps* with its brutal primitivism, and by Charles Ives (who was really discovered only in the second half of our century). In Ives's music there is almost everything: music about music, folk tunes, minimal music (similar to Eric Satie's), atonality, polyrhythmics, tone clusters, quarter-tones.

On the eve of the First World War works were composed that sounded like presentiments of the bloody slaughter to come: Stravinsky's *Sacre* (1911),

Webern's *Orchesterstücke*, op. 6 (1909), and Alban Berg's *Drei Orchester-stücke* (1914). The alarming signals of modern music, however, were perceived only by a small enlightened elite. The mass of fans of classical music refused to listen to such cacophony. In Vienna doctors even attested that listening to Schönberg's *Pierrot Lunaire* (composed 1912 in free atonality) would damage the nervous system.[55]

During the late 1920s the experimental mood that had animated modern music in the late *fin de siècle* was increasingly overlapped by the striving for a return to order (paralleling similar trends in politics), which appears in Schönberg's twelve tone system or in Stravinsky's neo-Classicism. And if we turn from the exceptional music life of cities such as Berlin, contemporary 'serious' music was further pushed into a ghetto.

Finally, the dictatorial regimes of the 1930s in many countries (including the Soviet Union) marginalized the avant-garde and depressed contemporary composition to the level of taste of dumb cultural bureaucrats. At least on the European continent, modern music could never recover from the authoritarian repression of the 1930s.

But political constraint only intensified and accelerated a development which had begun in the nineteenth century: the cleavage between contemporary composition and the taste of the broad public. This fatal process continued after the Second World War. Serious modern music became the esoteric arena of ever smaller circles of intellectuals. The first performances of many early works of Schönberg, Stravinsky and Paul Hindemith had been accompanied by scandals and scuffles. After 1945 contemporary music was beyond public controversy. Whatever therefore the *fin de siècle* of our time is going to bring forth, its avant-garde music will attract less public attention than that around 1900 – despite the many signs of the revival of a *fin-de-siècle* mood around us.

NOTES

I owe many thanks to my friends R. Kannonier, H. Rögl and A. Staudinger for commenting on the first draft of the article. I am especially grateful to Fred Prager, who did much more than merely correct my English.

1 N. Tschulik, *Musiktheater in Österreich* (Vienna, 1984), pp. 14–29, 45–7; R. Werba, *Maria Jeritza* (Vienna, 1981), pp. 43–4.
2 Cf. W. Niemann, *Die Musik der Gegenwart* (Berlin and Leipzig, 1913); A. Baumgartner, *Musik des 20. Jahrhunderts* (Salzburg, 1985).
3 K. Honolka, *Die Oper ist tot – die Oper lebt* (Stuttgart, 1986), pp. 26, 32.
4 Cf. Niemann, *Musik*, p. 217.
5 K. Blaukopf, *Gustav Mahler* (Munich, 1980), pp. 180–94; *Neue Freie Presse* (Vienna), 11 May 1883.
6 Adorno's idea about the breakthrough function of chamber music points in the

same direction. Cf. Th. W. Adorno, *Einleitung in die Musiksoziologie* (Reinbek nr. Hamburg, 1968), pp. 103–7.

7 Th. W. Adorno, *Philosophie der neuen Musik* (Frankfurt-on-Main, 1978), p. 175.

8 P. Bekker, *Gustav Mahlers Sinfonien* (Tutzing, 1969), pp. 9–35.

9 For detailed comments see H. H. Stuckenschmidt, *Neue Musik* (Frankfurt-on-Main, 1981).

10 The following remarkable sentence is to be found in a *Compendium of Practical Musick* of 1667: 'I am slow to believe that any good musick … can be composed in Quarter-Tones, although I hear some talk much of it.' Quoted in *The Oxford Companion to Music* (Oxford, 1947), p. 575.

11 It would be worth considering the different patterns of development of *fin-de-siècle* music in the core and the periphery regions in a separate article.

12 E. Friedell, *Kulturgeschichte der Neuzeit*, vol. II (Munich, 1976), p. 133.

13 W. Schivelbusch, *Lichtblicke. Zur Geschichte der künstlichen Helligkeit im 19. Jahrhundert* (Frankfurt-on-Main, 1986), pp. 67–70; *Allgemeine Geschichte der Technik von 1870 bis etwa 1920* (Leipzig, 1984), pp. 48–58, 220–41.

14 Cf. E. R. Tannenbaum, *1900. Die Generation vor dem Grossen Krieg* (Frankfurt-on-Main, Berlin and Vienna, 1978), pp. 242–8.

15 Friedell, *Kulturgeschichte*, pp. 1456, 1461.

16 Cf. H. Glaser, *Sigmund Freuds zwanzigstes Jahrhundert* (Munich and Vienna, 1976), pp. 53–4.

17 Friedell, *Kulturgeschichte*, pp. 1467–8; M. von Boehn, *Der Tanz* (Berlin, 1925), p. 120.

18 F. Ahlers-Hestermann, *Stilwende. Aufbruch der Jugend um 1900* (Frankfurt-on-Main, Berlin and Vienna, 1981), p. 21.

19 Concerning *Wandervogel* cf. C. Hepp, *Avantgarde* (Munich, 1987), pp. 11–42.

20 W. Schivelbusch, *Lichtblicke*, pp. 64–6.

21 Friedell, *Kulturgeschichte*, p. 1301.

22 Cf. Tannenbaum, *1900*, pp. 265–8; Blaukopf, *Mahler*, p. 127; Glaser, *Freud*, pp. 82–3, 153–4.

23 Tschulik, *Musiktheater*, pp. 64–74.

24 Cf. H. H. Eggebrecht, *Die Musik Gustav Mahlers* (Munich and Zurich, 1986).

25 Blaukopf, *Mahler*, p. 126.

26 N. Bauer-Lechner, *Erinnerungen an Gustav Mahler* (Leipzig, Vienna and Zurich, 1923), p. 147.

27 W. Felix, W. Marggraf, W. Reising and G. Schönfelder (eds.), *Musikgeschichte. Ein Grundriss*, part II (Leipzig, 1985), pp. 744–45.

28 Quoted in U. Appolonio, *Der Futurismus* (Cologne, 1972), p. 58.

29 F. Herzfeld, *Magie des Taktstocks* (Berlin, 1953), pp. 146–7. During one of these exotic *stagioni* the young Toscanini had his début as a conductor in Rio de Janeiro. Cf. H. Sachs, *Toscanini* (Munich, 1982), pp. 35–7.

30 *Musikgeschichte*, pp. 828, 833; H. Sirp, *Anton Dvorák* (Potsdam, 1939), pp. 104–15; S. Schmidt-Joos, *Das Musical* (Munich, 1965), p. 44.

31 P. Casals, *Licht und Schatten auf einem langen Weg* (Frankfurt-on-Main, 1974), pp. 72–91.

32 Herzfeld, *Magie*, p. 58; W. Jerger, *Die Wiener Philharmoniker. Erbe und Sendung*

(Vienna, 1942), pp. 58–9; W. Stresemann, *The Berlin Philharmonic from Bülow to Karajan* (Berlin, 1979), pp. 61–2.

33 Herzfeld, *Magie*, pp. 76–9; *Musikgeschichte*, pp. 602–3.
34 Cf. F.-P. Kothes, *Die theatralische Revue in Berlin und Wien 1900–1938* (Wilhelmshaven, 1977).
35 Concerning the origins of the Musical cf. Schmidt-Joos, *Musical*, pp. 33–41.
36 *Musikgeschichte*, pp. 252–6. There were also other contemporary sound reproduction systems like the Welte-Mignon and the Phonola processes, which enabled the direct recording of piano playing on paper rolls.
37 Casals, *Licht*, p. 85.
38 Schivelbusch, *Lichtblicke*, pp. 87–109.
39 Quoted in G. Salmen, *Musiker im Porträt 5. Das 20. Jahrhundert* (Munich, 1984), p. 150.
40 Quoted in H. C. Schonberg, *Die grossen Komponisten* (Berlin, 1986), p. 507.
41 Quoted in Niemann, *Musik*, p. 270.
42 Cf. P. Gradenwitz, *Musik zwischen Orient und Okzident* (Wilhelmshaven and Hamburg, 1977), pp. 324–5, 331.
43 Quoted in Sirp, *Dvorák*, p. 108.
44 Cf. Gradenwitz, *Orient*, pp. 22–6, 281–7. David also composed operas such as *The Pearl of Brasil* and *Lalla-Roukh*.
45 Ahlers-Hestermann, *Stilwende*, pp. 23, 31–3, 74, 84; Friedell, *Kulturgeschichte*, p. 1333.
46 Cf. W. Schivelbusch, *Das Paradies, der Geschmack und die Vernunft. Eine Geschichte der Genussmittel* (Frankfurt-on-Main, Berlin and Vienna, 1985), pp. 215–26.
47 Following Frederico Lorca, quoted in Gradenwitz, *Orient*, pp. 330–4.
48 K. Linke, 'Zur Einführung', in *Arnold Schönberg* (Munich, 1912), pp. 13–21.
49 Similar reflections should be entertained concerning Shostakovich's 'heroic' symphonies, composed *before* he was criticized by Stalin and Shdanov. For the history of orchestration in general cf. H. Raynor, *The Orchestra* (New York and London, 1978); A. Carse, *The History of Orchestration* (New York, 1964).
50 Cf. I. F. Belsa, *Alexander Nikolajewitsch Skrjabin* (Berlin, 1986), pp. 198–211; R. U. Ringger, *Von Debussy bis Henze* (Munich, 1986), pp. 26–7.
51 Quoted in P. Werckner, *Aufbruch in die Moderne*, in *Das Zeitalter Kaiser Franz Josephs* (Vienna, 1987), p. 227.
52 Quoted in P. Stefan, *Gustav Mahler* (Munich, 1912), p. 83.
53 Quoted in *Musikgeschichte*, p. 576.
54 Quoted in A. Janik and S. Toulmin, *Wittgenstein's Vienna* (New York, 1973), p. 101.
55 Stuckenschmidt, *Neue Musik*, pp. 82–3.

TWELVE

ॐ

THE TRANSFORMATION OF PHYSICS

ERWIN N. HIEBERT

REFLECTIONS ON THE PHYSICS DISCIPLINE

The end of the nineteenth century has been characterized by numerous authors as a time of intellectual and artistic decadence, political calumny, social discontent and widespread, general dissonance. By contrast it is universally asserted that advances in experimental and theoretical physics at the turn of the century set the stage for the revolution in physics that followed. It has become commonplace to view *fin-de-siècle* changes as a watershed separating the old physics from the new. In this context we will be referring to 'the transformation of physics' that took place in going from 'classical physics' to the 'new physics' of the twentieth century.

Unforeseen and abrupt as this transformation seems to have been, especially when examined with the aid of hindsight, it nevertheless can be said that most if not all of the decisive anchor points of the 'new physics' can be linked with components embedded in late nineteenth-century classical theory and practice. There were many contextual factors that made the 'new physics' possible. The establishment of research institutes and laboratories and the increased accessibility of scientific instruments were concurrent with the overhauling of methods of university instruction and laboratory practice. There was a gradual shift towards collaborative research that would have been beyond the reach of individuals. Above all the transformation of physics was facilitated by the birth of an expanding international consensus concerning the positive value of the natural sciences.

While the emphasis in this paper will fall on the discipline of physics itself, we recognize that the turn of the century also can be represented as a time when access to technological progress and mass participation in communication, transportation, domestic illumination, plumbing and central heating – that had been reserved for a privileged class – began to be extended to the public. Such changes run parallel with the development of physics; frequently experiment was ahead of theory, and sometimes technology was ahead of both. Evidence for the genuine and brisk transformation of physics that began in 1895 is exhibited most of all in the way that the experimental and theoretical subject matter of physics changed. The practice of doing physics was modified simultaneously with a restructuring of the professionalization of the discipline.[1]

The spontaneous and largely unanticipated disclosure of entirely new domains in physics and chemistry at the end of the century, such as X-rays, radioactivity, quantum theory and relativity, served to accentuate the differences in outlook that often were and still are alluded to in contrasting the progressive character of the natural sciences and the image of the so-called *fin-de-siècle* stalemate in social and political practice. Some of the expressions that came into vogue with *fin-de-siècle* reflections on the world of culture are: bourgeois decadence, intellectual bankruptcy, irrational escapism, freedom on the fringe of bored aestheticism, the abyss of freedom, fashionable despair, cultivated fatigue, and collapse.[2]

None of the negative expressions that have come to be associated with turn-of-the-century perspectives on literature, society, and the fine arts properly capture the state of affairs and intellectual climate in physics between 1880 and 1910. Nevertheless, it is pertinent to indicate at this point, but without entering into specifics, that the perceived upswing turn-of-the-century mood in physics by no means was thought by contemporaries to be the sole prerogative of the natural sciences. In fact there were many writers and artists who championed the dawn of a new day that, through release from the burdens of the past, would make available unimagined new literary and artistic possibilities. A vortex of unprecedented freedom, creativity and sensibility had been aroused, unloosed and set free. In music, for example, various musicologists, historians, composers and music critics have given positive appraisals for the period.

Before proceeding with an analysis of the preconditions and transformations that characterized turn-of-the-century physics, it is pertinent to specify what was meant by 'physics' at the time. To physics in the 1890s belonged 'the science or group of sciences, basically treating of the properties of matter and energy'.[3] In reference to domains or sub-disciplines within physics, this would have included, foremost, the study of matter in motion under the influence of forces, i.e. mechanics, but also thermal studies and thermodynamics, physical and geometrical optics, and the electromagnetic theory of radiation. The term 'classical physics' was not in widespread use until the 1920s. It was introduced to distinguish the 'new physics' from 'conclusions based on concepts and theories established before the discovery of quantum theory or relativity, etc.'.[4]

A concise and exemplary statement of what actually happened in physics that would bring the expression 'classical physics' into prominence, is given by Paul Dirac in 1930:

The classical tradition has been to consider the world to be an association of observable objects (particles, fluids, etc.) moving about according to definite laws of force, so that one could form a mental picture in space and time of the whole scheme. This led to a physics whose aim was to make assumptions about the mechanism and forces connecting these observable objects, to account for their behaviour in the simplest possible way. It has become increasingly evident in recent times, however, that nature works on a different plan. Her fundamental laws do not govern the world as it appears in our mental picture in any very direct way, but instead they control a *substratum* of which we cannot form a mental picture without introducing irrelevancies. The formulation of these laws requires the use of the mathematics of transformations. The important things in the world appear as the invariants (or more generally the nearly invariants, or quantities with simple transformation properties) of these transformations. The things we are immediately aware of are the relations of these nearly invariants to a certain frame of reference, usually one chosen so as to introduce special simplifying features which are unimportant from the point of view of general theory.[5]

It is evident from Dirac's statement that theoretical and mathematical physics would be given pride of place in the 'new physics' that came to be built around relativity theory and quantum theory. In these newly generated domains the reciprocity between experiment and theory was seen to be largely dominated by theories that are grandiose in claim and powerful in the suggestion of experiments that support the theory. The models for such majestic and commanding theories were inherited from the nineteenth century.

A retrospective examination of the most impressive theoretical landmarks in physics by the end of the nineteenth century reveals that three domains of 'classical physics' – mechanics, thermodynamics and electromagnetic theory – stand out conspicuously by virtue of the far-reaching consequences that can be drawn from a set of concise principles. These principles, in turn, can be derived from a surprisingly small number of axiomatic premises and phenomenological observations. By the end of the century considerable effort had been devoted to achieving some kind of deep-level integration of these three domains but without overall success. Enthusiasm for theoretical unification gave way to phenomenological expansiveness where novel discoveries did not fit into any of the known theoretical niches: X-rays in 1895, natural radioactivity in 1896, identification of the electron as a particle of discrete mass and charge in 1897, and by 1911 evidence that the atom was 100,000 times the size of its nucleus. Conceptually too, physicists were compelled to come to terms with quantized energy notions (1900), the relativity of space, time and motion (1905), and an internally structured atom where classical mechanics collapsed. Study of properties and processes for the atomic nucleus – for which there was no precedent, not even in chemistry or quantum theory – opened up new worlds that were inconceivably complex.

FRONTIERS OF PHYSICS

The transformation of physics was realized simultaneously at the frontiers of experimental, theoretical and mathematical physics. This division of scientific labour essentially had been put in place professionally during the last three decades of the nineteenth century. Prior to that time there basically were just 'physicists' whose expertise was dominant in one or more of the three areas. A few remarks will serve to clarify how physicists at the turn of the century sought to gain access to and integrate experimental, theoretical and mathematical physics.

The history of experimental physics, or at least what later generations referred to as experimental physics, can be traced over several centuries. The growth of physics and the recognition of its social value, notably after 1870, brought new significance to the role of experimentation and invention, its industrial patronage and its professional institutionalization. During the last three decades of the century the application of scientific principles, notably in the domain of electromagnetism, gave rise to an expansion in practical inventions that would lead to the perfection of telegraphy, telephone, incandescent electric lamps, induction coils and dynamo-driven electric supply stations. It therefore comes as no great surprise to see that towards the end of the century university posts in experimental physics increasingly came to be established, principally, one might suggest, to distinguish the pursuit of experiment as a speciality from mathematical and theoretical physics, but also to give such posts academic authority.

Mathematical physics, prominent throughout the nineteenth century, had been cultivated by both physicists and mathematicians who occupied chairs in mathematical physics, physics or mathematics, or any combination of them. This assimilation of skills reflects the need and the structure of the professional discipline of physics through most of its history. It also contributed substantially to the setting of the stage for the establishment of positions in theoretical physics by the end of the century.

In 1875, for example, a sizeable number of British physicists, such as Stokes, William Thomson, Maxwell and Tait, exhibited extraordinary competence in mathematics. Coincident with the political unification of Germany in the 1870s came the movement to reshape the institutional structure and training ideals in physics at the universities. Mathematics notably was given a new emphasis. Physicists like Helmholtz, Kirchhoff and

Hertz exhibited mastery in mathematics but were equally at home with theory and the experimental workshop. By 1880, in Germany, mathematical physics came to be looked upon as a special domain of physics. In France there was Cornu, and in America, Gibbs. A positive stimulus, that served to enhance the status and significance of both mathematical and theoretical physics, was provided by the rapid growth of investigations made possible by the refinement and proliferation of scientific instruments.

There also was a growing technical awareness of the relevance of physics in industry at the international level – a perspective that chemists had enjoyed for at least a century. William Thomson (Lord Kelvin) is a prime example of a physicist who, in addition to being one of the best mathematical physicists of his time, also was something of a technological entrepreneur; he commanded an in-depth knowledge of everything connected with electrical signalling, sensitive measuring devices, navigation, tides and waves.

The transformation of physics that is the focus of our concern here came more and more to depend on the mathematics of mathematicians, and especially on such as explicitly had extended their interests to specific topics in physics.[6] The unreasonable, almost uncanny pertinence and potency of mathematics for physics, as seen in the creation of relativity and quantum mechanics, became a much-discussed issue among physicists and epistemologists. In these discussions attempts were made to establish the ontological status of the formalisms that were generated. How was one to come to terms with formalisms – mathematically elegant and scientifically powerful – that were so effective in physics but so difficult to transpose into meaningful physical models – mechanical, thermodynamic or field theoretic? The new physics, as Dirac commented, led to the loss of mental models. They were replaced by invariants that were chosen for their simplifying features; they could be manipulated by mathematical transformations.

The crux of the matter was that the mathematical formalisms worked. They accounted for known phenomena, predicted new ones and led to theories and conceptual frameworks that did the same. When explanatory success was accompanied by theoretical, conceptual or mathematical complexity, physicists, then as now, explored strategic moves that would lead closer to a unitary physics. To elucidate what was meant by unity, of course, was open to debate. In 1900, speaking to an international audience in Paris, Henri Poincaré expressed the view that what was needed was not so much an abstract and general conception of the unity of nature, as a search for the sense in which nature might be conceived from a unitary point of view within the context of the available resources in experimental and theoretical physics.[7]

It was not until the 1870s that 'theoretical physics' came to be recognized as an autonomous domain within the physics discipline. Even then the opportunities for a career and a university post were rather occasional. Physicists such as Einstein and Gibbs, who by choice were comparatively far removed from direct access to experimental activities, pursued on their own what can be designated as theoretical physics. Others such as Bohr, Helmholtz, Larmor, Laue, Ritz and Wien were known primarily for their theoretical physics but stood in close contact with the experimental frontier. There were relatively few academic chairs explicitly established for theoretical physics, perhaps fewer than a dozen by 1905 – the date of publication of Einstein's special relativity theory.[8]

In comparison with experimental physics, theoretical posts, early on, did not always carry great prestige. In fact, an argument can be made, at least for turn-of-the-century Germany, that the most lucrative and desired professional university posts in physics were reserved for experimentalists and not for theoreticians. This imbalance in the discipline, in my opinion, goes a long way towards explaining why persons who did not have access to the best (i.e. experimental) positions in physics would have specialized in the more speculative and less traditional, i.e. theoretical, domains of physics. One might suggest, for example, that it was built right into the German university system that Jewish physicists would be forced, reluctantly – at least from their point of view as job-holders – to take up eccentric and controversial themes such as relativity, quantum theory and some aspects of nuclear physics. As it turned out, it is precisely in these new domains that the theoretical contributions of Jewish physicists became prominent.[9]

FIN-DE-SIÈCLE MENTALITY

From our comments thus far it will have become evident that the transition from classical to twentieth-century physics took place in a relatively unbroken and tranquil but reformist and spirited manner. That is to say, the transformation of the physics discipline was realized within an intellectual and social environment – mostly academia – that exhibited none of the stereotypical and demeaning referents that often, if not universally, came to be associated with '*fin-de-siècle*' mentality. How widely this polarization was thought to reach at the time depends on which authors, contemporary and later, are consulted. Even so a very prominent view is that the sciences everywhere were on the move while deterioration and retrogression were rampant in most non-science domains.

The most assertive expression of the uniquely progressive spirit in the physical sciences comes not from spokesmen within the physics community but from biologists and social scientists seeking to buttress their own scientific prestige by endorsing and appropriating to their own disciplines the most conspicuous accomplishments in physics. The positive reinforcement that physics enjoyed within the small and privileged circle of scientists served to generate within the minds of the general public a growing awareness of the importance of physics. This was accompanied by rising expectations concerning the potential social benefits of the technological by-products of physics.

The German electrophysiologist Emil Du Bois-Reymond stands out as one of the most domineering of nineteenth-century European scientists. He played an active role in promoting discussions on the connection between the natural sciences and the humanities. His research programme was based on developing an experimental science that would reduce physiological processes to electrical, molecular and atomic mechanism drawn from physics. He rejected the idea of 'vital force' in physiology. It was for him a metaphysical notion that violates the principles of conservation of energy. In his lectures of 1872 and 1880 he had brandished the expression *ignoramus – ignorabimus* (we do not know it – we never will know it) to characterize transcendental questions that are meaningless because scientifically unanswerable.[10] His polemical pronouncements gave rise to a polarization among scientists and philosophers that became a vehicle for scientific critiques of what were seen to be dogmatic and unreflective epistemologies of cognition. Within the context of debates on cultural, political and educational policy, at the end of the century, anti-metaphysical materialists used the *ignoramus-ignorabimus* image as a flag of convenience to espouse the cause of the emancipation of science from orthodoxy in philosophy and theology. All were ostracized in one way or another for their heretical philosophical positions. They none the less enjoyed wide readership.[11]

Du Bois-Reymond embraced a confidence in 'science that strides on victoriously towards a boundless future', where the scientist – as sworn witness 'before the tribunal of reality striving for knowledge of the universe as it actually is' – experiences a 'feeling of responsibility in presence of Nature's eternally inviolable laws'.[12] In comparing the progressive character of late nineteenth-century natural science with the 'falling-off' and 'at best stationary' condition of the arts, Du Bois-Reymond writes: 'No real civilization would exist without it [science], and in its absence nothing could prevent our civilization, including art and its master-works, from crumbling away again hopelessly as at the decline of the ancient world.'[13] Du Bois-Reymond wanted the natural sciences to occupy a position of primacy above all other branches of learning and arts, because he believed that only science was able to provide the basis upon which the ancillary furniture of healthy civilizations could thrive. Although he had no sympathy with Goethe's views on nature and science he valued Goethe's nimble-witted command of language: 'Goethe very truly observed – little thinking how harshly . . . his remark reflects on part of his own scientific work . . . that: Nature allows no trifling; she is always sincere, always serious, always stern; she is always in the right, and the errors and mistakes are invariably ours.'[14]

Towards the end of the century one encounters growing public support for an image of science as friend and ally of the masses – a point of view that went hand-in-hand with sentiments deploring the degradation of standards in the arts, literature, religion, politics and philosophy. In popular and polemic works, distributed far and wide, anti-metaphysical materialists, as we shall show, spread the gospel of an in-process transformation of science that would transcend the *fin-de-siècle* decadence taking place in those branches of learning having primarily a cultural character. For example, Karl Vogt, zoologist, geologist, marine biologist, champion of anthropological Darwinism and outspoken atheist, was skilled at cultivating the image of the scientist. Vogt was described as one who from time to time as the conscience of society 'steps out of the calm of the laboratory into the market-place of life and feels himself called upon to let all mankind take part in the spiritual blessings of scientific progress'.[15] Vogt had a gift for polemic and oratory. His materialist philosophy was laid down in 1853 in a caustic analysis of 'blind faith and belief' (*Köhlerglaube und Wissenschaft*). The work, published in several editions, caused a great commotion that to the end of his life was kept alive in his physiological letters. These are replete with catchy phrases that often were quoted to characterize crass materialism: 'The brain secretes thought as the kidney does urine', or 'thoughts are to the brain as the gall is to the liver or urine to the kidneys'.[16]

The most influential of the German materialists, Ludwig Büchner, came to fame with a popular scientistic and moralistic exploitation of the principle of conservation of energy, *Force and Matter*, a work first published in 1855 and in its eighteenth edition by the time of his death in 1899.[17] Towards the end of his life Büchner published a mock-heroic treatise, *At the Deathbed of the Century*, in which the steady advancement and benefits of the natural sciences were played off against the decadence exhibited in philosophy, religion, spiritualism, naturopathy, politics, anarchism, social questions, women's rights, the Jewish question and literature. He writes:

One might assume that the splendid advances in the sciences should have resulted in just as much progress in the thinking and meaning of mankind concerning the aim and purpose of existence. Miraculously, exactly the opposite is the case; this ranks among the many unclarified riddles and contradictions of world history. The greater the depth and compass of science on the one side, the greater the reaction against the conclusions that could be drawn from science . . .[18]

In his Janus-faced portrait of the state of affairs at the century's end Büchner gave an enthusiastic account of the splendid advances, discoveries and inventions in the natural sciences and especially in the physical sciences.[19] He also had kind things to say about studies in hypnotism and the shift that had taken place when psychology broke its alignment with philosophy and moved towards anthropology and psychiatry (*Seelenlehre*). By contrast Büchner saw that almost everything that falls beyond the boundaries of the natural sciences had deteriorated – had taken up partnership with the most gloomy and hopeless sentiments of mankind. In fact, he believed that in the world of culture, despair would produce negative pressures upon the future advancement of the sciences. Philosophy, he believed, had deteriorated to preoccupation with 'speculative solutions for the last and highest things', and to metaphysical talk about 'deriving the totality of being and thinking from an integrated all-encompassing principle that would solve the great riddle of the universe'.[20]

Religion and the religious lie – spread by state, church, judge and the educated modern priest – were seen to dominate the civilized world and had served to demoralize men's public and private lives. Spiritualism, as the retrograde movement of the mind (*geistiger Krebsgang*), and belief in ghosts and spooks, had infected millions. Politics without wisdom was the order of the day. Anarchism, wild and egoistic impulses, and antisocial instincts, were on the increase. The general esteem and standing of women had decreased from former times while their workload had increased. The florescence of anti-Semitism in the *Kaiserreich* was the disgrace of the century.[21] Art and literature were saturated with degeneration and mental laziness that was sickening, rotten, damaging, weak, miserable, tasteless, sensational, abnormal: 'It is the time of so-called decadence or decay which seeks to cover up, in its personalities as well as in the form or representation, its want of intellect and character in the depiction of extravagant, artificial, pathological feelings and situations.'[22]

The riptide of enthusiasm for the pursuit of science, in the midst of a perceived and, one might add, fabricated *fin-de-siècle* degeneration in morality, ethics, belief systems, art and literature, is nowhere more anxiously chased after than in the works of the zoologist Ernst Haeckel whose blending of monism, social Darwinism, pantheism and materialism seemingly answered some contemporary needs of the day. His 'scientific philosophy' was rooted in an uncompromisingly monistic empiricism, nurtured by harsh criticism of church dogma. In *The Riddle of the Universe* (1899), a work which found immediate popular acclaim and achieved great success in many editions and languages, Haeckel wrote:

At the close of the nineteenth century, before which we stand, one of the most remarkable spectacles is offered to the thinking observer. All educated persons are in agreement that in many respects this manifestation immeasurably outstrips all of its predecessors and has led to the solution of problems that were insoluble at first. Not only the unexpected theoretical progress in genuine knowledge of nature, but also the amazingly fertile, practical applications in technology, industry, communication, and so on, have given our modern cultural life a totally new special character. On the other hand, in important domains of intellectual life and social relations there is little or no progress to show over previous centuries, and unfortunately often even serious retrogressions. From this evident conflict there arises not only an uncomfortable feeling of inner disintegration and untruth, but also the danger of catastrophes in political and social spheres.[23]

TRANSFORMATION OF PHYSICS

We have sought here to characterize the main features of the scientific scene as it was represented in the reflections of scientists and self-christened, materialist philosophers at the turn of the century. The euphoria about science that was dramatized in their writings coincided chronologically with the *fin-de-siècle* decadence that was judged by them to be seeping into all areas of thought and action lying outside the province of science, i.e. those branches of learning regarded as having primarily a cultural character.

Physicists preserved a less sinister impression of the malaise of the time. On the one hand, they were less pessimistic about their surrounding non-scientific culture; or at least they were less outspoken about cultural degradation. On the other hand, physicists were not totally sanguine about the unbounded future of their own discipline. At most it was to be hoped that the rich harvest of new scientific discoveries might provide a promising point of departure for a critical, naturalistic, scientific humanism whose main objective it would be to organize scientific knowledge on behalf of human welfare. From an internal point of view, however i.e. from the standpoint of the physics discipline itself – the future, unlike pre-1895 physics, was unforeseeable, promising, uncharted.

During the last two decades of the nineteenth century, scientists had witnessed an expansive growth in the scope, content, practice and technological relevance of the natural sciences. In physics the maturity and refinement of theoretical principles was conspicuous, notably in continuum mechanics, thermodynamics and the electromagnetic theory of radiation. In the midst of these grand accomplishments, formidable phenomenological and theoretical difficulties, of course, were identified. In general, however, it was assumed that the elucidation of the most troublesome anomalies would depend less upon the discovery of new theoretical guidelines than upon successful integration into the body of what later came to be referred to as 'classical physics'. That is to say, the prevailing mood in physics was one that was oriented towards correlating newly discovered information with what already had been laid down. This perceived lull in physics prior to 1895 unquestionably was real. It nevertheless has received undue emphasis in the history of science, for with the benefit of hindsight it is tempting, and too easy, to pinpoint and contrast the explosive changes in the complexion of physics that occurred between the mid-1890s and 1905.

Not long after 1895, physicists were forced to recognize that their discipline was potentially open-ended to fundamental novelty in both experiment and theory. This mental switch, from seeming complacence to inquisitive expectations, had been accentuated just a few years earlier by high-level assertions that the future of physics lay mostly in mopping-up operations and refinements in what was already known. While there can be little doubt about the steady forward march of experimental physics and practice during the last two decades of the century, on the whole, conspicuous theoretical accomplishments were infrequent. This gave rise to the general opinion that perhaps the more important physical features of nature already had been discovered, and that improvements in theory were to be looked for mainly in the details rather than elsewhere on new theoretical frontiers.

The prominent physicist Gustav Kirchhoff, whose forte was theory but who also placed great value on the essential long-range need for experiment, was convinced that there were but slim chances of upsetting or even fundamentally revising the main theoretical pillars of physics. Kirchhoff's comprehensive lectures on mathematical physics are a living symbol of self-contained unitary physics from a phenomenological point of view.[24] The self-confident message concerning the advanced status of theory in physics is mollified only by accentuating the limitless frontiers of experimental refinement in basic theory.

One of the most frequently cited passages to illustrate the closure of physics at the end of the nineteenth century is the one made by Albert Michelson. In his Lowell Institute lectures of 1899 he said:

The more important fundamental laws and facts of physical science have all been discovered, and these are now so firmly established that the possibility of their ever being supplanted in consequence of new discoveries is exceedingly remote . . . Our future discoveries must be looked for in the sixth place of decimals.[25]

This sentiment represents vintage Michelson, for it was in keeping with his lifelong passion to develop ever more precise optical equipment for the measurement of the speed of light – a task he carried out with six-figure precision. Michelson was not merely asserting that the discovery of laws and facts would taper off; he was suggesting that experiments would show the way to the future. In this he was not so far off the mark. It was rather that he had too myopic a perspective on how radically experimental investigations might alter the theoretical structure of physics. 'It follows that every means which facilitates accuracy in measurement is a possible factor in a future discovery, and this will, I trust, be sufficient excuse for bringing to your notice the various methods and results which form the subject-matter of these lectures.'[26]

By the end of the first decade of the twentieth century sixth decimal place physics was passé. The discovery of X-rays, natural radioactivity and the electron paved the way for the study and theoretical interpretation of radiation and spectra, atomic and molecular theory, quantum theory and relativity. In 1911 Rutherford and others put forth a nuclear theory of the atom. In 1913 Niels Bohr published his planetary theory of the hydrogen atom based on quantum considerations. After 1920 particle-induced transmutation of elements became well known.

Apart from the transformation of physics associated with the enunciation of relativity theory, perhaps the most conspicuous *fin-de-siècle* watershed separating the 'classical physics' of 1895 from the 'new physics' of 1905 pertains to the status of the corpuscular theory of matter. Throughout the nineteenth century the atom, although discovered to be more or less ancillary to the mainstream of physical theory, was conceived of as a mechanical entity subject to attractive forces and possessing properties such as mass, density, impenetrability, elasticity, mobility and extension. Atomism and mechanism came to be so firmly held conceptually that most of the philosophical, physical and chemical debates surrounding the mechanistic interpretation of science spilled over into discussions about atomism, and vice versa.[27]

Towards the end of the century, however, many physical scientists felt that the atomic-molecular-kinetic model of matter was not deeply embedded in mechanics, thermodynamics, electrodynamics or structure of matter theory. It was widely understood among scientists that there was no adequate description or explanation of the physics and chemistry of atomic phenomena. Partial clues as to where the solution might be found came from a host of diverse puzzles generated from within physics and chemistry.[28]

The fundamental significance of the corpuscular theory of matter for physics came about only after the discovery of the electric atom (the electron), the planetary and nuclear models of the atom, the correlation of spectra with atomic structure, the quantum theory, the artificial transmutation of elements, the particle nature of all forms of radiation, and the wave nature of particles. By 1910 it had become evident that the atom was a complex, structured, unstable, dynamic unit not at all similar to the atom of Lucretius, Gassendi, Newton, Dalton, Maxwell or Kelvin.

CONCLUDING REMARKS

Michelson's 'sixth decimal place physics', as a maxim for the calm in 1899 that preceded the stormy first decade of the twentieth century, falls short in providing substantive insight into the major trends and climate of opinion prevalent among physicists at the time. Accordingly we offer an attempt to reconstruct a number of the most prominent landmarks current among members of the physics community around 1900, plus or minus five years.

In first place, a widespread belief existed – perhaps bordering on wishful thinking – that an expansive unity in 'classical' physical theory was feasible if not yet within reach. It is tempting to view such monistic perspectives as part and parcel of a larger doctrine of progress and the logical extension of nineteenth-century reductionist thought. By contrast, late nineteenth-century critical positivists such as Mach, Duhem and Poincaré maintained a brand of radical pluralism that, although rooted in scientific monism, was a monism of scientific methodology and not of theory. In any case, between 1900 and 1905 considerable emphasis was given to mastering the physics discipline in a unified way in order to encompass fundamental reformulations in physics indicated by new discoveries. Physicists, it seemed, were on the verge of a transformation of the discipline that, to a pre-eminent degree, would modify the thinking of scientists in all fields. Rightly or wrongly they felt that what was happening would revolutionize the whole domain of physics more than all that had gone before.

The self-confident and brazen elitism concerning the march of pure physics was not the only determinant for the new optimism. In another place I have referred to concomitant advances in technology as a factor:

The future of electrical technology . . . was seen to be very promising, indeed, although we recognize that much of what was known to be technically and economically feasible was communicated at the level of grand exhibitions and public demonstrations . . . Reflections on the state of science constitute a veritable hymn of praise for practical progress in electrical engineering: motors and dynamos with shuttle-wound armatures, polyphase transmission, electric induction machinery, frequency transformers, the telephone, the microphone, and wireless telegraphy. There is hardly a word about the use of combustion engines for transportation, but the number of articles devoted to the rosy future that was about to be ushered in by electrical means of communication is impressive to say the least.[29]

We have already referred, in the above, to the crucial role that was given to physics in the post-1895 discoveries associated with the corpuscular structure of matter. The complete switch of interest and confidence in structure of matter investigations around 1900 is nowhere more conspicuously seen than in the sudden way in which physicists and chemists retreated from their anti-atomistic positions. An examination of the unanticipated and spectacular experimental discoveries made during these years serves to show how dense was the terrain on which investigators were compelled to construct a new physics based on the corpuscular theory of matter.

The correlation of gravitational theory with spectroscopy at the end of the century was critical for the establishment of astrophysics as a major branch of physics. It served to reinforce the essential uniqueness of the atomic-molecular perspective throughout nature. Robert Woodward, Columbia University Professor of Mechanics and Mathematical Physics, wrote in 1904:

> It would be too bold, perhaps, to assert that the trend of accumulating knowledge is toward an atomic unity of matter, but the day seems not far distant when there will be room for a new *Principia* and for a treatise that will accomplish for molecular systems what the *Méchanique Céleste* accomplished for the solar system.[30]

In chemistry the atomic-molecular theory was, if anything, an even more sure-footed route towards understanding such fundamental issues as chemical spontaneity, equilibrium, structure and chemical kinetics. Physicist Professor Woodward, mentioned above, recognized this clearly when he said: 'If the progress of physics during the past century has been chiefly in the direction of atomic theory, the progress of chemistry has been more so. Chemistry is, in fact, the science of atoms and molecules *par excellence.*[31]

Various other trends are discernible in the physics community around 1900. One that merits special attention follows from the recognition that almost none of the new discoveries had been foreseen or predicted on the basis of established theoretical principles. This perception encouraged the taking of risks. Speculations about the unknown were made in hopes that empirical findings sooner or later either would validate a new idea or else be eliminated harmlessly from the record. The accent fell on the potentially positive incentives of imaginative and interrogative assumptions that might generate experimentally feasible and theoretically fertile consequences. The classical nineteenth-century categories of physics no longer were sacrosanct.

This generalization is not entirely warranted. 'Classical physics' never vanished from twentieth-century physics practice or textbooks. Many concepts and principles remained virtually unchallenged and, in fact, served as anchor points for the new physics – come what may. Prime examples in this category would include: the principles of Newtonian mechanics (at least in the limiting case), the principles of conservation of energy, Maxwell's electromagnetic theory (or some version of it) and the indispensability of an ordering of the chemical elements according to atomic mass and number.

Finally it is pertinent to call attention to a number of unsolved problems, puzzles and enigmas whose resolution was to be of crucial importance for future direction of physics. These issues were given high priority by physicists. For example, the assumption of a pervasive universal ether – the medium for all physical phenomena – was invoked as an intellectual necessity for explaining optical, thermal, electromagnetic and gravitational phenomena. The most recalcitrant problem connected with the ether was its function, the properties needed in order to fulfil that function and the relation of the ether – and sometimes of the plurality of ethers invoked – with mechanics, radiation theory and views on the constitution of matter. Perhaps matter or certain kinds of matter, electrons, for example, were composed only of electricity. The puzzles were not resolved; their resolution depended on other puzzles – such as: what is electricity? and what is ether?

The paradigm example of a deep puzzle brought on by a phenomenon totally unconnected with classical physics and chemistry was the discovery in 1896 of radioactivity. The spontaneous and uncontrollable disintegration of certain elements found in nature, opened up for fertile study the nature, properties and reactions of matter, and the forces that operate at the level of the atom and the nucleus of the atom. The planetary theory of the atom, nuclear theory, the identification of elementary particles and particle-induced transmutations of elements set the stage for the discovery of nuclear fission in 1939, just fifty years ago. When W. K. Clifford in the late 1870s reasoned, from the complexity of atomic spectra, that 'atoms must be at least as complex as a grand piano',[32] he could not possibly have known that the internally structured atom would turn out to be several orders of magnitude more complex than anyone had anticipated. However, the nuclear atom was found to be unmanageable not so much scientifically or technologically, but politically, and namely in those arenas of the world where the survival of mankind was to be placed in the hands of the major powers.

None of this could have been foreseen. It all began with intense and innocent curiosity about the nature of the physical world. In 1902 Ernest Rutherford wrote to his mother from McGill University:

I am now busy writing up papers for publication and doing fresh work. I have to keep going, as there are always people on my track. I have to publish my present work as rapidly as possible in order to keep in the race. The best sprinters in this road of investigation are Becquerel and the Curies in Paris, who have done a great deal of important work in the subject of radioactive bodies during the past few years.[33]

NOTES

1 For an analysis of the antecedents to the post-1900 modifications in laboratories in Britain, see R. Svierdrys, 'The rise of physics laboratories in Britain', *Historical Studies in the Physical Sciences*, 7 (1976), 405–36.

2 There are not many works in which *fin-de-siècle* physics has been analysed *per se*.

A comprehensive inventory of academic physics establishments at the turn of the century is provided by P. Forman, J. L. Heilbron and S. Weart, *Physics circa 1900. Personnel, Funding and Productivity of the Academic Establishments*, Historical Studies in the Physical Sciences 5 (Princeton, N.J., 1975). See also J. L. Heilbron, 'Fin-de-siècle physics', in C. G. Bernhard, E. Crawford and P. Sorböm (eds.), *Science, Technology and Society in the Time of Alfred Nobel* (Oxford, 1982), pp. 51–73. By contrast, the works on *fin-de-siècle* literature, culture, politics and the arts are immense, especially for Austria and France. The German literature on this period normally is treated under the heading of *Jahrhundertwende*. Monographs in many languages treat the period with perspectives both positive and negative.

3 *Oxford English Dictionary*, vol. III (1933), pp. 808–9.

4 *Oxford English Dictionary*, Supplement, vol. I (1972), p. 537.

5 P. A. M. Dirac, *The Principles of Quantum Mechanics* (Oxford, 1930), p. v.

6 The mammoth strides achieved in foundations of mathematics, beginning with C. F. Gauss in the middle of the nineteenth century, came to fruition in twentieth-century physics in the work of persons such as Felix Klein, David Hilbert, Hermann Weyl and Hermann Minkowski. There were other mathematicians who were less physics-oriented, but whose contributions nevertheless turned out to be crucial for advances in theoretical physics: Leopold Kronecker, Richard Dedekind, Georg Cantor, Gottlob Frege, Giuseppe Peano and Bertrand Russell.

7 H. Poincaré, 'Relations entre la physique expérimentale et la physique mathématique', in C. E. Guillaume and L. Poincaré (ed.) *Rapports présentés au Congrès International de Physique* (Paris, 1900), vol. I, pp. 1–29.

8 A list of theoretical chairs at this time would include: Kirchhoff, Berlin, 1875; Lorentz, Leiden, 1877; succeeded by Ehrenfest in 1912; Voigt, Göttingen, 1883; Volkmann, Königsberg, 1886; Planck, Kiel, 1885; Boltzmann, Vienna, 1902; Ernst Pringsheim, Breslau, 1905; and Sommerfeld, Munich, 1906.

9 See especially the article of Shulamit Volkov, 'Soziale Ursachen des Erfolgs in der Wissenschaft. Juden im Kaisserreich', *Historische Zeitschrift*, 245 (1987), pp. 315–42.

10 E. Du Bois-Reymond, 'Über die Grenzen des Naturerkennens' (1872) and 'Die Sieben Welträtsel' (1880), in *Reden* (Leipzig, 1886), pp. 105–40 and 381–417. The polemical statement of 1872, on p. 130 reads: 'In regard to the riddles of the material world the scientist long ago has become accustomed to pronounce his *Ignoramus* with brave renunciation [mit männlicher Entsagung] . . . In regard to the riddle about the essence of matter and force [Kraft], and how they are to be conceived, he once and for all must reach the much more difficult decision to accept the judgement: "*Ignorabimus*", (author's translation). Unless indicated otherwise, all translations from original works are done by the author.

11 Influential writers of this persuasion would include the Swiss zoologist and philosopher Karl Vogt, the Dutch physiologist Jacob Moleschott, the most influential nineteenth-century German materialist Ludwig Büchner, and the controversial German morphologist Ernst Haeckel. All were influenced by Ludwig Feuerbach. For an interpretative and contextual history of nineteenth-century German materialism, with focus on Feuerbach, Vogt, Moleschott, Büchner and

Czolbe, see: F. Gregory, *Scientific Materialism in Nineteenth Century Germany* (Dordrecht, 1977).

12 Du Bois-Reymond, 'On the relation of natural science to art', *Nature*, 45 (1891), 200–4 and 224–7. Address delivered at the annual meeting of the Royal Academy of Sciences in Berlin in 1890.

13 *Ibid.*, p. 200.

14 *Ibid.*

15 L. Büchner, *Im Dienst der Wahrheit. Ausgewählte Aufsätze aus Natur und Wissenschaft* (Giessen, 1900). Article on Karl Vogt (1896), p. 253–4.

16 *Ibid.*, p. 255.

17 L. Büchner, *Kraft und Stoff oder natürlich Weltordnung. Nebst einer darauf gebauten Moral oder Sittenlehre. In allgemeinverständicher Darstellung* (Frankfurt, 1855). The English edition first appeared in London in 1884.

18 L. Büchner, *Am Sterbelager des Jahrhunderts. Blick eines freien Denkers aus der Zeit in die Zeit* (Giessen, 1898), quotation on p. 9.

19 Apart from landmarks in Darwinian evolution, and the life and earth sciences, Büchner accentuated what he calls the great scientific upheavals (*Umwälzungen*) of the century: astrophysics, spectral analysis, photography, the revival of the Greek doctrine of immortality of the atom, radiation studies, fertility of the ether concept, the kinetic theory of gases, the discovery of argon and X-rays, the liquefaction and solidification of gases, the synthesis of organic compounds, and various technological accomplishments, conspicuously in electrochemistry and electrotechnology (the frontier science of the twentieth century). It is worth mentioning that Büchner refers to the face-abouts or upheavals (*Umwälzungen*) in science – without political overtones or reference to 'revolutions' – in the same sense in which Friedrich Engels employed the expression in his *Herr Eugen Dührings Umwälzung der Wissenschaft* (Leipzig, 1878).

20 Büchner, *Am Sterbelager des Jahrhunderts*, p. 61.

21 *Ibid.*, see especially pp. 141, 175, 229, 257 and 305.

22 *Ibid.*, p. 253.

23 E. Haeckel, *Die Welträthsel. Gemeinverständliche Studien über Monistische Philosophie* (Bonn, 1899), p. 3. The views of Lamarck, Darwin and Goethe ('the religion of the true, the good and the beautiful', p. 464) were given precedence. Whereas the work dealt primarily with anthropology, cosmology and psychology as a branch of physiology, it also touched upon physical principles such as the conservation of matter and energy, the kinetic theory, chemical atomism and affinity, and the imponderable ether (pp. 243–67). In spite of Haeckel's grandiloquent ideas of culture, the First World War brought forth in him, along with ninety-two of Germany's leading intellectuals, support for a 'manifesto to the civilized world' that 'affirmed the wisdom of German actions and ended with the flat assertion that German culture and German militarism were inseparable'. See M. J. Klein, *Paul Ehrenfest*, vol. 1, *The Making of a Theoretical Physicist* (Amsterdam, 1970), pp. 299–300.

24 G. Kirchhoff, *Vorlesungen über mathematische Physik*, 4 vols. (Leipzig, 1876–94). The 4th edition, reworked by Wilhelm Wien, appeared in 1897. Comprehensive

textbooks on 'classical physics' of this period and style would include as well: F. Neumann, *Vorlesungen über mathematische Physik* (7 vols., Leipzig, 1881–94); W. Voigt, *Kompendium der theoretischen Physik* (2 vols., Leipzig, 1893–6); and H. von Helmholtz, *Vorlesungen über theoretische Physik* (6 vols., 1897–1907). For a succinct discussion of German physics through the last quarter of the nineteenth century see: C. Jungnickel and R. McCormmach, *Intellectual Mastery of Nature. Theoretical Physics from Ohm to Einstein*, vol. II (Chicago and London, 1986), ch. 14, pp. 125–48.

25 A. Michelson, *Light Waves and Their Uses* (Chicago, 1903), pp. 23–5. A decade before this volume was published, its Polish-born author, then heading a new physics department at the University of Chicago, had already achieved an international reputation with his exact interferometric techniques. In 1907 he became the first American to gain the Nobel Prize, 'for his optical precision instruments and the spectroscopic and metrological investigations carried out with their aid'.

26 *Ibid.*, pp. 23–4.

27 See for example: E. Hiebert, 'The energetics controversy and the new thermodynamics', in D. H. D. Roller (ed.), *Perspectives in the History of Science and Technology* (Norman, Okla, 1971), pp. 67–86, and *idem*, 'Developments in physical chemistry at the turn of the century', in C. G. Bernhard, E. Crawford and P. Sorböm (eds.), *Science, Technology and Society in the Time of Alfred Nobel* (Oxford, 1982), pp. 97–118.

28 I may mention in this connection the most important developments: the discovery of X-rays in connection with cathode ray phenomena (Röntgen, 1895); the demonstration that a cathode discharge carries negative charge (Perrin, 1895); the announcement of the discovery of the new chemical element argon as a monatomic gas that had no valency, no chemistry and no place in the periodic table (Rayleigh, Ramsay, 1895); the discovery of the spontaneous disintegration of certain elements, i.e. radioactivity (Becquerel, 1896); the effect of a magnetic field on spectra, i.e. Zeeman's magneto-optic effect (1896); the Wilson cloud chamber experiments on the particle-induced condensation of water vapour in gases (1897); the discovery of the electron as a particle of discrete mass and negative charge (J. J. Thomson, 1897); the confirmation that cathode rays are particles of high velocity (about one-third the velocity of light) and negatively charged (Wien, 1897–8); the discovery of the corpuscular nature, charge and velocity of positive rays using combined electric and magnetic deflections (1898–9); the discovery and isolation of radium and polonium from pitchblende (the Curies, 1898); and the detailed and impressive experimental investigations on radioactivity undertaken by Rutherford and his collaborator, Soddy, while at McGill in Montreal between 1898 and 1907.

29 E. Hiebert, 'The state of physics at the turn of the century', in M. Bunge and W. R. Shea (eds.), *Rutherford and Physics at the Turn of the Century* (New York, 1979), pp. 3–22; quotation pp. 5–6.

30 R. S. Woodward, 'The unity of the physical sciences', *Congress of Arts and Sciences, Universal Exposition St. Louis 1904* (Boston, Mass., 1906), vol. IV, p. 8.

31 *Ibid.*

32 Quoted from O. Lodge, *Atoms and Rays* (London, 1924), p. 74.

33 Quoted from E. N. da C. Andrade, *Rutherford and the Nature of the Atom* (Garden City, N.Y., 1964), p. 55. The Nobel Prize for 1903 (discovery of spontaneous radioactivity and researches on radioactive phenomena) was shared by Henry Becquerel and Pierre and Marie née Sklodowska Curie. Rutherford received the Nobel Prize for chemistry in 1908 for his investigations into the disintegration of radioactive substances.

✧

THIRTEEN

A FEELING FOR THE 'WHOLE': THE HOLISTIC REACTION IN NEUROLOGY FROM THE *FIN DE SIÈCLE* TO THE INTERWAR YEARS

ANNE HARRINGTON

The first decades of the twentieth century form a peculiarly distinct intellectual chapter in the history of European clinical neurology. Sympathizers portray this period as a time in which a new generation of psychologically sophisticated researchers rebelled against the artificial machine-models of mind and brain favoured by the nineteenth century, and reaffirmed – in true Renaissance spirit – the inner irreducibility and outer organic unity of human mind and brain processes. More recent commentators within the field have taken a less rosy view of the events of this time, calling attention to discrepancies between the radical rhetoric of these so-called 'holistic' neurologists, and their actually quite conventional 'nineteenth-century' approach when faced with the nuts-and-bolts of individual cases.[1]

While modern critical assessments of the *fin-de-siècle* holistic rebellion in neurology vary, commentators are generally of one accord in considering the whole affair to be an 'in-house' quarrel, of likely interest only to practising clinicians or to specialists in the history of neurology. Modern historical studies of such *fin-de-siècle* creations as dynamic psychiatry and psychoanalysis go out of their way to emphasize the fundamental interdependence of these with a whole complex of cultural and social factors. Yet, strangely, there has been virtually no similar attempt to ground the story of holistic neurology in the wider context of European cultural history at the turn of the century.

The present essay represents a first attempt to do just that. It is not a comprehensive overview of general trends in the sciences of mind and brain in Europe at the turn of the century. It *is* an effort to relate the rise of holistic neurology to a number of other trends in psychiatry, psychology and biology; and to suggest some ways in which all these in turn might be related to the general cultural and social history of early twentieth-century central Europe, especially the German-speaking countries. My choice of geographical focus here is not arbitrary, for – like psychoanalysis and existential psychiatry – holistic neurology was, in its heart, a product of German-speaking science and philosophy. It is no accident that the same broad cultural environment which gave rise to such leading holistic neurologists as Constantin von Monakow and Kurt Goldstein should also have been the intellectual cradle of a Karl Jaspers, a Eugen Bleuler and a Sigmund Freud. Indeed, it is worth stressing that Freud himself played an early significant role in the holistic revision of nineteenth-century neurology; and, as will be seen, his activities in this respect significantly influenced several key aspects of his later psychoanalytic thinking. In addition (although the issue cannot be properly addressed in a brief paper such as this one), the relationship between the spread of psychoanalytic ideas on the one hand, and the rise of new dynamic approaches in neurobiology on the other, still remains to be fully clarified.[2]

THE CHALLENGE TO TRADITION

Holism arose as a self-conscious movement to discredit certain reigning doctrines of late nineteenth-century neurology and psychology. Consequently – especially in its early years – it tended to define itself largely in terms of what it rejected. Before we are in any position, then, to examine some of the positive alternative models of mind and brain offered by the holistic reformers (the second part of this essay), we must first attempt to understand holism in its negative face, and against the background of its nineteenth-century inheritance.

Concepts of brain-functioning in late nineteenth-century neurology

We begin then with the nineteenth-century doctrine of cerebral localization: the idea that higher cortical (mental) processes may be broken up into distinct functional units and correlated with discrete areas of the brain. The modern history of this idea dates back conventionally to the mid-1860s, when the French neuroanatomist Paul Broca managed to persuade his colleagues on the basis of certain clinico-anatomic evidence (speech loss coinciding with circumscribed damage to the brain) that the 'faculty of articulate language' had its seat in the left frontal lobe of the human cortex.[3] For the purposes of our story, though, these early localization theories are relatively peripheral, since they saw little significant input from German sources.[4] It took the pioneering work of two of their own countrymen, Gustav Fritsch and Eduard Hitzig, in 1870 to make German-speaking researchers really sit up and take notice of the new developments.

To understand the significance of the Fritsch and Hitzig work, it is first necessary to realize that, although it was well known in Broca's era that the spinal cord and subcortical regions of the nervous system served sensory-motor functioning for the body, it was generally believed that the cortex proper was exclusively reserved for the loftier functionings of mind. What Fritsch and Hitzig did, was to demonstrate that in fact the cerebral cortex plays a role in sensory-motor activity after all. Applying electrical currents to the brains of dogs, the two Germans were able to produce crude movements of the body, and found moreover that specific brain regions seemed responsible for specific movements.[5]

Now, if the cortex possessed 'motor centres', as Fritsch and Hitzig's work suggested, then it was logical to suppose, on analogy with the workings of spinal and subcortical structures, that it possessed sensory centres as well. And indeed the effort to identify these cortical motor and sensory centres would dominate experimental physiology in the last three decades of the nineteenth century.[6]

What, however, did this emerging new conception of the brain as a sensory-motor structure imply for the effort to correlate *mental* processes with discrete cortical areas? In 1874 a young German neurologist Carl Wernicke attempted a reply to this question with a now-classic monograph on the problem of language loss and cerebral localization, *Der Aphasische Symptomencomplex*. Significantly subtitled 'eine psychologische Studie auf anatomischer Basis', this study was offered as a first step towards a comprehensive neuroanatomy of mental functioning. Starting from the neuroanatomist Theodore Meynert's concept of the brain as a sensory-motor system of cells and fibres operating according to reflex laws, Wernicke argued that the idea that one could localize complex psychological processes such as 'speech' had been misguided. What was actually localizable were much simpler 'memories' of past sensory and motor experiences. These 'memories' served as the basic units of all mental functioning. They interacted and combined with each other along cerebral fibres in accordance with established psychological 'laws of association', generating in this way the full complexity of mind and consciousness.[7]

The success of the Wernicke 'associationist-connectionist' model of human higher cortical functioning was immediate, if not completely lacking in dissension.[8] Its establishment as a paradigm in clinical neurology (modified and developed in various directions by men like L. Lichtheim and, later, H. Liepmann) triggered what has come to be regarded as a 'classic' era in the history of the study of the human brain; an era which left behind a monolithic legacy of work on the no less 'classical' disorders of aphasia (loss of speech or – alternatively – loss of capacity for verbal comprehension); agnosia (loss of the capacity to recognize common objects or correctly interpret one's environment); and apraxia (loss of the capacity to perform willed, intelligent actions).[9]

Two difficult questions now suggest themselves. 1. Why, after three or more decades of apparent proven reliability and fruitfulness, should these classical ideas of higher brain functioning have suddenly come – in the early years of the new century – to seem self-evidently inadequate? And 2. given this sense that a thorough revision of reigning concepts was in order, why did the holists focus on the particular problems that they did?

The problem of 'recovery'

To begin, it is clear from the writings of the holists themselves, that the phenomenon of 'recovery' from brain damage stood out at the turn of the century as one of the most important perceived challenges to classical notions of cortical functional localization.[10] Increasingly it would be said that the simple fact that brain-damaged people can get better over time – can regain lost speech and movement – was simply incompatible with the nineteenth-century 'machine' model of the nervous system as a purely mechanical apparatus operating according to fixed laws of reflex and association. Machines do not repair themselves after suffering damage, and functions which 'reside' in certain fixed regions of the brain cannot reappear if their dependent brain-regions have been permanently destroyed.

The nineteenth-century localizers had attempted to account for recovery by arguing that undamaged parts of the brain were somehow induced to 'take over' responsibility for the lost functions of damaged areas, but that rigid localization of the original functions was not thereby negated. The holists would have none of that. It made no difference, they said, whether the newly responsible parts of the brain were understood to have participated in the functions of the damaged brain areas before injury or were thought to acquire their new physiological significance only afterwards. In either case, the principles of specific anatomic localization of functions had already been abandoned – and the way clearly signposted to a dynamic concept of the human brain, in which functioning was determined not by rigid structural arrangements, but by the ever-changing physiological reactions of the whole nervous system.[11]

The fallacies of 'associationism'

But 'recovery' was not the only issue at stake. Also generally critical to the holistic rejection of the classical ideas of mind and brain was the whole vexed issue of associationist psychology. When Wernicke declared his intention in 1874 to ground 'psychology' in an anatomical base, he was quite clear that it was associationism he had in mind. What, though, was this model of mind all about? Roughly speaking, it began with a rejection of the 'metaphysical' notion of innate 'faculties' of mind and asserted that all human knowledge and experience had its origin in sensation; that is, in sensory data acquired through the workings of the special senses. It then went on to affirm that, through various physiological processes, all such sensory data were combined and stored in such a way that they could later be revived by the brain in the form of 'representative images' or primitive ideas (*Vorstellungen*). These ideas – these atomistic units of thought – once revived, 'associated' with each other in accordance with certain fixed, rational 'laws'. The whole process was essentially automatic and passive.

The holists in the early twentieth century were all very self-conscious enemies of this 'atomistic' psychology. The neurolinguist Arnold Pick stated the case firmly in 1913:

If state-of-the-art pathological psychology previously represented one of the obstacles to a prosperous development of the field, it is easy to account for that. Above all, inherent to the psychology dominating aphasiology was that objectification [*Verdinglichung*], which was taken from Herbartian [associationist] psychology and whose deleterious effects (one need only think of the 'memory pictures laid down in cells') can be noted up to most recent times.[12]

As the holists themselves stressed, the new century had seen developments in experimental psychology which, in various ways, seemed to challenge the tenability of many of the old associationist ideas. In the first years of the new century, Oswald Külpe's school of experimental psychology at Würzburg (which influenced Pick) published a series of studies detailing the apparently unlawful – even irrational – way in which the mind 'associates' to nevertheless ultimately arrive at a 'rational conclusion', and stressing generally the relatively small role which consciousness and logic actually seemed to play in human thought.[13] Later, in the 1920s, the workers of the *Gestalt* school of psychology (who influenced later holistic neurologists like Head and Goldstein) would challenge the associationist model of mind still more decisively.[14]

The holistic neurologists were also convinced that their own observations of brain-damaged patients – no less than the findings of the new experimental psychologists – spoke clearly against the continuing viability of the classical associationist model of mind. In 1906 the French neurologist Pierre Marie had startled the scientific world with three papers on the problem of language disorder (or aphasia) and brain localization.[15] There he denied that there existed special visual or auditory 'verbal-images' in the brain, loss of which (through damage to special centres) leads to aphasia. So far as he could see, all the clinical evidence pointed instead to a view of aphasia as a generalized disorder of intelligence; a sort of dementia concerned particularly with that aspect of thought dependent upon language. In stating the matter so, Marie thus posed a clear challenge to one of the cornerstones of classical associatio-

nist-connectionist neuropsychology: namely, that *words* (or 'images' thereof)
– acting in association with each other and with primitive 'concept' (*Begriff*)
images – served as the building-blocks of speech and thought. For the holistic
neurologists that came to maturity in the wake of Marie's 'iconoclasm' (as
Henry Head would call it), it would seem increasingly clear that such an
atomistic theory of thinking and speaking was hopelessly out of touch with
the real-live behaviour of patients. As Head put it:

We neither think nor speak in combinations of verbal units. In order to understand the
morbid phenomena of speech they must be considered as a disturbance of progressive
acts, which cannot reach their proper conclusion. They are not due to disintegration of
isolated words strung together in sequence. Not only is it impossible to break up a
word into auditory and visual elements, but disease does not analyse a sentence into its
verbal or grammatical constituents . . . Speech, like walking, is an act of progression.[16]

The wider context: neo-Kantianism and neo-vitalism

Though it is true that the holists tended in their rhetoric to stress the clinical
and experimental basis of their quarrel with Wernicke and the other classical
localizers, it would be a mistake to accept that matters were really so simple.
For example, well before the holistic neurologists had taken it upon themselves to point out the fallacies of the associationist ideas, a new breed of
idealistically oriented post-Kantian philosophers had already attacked it on
epistemological grounds.[17] Their specific objections centred on the fallacies of
the so-called 'common sense' view of reality. The naïve man in the street
supposes that his knowledge of the external world is derived from trust-
worthy perceptions. By adding up all his various perceptual experiences, he
believes himself in a position to arrive at an ever more complete knowledge of
reality. This same 'common sense' epistemology, stressed the idealists, was
fundamental to associationist psychology – with its stress on the sensory basis
of all knowledge and its additive, passive view of cognition. Indeed,
associationism was often even more incautious than the man in the street,
since it supposed that even our subjective impressions about the outside world
could be explained in terms of that same outside world: namely, as end-
products of various physiological processes in our brains.

   All this, suspected these post-Kantian idealists, accounted for a good part
of the hegemony of the associationist model of mind during those brief but
heady years when German natural science was dominated by the anti-
vitalistic, positivistic ideology of men like Hermann von Helmholtz and Emil
Du Bois-Reymond. Unfortunately, ever since Kant it had been clear that
perception, far from being a straightforward passive experience, in fact
involved an active structuring of phenomena according to various a priori
mental categories and intuitive judgements (*Anschauungen*). This meant that

what we called the outside world must in the end be judged as much a construction of our own subjectivity as a 'discoverable' reality outside of us, since our ideas or experience about something could in no sense be supposed to correspond to the 'thing-in-itself'. For these philosophers, the necessary limits that this fact placed on empirical knowledge justified a turning away from such an inadequate approach to truth, and prompted an appeal to other ('higher', intuitive or subjective) forms of knowing not dependent upon sense experience and dull analytic reasoning.

In fact there was more than one way to read Kant, and in their own way the positivists were quite aware of the epistemological problems raised by the Kantian critique. However, where idealists believed Kant to have discredited the pretensions of empirical science, positivists like Du Bois-Reymond and Helmholtz combined an acknowledgement of the limits of scientific knowledge with an unshaken faith in the scientific method as the only reliable means to knowledge, however ultimately finite. These men admitted that science could never hope to know the 'thing-in-itself', but they argued (with varying degrees of persuasiveness) that the relationships it discovered through experience corresponded in a consistent manner to relationships that existed in nature itself – somewhat like (to use an analogy from Helmholtz) 'a statue . . . has the same corporeal form as the human being after which it was made'. It was only later, under men like Ernst Mach, that this correspondence theory of knowledge would itself be challenged, and positivism would take on the far more radical form that characterized it at the turn of the century.[18]

Whether the positivistic philosophy of the Helmholtz school can be fairly judged as legitimate an offspring of the Kantian critique as idealism is almost beside the point. In any polemical controversy, fairness towards the adversary is hardly a high-priority concern. All that is important to note here is the extent to which idealism had come to dominate educated thinking during the years when the neurological holists first took it upon themselves to examine the foundations of their discipline. In this respect, it is surely significant that some of these men – I am thinking here especially of Kurt Goldstein – openly admitted their attraction to idealism, and stressed the methodological limits of natural science in their own writings.[19] The question thus arises: To what extent does holistic neurology's assault on the fallacies of associationism in the early twentieth century qualify it as a part of this much more broadly based post-Kantian reaction against the perceived epistemological arrogance of late nineteenth-century empirical science?[20]

Similarly, how far can we understand the sudden emphasis within holistic neurology on the dynamic, self-regenerating capacities of the brain – focused, as we have seen, around the clinical issue of 'recovery' – as simply one more expression of a growing general disenchantment in early twentieth-century central Europe biology with materialistic metaphysics and reductionism in the life sciences? From the neo-vitalistic biology of Hans Driesch, the 'Umwelt' ethology of Jacob von Uexküll, the 'personalistic' psychology of William Stern, the 'creative evolution' of Henri Bergson, the probings of the zoologist Karl von Frisch into the inner world of bees and fish, the existential psychiatry of Karl Jaspers, and – on a somewhat different level – the psychoanalysis of Sigmund Freud, the trend in the sciences of life and mind at this time was increasingly subjectivist and non-reductionist; increasingly towards a view 'in which life, instead of being interpreted from beneath in terms of supposed physical and chemical processes of accretion and blind interaction, somehow sets the stage upon which physical and chemical realities can occur'.[21] In physiology, the new emphasis was on dynamic, systems-oriented models of functioning; in psychology, on such previously neglected issues as motivation and the nature of instinctual life.[22] It seems quite self-evident that the upheavals and challenges preoccupying clinical neurology at this time cannot be understood apart from this much more broadly based reorientation in psychology, psychiatry and physiology.[23]

Nor can this general reorientation in the life sciences – in which neurology shared – be properly understood without reference to the wider cultural and social conditions within which early twentieth-century biology found itself. Very briefly put, we are concerned here with a time in which European intellectuals were increasingly speaking out against what they perceived as the nihilistic consequences of positivism, materialism and 'scientism' overall in modern thought. These sentiments were generally part and parcel of a no less powerful concern with the fatal loss of humanity caused by the mechanization, industrialization and super-compartmentalism of modern living. Once this is understood, one sees too how it is hardly coincidental that a so-called 'holistic biology' should have taken root in the German-speaking countries during a period when these elites had turned references to 'whole-ness', 'oneness', the 'whole' (Ganzheit, Einheit, das Ganze) into slogans for their fight against the shallow individualism of modern life and their effort to reclaim the essential spiritual values of German Kultur. Ernst Troeltsch was proclaiming nothing particularly novel when, in a pro-war 1914 speech that would quickly become renowned, he identified 'wholeness' as one of the key saving 'ideas of 1914'.

The first victory we won, even before the victories on the battlefield, was the victory over ourselves . . . A higher life seemed to reveal itself to us. Each of us . . . lived for the whole [das Ganze], and the whole lived in all of us. Our own ego with its personal interests was dissolved in the great historic being of the nation. The fatherland calls! The parties disappear . . . Thus a moral elevation of the people preceded the war; the whole nation was gripped by the truth and reality of suprapersonal, spiritual power.[24]

HOLISTIC ALTERNATIVE APPROACHES TO MIND AND BRAIN

The extent to which the 'saving ideas' of holistic biological thinking may have reinforced, rationalized or simply reflected the social and political hopes of the intellectual classes at this time is an important question that remains still to be explored, and will not be discussed here (but cf. below and note 24). In this section of my paper, I intend simply to survey a few of the most important alternative models of mind and brain to emerge out of the holistic critique, and to illuminate at least some of the concrete links between these models and various more broadly based shifts in the sciences of mind and brain from the *fin de siècle* to the interwar years.

The legacy of Hughlings Jackson

I begin, then, with the work of the late nineteenth-century British neurologist John Hughlings Jackson (1835–1911). Although it is true that the holistic neurologists maintained an antagonistic – or at least highly critical – attitude towards the majority of their late nineteenth-century forebears, they did make a very pointed exception in the case of this one man. As early as 1891, Sigmund Freud in Vienna pronounced Jackson the chief inspiration behind his proposed revisionist approach to the problem of speech disorders and cerebral localization. The pioneering neurolinguist Arnold Pick in Prague dedicated his 1913 *Die Agrammatischen Sprachstörungen* to Jackson, whom he called 'the deepest thinker in neuropathology of the last century'. The English holistic neurologist Henry Head called Jackson 'one of the most remarkable pioneers in this field of research . . . [whose] aphoristic dicta fell upon deaf ears'. In Germany, Kurt Goldstein sighed – 'Had one followed Jackson, how many errors would have been avoided!' And in Switzerland, Constantin von Monakow and R. Mourgue, in their 1928 *Introduction biologique de la neurologie et de la psychopathologie*, devoted more space and care to Jackson's work than to any other outside author mentioned in their book.[25]

A maverick in his own time – to a large extent respected for his philosophical profundity but also often misunderstood for the same reason – Jackson's essential legacy to the twentieth-century holists was a dynamic, functional (rather than strictly anatomical) model of mind/brain functioning conceived in hierarchical terms. Drawing on the evolutionary philosophy of the English philosopher Herbert Spencer, this nineteenth-century neurologist started out from the premise that the nervous system had evolved over time into a pyramid of increasingly complex functions. More complex and specialized functions (associated in human beings with consciousness and rational thought) represented a higher, later level of evolution than simpler, more automatic (para-rational or emotionally driven functions) that had been acquired at an earlier stage of human evolution. As Jackson saw it, the higher levels of the brain not only had their own special functions to carry out; they also had the thankless task of controlling or 'keeping down' the lower levels. However, in various forms of neurological disorder and in most forms of insanity, such high-level control was lost, and one was then witness to a 'welling up' of suddenly uncontrolled primitive forms of brain-functioning. This twofold process of high-level function loss and low-level function release was understood by Jackson to be a reversal of the individual evolutionary process. It was a descent to a more primitive, automatic and emotional state of functioning which, following Spencer, Jackson called 'dissolution'.[26]

Sigmund Freud's On Aphasia *and the rise of psychoanalysis*

For the majority of late nineteenth-century neurologists in England and elsewhere – essentially concerned with mapping the sensory-motor 'carto-graphy' of the cognitive functions of the brain and relatively at a loss when it came to questions about the dynamic physiological-emotional forces that drove it to behave as it did – the Jacksonian model of mind and brain was perplexing and largely indigestible.[27] But the intellectual climate had already begun to change by 1891, the year Sigmund Freud turned to Jackson's work as the starting point for his critique of the classical localizationist approach to speech disorders. In continental Europe especially, questions about the dynamics of emotion, instinct and will in mental life (questions that had long obsessed some of the best philosophical minds of these countries) were finally beginning to make inroads into the biological and medical sciences. In the context of this growing interest, it seems that Jackson's work – even while it was steeped in a British philosophical tradition otherwise relatively alien to most of the German-speaking holists – could not help but impress. Thus Freud declared:

In assessing the functions of the speech apparatus under pathological conditions we are adopting as a guiding principle Hughlings Jackson's doctrine that all these modes of reaction represent instances of functional retrogression (dis-involution) of a highly organized apparatus and therefore correspond to earlier states of its functional development. This means that under all circumstances, an arrangement of associa-tions which, having been acquired later, belongs to a higher level of functioning, will be lost, while an earlier and simpler one will be preserved.[28]

For Freud, it was clear that the classical view – that all aphasic syndromes could be explained as a simple consequence of lesions in or between three main language 'centres' in the brain – failed to account for a wide range of the phenomena actually seen in aphasic patients. Freud called particular attention to Jackson's discussion of so-called 'recurrent utterances': various stereotyped 'automatic' forms of verbal expression which persist in otherwise speechless patients. If the Germans were right and aphasia did indeed result from damage to linguistic centres in the brain, then language should be uniformly disordered; it was incomprehensible that a tiny cluster of nervous arrangements serving a few sentences could persist in isolation. On the other hand, Jackson had shown how a lesion to an isolated part of the brain could throw the whole system into a state of psycho-nervous dissolution: a process in which various emotional and automatic forms of speech (swearing, exclamations, stereotypical utterances) might indeed be preserved, even while the capacity for highly flexible, conscious utterances (language proper) is lost.

Although a substantial early contribution to the holistic neurology critique in its own right, the Freudian 1891 monograph *On Aphasia* is perhaps even more significant for the influence it had on Freud's later psychoanalytic thinking. Numerous Freudian scholars have documented the way in which the Jacksonian doctrine of 'dissolution' would later be transformed by Freud into the psychoanalytic concept of libidinal 'regression'. A number have also proposed a link between Freud's early interest in Jackson's work on 'recurrent utterances' in aphasia, and certain aspects of his later thinking on such matters as hysterical symptoms, compulsive behaviour and the use of words in dreams.[29] Be that as it may, Freud's intellectual debt to Jackson – while perhaps it does not allow us to see psychoanalysis as some sort of offshoot of holistic neurology – does at least underscore the extent to which the latter was part and parcel of much more general conceptual changes in the mind and brain sciences during the first decades of the twentieth century.

Von Monakow on 'diaschisis' and the 'horme'

Freud's contemporary, the Russian-born Swiss neurologist Constantin von Monakow (1853–1930), offers himself as another instructive example of a man whose early dissatisfaction with reigning ideas in classical neurology ultimately evolved in directions far removed from the esoteric world of brain-disorder.

The von Monakow notion of 'diaschisis' or cerebral shock – first developed by him in a 1902 lecture, 'Über den gegenwärtigen Stand der Frage nach der Lokalisation im Grosshirn' – seemed at first to be nothing more than an explanation for the problem of recovery in brain-damage. Properly understood, however, it became clear that the concept opened the door to a radically new approach to the nature of cerebral localization.

As von Monakow saw it, classical localizationist theories all ultimately fell short of accounting for the recovery problem because they failed to recognize that a lesion to the brain not only put the lesioned brain-part out of commission: it also had the effect of throwing the entire brain into a state of sympathetic shock (diaschisis). For this reason, a freshly injured patient might show a variety of disabilities stemming from disordered brain-areas far from the actual lesion, and which could be expected to vanish over time as the nervous system once again stabilized itself. The underlying assumption here was that every part of the brain could affect every other, and that breakdown (and recovery) of function ultimately had to be understood in terms of the dynamic working of the whole.

Von Monakow did not deny the possibility of cerebral localization of function, but he stressed that it had to be answered in a new way – one which took account of the *temporal* factors operating within the three-dimensional world of brain functioning ('chronogenic localisation'). According to von Monakow, a neurologist must not only consider the history of his patient's injury (its onset and various stages of functional loss and recovery), but also the total phylogenetic and ontogenetic development of the function in question. In other words, complex psychological functions had to be understood as processes which evolved and unfolded in time; their relationship to a spatial object like the brain was similar to that of a melody to a music box. Nobody would attempt to 'put the melody (or some bars of it) into locally circumscribed parts of the [music box] cylinder'. Similarly, the neurologist must never think of localization of function in the brain 'as represented by geometrical lines in certain groups of gyri in adult man'.[30]

Von Monakow freely acknowledged the extent to which Hughlings Jackson had anticipated him in many of his ideas. He also felt, though, that Jackson's vision of the nervous system was ultimately incomplete, since – hampered by the nineteenth-century mechanism of the Spencerian evolution on which it was based – it could not account for the *creative* and *purposive* qualities of the nervous system when it was acting as a whole. The analogy between the functioning of a music box and the functioning of a human brain was actually not an exact one, since the latter was

not mechanically predetermined . . . as is the case of the music box . . . Psychological phenomena . . . presuppose the existence of a social human milieu, which has a development that is really creative in the sense of being unpredictable . . . Chronogenic synthesis is an emergent property of the [mechanistic] phase preceding it, although in latent form; it distinguishes itself qualitatively from that phase, however, through its creative activity.[31]

The dynamic element missing from the Jacksonian schema would be supplied by von Monakow in his concept of the 'horme'. Indebted to the 'évolution créatice' and 'élan vital' of the French philosopher Henri Bergson,[32] and again to the concept of inherited memory (or 'mneme') developed by the German zoologist Richard Semon,[33] von Monakow's horme was a self-actualizing biological force whose exact nature (physiological, chemical, psychic?) remained somewhat unclear. In animals, it manifested itself in that life-enhancing, unlearned behaviour scientists called 'instinct'. In that very special animal known as man ('der Riesenprotoplasma Mensch'), it actualized itself additionally as the 'Syneidesis' or biological conscience ('biologischen Gewissen'), which was the source of the individual sense of right and wrong, and the unconscious basis of all those formalized concepts that make up moral law in society.[34]

The heavy ethical responsibilities which von Monakow imposed upon his horme must be understood in the context of this neurologist's hope that biology (and especially the new principles of holistic neurology) might offer mankind a source of enduring values in a world torn apart by nationalist rivalries and alienated from its true roots.[35] Deeply shaken by the events of the First World War,[36] von Monakow came in the interwar years to share the deep pessimism and sense of crisis of so many of his contemporaries. His attempt to use the life sciences as a beacon to cut through the moral darkness of the post-war years and reveal the road to spiritual renewal was also far from exceptional for his time. The early founder of *Gestalt* psychology, Christian von Ehrenfels, came during this period to look upon his concept of *Gestalt* (literally, 'form' or 'configuration') as a metaphysical ordering-principle that was mankind's only defence against racial degeneration and cosmic entropy. The biologist Hans Spemann – with his concept of the 'organizer' as a critical force in foetal development – would argue that his embryological research illuminated enduring values that would be important to the moral education of future generations.[37]

The 'organismic' existentialism of Kurt Goldstein

Von Monakow's younger contemporary, the German–American neuropsychiatrist Kurt Goldstein (1878–1965), was quick to recognize the value of his Swiss colleague's work and the similarities of certain of their views.[38] Ultimately, though, the critical moral lesson he would draw from his own neurological work set him in quite a different framework from the latter. A student of Carl Wernicke and Ludwig Edinger at the turn of the century (he published his first scientific papers in 1903), Goldstein survived the First World War, imprisonment in Berlin under the Hitler regime, escape and exile in Amsterdam, and finally emigration to the United States, where he died in New York City in the mid-1960s. His formidable intellectual career thus spans the years from the late nineteenth century to the present age – making him a particularly appropriate figure with which to close our brief probe into the *fin-de-siècle* phenomenon of holism and its legacy.[39]

Appointed to the staff of the university psychiatric clinic of Königsberg shortly after the turn of the century, Goldstein found himself increasingly frustrated by the therapeutic barrenness of the then-dominant approach to understanding mental disorders developed by the Munich psychiatrist Emil Kraepelin. Kraepelin's emphasis on inherited constitutional factors in a wide range of psychoses had encouraged many medical men to believe that if they made an accurate diagnosis based on Kraepelin's nosology and then arranged for their patient to receive proper custodial care, they had done all that could reasonably be expected of them.[40]

Goldstein's desire to create an alternative to the 'therapeutic nihilism' of Kraepelin's psychiatry seems to have been a powerful (if generally unspoken) shaping force behind many of his later key ideas.[41] After the First World War, he joined forces with a psychologist, Adhémar Gelb, in founding the government-supported Institut zur Erforschung der Folgeerscheinungen von Hirnverletzungen at Frankfurt, dedicated to the study – and ultimate rehabilitation – of brain-damaged and psychologically scarred soldiers.[42] The years in Frankfurt saw the development of most of the key elements of Goldstein's mature 'holistic-organistic' approach to the problem of psychopathology. It was not until 1934, however – while in forced exile in Amsterdam – that he was able to consolidate these elements in the work destined to stand as his magnum opus: *Der Aufbau des Organismus. Einführung in die Biologie unter besonderer Berücksichtigung der Erfahrungen am kranken Menschen.*[43]

The starting point of Goldstein's essential holistic philosophy preceded even the Frankfurt years, dating back to his early experiences at Königsberg. There he had become quickly dissatisfied with the established procedure of medical diagnosis which analysed a disease in terms of a handful of preselected outstanding symptoms – and then treated all other manifestations of pathological functioning as simple concomitants that could be more or less disregarded. It began to seem to Goldstein that this arbitrary fragmentation of the total clinical picture pointed to 'a basic problem in our scientific approach to understanding the behaviour not only of patients but of living beings in general'.[44]

The alternative was to make no prejudgements about the greater importance of one symptom over another, but simply to study the patient 'phenomenologically'.[45] This concern with the total functioning of the patient led Goldstein to denounce both the classic nineteenth-century approaches to cerebral localization and the no less atomistic, reflex-oriented approaches to mind and brain activity of his own time. Pavlov's work on conditioned reflexes – which artificially isolated aspects of behaviour for the purposes of analysis – came in for special criticism, but even the more flexible Sherringtonian model of reflex integration was not spared from attack.[46]

For a time, Goldstein thought he had found an alternative model of mind/ brain functioning in the new *Gestalt* psychology of men like Wolfgang Köhler, Max Wertheimer and Kurt Koffka. Ultimately, though, he would use their ideas to create his own formula. This was based on the idea that cerebral activity was indeed always a total process, but one with constantly changing regional accents: a perpetual physiological interplay of *figures* and *backgrounds*.[47]

Gestaltian ideas were first formally applied by Goldstein and Gelb in the analysis of their First World War patient *Schn*, suffering from visual agnosia. On superficial examination, the patient failed to exhibit any obvious perceptual defect; but over time it became clear that he had simply learned to mask his disorder through an elaborate tracking-system (involving rapid, minute head movements) that allowed him to infer from isolated cues the nature of the object he was meant to identify. On the basis of this case, it began to be argued that, rather than reacting piecemeal to localized brain-injuries, patients compensate for their defects by adjusting their total set of responses to a reduced level of functioning.

The holistic principles learned from studying perceptual disabilities would ultimately be applied by Goldstein equally to language and cognitive disorders. Thus he would teach that language must be seen not as an isolated skill, but as a mode of functioning that permeated the individual's total mental orientation. Above all, language allowed for the possibility of abstract thought: what Goldstein called 'categorical behaviour'. He contrasted this advanced mental state with the more primitive 'concrete' mental attitude caused by brain-damage, and associated with the disorder most people called aphasia. This was characterized by a preoccupation with sense impressions of the moment and with concrete things in their immediate uniqueness. On this lower level, patients largely failed to appreciate the significance of words as symbols – as tokens denoting abstract categories to which specific objects in the real world belonged. Instead they tended to use words as if they were concrete qualities of the specific objects in question. That is to say, such a patient might accurately describe an object as 'cherry-coloured', but deny or fail to see that this same object could be grouped with a crimson-coloured object under the abstract category 'red'.[48]

These new approaches to the problems of language and its relationship to the inner subjectivity of the patient were to have a significant influence on the psychology and philosophy of Goldstein's time. Soon the Frankfurt Institute was attracting such distinguished visitors as the phenomenological philosopher Aron Gurwitsch, the psychoanalyst Frieda Fromm-Reichmann, the psychologist Egon Weigl and the neo-Kantian philosopher Ernst Cassirer, Goldstein's cousin. Indeed, the latter's master-work, the three-volume *Philo-*

sophie der symbolische Formen (1923–9), was importantly influenced by the principles of holistic neurology developed by Goldstein and Gelb after the war, as well as by the similarly oriented writings of men like Hughlings Jackson.[49]

Goldstein was also well aware that his concepts had a number of key points in common with the teachings of Hughlings Jackson on 'evolution' and 'dissolution', as well as with the latter's distinction between true language and the inferior ways in which a patient may 'use' words in behaviour. He clearly parted company with his nineteenth-century forebear, however, when he came to consider the alleged *motivational* factors responsible for the patient's descent into dissolution. As Goldstein saw it, a patient's stabilization at a reduced level of functioning was not simply a result of inevitable physiological forces. It was also an adaptive reaction to unbearable existential stress. To realise that one was no longer fit to carry out tasks of which one was formerly capable represented for the brain-damaged patient a terrible revelation, a confrontation with a loss of 'essence' or self-identity. The usual effect of the experience was to plunge the afflicted patient into a state of severe anxiety. Goldstein called this a 'catastrophic reaction'. He argued that the solution normally chosen by a patient to escape 'catastrophe' was simply to take himself out of situations where it was likely to be provoked. That is to say, such, it became also clear that becoming healthy always involved a *choice* on reached a point where he existed in a milieu (Goldstein himself generally used the term *Umwelt* employed by Uexküll) that was suited to and did not threaten his new, more limited 'essence' or essential self.

Goldstein's existential concepts of 'essence' and 'catastrophe' stand as his final answer to the therapeutic nihilism of his nineteenth-century heritage. It was now clear that even where a patient obviously could not be 'cured' – i.e. returned to his pre-injured state – that did not mean he could not be helped back to health. Becoming healthy ('Gesundwerden') had, however, to be understood in a new way, as a redefining of the relationship between the individual (his holistic 'essence') and his milieu or *Umwelt*. Understood as such, it became also clear that becoming healthy always involved a *choice* on the part of the patient to accept certain environmental restrictions for the privilege of regaining coherence and meaning in his life. Health therefore took on the status of an existential value. At the same time, the healing process through which doctor and patient together identified and re-established the latter's 'essence' was understood by Goldstein to involve a special intuitive act of understanding that, in the final analysis, took biology outside of the realm of natural sciences. In these final formulations of a man whose life spanned an era, clinical neurology had moved about as far from its positivistic, mechanistic nineteenth-century roots as it was possible to go.[50]

NOTES

1 The classic historically oriented defence of the new holistic ideas can be found in Henry Head's 1926 *Aphasia and Kindred Disorders of Speech* (Cambridge), vol. I. Walther Riese is unquestionably the most eloquent defender of holistic neurology as a watershed in the history of thinking about mind–brain relations: see, e.g., his 1959 *A History of Neurology*, MD Monographs on Medical History (New York), and his 1960 'Dynamics in brain lesions', *Journal of Nervous and Mental Disease*, 131, 291–301. The key historical paper in the literature essentially concerned to portray holism as a regrettable lapse from late nineteenth-century standards of clinical observation and anatomical analysis is Norman Geschwind's 1964 'The paradoxical position of Kurt Goldstein in the history of aphasia,' in R. S. Cohen and M. W. Wortofsky (eds.), *Selected Papers on Language and the Brain: Boston Studies in the Philosophy of Science*, vol. xvi (Dordrecht, Holland, 1974), pp. 62–72.

2 In Constantin von Monakow's major 1928 opus on the premises of holistic neurology, *Introduction biologique à l'étude de la neurologie et de la psychopathologie* – written in conjunction with the French neurologist R. Mourgue – Freud is the second most frequently cited author, after Monakow himself. It seems likely that Monakow was influenced in this respect by the psychoanalytically-oriented psychiatrist Eugen Bleuler with whom he was in regular contact in Zürich.

Kurt Goldstein struggled more than once with the problem of psychoanalysis' relationship to the new dynamic developments in neurological thinking. See Goldstein, 'Die Beziehungen der Psychoanalyse zur Biologie', *Bericht über den II. allgemeinen ärtzlichen Kongress für Psychotherapie in Bad Nauheim, April, 1927* (Leipzig, 1927), pp. 15–52; 'Beziehungen zwischen Psychoanalyse und Physiologie', *Zentralblatt für gesamte Neurologie und Psychiatrie*, 47 (1927), 160–1; 'The concept of transference in treatment of organic and functional nervous diseases', *Acta psychotherapeutica, psychosomatica et orthopaedagogica*, 2 (1954), 334–53; also 'Notes on the development of my concepts', *Journal of Individual Psychology*, 15 (1959), 5–14.

3 I have discussed some of the problematic aspects of Broca's localisation work in my book *Medicine, Mind and the Double Brain* (Princeton, N.J., 1987), pp. 35–49. See also W. Riese (1947), 'The early history of aphasia', *Bulletin of the History of Medicine*, 21, 322–34; and F. Schiller, *Paul Broca: Founder of French Anthropology, Explorer of the Brain* (Berkeley and Los Angeles, 1979).

4 This is not to overlook the fact that certain leading German *Somatiker* psychiatrists at this time – Wilhelm Griesinger, Theodor Meynert, to name only two of the most prominent – were committed in a general way to the concept of cerebral localization as an ideal which would ultimately allow for the creation of a comprehensive somatic model of mental activity. I am here only speaking of the relatively lukewarm German response to France's localization of a 'language faculty' in the cortex. I see nothing surprising about this response, given the growing nationalistic sentiment and anti-French feeling in the German states at this time. The Franco-Prussian War of 1870–1 and the unification of Germany

under Bismarck came less than a decade after Broca in Paris opened up the cerebral localization issue with his clinical work on the patient 'Tan'.

5 G. Fritsch and E. Hitzig (1870), 'Über die elektrische Erregbarkeit des Grosshirns'. In Eng. trans. in G. von Bonin, (ed.), *Some Papers on the Cerebral Cortex* (Springfield, Ill., 1960). For a stimulating, if perhaps still inconclusive study arguing for a deeper link between the sudden German interest in the problem of cerebral localization after 1870, and various wider institutional and political tensions in German society of the time, see P. J. Pauly, 'The political structure of the brain: cerebral localization in Bismarckian Germany', *International Journal of Neuroscience*, 21 (1983), 145–50.

6 See, e.g., David Ferrier's 1876 *The Functions of the Brain* (London); and Hermann Munk's 1881 *Uber die Funktionen der Grosshirnrinde: Gesammelte Mittheilungen aus den Jahren 1877–80* (Berlin).

7 C. Wernicke, *Der Aphasische Symptomencomplex: Eine Psychologische Studie auf Anatomischer Basis* (Breslau, 1874).

8 The dissenting work of the internist and neurologist Adolf Kussmaul in the late 1870s may be mentioned in this connection. See G. Oepen, 'Vorläufiges und Gültiges – Kussmauls "Die Störungen der Sprache" und die heutige Aphasiologie', in F. Fluge (ed.) *Adolf Kussmaul: Seine aktuelle Bedeutung für Innere Medizin und Neurologie* (Stuttgart, 1985), pp.23–31. (I am indebted to Professor Eduard Seidler at Freiburg for bringing this volume to my attention.) The special dissenting case of Hughlings Jackson in England is discussed later in this essay.

9 For a variety of perspectives on the classical era of cerebral localization theory and research, see E. Bay, 'Die Geschichte der Aphasielehre und die Grundlagen der Hirnlokalisation', *Deutsche Zeitschrift Nervenheilkunde*, 181 (1961), 634–46; the historical introduction in J. M. Nielsen, *Agnosia, Apraxia, Aphasia: Their Value in Cerebral Localization* (New York, 1946); W. Riese, *A History of Neurology*, MD Monographs on Medical History (New York, 1959); H. Hécaen and G. Lanteri-Laura, *Evolution des connaissances et des doctriness sur les localisations cérébrales* (Bibliothèque Neuro-Psychiatrique de Langue Française) (Desclée de Brouer, 1977).

10 The recovery issue is especially stressed by Walther Riese – holist neurologist turned historian – in his various accounts of the holist movement in neurology. He goes so far as to identify it as *the* problem 'at stake'. See his 1959 *History of Neurology* (cited n. 1), pp. 126–7.

11 The above two paragraphs largely follow the arguments set out by Walther Riese in his (1960) 'Dynamics in brain lesions', in W. Riese, *Selected Papers on the History of Aphasia* (Neurolinguistics, vol. 7) (Amsterdam and Lisse, 1977), p. 71; and his (1963) 'Dynamic aspects in the history of neurology', in L. Halpern (ed.) *Problems of Dynamic Neurology* (Jerusalem, 1963), p. 21.

12 A. Pick (1913), *Die agrammatischen Sprachstörungen. Studien zur psychologischen Grundlegung der Aphasielehre*, Facsimile reprint edition (Berlin and Heidelberg), p. 3.

13 H. Decker, *Freud in Germany: Revolution and Reaction in Science, 1893–1907*, Psychological Issues, Monograph 41 (New York, 1977), pp. 216–19.

14 See T. Hermann, 'Ganzheitspsychologie und Gestalttheorie', in *Die Psychologie des 20. Jahrhunderts*, vol. I, *Die europäische Tradition* (Zürich, 1976), pp. 573–658.

15 Pierre Marie (1906), 'Revision de la question de l'aphasie: la troisième circonvolution frontale gauche ne joue aucun role special dans la fonction de langage', *Semaine médicale*, 241–7; 'Revision de la question de l'aphasie: que faut-il penser des aphasies sous-corticales (aphasies pures)?', *Semaine médicale*, 493–500; 'Revision de la question de l'aphasie: l'aphasie de 1861 à 1866, essai critique historique sur la génèse de la doctrine de Broca', *Semaine médicale*, 565–71.

16 Head, *Aphasia and Kindred Disorders of Speech*, vol. I, p. 120.

17 I am indebted for much of this paragraph and the following to Fritz Ringer's analysis in *The Decline of the German Mandarins: The German Academic Community, 1890–1933* (Cambridge, Mass., 1969), pp. 90–3.

18 In a critique of an earlier draft of this paper, Dr M. Teich at Cambridge University expressed his view that, while Helmholtz and Du Bois-Reymond may well have been anti-vitalists, their deep concern with the issues arising out of Kant's critique of the knowability of the 'thing-in-itself' forbids any description of them as 'positivists'. While I am grateful to Dr Teich for taking the time to draw my attention to certain problematic points in my analysis, I have nevertheless chosen to retain the term 'positivist' in my revised discussion of the Helmholtz School. As I suggest in the text, my understanding of nineteenth-century positivism in no sense excludes a capacity to be preoccupied with the epistemological issues raised by the Kantian critique. Quite the contrary, such epistemological concerns represented an essential cornerstone of what was called 'positivism' during this time. As Maurice Mandelbaum writes in his chapter 'Ignoramus, ignorabimus: the positivist strand' (*History, Man, and Reason: A Study in Nineteenth-Century Thought*, Baltimore, Md, 1971), positivism

> arose in the mid-nineteenth century and returned to a position which was ... similar to that of Kant: our knowledge is circumscribed by the limits of sensibility and by the manner in which our minds organize that which is immediately presented to us . . . After the middle of the century, this was one of the characteristic marks of positivism among scientists and scientifically oriented philosophers. As a consequence, these later positivists placed heavier stress than had Comte or Mill upon the distinction between that which is knowable and that which exists in itself. They justified the distinction by appealing to the fact that knowledge depends upon sense experience, and what we are capable of directly experiencing is a function of the sense-organs we possess. (p. 289).

19 In his later reflections on the development and wider philosophical context of his thinking, Goldstein wrote: 'I agree with the existentialist concept [in psychiatry] in so far as I also deny that biological phenomena, particularly human existence, can be understood by application of the methods of natural sciences. But I differ in the meaning of the term existence. It means for me an epistemological concept based on phenomenological observations.' And elsewhere: 'My introduction of the concept of "existence" in the interpretation of human behavior – much as it developed from observations – ultimately goes back to Kant's transcendental theory of knowledge.' K. Goldstein (1959) 'Notes on the development of my

concepts', in A. Gurwitsch, E. M. Goldstein Haudek and W. E. Haudek (eds.), *Kurt Goldstein. Selected Papers/Ausgewählte Schriften* (The Hague, 1971), pp. 11–12, II.

20 See S. H. Hughes (1958), *Consciousness and Society: The Reorientation of European Social Thought, 1890–1930* (Hassocks, Sussex, 1986).

21 G. Murphy, 'Personal impression of Kurt Goldstein', in M. Simmel (ed.), *The Reach of Mind: Essays in Memory of Kurt Goldstein* (New York, 1968), p. 34. Cf. P. L. Entralgo and A. A. Tenlon, 'La mentalidad bio-patologica', in P. L. Entralgo (ed.), *Historia Universale de la Medicina*, vol. VII, *Medicina actual*, (Barcelona and Madrid, 1978), pp. 197–202; Hughes, *Consciousness and Society*: K. Goldstein, 'Die ganzheitliche Betrachtung in der Medizin', in T. Brugsch (ed.), *Einheitsbestrebungen in der Medizin* (Dresden and Leipzig, 1933), pp. 143–58; T. Von Uexküll, 'The sign theory of Jacob von Uexküll', in M. Krampen, K. Oehler *et al.* (eds.), *Classics of Semiotics* (trans. of *Die Welt Als Zeichen*, 1981, (New York and London, 1987), pp. 147–89; S. Casper, 'Die personalistische Weltanschauung William Sterns' (Repr. from *Die deutsche Schule*, 1931, vol. 35); W. Schmitt, 'Karl Jaspers und die Methodenfrage in der Psychiatrie', repr. *Klinische Psychologie und Psychopathologie*, 8 (1979), 74–82 (Stuttgart).

22 To a certain extent, this trend spread beyond the strict geographical borders of central Europe to the Anglo-American scene, where, however, the social and philosophical context was naturally rather different. In England, Sir Charles Scott Sherrington's 'integrative' model of reflex nervous action would roundly overturn the nineteenth-century view of the organism as a bundle of sensory-motor reflex arcs, and stress the extent to which sensory input at one level of the system modifies input at another, leading to a unified, hierarchical pattern of biologically purposive behaviour. His countryman and contemporary, William McDougall, would develop a model of human motivation based on his concept of the 'horme', a unit of biologically purposive energy which more or less corresponded to the 'instinct' concept of other authors. In the United States, Walter B. Cannon's work on the role of the sympathetic nervous system would cast new light on the bodily changes associated with emotional arousal – especially the so-called 'fight or flight' response.

23 It is interesting that a trend towards 'holistic' subjectivist ways of thinking about phenomena should have seen certain parallels in the physical sciences of this same period, struggling to absorb the implications of the breakdown of Newtonian mechanics. Some of the holistic neurologists were also aware of the broad similarities between their own changing preoccupations and those of the physicists. See, e.g., M. Minkowski on Constantin von Monakow in his memorial tribute, 'Constantin von Monakow, 1853–1930', *Archiv für Neurologie und Psychiatrie*, 27 (1931), 37.

The remarks of Wolfgang Köhler – one of the leaders of the *Gestalt* school of psychology that strongly influenced men like Goldstein – are also of interest: 'Until recently it has been impossible to give conclusive answers to the speculations of additive thinking; *now*, however, from physics, comes evidence to *demonstrate* the errors of such thinking'. *Die Physischen Gestalten in Ruhe und in stationären*

Zustand. Eine naturphilosophische Untersuchung (1920), repr. in W. Dennis (ed.), *Readings in the History of Psychology* (New York, 1948), p. 527.

24 The Troeltsch quote was cited from Fritz Ringer's *The Decline of the German Mandarins* (Cambridge, Mass., 1969), p. 181. See also Ringer's general analysis of the issues only touched on here, esp. chs. 5–7.

Although I am still sifting it out, there is also more direct evidence for a link between broad cultural disaffection in Germany, calls for spiritual revival, and the new holistic trends in neurology. Consider, for example, the early (1913) remarks of Kurt Goldstein – later to become Germany's leading holistic neurologist – linking modern industrial living and materialistic trends in modern thinking to racial degeneration, as seen above all in the recent sharp rise of nervous disorders among the general public (*Über Rassenhygiene*, Berlin, 1913).

25 Freud (1891), *On Aphasia: A Critical Study* (London, 1953); Pick, *Die agrammatischen Sprachstörungen* (Berlin, 1913); Head (1926), *Aphasia and Kindred Disorders of Speech* (New York, 1963), p. 30; Goldstein, *Über Aphasie* (Zurich, 1927), p. 11; Monakow and Mourgue (1928), *Biologische Einführung in das Studium der Neuropathologie und Psychopathologie*, tr. E. Katzenstein (Stuttgart and Leipzig, 1930).

26 The best single source for Jackson's thought is the two-volume *Selected Writings of John Hughlings Jackson*, ed. J. Taylor (London, 1932).

27 See on this issue, e.g. J. Durant, 'The science of sentiment: the problem of the cerebral localization of emotion', in P. Bateson and P. Klapper (eds.), *Perspectives in Ethology* (London, 1985). Consulted here only in draft form.

28 Freud, *On Aphasia*, p. 87.

29 For discussions of the link between the Jacksonian concept of dissolution and the Freudian concept of regression, see, e.g. W. Riese, 'Freudian concepts of brain function and brain disease', *Journal of Nervous and Mental Diseases*, 127 (1958), 287–307; and S. Jackson, 'The history of Freud's concepts of regression', *Journal of the American Psychoanalytic Association*, 17, no. 3, 743–84. For a sampling of discussions on Freud's later use of Jackson's ideas on 'recurrent utterances', see J. Forrester, *Language and the Origins of Psychoanalysis* (London and Basingstoke, 1980); E. Stengel, 'Hughlings Jackson's influence on psychiatry', *British Journal of Psychiatry*, 109 (1963), 348–55. Some attempts to push the case for a psychoanalytic debt to Jackson beyond these two key issues can be found in S. P. Fullinwider, 'Sigmund Freud, John Hughlings Jackson, and speech', *Journal of the History of Ideas*, 44 (1983), 51–8; and chapter 8 of my own *Medicine, Mind and the Double Brain*, 'Freud and Jackson's double brain: the case for a psychoanalytic debt'.

30 Von Monakow (1911), 'Lokalisation der Hirnfunktionen', tr. in G. von Bonin (ed.), *Some Papers on the Cerebral Cortex* (Springfield, Ill., 1960), pp. 231–50.

31 Von Monakow, and R. Mourgue (1927), *Biologische Einführung in das Studium der Neurologie und Psychopathologie*, tr. E. Katzenstein (Stuttgart and Leipzig, 1930), pp. 27–8.

32 Bergson's involvement with the holistic trend in neurology actually goes beyond his immediate influence on von Monakow. His 1896 *Matière et mémoire* also

contained a harsh critique of the classical localistionist approach to the problem of aphasia which served as a springboard to a discussion of the way in which memory serves to bind existence together and make it continuous.

33 For the relevant works of Semon, see his *Die Mneme als Erhaltendes Prinzip im Wechsel des Organischen Geschehens* (Leipzig, 1904), and *Die mnenischen Empfindungen. Erste Fortsetzung der Mneme* (Leipzig, 1909).

34 See Monakow's *Introduction biologique à l'étude de la neurologie et de la psychopathologie*, written in 1927 with the French psychologist R. Mourgue. Cf. the early 'Gefühl, Gesittung und Gehirn', *Arbeiten aus dem Hirnanatomischen Institut in Zürich*, 10 (1916), 115–213; the later 'Die Syneidesis, das biologische, Gewissen', *Schweizer Archiv für Neurologie und Psychiatrie*, 29 (1927), 56–91; and Monakow's final work, 'Religion und Nervensystem (Biologische Betrachtungen)', *Schweizer Archiv für Neurologie und Psychiatrie*, 26 (1930), 63–83.

35 Walther Riese asserts that those 'close to Monakow' knew how he resisted the increasingly parochial nationalistic tendencies of his time, and cherished instead ideals of cosmopolitanism and world citizenship. Riese (1958), 'The principle of diaschisis', in R. Hoods and Y. Lebrun (eds.), *Selected Papers on the History of Aphasia* (Amsterdam, 1977), p. 125.

36 Von Monakow's unpublished papers (today held at the University of Zürich) include a number of manuscripts dating from the war period, and dwelling on the causes of war, as well as the purpose generally of life, of reproduction, maturity, old age, degeneration, death, and the noble and base emotions. Alfred W. Gübser at Zürich worked through much of this material in the late 1960s, but his resulting article, 'Constantin von Monakow und der Erste Weltkrieg', was never published. (See his reference to the piece in C. von Monakow, *Vita Mea/Mein Leben* ed. W. Gübser and E. H. Ackerknecht, Berne, Stuttgart and Vienna, 1970, p. 261.) I am intending, in a future publication of my own, to explore this manuscript material as part of a larger study of holistic neuro-biological thinking in the German-speaking countries from the First World War to the rise of the Third Reich.

Von Monakow continued to dwell upon the biological significance of the Great War for the rest of his life. In light of the events that followed, there is a certain ironic interest in his final suggestion, made shortly before his death in 1930, that the war had perhaps been the birth pains of a spiritual revival – 'a stormy preliminary phase ... of a powerful spiritual world movement' – which was only now making its presence felt, especially among the young (Monakow, 'Religion und Nervensystem (Biologische Betrachtungen)', *Schweizer Archiv für Neurologie und Psychiatrie*, 26 (1930), 80).

37 Ehrenfels developed these ideas in his 1918 *Kosmogonie*. See W. Johnston, *The Austrian Mind: An Intellectual and Social History, 1848–1938* (Berkeley and Los Angeles, 1972), p. 305; see also p. 329, where Johnston discusses the ideological uses of the concept of *Gestalt* in the work of that arch-polemicist for Aryan 'racial purity', Houston Stewart Chamberlain. On Spemann, see Paul Weindling, 'Weimar eugenics: The Kaiser Wilhelm Institute for Anthropology, Human Heredity and Eugenics in social context', *Annals of Science*, 42 (1985), 307, and esp. T. J. Horder and P. J. Weindling, 'Hans Spemann and the organiser', in T. J. Horder, J.

A. Witkowski and C. C. Wylie (eds.), *A History of Embryology* (Cambridge, 1986), pp. 183–242.

38 See K. Goldstein, 'Konstantin [*sic*] von Monakow', *Deutsche Zeitschrift für Nervenheilkunde*, 120 (1931), 1–7.

39 While there is no definitive biography of Kurt Goldstein, Marianne L. Simmel's lovingly edited book, *The Reach of Mind: Essays in Memory of Kurt Goldstein* (New York, 1968), contains a number of illuminating contributions as well as a full bibliography of Goldstein's writings over more than sixty years. Also valuable for historical orientation during the later period of Goldstein's career is the work on the Jewish Berlin hospital Moabit, where Goldstein served as head of the Neurology Department from 1930 to 1933: C. Prosee and R. Winau (eds.), *Nicht misshandeln: Das Krankenhaus Moabit. 1920–1933: Ein Zentrum jüdischer Ärtzte in Berlin; 1933–1945: Verfolgung. Widerstand. Zerstörung*, Stätten der Geschichte Berlins, B. 5 (Berlin, 1984). A useful source book for Goldstein's thought itself is A. Gurwitsch, E. M. Goldstein Haudek and W. E. Haudek, (eds.), *Kurt Goldstein. Selected Papers/Ausgewählte Schriften* (The Hague, 1971).

40 See Goldstein (1959), 'Notes on the development of my concepts', in *Selected Papers/Ausgewählte Schriften*, p. 2; Decker, *Freud in Germany*, p. 69.

41 Similar sentiments may also have influenced the orientation of Goldstein's 1913 *Über Rassenhygiene*. This argued that the inherited causes of degeneration had been exaggerated by the scientific community, and that in fact a great deal could be done to improve the quality of the German race through education and other practical social programmes designed to help the populace adjust itself to the still unaccustomed new pressures of modern technological culture.

42 On the problem of rehabilitation, see Goldstein, *Die Behandlung, Fürsorge und Begutachtung der Hirnverletzten. Zugleich ein Beitrag zur Verwendung psychologischer Methoden in der Klinik* (Leipzig, 1919).

43 The Hague, 1934. This book was published in English translation five years later under the title *The Organism. Holistic Approach to Biology derived from Pathological Data in Man*, with a foreword by Karl S. Lashley (New York, 1939).

44 Goldstein, 'Notes on the develoment of my concepts', p. 2.

45 'Phenomenology' was a term that had become associated in Goldstein's day with a movement in German philosophy loosely grouped around the leadership of Edmund Husserl. The professed aim of this movement was to bracket ('einklammern') all presuppositions of a metaphysical or epistemological nature, and simply to focus on the essence of experience directly apprehended. Goldstein would later acknowledge an intellectual debt to Husserl, and several of the second generation of phenomenological philosophers – notably Maurice Merleau-Ponty in France – would later interpret Goldstein in the context of their own philosophies.

46 See e.g. Goldstein, *Über Aphasie* (Neurologische und Psychiatrische Abhandlungen aus dem Schweizer Archiv für Neurologie und Psychiatrie, ed. C. von Monakow), Heft 6 (Zürich, Leipzig and Berlin, 1927), pp. 25, 146–7. Cf. also note 22.

47 W. Riese, 'Kurt Goldstein – the man and his work', in Simmel (ed.) *The Reach of Mind*, (New York, 1968), pp. 18–19.

48 See A. Gurwitsch, 'Gelb-Goldstein's concept of "concrete" and "categorical" attitude and the phenomenology of ideation', in Simmel (ed.), *The Reach of Mind*, pp. 119–42; Goldstein and Gelb, 'Psychologische Analysen hirnpathologischer Fälle. XI. Über Farbenanamnesie, nebst Bemerkungen über das Wesen der amnestischen Aphasie überhaupt und die Beziehung zwischen Sprache und dem Verhalten zur Umwelt', *Psychologische Forschung*, 6 (1925), 127–86.

49 See e.g. E. Cassirer, 'Etude sur la pathologie de la conscience symbolique', *Journal de psychologie normale et pathologique*, 29 (1929), 289–336, 523–66.

50 See Goldstein, 'Zur Problem der Angst', *Allgemeine ärtzliche Zeitschrift für Psychotherapie*, 2 (1927), 409–37; 'Die ganzheitliche Betrachtung in der Medizin', pp. 149–52, 155–8; 'Health as value', in H. Maslow (ed.), *New Knowledge in Human Values* (New York, 1959), pp. 178–88; 'Notes on the development of my concepts', in *Selected Papers/Ausgewählte Schriften*, pp. 7–9.

🙂

FOURTEEN

BIOLOGY AND BEAUTY: SCIENCE AND AESTHETICS IN *FIN-DE-SIÈCLE* GERMANY

KURT BAYERTZ

ART AND EVOLUTION

In 1899 – the *fin de siècle* had reached its culmination – the biologist Ernst Haeckel propounded an amalgamation of artistic creation and scientific knowledge unknown up to then:

The remarkable expansion of our knowledge of nature, and the discovery of countless beautiful forms of life, which it includes, have awakened quite a new aesthetic sense in our generation, and thus given a new tone to painting and sculpture. Numerous scientific voyages and expeditions for the exploration of unknown lands and seas, partly in earlier centuries, but more especially in the nineteenth, have brought to light an undreamed abundance of new organic forms. The number of new species of animals and plants soon became enormous, and among them (especially among the lower groups that had been neglected before) there were thousands of forms of great beauty and interest, affording an entirely new inspiration for painting, sculpture, architecture, and technical art. In this respect a new world was revealed by the great advance of microscopic research in the second half of the century, and especially by the discovery of the marvellous inhabitants of the deep sea, which were first brought to light by the famous expedition of the *Challenger* (1872–6). Thousands of graceful radiolaria and thalamophora, of pretty medusae and corals, of extraordinary molluscs and crabs, suddenly introduced us to a wealth of hidden organisms beyond all anticipation, the peculiar beauty and diversity of which far transcend all the creations of the human imagination.[1]

Haeckel did not limit himself to such general explanations. The same year the first set of an extensive series, containing a hundred large unbound folio illustrations, appeared under the title *Kunstformen der Natur* (*Artistic Forms in Nature*), drawn from illustrations for earlier works of Haeckel's. His stated purpose with this collection was to make available to the public the beauty and the richness of forms in the organic world – above all of the radiolaria, medusas and foraminifera that he had described in detail and depicted in his scientific publications. The similarity in appearance between these lower animals and forms used in the art of his time strikes the eye. The same burgeoning lines and rhythmic forms of Haeckel's plates are to be seen in the swirling ornamentation of the new art movement *Jugendstil*. It is not surprising, therefore, that Haeckel's work soon acquired supporters among the fine artists of his day. The sculptor Hermann Obrist, for example, tried to employ the forms Haeckel had made public in his fountains and sculptures, and referred explicitly to Haeckel in his theoretical writings.[2] In a later work Haeckel mentioned, not without pride, the French architect René Binet, who had become famous for his highly detailed *Jugendstil* buildings for the World Exhibition in Paris in 1900. Binet had presented the forms of microscopic organisms as the aesthetic model for numerous drawings in the book he published in 1902 entitled *Esquisses décoratives* (*Decorative Sketches*). He referred explicitly to Haeckel's *Kunstformen der Natur*, saying that the lower forms of life depicted there were a main source of inspiration for his decorative fantasy. These forms were also made much use of in the handicrafts, as Haeckel mentions in the same text:

I have further experienced first-hand how beautifully the charming artistic forms of the above-mentioned groups – especially those of the amazing structures of the microscopic protista – can be employed ornamentally: I have received numerous gifts since the publication of my *Kunstformen* – pieces of furniture and other household articles, plates, cups, pillows, bags, etc. – that have been tastefully decorated with the forms of the protista.[3]

Evolutionary aesthetics

Not only artistic production, but also aesthetic theory, was influenced by evolutionary theory at the *fin de siècle*. The leading German *Jugendstil* magazine *Pan* published an article in 1899 entitled 'Evolutionary Theory and Aesthetics', which began with the following passage:

Evolutionary theory is as old as the world. We can perceive its traces – beginnings and elaborations – in all cultures, as well as in our own. We've become accustomed to identifying it with the name Darwin because he was the first to give it, within certain limits, a scientific foundation. Since Darwin – who only made a beginning – we've come to see the world in the light of this theory. Everywhere forces are at work extending its limits, and an unsuspected deepening of our understanding of the world will follow from it. Only to the extent that a modern aesthetics is founded on this theory will the striving of our age be satisfied.[4]

Darwin's theory was especially attractive to music aestheticians. H. Berg had already tried in 1879 – in a somewhat crude attempt – to derive music from the rutting cries of the apes. Other theoreticians followed his lead, at least in so far as they attempted to explain the development of music by natural selection.[5] Haeckel himself provided an important stimulus in this direction with the 'monistic' philosophy he propounded in many of his works, impulses that were taken up and expanded systematically by his followers.

In the present essay I would like to investigate the highly influential concept of 'evolutionary aesthetics', focusing above all on one of its less conspicuous aspects. My main interest is not in the theoretical claims of the aesthetic theory inspired by Haeckel, or in its validity or justification, but in the problem that these claims were intended to provide a resolution to. The historical emergence, establishment and institutionalization of the natural sciences in the nineteenth century did not, in fact, have only the positive consequences for art and aesthetics that Haeckel emphasized. By undermining the metaphysical assumptions on which both traditional philosophical aesthetics and artistic production were based, the natural sciences presented above all a problem, if not a threat, to both. The influence of the sciences – above all of the evolutionary theory – on *fin-de-siècle* aesthetics was not limited to its 'exoteric' moment: in the transfer of biological concepts and explanatory models on to art. My thesis is that the emphatically harmonious picture presented by Haeckel and his monistic followers of the relationship between evolutionary theory, on the one hand, and art and aesthetics, on the other, must be understood more as a reaction to the problem posed by science, i. e. as the attempt to ward off the threat it represented.

METAPHYSICAL DISILLUSIONMENT

The shock caused by Darwin's theory to the philosophical foundations of the West has often been described: the ground was suddenly pulled away from under man's traditional understanding of his origins and position in Nature. Less attention has usually been paid to the fact that this theory also produced a cultural shock, calling into question traditional convictions as to the origins of beauty and, as a result, the foundations of art.

From harmony to horror

By emphasizing the limitations of all resources and the resulting competition among organisms, Darwin's theory undermined what had until then been the dominant physico-theological conception of a peaceful, harmonious Nature, substituting for it a new, thoroughly unidyllic image. The young Ernst Haeckel himself had already described this new understanding of Nature in his *Natürliche Schöpfungsgeschichte* (*Natural History of Creation*) in 1868:

If one observes more closely the communal life and the mutual relations of plants and animals (including man) one discovers everywhere, and always, the opposite of that pleasant and peaceful communal life that the goodness of the Creator is supposed to have provided his creatures with; on the contrary, one sees everywhere a pitiless struggle of all against all. Nowhere in Nature, wherever one may turn one's eyes, does one find that idyllic peace so praised by the poets – one finds struggle everywhere, a striving for self-preservation and for destruction of one's immediate enemy, as well as of one's neighbour. The motive force of life is, consciously or unconsciously, passion and egoism. The famous lines of the poet: 'Wherever man has not appeared with his torment, Nature is complete', while beautiful are, unfortunately, not true. Man, moreover, is in this regard, no exception from the rest of the animal world.⁶

From the perspective of natural selection Nature was transformed into a battleground in which there was no more place for beauty. Darwin's theory seemed to possess an immanent urge to disabusal, discovering struggle and destruction where once harmony and beauty had been found. A striking example of this is the following passage from the philosopher Friedrich Albert Lange:

A hundred years ago one of the favourite themes of popular and scientific writings was the purposefulness of Nature – how everything worked so well together to ensure the survival of all living things on Earth, and how every need was provided for by special, ingenious arrangements. Today a corner of the veil concealing the secrets of Nature has been raised and we have gained insight into the way in which that purposefulness has come about . . . We have come to recognize that the means by which Nature achieves survival, recognizable beneath its manifold appearances, is nothing but the repeated, immense *waste* of new lives and the prompt destruction of the countless germs and living things that haven't had the good fortune to find themselves on the narrow path of favoured development.⁷

In his famous *History of Materialism* Lange describes Darwin's theory in detail once again, emphasizing the blindness and brutality of Nature in its treatment of its creatures, a fact that undermines every theology or anthropomorphism.⁸ To sum up: Only an aesthetic of *horror* seemed possible in Darwin's day, an aesthetic which – as was tersely expressed by the poet Tennyson – was based upon a Nature 'red in tooth and claw'.

It is clear that this new understanding of Nature is closely connected with social changes in the nineteenth century. Contemporaries often referred to the similarities between the Darwinian mechanism behind evolution and the structures of early capitalism, which made the 'struggle for survival' seem a projection of economic competition on to Nature. But even those who would consider it an exaggeration to find a reflection of social conditions in the concepts and claims of Darwin's theory could not deny that socio-economic developments in the nineteenth century had undermined step by step the traditional conception of an all-inclusive harmony and purposefulness in Nature. It is in this sense that Darwin's theory was more than just a theory of organismic evolution: it also expressed the new social experience of those in the progressive industrial societies.

In Germany this socio-economic transformation had also begun already when Darwin's theory first became known. The basic elements of such a conception of Nature were not completely new. Schopenhauer had, before Darwin, developed a pessimistic metaphysics in which the real world was identified with blind movement, evil and the irrational. The young Nietzsche became acquainted with both the theory of evolution and Schopenhauer's philosophy in the same year,[9] and the two became inseparably joined in his thought: the one confirmed scientifically what the other had formulated philosophically. Despite his repeated attacks against Darwinism – 'a philosophy for butchers' apprentices'[10] – Nietzsche's philosophy was deeply influenced by the theory of evolution, and especially by the idea of natural selection. Fundamental to his thought is the ruthlessness of Nature, the brutality associated with almost all life processes, and the irrational quality of reality, all of which he found confirmed in the theory of evolution and in other scientific theories.[11] Nietzsche's philosophy is the most striking illustration of my basic thesis that science presented a *problem* for aesthetic theory.

The problem was magnified by changes in German society during the time when Nietzsche was developing his philosophy. He felt that with Germany's development into a modern society all possibility of a genuine and great culture – as he had seen embodied in ancient Greece – had been destroyed. The expansion of a capitalist economy, based on money and profit, in the *Gründerjahren* following the victory over France in 1871, seemed to him no less a threat than the growth of mass democracy and the emergence of the socialist movement. Just as he saw in the sciences of his day above all the destruction of traditional rationalistic metaphysics, so he found only signs and causes of decay in the social developments of his time. Neither the moral ideas of the humanistic-Christian tradition, nor the political ideals of the Enlightenment seemed to him strong enough to be able to maintain themselves in the face of political and scientific realities. Nietzsche's whole philosophy was based on the assumption that any attempt to hold on to these ideals was cowardly and dishonest, and this led him to the decision to reject every attempt at reconciliation, extenuation or compromise. Wherever he sensed a tendency to attenuate the pessimistic consequences of the sciences or, above all, to reconcile traditional European values with the new scientific view of the world, he reacted with enmity and scorn. For example, he attacked David Friedrich Strauss with bitter sarcasm for attempting to make Darwin's theory the basis of a pleasant, optimistic theory of progress. Filled with contempt, Nietzsche says that Strauss draws about himself the matted robe of our ape genealogy and praises Darwin as one of the greatest benefactors of the race, but pulls back from drawing consequences out of the theory of evolution. He refuses to make the *bellum omnium contra omnes* and the prerogative of the stronger into the foundation of a new morality that would call into question the dominant social morality. Strauss goes to great but vain efforts to avoid the insight that the universe is nothing more than 'an inflexible clockwork' that threatens to crush man.[12]

Art as compensation

Nietzsche's metaphysics is consequential, but hardly tolerable. In his first published work, *The Birth of Tragedy* (1872), he raised the question, therefore, of whether and how existence could be endured under such conditions. His answer was: It is art that makes life bearable and possible. The ancient Greeks had already had 'the extreme distrust of the titanic forces of Nature' that he had absorbed from Schopenhauer and found reinforced in the science of his day, especially in Darwin's theory. 'The Greeks were familiar with and had felt the horror and dreadfulness of existence', he says, but they hadn't reconciled themselves to what afflicted and threatened them: It was through tragic drama:

that the profound Hellenes, singularly gifted for experiencing the most delicate and the most extreme sufferings, consoled themselves. Tragedy kept them from yielding to the temptation of longing for a Buddhistic renunciation of will on facing the horrible destructiveness of so-called world history and the brutality of Nature. It is art that saved them and through art life itself is saved ... Art, at this point of greatest danger of the will, approaches in the guise of a healing, saving sorceress. Only it is able to transform the feeling of nausea at the horribleness or absurdity of life into conceptions that can be lived with, the *sublime* as the artistic subduing of horror, and the *comic* as the artistic release from nausea at the absurd.[13]

Throughout all the changes his aesthetic theory underwent Nietzsche retained this conception of the function of art. This is expressly stated in the introduction to the new edition of his first book. He says that what he had early come to understand was something terrible and dangerous: 'Today I would say that it was the very *problem of science* – science conceived of for the first time as problematic, as questionable.' What is referred to here as the 'problem of science' is the destruction of the anthropocentric and anthropomorphic concept of Nature, which made it impossible for man to feel at home in Nature any longer. Science undermines the traditional values without being able to create new ones. Against this background Nietzsche characterizes art 'as the only real metaphysical activity' of man and repeats that 'the existence of the world is only justified as an aesthetic phenomenon'.[14]

None the less, although art appears as the 'metaphysical solace' enabling man to continue living in a brutal and alien Nature, it is still not contrary to Nature, but itself a product of it. Nietzsche speaks of an 'artistic power of the whole of Nature', which uses the artist as its medium. The artist's subjectivity disappears during aesthetic production, becoming one with Nature, with

Being: 'Only in so far as the genius in the act of creation coalesces with the original artist of the world does he know anything about the eternal essence of art.'[15] Nietzsche's aesthetics is by no means inimical to Nature; he finds that art is an expression of Nature and the return of man to its womb. This double aspect of art – at once a product of Nature and a trick to seduce man into going on living – was developed by Nietzsche at greater length in his later works. There a narrower, bio-physiological language, centred about the concept of 'life',[16] increasingly comes to replace the general categories of 'Nature' or 'Being'. Above all in the literary remains of the 1880s he elaborates a 'physiology of art', drawing on the contemporary biological sciences. Radicalizing his original conception, he characterizes aesthetic sensitivity as innate and inherited, interpreting it as an expression and transformation of the sexual drive and associating it above all with intoxication. Beauty or ugliness serve only as symbols for that which sustains and furthers life, or inhibits it.

What we find instinctively repugnant, aesthetically, has proven through mankind's long experience to be injurious, dangerous and worthy of mistrust: the aesthetic instinct that finds sudden expression (in disgust, e.g.) issues from a rational judgment. *Beauty*, therefore, belongs to the general category of biological values including the useful, the beneficial and the life-sustaining. The association is not direct but due to the fact that a large number of stimuli that remind us from afar of useful things and conditions, and are associated with them, awaken the feeling of beauty in us, i.e. increase our feeling of power. This means that Beauty and Ugliness are recognizable as depending upon our lowest *survival values*. To attempt to understand Beauty or Ugliness without such a foundation is pointless.[17]

Central here is the fact that this reduction of aesthetics to biology is meant not simply descriptively but also normatively. For Nietzsche 'life' has been placed among the highest values for judging aesthetic creation. He repeatedly attacks the conception of art as a value in itself – as propagated in *l'art pour l'art* – as well as all attempts to see in art a means to the moral improvement of man, insisting instead on art as a means of intensifying life: 'Art and nothing but art! It is she that makes life possible, who seduces us to live, the great stimulus of life. Art is the only effective counterforce to the will to deny life.'[18]

PHILOSOPHICAL *JUGENDSTIL*

In the second half of the nineteenth century it was science that raised the basic difficulty for an aesthetic perception of Nature. The empirical sciences had driven man from the centre of creation and destroyed the teleological orientation of life about him as the highest being. They had reduced the natural processes known to us to abstract, mathematically formulated laws, and transformed the Universe into a mechanism devoid of living spirit. The philosophy of Nietzsche is, to be sure, an extreme case but it throws light on to a problem that troubled not only Nietzsche: scientific truth seemed to have made an aesthetic conception of Nature inconceivable, calling into question the natural foundations of art as such. It was on the relationship of art to truth that he had first begun to reflect seriously, he wrote even in 1888, and he still faced 'the dichotomy with a holy dread'. *The Birth of Tragedy* had been dedicated to this question: the faith in art he proclaimed there was founded upon the quite different conviction 'that it is not possible to live with the truth'.[19] It can't be doubted that the assumed harmony of aesthetics and science, of art and Nature, of beauty and truth, that had been traditional in Western culture had been destroyed. But was it necessary to go to the extreme Nietzsche did in emphasizing the dichotomy? Couldn't one take a less dramatic view of things? Were all attempts at reconciliation futile?

The spiritualization of matter

Ernst Haeckel was among those seeking a reconciliation, who attempted to subsume the results of the exact sciences into a satisfying philosophico-aesthetic conception of Nature. He had already, as a student in Würzburg, expressed dissatisfaction with the positivistic conception of science that was gaining in influence during his day. In a letter to his parents he wrote about his teacher Rudolph Kölliker:

He gave a very attractive philosophical introduction to physiology in which he defined quite clearly the outlook of the scientist, distinguishing it completely from that of the ordinary human being. The scientist must proceed purely empirically and critically; he is allowed to engage only in objective research, making observations and experiments, at most setting up or deriving general laws from the information he's obtained. He is never to make teleological, idealistic or dynamic judgements; that is, natural philosophy is forbidden to him. Although I have to accept this concrete-empiric method of research in its absolute objectivity, I must confess that it doesn't satisfy me: I am attracted to, indeed have a need for, a general philosophical perspective, which would offer an overview of the whole after the concrete details had been investigated.[20]

In 1860, when Ernst Haeckel became familiar with Darwin's theory, he found in it not only a technical tool for answering biological questions, but above all the foundation for the 'general philosophical perspective, which would offer a view of the whole' that he'd been long searching for. From the very outset his engagement on behalf of Darwin's theory and his populariza-tion of it were bound to a tendency to reinterpret it: Darwin had concentrated on the mechanism of natural selection, whereas Haeckel emphasized the process of evolutionary change and the fact of the descent of man. In 1866 Haeckel, in his *Generelle Morphologie*, generalized the concept of evolution to a 'monistic' world-view according to which all the phenomena of the

Universe – from the most remote heavenly body to the minerals, primitive plant life and animals on Earth, up to a man and his highest achievements – were only stages of an immense developmental structure. The Universe formed an evolutionary whole in which all the higher forms were presaged in the lower ones, so that nowhere were there any discontinuities to be found. Haeckel argues in particular against the assumption of a discontinuity in the emergence of mind and spirit from pure matter. For him 'monism' means, above all, the recognition that even the highest intellectual capabilities of man had their roots in the instincts of animals, in the sensitivity to stimulation of the plants and the reactivity of micro-organisms. For him even individual cells have a 'soul' (*Seele*) – and, since it isn't possible for the souls to have arisen out of nothing, he was convinced that the whole of inanimate Nature possessed spiritual qualities. His last work bore the title *Kristallseelen. Studien über das anorganische Leben* (*The Souls of Crystals. Studies of Inorganic Life*). The Universe – both the animate and the inanimate part – is by no means dead and purely material, but living and filled with soul.

Given these assumptions it seemed that the beauty of Nature, which had threatened to be lost in the face of the 'struggle for survival', could be regained. Monism is an attempt to requicken the frozen image of Nature that dominated scientific rationalism and to counter the scientific de-spiritualization of Nature by a reawakening of pantheism. Haeckel himself emphasized this:

The most frequent criticism made today of the natural sciences and, in particular, of its most promising discipline, evolutionary theory, is that it has reduced living Nature to a soulless machine, banished all ideals from the real world and destroyed its poetry. We are convinced that our unbiased, comparative and genetic observations on the life of the spirit refutes that erroneous criticism ... To be sure, we no longer have today the nymphs and naiads, the dryads and oreads the ancient Greeks peopled their springs and rivers, their forests and mountains with; along with the gods of Olympus they are long gone. But the place of these manlike demigods has been taken by the countless elementary spirits of the cells. And if there is a concept that is poetic in the highest degree then it is certainly the clear recognition that in the smallest worm and the most unpresupposing flower there dwell thousands of fragile autonomous spirits.[21]

The productivity of Nature is emphasized now, its ceaseless transformation and the creation of ever new forms, whereas the 'struggle for survival' and the destruction of countless organisms are reduced to mere means for bringing about the continual transformation of organic forms. By identifying evolution with progress Haeckel secretly rehabilitated teleology: it was assumed that Nature had an inclination to produce ever better, higher and more perfect forms. In his *Welträtsel* (*Riddle of the Universe*) Haeckel presented a picture of Nature and its beauties which contrasted with that of the pre-Darwin era only in so far as it replaced a personal Creator with – an equally wise and beauty-producing – pantheistic God – Nature.

Surrounding nature offers us everywhere a marvellous wealth of lovely and interesting objects. In every bit of moss and blade of grass, in every beetle and butterfly, we find, when we examine it carefully, beauties which are usually overlooked. Above all, when we examine them with a good microscope, we find everywhere in nature, a new world of inexhaustible charms.[22]

From here it is not very far to the philosophical *Jugendstil* as it was developed and propagated above all in the 1890s by the supporters of Haeckel's monism. The Darwinian 'struggle for survival', which had once undermined the physico-theological idyll, was now employed to revive it: Bölsche speaks of it as of a God that turns everything to the good and dispenses blessings on all sides.

The vast struggle for existence that rages among the free-soaring heavenly bodies as well as among the elements on Earth, among simple chemical substances as well as among the mysterious structures of organic life, is only the enduring well-being of the generations that have come into harmony with their surroundings. Nature itself is, in this sense, filled with a deep, necessary ideality; wherever its development is the fullest, this ideality is expressed in the closest approach to the principle of the greatest good for the greatest number, in which every single individual participates. However obscure the general course of existence might appear to our understanding, the only clear line that we can follow in the system of creation is the ideal path towards harmony, towards what has achieved stability in all directions, towards what is normal and happy in its existence. It is the only motive idea that appears with some degree of clarity out of the incredible complexity of events, and of which we can say: it embodies a goal, a termination.[23]

The philosophical writer Bruno Wille went a step further: for him the Universe is not only composed of harmonious individual beings, but is itself a harmonious individual being with 'an individual spirit', inwardly related to man. In the novel *Offenbarungen des Wacholderbaums* (*Revelations of the Juniper Tree*) he defines 'organism' as: 'a harmonious structure intended for survival or even for an increase in its harmony'. In this sense, the hero of his novel repeatedly says, the world is an organism:

a living form – a structure with a certain harmony or unity – and this unity sustains itself successfully – even has principles of development that are directed towards an increase in harmony. This suffices for me to justify the conclusion that the world is an autonomous, growing harmony, a living structure – and as such is my equal, to be interpreted according to the pattern of my own being, that is, with a uniform inner life and an individual mind.[24]

Evolution through love

Viewed from the perspective of natural selection, Nature seemed to be transformed into a battleground in which there was no longer any room for beauty. But Darwin's concept of natural selection is ambiguous. Beside 'natural selection' Darwin also uses the expression 'sexual selection'. It was through the latter that he had discovered the way to an evolutionary explanation of the richness of forms and colours in organic nature. In the *Origin* Darwin had described the emergence and evolution of the song and plumage of birds.

The rock-thrush of Guiana, birds of Paradise, and some others, congregate; and successive males display their gorgeous plumage and perform strange antics before the females, which standing by as spectators, at last choose the most attractive partner . . . I can see no good reason to doubt that female birds, by selecting, during thousands of generations, the most melodious or beautiful males, according to their standard of beauty, might produce a marked effect.[25]

This principle of sexual selection is evidently transferable to man. In his later work, *The Descent of Man*, Darwin interpreted the human sense of beauty as a product of sexual selection. If one assumes then that this sense of beauty – together with the other ideals – directs all human action, and that every human being '[is possessed of] the ideal image of a human being of the most beautiful form, the greatest spiritual strength and the most superb character ethically',[26] and selects his sexual partner to fit this ideal, then one can conclude that there is a general tendency to an increase in beauty (as well as in intelligence and moral strength) in mankind. This is precisely what Bölsche claimed: 'For thousands of years sexual choice has followed these simple demands: for a morally superior character, a more pleasant temperament, a quicker intelligence, a more beautiful, more harmonious, healthier and stronger body (for health is *one* form of beauty!)[27]

The monistic aestheticians did not limit themselves to this evolutionary explanation of the preference for certain facial and body forms. Bölsche published, over the years 1898 to 1901, his three-volume work *Das Liebesleben in der Natur. Eine Entwicklunggeschichte der Liebe* (*Love-life in Nature: An Evolutionary History of Love*) in which he presented a reformulation of evolutionary theory based completely on the principle of love. In it he describes the double aesthetic dimension of his work. Firstly, Bölsche went to great pains to give a stylistically attractive presentation of his view of evolution. The work is based on scientific research, he says in the introduction to the revised edition, but is not intended as a simple popularization of its results. The world-view that he has constructed with the help of the results of biological research has to be understood as a 'personal, subjective work'. From the beginning he had no doubts as to the external form his work was to take, he continues: 'It would have to be essentially an aesthetic one. I am of the opinion that art provides the bridge from the strict scientific discipline – where certain facts that are partially or completely true have been collected – to the controlling world of thought, which is in search of the whole.'[28] One could describe Bölsche's project as the attempt to aestheticize evolutionary theory.

Secondly, Bölsche universalizes Darwin's principle of sexual selection by turning it into a universal metaphysical law controlling all of Nature. His dedicating the whole of the seventh book of his *magnum opus* to sexual selection is not, he says, out of interest in its zoological significance but rather in its 'so-called "world-logical" aspect'.[29] His claim is no less than that love is a powerful motive force of evolution not only in the animal kingdom but also in all of organic and inorganic matter. Love is inherent in the cosmos as a whole, finding expression as the tendency to an increase in harmony and beauty. Man, in forming beauty in his aesthetic creations, is only following this inherent tendency of Nature and bringing it to completion. Even the most sophisticated works of art are only the expression of the principle equating love with evolution, which rules all of Nature. Here Darwin's theory of sexual selection becomes the foundation of a metaphysics of love that issues from Bölsche's wish to oppose a 'warm', emotional, optimistic, friendly image of Nature to the 'cold' one of rationalistic science. He insists that, in defining Nature, one has to take the concept of 'whole' seriously:

Nature is not simply force and matter, but also human spirit. It is not only the planetary system, but also Kepler who calculates the laws of planetary motion. It is Nature, in fact, that wrote Goethe's 'Faust' and created Beethoven's symphonies, that formed the Venus of Milo and painted the Sistine Madonna and the Last Judgment . . .[30]

The re-enchantment of the world

Bölsche, who had begun as a proponent of literary realism and ideas of social reform,[31] took leave of social reality with this philosophy of love. In three voluminous books he develops his myth of love in Nature, which one might say embodied negatively the reality of Imperial Germany: the beauties of organic nature contrasted with the uncontrolled growth of industrial centres and slums, the universal love contrasted with an undemocratic state based on class, and the evolutionary tendency towards an increase in harmony contrasted with the creation of a navy and colonial policy. In the same manner, the *Jugendstil* in art tried to remove itself from the social realities of its time and to present, in its floral ornamentalism, a natural organic world in opposition to the industrial reality at the turn of the century.[32] This flight from society into Nature is characteristically expressed in the sigh of relief of the hero in Wille's *Offenbarungen des Wacholderbaums*, when he returns to his rural idyll from a visit to the city:

I'm a man of the open air, have my roots in Nature, a brother of the plants. I'm distracted and disturbed by the confusing crowds – it's only alone that I find harmony and communion with myself, and feel in good spirits . . . Oh, the dirt! Every night it's swept up by an army of street-cleaners, but it's always there once again, filling all of life. If one sits down to breakfast feeling revived in the morning one finds the newspaper. And what is it filled with? With everything that panders to a crude interest – the greedy squabbling of the politicians, war, the exploitation of the colonies, trials, accidents, suicides, robberies, crimes of passion and murders. Everything is described in the minutest detail and with great clarity, to satisfy the crudest taste. There are no refined sentiments, no cultivated feeling for beauty, no contemplative appreciation.[33]

But it is not only in the tendency to flight from social reality that the philosophical and the artistic *Jugendstil* resemble each other. Monistic pantheism offers a world-image that exactly suits the aesthetic vogue of the day, with its description of Nature as an all-encompassing organism that is animated throughout, and flooded with, spirit, which is in essence productive, continually creating new forms and progressing to ever more perfect harmonies. Just as the philosophy of monism wanted to go beyond the dead 'matter' the Universe was said to consist of, in quest of the 'life' and 'spirit' they believed to be pulsing in it, the purpose of the ornamentalism of the *Jugendstil* was not simply to reproduce the forms of Nature but to make visible the 'spirit' behind the forms. It is here that the special character of this ornamentalism can be found, which distinguishes it from all earlier ornamental art forms. Even the most abstract patterns 'corresponded to or embodied certain feelings or "experiences" according to the theory of the *Jugendstil*'.[34] It is not by accident, then, that Haeckel's *Kunstformen der Natur* was made use of by the artists of his day. His monistic pantheism can be taken as a 'philosophical *Jugendstil*' above all because it expresses conceptually the artistic practice of the *Jugendstil*. Both envisage a Nature that is healthy and beautiful, creative and harmonious, rhythmically progressive and self-perfecting in contrast to the soulless Nature of science, technology and industry. If one considers that Haeckel's conception of beauty had already been formed – before his acquaintance with Darwin's theory – in the classically influenced spiritual climate of the 1850s, and that his pantheistic philosophy had already emerged, under the influence of Goethe, before his conversion to evolutionism, it becomes clear that his philosophical programme was intended to reawaken a pre-modern conception of Nature. In 1879 he still felt committed to the ideals of the *true*, the *good* and the *beautiful*, which he wanted to 'lend the character of noble goddesses'[35] – just as the classical poetry of ancient Greece had embodied their moral ideals in the forms of gods.

One doesn't need much fantasy to imagine how Nietzsche would have reacted to this monistic attempt to re-enchant the world. Nietzsche would have made the same criticism of Haeckel, Bölsche and Wille that he had of Strauss: that they were dishonest and cowardly in fleeing before the irritating and frightening consequences of science in general – and of evolutionary theory in particular – by trying to immunize the old ideals against the subversive force of science. It was not Darwinism that Nietzsche criticized in *Unzeitgemässe Betrachtungen* (*Untimely Meditations*), but its inconsequential and conciliatory reception by Strauss. If one invoked the revolutionary success of evolutionary theory, then one also had to follow its consequences to the bitter end. One couldn't simply ignore the consequences for the foundations of Western culture and its sacred traditional values and ideals – moral as well as aesthetic. But Bölsche and Haeckel refused to consider a revaluation of all values and a radical anti-moralism such as Nietzsche was calling for, as they identified closely with traditional aesthetic and moral values. None the less, it is possible to see in their aesthetic philosophy a certain fulfilment of the hope that Nietzsche – even in 1872 – projected into the ancient world: 'society and the state, indeed all the divisions between men, yield to an overwhelming feeling of unity that returns us to the heart of Nature'.[36]

THE LEGACY

Nietzsche's philosophy and Haeckel's monism represent two influential positions in the broad spectrum of biologistic thought at the turn of the century.[37] The theory of evolution had become an intellectual fad at that time – everything was interpreted in evolutionary terms. It would have been surprising if it had not also been applied to art. One can then see 'evolutionary aesthetics' as part of a broad movement beginning in the second half of the nineteenth century, and continuing on into our own time, the goal of which is to be found in scientific theory of art. Although such attempts have been criticized from the outset,[38] this opposition has had little effect on the attractiveness of the Darwinistic paradigm in aesthetics. Aesthetic evolutionism – as well as the epistemological, social and ethical Darwinism of the nineteenth century – has its contemporary supporters and proponents.[39]

It is not, however, the application of biological theory to art that makes the 'evolutionary aesthetics' of the *fin de siècle* a potential legacy for the present. It should be clear that neither the ideas of the monists nor the philosophy of Nietzsche can be limited to such a transfer of concepts and explanatory models. Essential, in both instances, is the metaphysical disillusionment resulting from the growth of the empirical sciences. This is obvious with Nietzsche, as he makes this experience a central question of his philosophy, accepting the challenge it presents. The destruction of teleology and of anthropomorphism are indisputable facts for him, which he greets as a liberation from traditional illusions. Only at first does it seem that this claim is not applicable to Haeckel. But if one looks a bit closer one finds, beneath the superficial scientism of his philosophy, a sense of the dangers inherent in science. His proclamation of a 'monistic religion'[40] is the strained attempt to manoeuvre about the realization that positive science can destroy (old) values, but hardly create (new) ones. His conjuring up of the three classical rational ideals of truth, beauty and goodness cannot conceal the implicit insight that the unity of the three had been long lost.

Both philosophies are a legacy for the present more because the problem they went to great lengths to solve has found no resolution up to the present day. It is not necessary to call to mind all those lesser Nietzsches of recent times who have proclaimed the end of Enlightenment and rationality, as well as the decline of science and modernity, to be aware of the fact that science has remained a problem. It is therefore hardly surprising that – *mutatis mutandis* – the fronts haven't changed since those days. On the one hand we have the Existentialists – more or less heroic – who remind us 'that the problem of meaning is the one to which no scientific answer ever could be provided', and that science casts us into an absolute isolation:

The scientific approach reveals to Man that he is an accident, almost a stranger in the Universe, and reduces the 'old alliance' between him and the rest of creation to a tenuous and fragile thread. None of the gracious or frightening myths that he had dreamed, none of the hopes he had tenaciously entertained, none of the certainties that had formed the structure of his moral and social life for thousands of years, can stand anymore.[41]

On the other hand, just as at the end of the last century, there is protest against such a severe philosophy. Theoreticians and prophets have emerged who attack the fatal dualism of matter and spirit, of subject and object, wanting to replace it by a new unity of man and Nature. The Haeckels and Bölsches of our day tell us the same tale as did the philosophical *Jugendstil* of the nineteenth century did in the language of Darwinism: they propound the evolution of the Universe 'as a whole', but in terms of autopoesis and autocatalysis, of dissipative structures and non-linear processes, of fluctuations, hypercycles and ecological systems. They tell us the story of a Self-Organizing Universe that man, with all his creations, including art – 'the creative process appears as an aspect of evolutionary self-organization' – is an integral part of. And, just as a hundred years ago, evolutionary self-organization provides us with meaning without charge, since God, of course, is also an integral part of this process: 'He is evolution.'[42] The closer we get to the *fin de siècle* of the twentieth century, the more euphoric become the prophecies of the 'New Age' we are moving irresistibly towards by the agent of self-organization: it would seem that turns of the century bear an inherent tendency to harmony and reconciliation.

NOTES

1 E. Haeckel, *The Riddle of the Universe. At the Close of the Nineteenth Century*, trans. Joseph McCabe (London, 1900), p. 349.
2 Cf. C. Kockerbeck, *Ernst Haeckels 'Kunstformen der Natur' und ihr Einfluss auf*

die deutsche bildende Kunst der Jahrhundertwende (Frankfurt-on-Main, Bern and New York, 1986).

3 E. Haeckel, *Die Natur als Künstlerin* (Berlin, 1924), p. 15.

4 E. Freiherr von Bodenhausen, 'Entwicklungslehre und Aesthetik', *Pan*, 4 (1899), 236. Konrad Lange developed a detailed theory of art based on evolutionary concepts in his book: *Das Wesen der Kunst* (Berlin, 1901).

5 H. Berg, *Die Lust an der Musik* (Berlin, 1879). E. Kulke, *Über die Umbildung der Melodie. Ein Beitrag zur Entwicklungslehre* (Prague, 1884); R. Wallaschek, *Anfänge der Tonkunst* (Leipzig, 1903); O. Koller, 'Die Musik im Lichte der Darwinschen Theorie', *Jahrbuch der Musikbibliothek Peters*, 7 (1900), 37–50.

6 E. Haeckel, *Natürliche Schöpfungsgeschichte. Gemeinverständliche wissenschaftliche Vorträge über die Entwicklungslehre*, 9th revised and expanded edition (2 vols., Berlin, 1898), vol. I, p. 17.

7 F. A. Lange, *Die Arbeiterfrage. Ihre Bedeutung für Gegenwart und Zukunft*, 6th edn (Winterthur, 1909), p. 1.

8 F. A. Lange, *Geschichte des Materialismus und Kritik seiner Bedeutung in der Gegenwart*, reprt. (2 vols., Frankfurt-on-Main, 1974), pp. 685–727.

9 Nietzsche became familiar not only with Darwin's theory of evolution over Lange's *Geschichte des Materialismus*, but also with numerous other scientific concepts and concepts of natural philosophy.

10 F. Nietzsche, *Nachgelassene Fragmente, Sämtliche Werke: Kritische Studienausgabe*, vol. VIII, ed. G. Colli and M. Montinari (Munich and New York, 1980), p. 259.

11 Around 1882 Nietzsche, referring to the astrophysical ideas of his day, wrote: 'We have to beware of thinking that the Universe is a machine; it has certainly not been constructed with any goal in mind and we do it too great an honour to use the word "machine" in reference to it. We must beware of assuming that something so structured as the cyclic movements of our neighbouring stars can be found everywhere – simple observation of the Milky Way alone makes it conceivable that there are much cruder and more contradictory motions – stars, for example, that move eternally in straight lines, or whatever. The astral order we live in is an exception; this order, and the long period of time resulting from it, has made possible the exception within the exception – the emergence of organic life. But viewed as a whole the Universe is in eternal chaos, not in the sense of its not being controlled by necessity, but that it lacks order, articulation, form, beauty, wisdom and all the other aesthetic qualities one might think of.' F. Nietzsche, *Die fröhliche Wissenschaft, Sämtliche Werke*, vol. III, pp. 467ff.

12 F. Nietzsche, *Unzeitgemässe Betrachtungen, Sämtliche Werke*, vol. I, pp. 194 and 199. It is in *Die fröhliche Wissenschaft* (*The Gay Science*) that Nietzsche calls every attempt to establish a harmonious image of Nature naïve or self-deceptive. He speaks of the nausea that overcomes him facing the attempt 'to refashion the incredibly derivative, late-appearing, rare and coincidental phenomena we find on the surface of the Earth into something essential, generally valid and eternal, such as can be found in all those that call the Universe an organism'. Nietzsche, *Die fröhliche Wissenschaft*, p. 467.

13 F. Nietzsche, *Die Geburt der Tragödie, Sämtliche Werke*, vol. I, pp. 35 and 56ff.

14 F. Nietzsche, *Die Geburt der Tragödie. Versuch einer Selbstkritik, Sämtliche Werke*, vol. I, pp. 13 and 17.

15 F. Nietzsche, *Die Geburt der Tragödie*, pp. 56, 30 and 48.

16 Herbert Schnädelbach gives a short, informative explanation of the specific meaning of this concept in the German 'Lebensphilosophie' of the nineteenth and twentieth centuries in chapter 5 of his book: *German Philosophy, 1831–1933* (Cambridge, 1983).

17 F. Nietzsche, *Nachgelassene Fragmente, Sämtliche Werke*, vol. XII, p. 554.

18 F. Nietzsche, *Nachgelassene Fragmente, Sämtliche Werke*, vol. XIII, p. 521.

19 *Ibid.*, p. 500. Just before this Nietzsche says: 'The truth is odious: *it is art* that keeps us from being destroyed by truth.'

20 E. Haeckel, *Biographie in Briefen*, ed. G. Uschmann (Leipzig, Jena and Berlin, 1983), p. 21.

21 E. Haeckel, 'Zellseelen und Seelenzellen', in *Gemeinverständliche Werke*, vol. V (Leipzig and Berlin, 1924), pp. 194ff.

22 Haeckel, *The Riddle of the Universe*, p. 350.

23 W. Bölsche, *Die naturwissenschaftlichen Grundlagen der Poesie. Prolegomena einer realistischen Ästhetik*, repr. (Munich and Tübingen, 1976), p. 49. On Bölsche cf. A. Kelly, *The Descent of Darwin. The Popularization of Darwinism in Germany, 1860–1914* (Chapel Hill, N.C., 1981), ch. 3.

24 B. Wille, *Offenbarungen des Wacholderbaums*, new edn (Pfullingen, n.d.), vol. I, p. 135. Wille refers here explicitly to Nietzsche, criticizing his pessimistic metaphysics.

25 C. Darwin, *On the Origin of Species*, facsimile of the 1st edition (Cambridge, Mass. and London, 1964), p. 89.

26 W. Bölsche, *Das Liebesleben in der Natur. Eine Entwicklungsgeschichte der Liebe*, vol. II/1, expanded and revised edition (Jena, 1917), p. 349.

27 *Ibid.*, p. 350. Four pages later one of the darker aspects of Bölsche's aesthetic evolutionism appears: 'There is a movement in all races towards noble types thanks to the slow workings of selection due to love; and among these noble types there is a tendency leading up to the European who, however one might be opposed to the idea, represents, in the harmoniousness of his bodily forms, the highest and purest noble type of mankind' (p. 344).

28 *Ibid.*, vol. I, pp. viii ff.

29 *Ibid.*, p. 351.

30 *Ibid.*, vol. II/2, p. 727.

31 Cf. Kelly, *The Descent of Darwin*, p. 131. Bölsche was a long-time supporter of the German Social Democrats, differing in this regard from Haeckel, who was strictly anti-socialist, Cf. K. Bayertz, 'Darwinism and scientific freedom. Political aspects of the reception of Darwinism in Germany, 1863–1878', *Scientia*, 188 (1983), 297–307.

32 D. Sternberger, 'Jugendstil. Begriff und Physiognomik', in *Jugendstil*, ed. J. Hermand (Darmstadt, 1971), p. 33.

33 Wille, *Offenbarungen des Wacholderbaums*, vol. II, pp. 60ff.

34 Sternberger, 'Jugendstil', p. 32.

35 Haeckel, *The Riddle of the Universe*, p. 344.

36 Nietzsche, *Die Geburt der Tragödie*, p. 56.

37 Martin Heidegger, in a lecture in 1936–7, denied that this is true of Nietzsche's aesthetics: 'However often Nietzsche might have fallen into a fateful physiological-naturalistic language with regard to art -- in his writings and even in his own thoughts – one misunderstands him fundamentally when one takes these physiological ideas out of context and presents them as a "biologistic" aesthetics.' M. Heidegger, *Nietzsche*, vol. I (Pfullingen, 1961), p. 149. Heidegger, however, does not adduce any evidence in support of his claim, as Walter Schulz points out: 'Nietzsche begins with a *scientific-biological* anthropology – to deny or qualify this point, as some important commentators, above all M. Heidegger, have done, is simply wrong.' W. Schulz, 'Funktion und Ort der Kunst in Nietzsches Philosophie', *Nietzsche-Studien*, 12 (Berlin and New York, 1983), p. 6. Cf. also H. Pfotenhauer, *Die Kunst als Physiologie. Nietzsches ästhetische Theorie und literarische Produktion* (Stuttgart, 1985), pp. 20ff.

38 Cf. J. Volkelt, 'Die entwicklungsgeschichtliche Betrachtungsweise in der Ästhetik', *Zeitschrift für Psychologie und Physiologie der Sinnesorgane*, 29 (1902), pp. 1–21.

39 Cf. D. Morris, *The Biology of Art* (New York, 1962); E. O. Wilson, *Sociobiology. The New Synthesis* (Cambridge, Mass., 1975), p. 564; B. Rensch, *Psychologische Grundlagen der Wertung bildender Kunst* (Essen, 1984).

40 Haeckel, *The Riddle of the Universe*, pp. 339–54.

41 J. Monod, 'On values in the age of science', in *The Place of Values in a World of Facts*, ed. A. Tiselius (Stockholm, 1970), pp. 20 and 24. It is hardly by coincidence that Monod refers explicitly to Nietzsche: 'We must start from an absolute *Tabula rasa*; we must go further and deeper than Nietzsche's prophetic "Gott ist tot", for, not only is God dead, but also his various romantic, historicist and progressist substitutes' (p. 25).

42 E. Jantsch, *The Self-Organizing Universe. Scientific and Human Implications of the Emerging Paradigm of Evolution* (Oxford, 1980), pp. 286, 308.

☙

FIFTEEN

THE UNMASTERED PAST OF HUMAN
GENETICS

MIKULÁŠ TEICH

> For the past few years I have looked back into the history of my field, genetics,
> and I have published my findings.[1] If I had to summarize them in one sentence I
> would write: 'The rise of genetics is characterized by a gigantic process of
> repression of its history.' Benno Müller-Hill, 'Genetics after Auschwitz',
> *Holocaust and Genocide Studies*, 2 (1987), 3–20 (p. 3)

This harsh judgement of the internationally respected member of the Genetics
Institute of the Cologne University (FRG) rests, among others, on his
examination of documentary material in the Federal Archives (*Bundesarchiv*)
at Koblenz. There Benno Müller-Hill apparently was the first person since the
war (in 1981) to study archival items which, together with other primary and
secondary sources, disclosed to him 'that so many German professors of
psychiatry, anthropology or human genetics used their knowledge to have
their patients or clients mutilated or killed by others in the name of science'.[2]

An integral feature of how this came about were the methodological
elements within human genetics that grew out of the amalgam of Weismannian and Mendelian approaches to heredity since the turn of the century. A
major effect of this development was the assumption regarding the intrinsic
role of the hereditary endowment in determining social, national and racial
differences between people. Related, and no less significant, was the contemporary concern with the danger of losing one's 'superior' genetic heritage
through interbreeding with persons considered genetically 'inferior'. Ideas
about genetic degeneration became fused with the *fin-de-siècle* alarm at the
dismantling of the seemingly solid foundations of the nineteenth-century
world, beset by social, economic, imperial and racial issues.

What interests us about this socio-genetic interplay is that it set a course,
well into the twentieth century, that was to push geneticists into embracing
the position that the control of human heredity in desired directions (racial,
physical, mental) was on hand. What follows is an attempt to explore its

conceptual and methodological underpinnings – a skirted issue in the history of human genetics.

GENES, GENOCIDE AND GOD: OTMAR VON VERSCHUER

Müller-Hill lists several names, including Professor Otmar von Verschuer, whose investigations into the hereditary disposition to diseases, particularly tuberculosis, in identical twins had gained him international reputation between the two world wars.[3] Heredity in man could not be studied by the same experimental methods employed for plants and animals. This is where the collection and analysis of data on identical (but also non-identical) twins came in because it was taken for granted that they would reveal the effect of nature (heredity) as opposed to nurture (environment).

In a lecture delivered before the Royal Society of London (8 June 1939) Verschuer – since 1935 full professor and head of the newly founded Institute for Hereditary Biology and Racial Hygiene at Frankfurt-on-Main – made it clear that in his view nature takes precedence over nurture.[4] He found evidence for this not only in his own studies regarding susceptibility to tuberculosis in twins but also in investigations by others into the mental traits of children in 'twins camps'. These were two camps where twins from Berlin and other towns were brought to spend a six-week holiday under observation. The case material resulted from registering the children's behaviour from the time they got up in the morning until they went to bed in the evening. In addition, the children were subjected to 'unobtrusive' experimental psychological tests.

Verschuer found this procedure (due to K. Gottschaldt who was in charge of the Department for Hereditary Psychology at the Kaiser Wilhelm Institute for Anthropology, Human Heredity and Eugenics in Berlin-Dahlem) highly appealing. It was a way, he believed, towards securing a satisfactory set of data on twins which was hard to come by. Verschuer returned to this theme somewhat later in the year during the Seventh International Genetical Congress in Edinburgh (23–30 August 1939) in a contribution concerned with gene analysis in human beings. In the version published in the *Proceedings* of the Congress he stressed that here the progress depended on large-scale studies of twins the value of which in Germany was fully appreciated. While keeping clear of racialism, Verschuer went out of his way to bring home to Congress participants the vital support given by the German health service to systematic twin and family studies and hereditary surveys, carried out in several research institutes.[5]

Within a few years, Nazi state-supported twin studies came into being in another camp. True, it was not a holiday camp but the concentration camp at Auschwitz where the camp doctor, Joseph Mengele, applied the twin method on Jews and gypsies by infecting them with typhoid. It was part of a large-scale research project concerned with racially conditioned susceptibility (resistance) to various infectious diseases. In it Verschuer, who by 1942 became the Director of the Kaiser Wilhelm Institute for Anthropology, Human Heredity and Eugenics in Berlin-Dahlem, was in various ways directly involved.[6] Not surprisingly, since a year before in the first edition of his *Leitfaden der Rassenhygiene* (Manual of Racial Hygiene) Verschuer demanded 'a new total solution of the Jewish problem.[7] As to gypsies in Germany, Verschuer expected a speedy legal provision for dealing with them since he regarded them to be overwhelmingly (90 per cent) hybrid people, composed largely of asocial and inferior individuals.[8] That Verschuer had an overtly racist perspective on genetics is shown by the following quotation taken from the closing paragraph of the book's introduction:[9]

The first pioneering works and discoveries regarding race, selection and heredity were published in the second half of the previous century. It took a generation to build the edifice of a science, which could assume responsibility for handing over its tools into the hands of the statesman. Decisive for the history of a people is what the political leader recognizes as essential in the results of science and puts into effect. The history of our science is most closely connected with German history of the most recent past. The Führer of the German *Reich* is the first statesman who has made knowledge of biological inheritance and racial hygiene a leading principle of government policy.

After the Nazi era Verschuer's scientific standing in (West) Germany remained undamaged. In 1951 he was appointed Director of the newly founded Institute of Human Genetics at Münster University. In 1952 he became Chairman of the German Society for Anthropology. In 1954 he rose to the position of Dean of the Medical Faculty at Münster. In 1956, when he was sixty, Verschuer was explicitly described as the 'leading German human geneticist'. In keeping with this assessment, he was nominated Chairman of the German Committee entrusted with preparations for the First International Congress of Human Genetics held in Copenhagen in 1956.[10]

   This brings us to the question of the impact of changed post-war political and ideological climate on Verschuer's genetical thinking. This may be gleaned from his lecture on 'The application of knowledge of general genetics to man and its limitations', given before the Academy of Sciences and Literature in Mainz on 18 November 1949.[11] In it Verschuer again stressed that human genetics depended methodologically on twin studies. But Verschuer avoided any mention of the way such studies had degenerated in Auschwitz, including his own part in it. He turned instead to a discussion of human inheritance at an 'elevated' level, as it were. It amounted to this: How to reconcile genic determinism with free will. For Verschuer God was the solution which he summed up as follows:[12]

Our conviction that man is free is not affected by knowledge that a hereditary constraint [*erbliche Gebundenheit*] exists. But it is my opinion that recent scientific knowledge has sharpened our vision and removed a few obstacles so that the way is free to a new turning to God – above all in scientific circles [*gerade im Kreise der Wissenschaft*].

THE BEST WORK ON HUMAN HEREDITY – ACCORDING TO H. J. MULLER (1933).

The career of Verschuer is of interest in more than one respect. After Germany's defeat in 1918 the *Oberleutnant* and regimental adjutant Verschuer, descending as he did from a military family, was greatly disappointed with having to leave the army. He then enrolled as student of medicine at Marburg University where he soon had the opportunity to exercise his military skills. As First Adjutant in the Marburg Student Voluntary Corps (*Freikorps*), he took a prominent part in putting down Communists in Thuringia in 1920.

There was nothing exceptional about the German officer *manqué* Verschuer embracing the views of the political right in the 1920s. What is material, in the context of this essay, is that he came to combine them with interpretations of the principles of human genetics along eugenic-racialist lines. Of the writings in this area, the most influential was the two-volume treatise by E. Baur, E. Fischer and F. Lenz, the first edition of which appeared in 1921.[13] In 1941 Verschuer, by his own account, traced the beginnings of his interest in human inheritance, racial science and racial hygiene to this text:[14]

To the work of E. Baur, E. Fischer and F. Lenz whose first edition appeared twenty years ago goes the main credit for the inner framework of our science. I regard it as a particular favour of fate that already as student and *Assistent* I was allowed to establish personal contact with these pioneers of racial hygiene to whom I owe most valuable impulses and encouragement for my scientific development.

In 1931 the English version of volume I (third edition) appeared under the title *Human Heredity*. Two years later the book was reviewed by H. J. Muller[15] who pronounced it 'the best work on the subject of human heredity which has yet appeared'. Such praise from one of the leaders in the field[16] is notable, but before discussing the review let us briefly examine the contents of the book. Divided into five sections, the first, written by Erwin Baur, provided an outline of the principles of genetics. The second, by Eugen Fischer, concentrated on racial biology. The third, fourth and fifth sections were by Fritz Lenz. In these Lenz dealt with pathological hereditary trends, methods of study of human inheritance and the heredity of mental gifts.

In his review of the book Muller described Erwin Baur as 'the leading geneticist of Europe engaged in active work at the present time'. It is not surprising, therefore, that he commended the first section 'of the book highly, along with everything else that has issued from Baur's pen'. None the less, Muller provided two instances in which he disagreed with Baur. He took exception to Baur's suggestion that human heredity might not be exclusively Mendelian.[17] Moreover, he objected to Baur raising the possibility that mutations might be produced by alcohol, inbreeding and crossbreeding.

Muller's review also included critical observations bearing on the doctrine of relative, congenital, racial superiority of Nordics over Jews and Negroes. There can be no doubt that all three authors – not just Fischer and Lenz, whom Muller took to task for this – subscribed to the view that there were innate qualitative disparities between races and that race crossing was detrimental.

HISTORY OF HUMAN GENETICS: ERNST MAYR AND ALFRED BARTHELMESS

There is an animated reappraisal taking place of the long-held view that Hugo de Vries, Carl Correns and Erich von Tschermak-Seysenegg rediscovered Mendel's work in 1900.[18] Whether or not one regards the papers published by the three botanists in that year as rediscovery or 'rediscovery' papers, they mark the take-off of the 'edifice of science' invoked by Verschuer. From then on within the space of four decades, the science – soon to be called genetics – came uncommonly rapidly into its own.[19]

Although genetics has a relatively short past, it is not an altogether neglected area of history. Even seventeen years ago, Ernst Mayr in a major historiographical overview of works on the development of genetics could write:[20]

Except for the study of Darwin, there is perhaps no other area in biology the history of which has been dealt with as frequently and with as much competence as the history of genetics . . . what is perhaps most interesting is the fact that with a few exceptions, all these books and articles were written by members of the genetics establishment. And, since some of these geneticists belong to different schools within the field, they sometimes provide slightly different views or at least emphases concerning the same developments.

Extensive and insightful as Mayr's piece is, it contains nothing on the history of human genetics. Perhaps the author, an eminent evolutionary biologist and explorer in biological thought, had deliberately chosen not to pursue this area of genetics in the first place. Be that as it may, Mayr lists a number of books 'on the history of classical genetics (or certain aspects of it)' which might be expected to pay attention to human genetics. Let us examine, then, what these works have to offer on this aspect of the science.

Among them the first publication which falls into this category is by the German geneticist Barthelmess whose observation concerning the rapid development of the science of heredity has already been noted. Actually, it was precisely this that prompted Barthelmess to produce a kind of source book in genetics by using material from original scientific writings as part of the running text. The intention behind his enterprise was to motivate the geneticists to pause, to look back, to take stock of their discipline. To do it adequately, Barthelmess was well aware, demanded the inclusion of the issues arising out of the application of genetics to human beings. This encompassed, as he wrote, 'above all eugenics, the class issue, free will, heredity of the mental make-up and such like matters'. But these topics were kept out of the book for the following reason. To do them justice, Barthelmess argued, required addition of more material and this would have greatly exceeded his allocated publication space.[21]

Mayr's booklist includes two standard histories of genetics, both of which might be presumed to take account of human genetics. Written by two distinguished American geneticists, A. H. Sturtevant and L. C. Dunn, both books were published in the centenary year (1965) of Mendel's report on his hybridization of varieties of the edible pea.[22]

HISTORY OF HUMAN GENETICS: A. H. STURTEVANT

In his work, Sturtevant addressed the topic of human genetics separately in the book's penultimate chapter, entitled 'The Genetics of Man'.[23] Sturtevant began by stating that man is in many ways a very unsuitable object for the study of genetics. He explained his reservation as follows: 'Families are too small for dependable determination of ratios, desired test matings cannot be made, and study of more than a very few generations for any particular purpose is not often possible.'

Despite Sturtevant's initial unfavourable assessment of man as an object of genetic study, he none the less stated that because 'the social implications of human genetics are so great . . . the subject *must*[24] be investigated'. Moreover, Sturtevant pointed out that due to advances in a wide range of branches of science (from anatomy to population genetics) there was more comprehensive information available on man than on any other organism.

This is certainly true of the human blood which, because of its accessibility as well as cardinal physiological importance, is historically one of the most investigated living tissues. It is, therefore, no accident that there has long been a continual interaction between the study of the properties of blood (blood groups, haemoglobin types) and the growth of genetics. The scientific and practical extension of these developments, as noted by Sturtevant, have been prominent in the fields of medicine, immunology and physical anthropology.

But what emerges from Sturtevant's account, in the first place, is that to substantiate Mendelian inheritance in man, encompassing both physical and mental traits, is by no means an easy task:

There is an unfortunate tendency, however, to accept cases as established when the evidence is so weak that it would not be considered conclusive for any organism other than man . . . The more obvious and familiar human differences, such as stature, hairform and color, eye color, skin color, right- vs. left-handedness, or fingerprint patterns, although obviously inherited, are difficult to analyze . . . Even more difficult to analyze are mental properties and, obviously, these are the human characteristics that are of the greatest interest and importance to society . . .

Having thus underlined the uncertainties when it comes to pinning down the genetic basis of physical and mental differences between human beings, Sturtevant turned his attention to the problem of racism. For our purposes the manner by which the *geneticist* Sturtevant disposed of racism is of manifest interest.

At first Sturtevant seems to claim that geneticists, in general, cannot be blamed for giving scientific credibility to the view which differentiates between 'superior' and 'inferior' races in terms of innate mental traits. This, he argued, was essentially a postulate elaborated by non-scientists:

The difficulties of objective study of mental differences reached their maximum in the case of racial differences. If it be admitted that there are inherited individual differences, then on general grounds one must conclude that there are statistical differences between races. If one is inclined to look upon individual mental differences as largely genetic in origin, he then is likely to consider the observed (or imagined) cultural differences between races as being genetically determined and to conclude that some races (inevitably including the one to which he belongs) are inherently superior. The extreme examples of this attitude have not usually been scientifically trained . . .

After writing these words, Sturtevant appears to have recognized that they conveyed a too simple (if not distorted) picture of what happened in the history of human genetics between 1900 and 1940. In any event, he then added the following qualifying remark:

There have, however, been biologists with some background in genetics who have leaned in this direction. Since *racism*[25] is a dirty word it is perhaps kinder (and certainly more agreeable to the writer) not to name them.

By avoiding addressing the issue directly, Sturtevant actually was posing a further question. Why should he, in 1965, an eminent geneticist deeply interested in the history of his discipline, be at a loss to look below the surface and examine the relationship between genetics and racism in the context of scientific history? Particularly so, since he ended the chapter by discussing eugenics as part of the history of genetics and quite properly, too. One motive in doing so may have been his doubts about the claim that race crossing is harmless.[26]

The fear of racial degeneracy arising out of race crossing – we are looking at the United States, Great Britain and Germany – was by no means a negligible factor in the eugenics–genetics liaison during about 1900–50.[27] The belief in the possibility of improving the genetic constitution of mankind was, in general, another factor. It found expression in the renowned 'Geneticists' Manifesto' (about which more is to come) at the Seventh International Congress of Genetics in Edinburgh in 1939.

To return to Sturtevant, it is worth while to note his observation that about 4 per cent of human infants have been born with one or other physical or mental deficiency. About half of these congenital disabilities have been considered to be of genetic origin. This leads him to state: 'If it were possible to eliminate these by preventing their birth, this would obviously be a great advantage to society, in economic and, especially, in humanitarian terms.'

But after voicing this conditional support for eugenics, Sturtevant cautions against the optimism that geneticists displayed during the first decades of the twentieth century towards negative eugenics. That is, towards (statutory) moves to reduce if not eliminate hereditary physical and mental defects: 'In the early days of Mendelism, there were many people who felt that this objective could be rather simply achieved, but with increased knowledge this hope has been somewhat dimmed.' The interest of these passages lies in the fact that they reveal Sturtevant's ambivalent attitude towards the eugenic target of improving heredity in man by preventing the propagation of undesirable genetic constitutions.

Sturtevant was no less ambivalent when he assessed 'positive' eugenics, the aim of which has been to bring forth human beings endowed with desirable genetic traits. Sturtevant clearly indicates that the science of genetics has made this a possibility:

It is evident that animal breeders have, by selection from mixed populations, produced many reasonably uniform breeds, possessing desired characteristics and including many individuals more extreme in these respects than any found in the original population. There is no reason to doubt that similar results could be obtained with human populations.

For Sturtevant 'positive' eugenics was scientifically feasible but socially and politically an awkward matter, involving a series of difficulties of which the greatest is:

Who sets the goals? Who functions as the animal breeders have, in determining the basis of selection? Obviously no sane person would want a Hitler to have this power and responsibility, and most of us would agree with Bateson in mistrusting even a committee of Shakespeares.

HISTORY OF HUMAN GENETICS: L. C. DUNN

When we turn to the other noted history of genetics, we find that human genetics receives marginal attention. L. C. Dunn's account essentially ends in 1939. He obviously felt – the following statement indicates it – that scientific activity in this area had actually not forged ahead before then, and therefore, there was not much to discuss:[28] 'Human genetics could have got underway in 1902,[29] or certainly following Weinberg's lead in 1908[30] but in fact made little progress until thirty to forty more years had passed.'

Dunn's opinion that human genetics developed slowly during the first four decades of this century is notable, given the rapid growth of genetics as a whole during the same period. The slower progress of this field may have been due to human genetics' failure to make adequate use of the technical and analytical means (for example, cytology) employed so successfully in non-human genetics. Moreover, it must be remembered that the procedure of crossbreeding, in contrast to plant and animal genetics, could not be realized in the framework of human genetics. Yet however much these factors, acknowledged by Dunn, retarded the growth of human genetics during what he called its 'adolescent period', he nevertheless put the bulk of the blame for the lack of progress in this area on the negative influence of eugenics.

This much emerges from Dunn's revealing Presidential Address to the American Society of Human Genetics in 1961.[31] There he set out his general views as follows:

Progress in human genetics seemed to have been impeded less by lack of means than by lack of a clear scientific goal, and this at a time when the major problems of genetics were taking a clear form. The particular nature of the transmission mechanism of heredity had focused attention on the means by which genetic elements reproduce and maintain their continuity with opportunity for change and evolution, and on the means by which genes control metabolism and development. But most observations on human heredity were not oriented in any clear way toward such problems. Matters of greater moment seemed to be the inheritance of 'insanity', of 'feeblemindedness' and other then vaguely defined mental ills, the effects of parental age or alcoholism or social status on the offspring, and similar studies pursued for immediate social ends.

Already this passage throws a good deal of light upon the differences in the approaches of Dunn and Sturtevant to the historical relations of eugenics and genetics. In fact, Dunn's discussion of this subject is superior to that of Sturtevant in at least two respects. First, Dunn brought into the picture a broader, international, perspective by paying attention to developments in Britain, the USA, Germany and the USSR. Second, he subjected the eugenics–genetics interplay to a more concrete critical analysis.

In 1961 it was not a common thing to proclaim that the 'first proponents of eugenics in the U.S.A. . . . were thoroughgoing Mendelians, and eugenists because they were Mendelians'. It was also not in vogue to spell out that 'Verschuer . . . has not to my knowledge publicly altered his position on enforced race hygiene'. Further, he gave a contemporary example of the way internationally reputable human geneticists had been evaluating data and reaching conclusions in racialist terms:

Human genetics has today become a useful contributor to anthropology, mainly through gene frequency studies, and by the application of good objective methods generally untinged by racialism. However, there are still reminders of the uncritical use of what look like genetical methods applied to racial anthropology. What shall one say, for example, when three authors, after anthropometric examination of 44 Italian war orphans of whom the father was unknown but assumed to be 'colored' draw sweeping conclusions concerning heterosis ('established with certainty'), inheritance of erythrocyte diameter ('very convincing') and other statements not supported by evidence. Yet these are statements made in 1960 by Luigi Gedda and his co-workers Serio and Mecuri in their recent book Meticciato di Guerra. R. R. Gates, who writes an introduction in English to this elaborate book refers to it as an important contribution to what he calls 'racial genetics'. Others will have greater difficulty in detecting any contribution to genetics, but may see in it, as I do, a reflection in 1960 of the uncritical naiveté of that early period of human genetics which delayed its progress. And the same year – 1960 – sees also the appearance of a new journal 'Mankind Quarterly' devoted in part to racial anthropology of the above kind (again described as such by one of its editors – R. R. Gates) and embodying racist attitudes of the earlier period. Truly the past is not yet buried, and human genetics, in spite of its recent evidences of new life, is still exposed to old dangers.

Last but not least, it is worth pointing to Dunn's critique of Muller's enduring commitment to eugenic beliefs and programmes. Of the latter, the most notorious was that proposed in Muller's book *Out of the Night: A Biologist's View of the Future* (1935), reiterated in 1959.[32] His idea was to set up a bank for preserving the sperm of selected 'outstanding' donors which, by way of artificial insemination, was to be employed to improve the quality of human stock. This, Dunn felt, he was unable to support:

To me such schemes seem to express the same sort of benevolent utopianism as did some of Galton's proposals of 60 years ago, but now they must be viewed in the light of some actual experience with them. Then as now they were backed by the prestige of men of deserved eminence in science, then of Galton, today of Muller, but this did not save the earlier programmes from grave misuse and ultimate damage to both human society and science. In fact the high scientific standing of their proponents increases the dangers of uncritical acceptance of them as bases for social and political action, with the ever attendant risk of loss of public confidence in genetics as applied to man if or when their unsoundness becomes manifest.

But the reader should not be led to believe that Dunn's negative assessment of Muller's eugenic programme was shared universally by contemporaries. Thus, at the same time, G. Pontecorvo – one of Muller's notable collaborators – sought to defend it as follows:[33] 'His outlook on the prospects of mankind – dismissed as utopian by obscurantists – is the result of a powerful mind combined with kindness and a deep sense of justice.'

THE 'GENETICISTS' MANIFESTO'

At this juncture, it is pertinent to examine the already mentioned 'Geneticists' Manifesto' of 1939. This is the name given to a statement, signed – in the first place – by seven participants in the Seventh International Genetical Congress in Edinburgh in response to the following question: 'How could the world's population improve most effectively genetically?' Exactly to whom it was addressed – by the American scientific journalist Watson Davis – is not clear. According to the 'Reports from the Genetics Congress' in the *Journal of Heredity*, which comprised the text of the 'Manifesto',[34] it 'was prepared *jointly* by a group of those to whom it was addressed . . .'[35] Also the word 'jointly' raises an element of an uncertainty about the extent of H. J. Muller's authorship of the 'Manifesto' to whom it is generally ascribed – it is included in his selected *Studies in Genetics*.[36]

Be that as it may, the 'Manifesto' constitutes a major document reflecting the attitude of humanitarian geneticists at the end of the thirties to the social application of their science. The 'Manifesto' declares that 'the effective genetic improvement of mankind', with which it is concerned, 'is dependent upon major changes in social conditions, and correlative changes in human attitudes'. They are discussed thematically in six propositions.

The first states that the economic and social conditions should be such as 'to provide approximately equal opportunities for members of society instead of stratifying them from birth into classes with widely different privileges'.

The second demands the removal of race prejudices and 'the unscientific doctrine that good or bad genes are the monopoly of particular peoples or of persons with features of a given kind'. To eradicate such opinions, it stressed, necessitates the elimination of political and economic conditions which promote hostilities between different peoples, nations and 'races' [*sic*], leading to war and economic exploitation. And for this to take place, it is suggested, 'some effective sort of federation of the whole world, based on the common interests of all its peoples has to be set up'.

The third proposition focuses on the need for social and material improvements in the situation of women, especially mothers. This, it is argued, involves giving the woman special protection to ensure that 'her reproductive duties do not interfere too greatly with her opportunities to participate in the life and the work of the community at large'.

The fourth represents a plea for a 'rational' approach to procreation. As it touches directly the theme of this essay, it is quoted at length in order fully to bring its argument to the fore:

A fourth prerequisite for effective genetic improvement is the legalization, the universal dissemination and the further development through scientific investigation, of ever more efficacious means of birth control, both negative and positive, that can be put into effect at all stages of the reproductive process – as by voluntary temporary or permanent sterilization, contraception, abortion (as a third line of defense) control of fertility and of the sexual cycle, artificial insemination, etc. Along with all this the development of social consciousness and responsibility in regard to the production of children is required, and this cannot be expected to be operative unless the above mentioned economic and social conditions for its fulfilment are present and unless the superstitious attitude towards sex and reproduction now prevalent has been replaced by a scientific and social attitude. This will result in its being regarded as an honour and a privilege, if not a duty for a mother, married or unmarried, or for a couple, to have the best children possible, both in respect of their upbringing and of their genetic endowment, even where the latter would mean an artificial, though always voluntary control over the processes of parentage.

Such a rational approach to human reproduction, the fifth proposition contends, presupposes the spread of knowledge of biological and genetical principles among ordinary people. While acknowledging the complementary role of heredity and environment, this proposition rejects the view that better environmental conditions improve human heredity. Instead it gives the pride of place to selection:

The intrinsic (genetic) characteristics of any generation can be better than those of the preceding generation only as a result of some kind of *selection*, i.e., by those persons of the preceding generation who had a better genetic equipment having produced more offspring, on the whole, than the rest, either through conscious choice, or as an automatic result of the way in which they lived. Under modern civilized conditions such selection is far less likely to be automatic than under primitive conditions, hence some kind of conscious guidance of selection is called for. To make this possible, however, the population must first appreciate the force of the above principles, and the social value which a wisely guided selection would have.

As for the sixth and final proposition, its theme is the nature of social circumstances in which conscious selection, indeed knowledge of human genetics as a whole, is to be applied in the interest of 'the good of mankind at large'. For this to happen, it claims, society has to be motivated, and this 'in turn implies its socialized organization'. Without elaborating on the manner of its attainment, or indeed even on its form, the 'Manifesto' concludes with the bold proclamation that biological (genetical) knowledge can produce geniuses in a relatively short time:

A more widespread understanding of biological principles will bring with it the realization that much more than the prevention of genetic deterioration is to be sought for and that the raising of the level of the average of the population nearly to that of the highest now existing in isolated individuals, in regard to physical well-being, intelligence and temperamental qualities, is an achievement that would – so far as purely genetic considerations are concerned – be physically possible within a comparatively small number of generations. Thus everyone might look upon 'genius', combined of course with stability as his birthright. And, as the course of evolution shows, this would represent no final stage at all, but only an earnest of still further progress in the future.

HUMAN HYBRIDIZATION IN HISTORY: J. S. HUXLEY

Given the protagonists and the nature of the 'Manifesto', and the occasion and the timing of its proclamation, it is curious that it has aroused little notice from historians of genetics.[37] The 'Manifesto' raises the vexing problem – in the light of history – that its signatories drew on the same principles and methods of genetics as did Fischer, Lenz, Verschuer and others in Nazi Germany, who had promoted and abetted measures for racial improvement.

Take the attitude of British and American geneticists to race mixture. According to Provine, only slowly did they reverse their opinion on this question between 1930 and 1950. That is, from thinking that race crossing was undesirable, they gradually proceeded through agnosticism to accepting that 'wide race crosses were at worst harmless'. Inasmuch as the British and American geneticists shifted their position on miscegenation, Provine observes, they were motivated by humanitarian impulses. They were horrified by the practical outcome of the Nazi racial doctrine. At the same time, Provine makes the crucial point that the transformation in outlook did not come about because of any fundamental change in the basic theory of genetics or through new scientific evidence.[38]

Thus, Sturtevant was not the only prominent member of the Anglo-American genetics community who, by 1950, still entertained doubts regarding the harmlessness of race mixture. In September of that year a meeting was held at Ohio State University in Columbus, to celebrate the fiftieth anniversary of the rediscovery of Mendel's work – the Golden Jubilee of Genetics. Some of the most distinguished contemporary workers in the field were invited to present papers, amongst them the influential Julian S. Huxley, one of the 'Seven' who first signed the 'Manifesto'. In an ambitious attempt to cover the growth of genetics since the rediscovery of Mendel's work, its connection to the study of evolution, and the history and future of man, Huxley touched on the genetic aspects of race mixture and had the following to say:[39]

In man, the probable production of a certain number of 'disharmonic' types through wide crossing will certainly be offset and may well be outweighed by that of valuable new recombinations: but we must not imagine that all the effects of 'racial' crossing in man are necessarily good, and may not include certain undesirable genetic results.

Hence fifteen years after co-authoring a widely acclaimed critique of the Nazi doctrine of 'racial purity',[40] Huxley did not exclude the feasibility, if not truth, of one of its basic tenets: the injurious consequences of race mingling. He now spoke only of 'the errors of racism' and links them to 'the errors of eugenics when treated as a dogma and not as an applied science'. The reaction to these errors Huxley found 'natural' but he feared the consequences of the perception of hereditary differences among human individuals and groups: 'At the moment it is socially and intellectually fashionable to minimize or even to deny such genetic differences.' This approach brought him into an uncomfortable proximity to views adopted by the Nazi geneticists:

It is also true that, in many kinds of human social system, a small minority, if possessed of the right genetic qualities as well as of appropriate traditions and of social or political power, can effectively dominate a much larger group. It seems fairly clear that many conquering minorities, like the Moguls, or the Normans, or the Watusi, were selected for genetic qualities conducive to what is broadly called leadership before conquering the people over whom they later ruled – who in their turn may often have been pre-selected for patience or docility. When the dominance of a minority has continued for long periods, it will generally be found that either inbreeding or some form of mate selection has been at work to perpetuate the genetic differences between dominant and subordinate groups. But when there has been random outcrossing, and still more when, as after the early conquests of Islam, there has been polygyny together with mate selection that has not been concerned with qualities making for leadership the genetic differential can be, and has been, rapidly dissipated.

So much for an elitist reading of history – by the middle of the twentieth century – by a leading British biologist, renowned for his liberalism and humanitarianism, in the name of genetics, 'the most rigorous of all biological disciplines, and of the utmost importance for the understanding of social affairs'.

CERTAINTIES AND FALLACIES

Julian Huxley belongs to a long line of scientists, since human genetics took off early this century, claiming an unwarranted scientific insight into human heredity, including its control. This brought into existence the benevolent 'Geneticists' Manifesto', but also the murderous applications of genetics in Nazi Germany.

After the Second World War, the Eighth International Congress of Genetics (which met in Stockholm in July 1948) offered the first big and appropriate opportunity for geneticists to examine critically these events in some depth. But, apparently, there was no urge to do so judging by the manner Muller, in his Presidential Address, dealt with them.[41] Regarding the 'Geneticists' Manifesto', Muller reaffirmed that he stood by its principles. In addition, giving way to elitism, Muller elaborated that 'sound genetic selection' could be carried out voluntarily and responsibly only 'by persons whose educations and circumstances of living predispose them to regard suitable conduct along such lines, taken with appropriate, considered advice, as being indispensable to the attainment of their higher satisfactions'.

As for the field of human genetics under the Nazi regime, Muller dismissed it out of hand in only three sentences. It was, he stated, distorted and misused in the interests of a barbaric state policy controlled by 'supremely self-confident officials sporting a veneer of science'. At the same time, Muller did recognize the danger posed by 'the increasing influence of ex- or not-so-ex-Nazis among the staffs of the German universities in the Western zones'.

In fact, Muller was more concerned with the genetics controversy in the Soviet Union as the repugnant example of state interference with science. In this sense, the situations in the Soviet Union and Nazi Germany appeared to him to be similar. Regarding the Soviet Union, central to Muller's critique is the condemnation of the officially supported doctrine of inheritance of acquired characters in the name of dialectical materialism, which he characterizes as[42] 'a fixed all-embracing and mystical creed, one old-fashioned in its design and full of shibboleths, that claims to underlie all other thought'. This latter opinion may be compared with that of Haldane in the concluding paragraph of his congressional paper dealing with the human mutation rate. The arguments therein, Haldane went out of his way to stress, 'were propounded under the influence of the philosophy to which our president referred in somewhat unfavourable terms'. Beyond that, Haldane concretely voiced two caveats regarding the study of the rate at which human genes mutate. First, he maintained that any such study required special statistical methods. Second, and most important, this research, he warned, demanded particular care on the part of the investigator 'to avoid the rather numerous fallacies which beset human genetics and which are particularly liable to deceive workers whose previous experience has lain in the experimental study of plant and animal genetics'.[43]

Underlying Haldane's reservations was the fundamental fact that cross-breeding experiments employed in plant and animal genetics were inapplicable to the study of human inheritance. Hence the particular significance in developing the statistical empirical approach to human genetics through population genetics. But, for all its growth, population genetics was a matter of theory rather than practice at the time. This was pointed out by the leading American human geneticist L. H. Snyder during his Presidential Address to the American Society of Human Genetics as part of the Golden Jubilee celebration of genetics at Columbus.[44]

Unfortunately, theoretical considerations of population genetics are far in advance of empirical investigations. There is as yet insufficient realization of the necessity of carefully collected field data on the genetics of human populations.

Here special mention must be made of Lionel S. Penrose, who held the Galton Chair and headed the Galton Laboratory at University College, London between 1945 and 1965. Since he entered the field of human genetics (1931) until the time of his death (1972) he consistently opposed claims that knowledge regarding human genetics allows improvements of human stock by selective breeding in desirable directions. It cannot be an accident that his name is not to be found among the leaders in the field who signed the 'Geneticists' Manifesto'. In harmony with this stand, Penrose's voice against jumping too readily to conclusions was raised in his paper at the Golden Jubilee celebration:[45]

Eugenical thought has tended to accept uncritically certain assumptions. The first is that we know what phenotypes are desirable, and alternatively, that some social or national groups are essentially more desirable than others. Secondly, it is believed that extremely desirable and undesirable characters breed true; that is to say, the influences of environment and of dominance, overdominance and genetical modification are neglected. Furthermore, fertility is supposed to be a quality depending upon social environment rather than upon genetical constitution. Our knowledge of human genetics at the present time, however, is sufficient to raise serious doubts as to the truth of these assumptions. The relationship between gene and phenotype is often so complex that, even if we are satisfied about the undesirability of a given phenotype, the genes contributing to it may not necessarily be bad for the species. It is difficult to decide whether any gene is good or bad.

Twelve years later, new heights in the debate between proponents and opponents of human stock breeding were reached at the international symposium titled *Man and His Future*, arranged by the CIBA Foundation in London. Perhaps nothing epitomizes better the clash between those who spoke out for or against eugenic programmes there than the exchange of words between Peter B. Medawar (Nobel Prize for Medicine 1960) and Julian Huxley. The relevant passages read as follows:[46]

Medawar: What frightens me about Muller and to some extent Huxley is their extreme self-confidence, their complete conviction not only that they know what ends are desirable but also that they know how to achieve them. I can perhaps imagine approving of the kind of scheme Muller has outlined if he put it in this way: 'we don't really know about human inheritance but with the co-operation of a number of volunteers let us put my scheme into practice and perhaps we shall learn from it'.
Huxley: But surely Muller's point, and certainly mine is not to think in terms of any definite eugenic ideal; the aim that I have in mind is the very general one of gradual improvement.
Medawar: But you don't know how to do it! May I challenge you to explain Evelyn Hutchinson's paradox about homosexuality? The proportion of homosexuals has probably not declined over the period of recorded history: yet according to all selection theories which we are so confident about, the proportion should have

declined on the reasonable grounds (a) that homosexual tendencies are to some extent genetically determined and (b) that homosexuals are on the whole less fertile (even if fractionally less fertile) than normal people. It follows that the genetic endowments that make for homosexuality or parasexuality in general should have declined. In fact they have done nothing of the kind. This means either that so deep-seated a trait as parasexuality or homosexuality is not genetically determined or that we don't really understand the mechanism of its inheritance.

Huxley: I didn't know about this paradox, and am afraid I can't answer that point. In any case I want to look at the problem from another angle. You say we must know more about human genetics before we can think about improvement. I really don't see why. Darwin knew nothing about the details of reproduction, still less about genetics, and yet he was able to deduce a set of principles and a general theory of evolutionary transformation which have stood up to the test of time. Our new knowledge is merely permitting us to fill in the details and add a few minor modifications. What I want to stress is that if we can find the right method of exerting selective pressure, we could make for human genetic improvement. We must do it by way of experiment.

It should be added that since these words were printed twenty-seven years ago there is ample evidence that the issue of advancing unjustified assertions about social aspects of human genetics remains.[47]

CONTINUITY OF THE GERM PLASM, INHERITANCE OF ACQUIRED CHARACTERS AND THE CENTRAL DOGMA

To explain this there are more factors to be considered than is possible within the scope of an essay such as this. They include the issue, raised by Provine, regarding the scientific methodology and intrinsic developments of human genetics of which one aspect has attained incalculable historical significance. That is, the perception of nature–nurture interaction that has come to pervade the genetic scene since the early 1900s. It has grown out of merging Mendelian principles of inheritance and August Weismann's theory of the continuity of the germ plasm (1885–92), coupled with his experimental evidence for the non-inheritance of acquired characters (1888–1913). Weismann himself, as has been noted before by the eminent geneticist Curt Stern, looked upon the rediscovery of Mendel's rules 'as a confirmation of the basic tenets of the theory of the germ plasm'.[48]

According to the historian Garland Allen (1975), there has been a negative reaction to Weismann by biologists in the twentieth century. Weismann has been judged, Allen explained, to have been too speculative on the theoretical side and morphological on the practical side.[49] A somewhat different appraisal emerges from the papers presented by biologists and historians to the Weismann-Symposium held at the University of Freiburg in 1984. Thus the zoologist K. Sander, the editor of the publication containing the papers, writes in the preface:[50]

Despite apparent weakness, the germ plasm theory, logically derived and clearly formulated acquired deep influence on biological thought and research. It widened Darwinism into neo-Darwinism which, at first, in England was called Weismannism. If offered decisive impulses to investigations in developmental biology (*entwicklungsbiologische Forschung*), and intellectually paved the way to rediscovery of Mendel's rules and the chromosome theory of inheritance.

The historian Gloria Robinson, dealing with Weismann's hereditary theory, ends her contribution to the Symposium as follows:[51]

Weismann's theory of a germ plasm apart from somatic influences, his stand against the inheritance of acquired characters, and his continued emphasis on the action of natural selection appear clearly today as a lasting influence in biology.

Frederick B. Churchill's discussion of the 'continuity of the germ-plasm as a prelude to genetics' is characteristically cautiously worded. Nevertheless, he also notes:[52]

By putting the emphasis on the germ-plasm, which he identified with the chromosomes, Weismann rode the crest of a newly breaking wave. With the invaluable assistance from his student Chiamatsu Ischikawa, Weismann moreover contributed considerably to the momentum of that wave. In a series of studies on the expulsion of polar bodies, culminating with his important treatise of 1891 on *Amphimixis*, Weismann demonstrated the process of reduction division that, with a few modifications, to be sure, was absolutely essential for the appreciation of Mendelian genetics.[53]

Ernst Mayr evaluates similarly the historical place of Weismann's assumption regarding reduction division of the germ plasm and particulate inheritance (in terms of a series of hereditary units) when he states:[54] 'These postulates laid the foundations for Mendelian genetics (as clearly stated by Correns), and Mendelian genetics in its turn validated Weismann's theories.'

The parentship of the principle of the continuity of the germ plasm (as that of twin research) belongs to Francis Galton. It can be traced – since the mid-1860s – to his espousal of the hereditarian position that nature overrides nurture, which underlay his opposition to inheritance of acquired characters. From the confluence of these approaches and beliefs Galton construed eugenics as a kind of socio-biological branch of science, centring on improvement of human inheritance – along racial and class lines – by selective breeding. But it was from Weismann that was to come what biologists gradually took to be a telling blow against the inheritance of acquired characters.[55]

What he had shown was that tail amputations in mice over generations produced no hereditary effects. The issue of the inheritance of acquired characters has been largely ignored by historians, not least because of its association with Lysenko's work which has been dismissed as pseudoscientific.[56] No doubt, this was also what the Russian embryologist cum historian of science L. I. Blacher (Blakher) felt when he was writing his notable and virtually only historical study of the subject (1971). Given Blacher's critical attitude towards claims regarding inheritance of acquired traits, his assessment of Weismann's part in making it invalid in the eyes of the biologists is of interest:[57]

In essence, Weismann's most important contribution was not the definitive resolution of the question of the transmission of mechanical injuries but a new methodological approach to the discussion of the whole problem of inheritance of acquired traits. After Weismann's investigation in spite of all its naiveté from a modern viewpoint it became perfectly clear that *a priori* argumentation, by whatever 'higher arguments', was completely inadequate to answer the question of the transmission of any acquired trait. The natural method by which to silence the disputing parties was the experimental method. It was only after Weismann's experiment amputating mouse tails conducted, incidentally, without sufficiently strict observance of the methods of investigation, that investigators realized that strict criteria for such experiments should be worked out. These included determining the genetic purity of the original experimental material and providing precise quantitative data of traits in terms of size and number.

There can be no doubt that a full understanding of the history of genetics in general, and human genetics in particular, can only come about when also appropriate weight is given to the persisting influence of Weismann's ideas and work on the minds of geneticists. That is, the influence emanating from the mixture of Weismann's concept of the independence of germ line and soma, and experimental data for the non-inheritance of acquired characters.

To see this contention in historical perspective, it is possible to refer to the following comment by Mayr:[58]

To a modern, fully convinced of the impossibility of an inheritance of acquired characters, Weismann's arguments seem most persuasive . . . but the conclusive refutation of the principle of the inheritance of acquired characters was not achieved until the 1950s, through the so-called central dogma of molecular biology.

This passage reiterates a formulation which Mayr employs in his major historical *opus* two years earlier.[59] There he attempts to summarize – as he stresses – provisionally 'in few sentences the major concepts that have emerged from the mass of researches from 1865 to 1980'. The relevant – sixth – point of the summary reads as follows:

The pathway from the DNA of the genome to the proteins of the cytoplasm (transcription and translation) is strictly a one-way track. The proteins of the body cannot induce any changes in the DNA. An inheritance of acquired characters is thus a chemical impossibility.

It has to be said that the summary – in eight points – turns out to be different from what the reader may have expected. It concentrates exclusively on the consequences arising out of the discovery of DNA, while keeping clear of the conceptual developments before then. Indeed, the course that Mayr charts for the summary is indicated in the first point:

The most spectacular and – until the 1940s – totally unexpected finding is that the genetic material, known to consist of DNA, does not itself participate in building the body of a new individual but merely serves as a blueprint, as a set of instructions, designated as the 'genetic program'.

GENE AND ENVIRONMENT

As it happens, a year later after these words appeared in print, a collection of articles was published that touches closely not merely the subject matter of Mayr's summary but of this essay as a whole. Of particular interest is the introductory article 'The General Idea' by the Cambridge biochemist Tim Hunt, who is also one of the editors of the volume.[60] As Hunt explains, there are two principles that make up the General Idea:

The first principle is the Sequence Hypothesis; the idea that the sequence of amino acids in proteins is specified by the sequence of bases in DNA and RNA. The second principle is the famous 'Central Dogma'; not DNA makes RNA makes Protein, but the assertion that 'Once information has passed into protein it cannot get out again'.

Reflecting, as it does, a shift of mood among the workers in the field, the volume points to limitations of the General Idea. They are connected with experimental evidence invalidating the conclusive argument offered, as we have seen, in support of the non-inheritance of acquired characters. It should not be forgotten how much this owes to the biochemical approach having been superseded by the infiltration of the theory of information into molecular genetics, which has come home to roost:

... DNA is recognized by proteins in much the same way that they recognize any other substrate, and proteins control the expression of the information contained in the linear strings of bases ... Evidently, proteins recognize the right sequence when they see it. At which point, the General Idea has to give up, because the proteins' trapped information is being used to control the flow of information from DNA. There is no more logic in that than in the recognition of glucose-6-phosphate by glucose-6-phosphate dehydrogenase. Certainly nothing to be dogmatic about.

The point advanced by Hunt is that there is more to life than to view it in terms of genetic programming by DNA. He finds this approach wanting when it comes to the understanding of chemical, structural and physiological changes at the cellular level. Recently John Cairns, Julie Overbaugh and

Stephan Miller published a paper the main purpose of which 'is to show how insecure is our belief in the spontaneity (randomness) of most mutations. It seems to be a doctrine that has never been properly put to the test.' They report that the presence of lactose in the culture medium affects the mutation rate of a gene controlling lactose metabolism in *E. coli*. Discussing the possible processes that can generate such a situation, they conclude:

Each of these processes could allow individual cells to subject a subset of their informational macromolecules to the forces of natural selection. Each could, in effect, provide a mechanism for the inheritance of acquired characteristics.[61]

During the 1940s and 1950s the link between DNA and genes had been established. A most important consequence of this development has been the reinforcement of the traditional distinction fostered by the geneticists, between the hereditary constitution (genotype) and the appearance of the organism (phenotype).[62] Here it is apt to refer to the opinion, stated recently, of one of the stimulating contemporary writers on biological matters:[63]

In classical genetics the 'phenotype' of an individual is its structure and behaviour, and its 'genotype' is its genetic constitution. The distinction reflects the more fundamental one between a mortal body and a potentially immortal genetic message . . . Even if life elsewhere uses a genetic material different from DNA, I think that the distinction between genotype and phenotype will remain. There are two reasons for this. One is that most acquired characters are disadvantageous – they are results of injury, disease, and old age. Hence a hereditary mechanism which transmitted them would result in continued degeneration. A sharp distinction between soma and germ line makes it possible to prevent acquired characters from being transmitted. But there is a second reason . . . The distinction between genotype and phenotype reflects a division of labour between nucleic acids and proteins.

As we have seen, this approach is being seriously called in question.[64] Related to this is the objection to the currently so fashionable treatment of biological development as if it were analogous to a computer programme. Among the critics of such a conception the evolutionary geneticist Richard Lewontin occupies an important place.[65] Lewontin's starting position is that organisms, including human beings, develop continuously throughout their lives under the influence of mutually interacting genes and environment. This leads him to stress that the accepted distinction between genotype and phenotype is simplistic and undialectical. Thus, according to him: 'We do not inherit our phenotypes. They develop throughout our lifetimes partly as a consequence of our genotypes – but only partly.'

With respect to the relation between the genes and the organism Lewontin pinpoints three commonly held errors. The first error concerns the assertion that genes determine the phenotype which Lewontin states is, in general, false. That it applies to blood groups is the exception rather than the rule. The second error refers to the claim – for which Lewontin finds no evidence – that in different environments genotypes possess different capacities. The third error relates to the statement that genes determine tendencies. 'This', Lewontin declares, 'is the subtlest of the errors because it is framed in tentative terms and seems to take into account the environment in which an organism develops.' The conception of 'genetic tendencies' in human beings entails, Lewontin contends, a notion of 'normal human environments'. But to specify the nature or properties of a normal human environment is virtually impossible.

Against this Lewontin espouses the 'norm of reaction' as the concept on which the understanding of the gene–organism relation turns. 'All that genes ever do', Lewontin states, 'is to specify a norm of reaction over environ-ments.'[66] Consistent with these considerations Lewontin writes:

No notions of determination, or tendency, or capacity have any meaning for describing the relations between genotype and phenotype. The phenotype is the unique consequence of a particular genotype in a particular environment.

Whether the concept of norm of reaction provides the avenue to a deeper understanding of the heredity–environment problem in human beings remains to be seen. The one established norm of reaction for a human trait is the immensely important phenomenon of the specificity of an antibody–antigen reaction. Lewontin himself points to two difficulties regarding the study of norms of reaction to human traits. One is the absence of knowledge of environmental facts, relevant to the development of most human traits. The other difficulty is connected with the limitation inherent in the identicals method. There is no practical possibility to produce large numbers of genetically identical human individuals and raise them in controlled environments.

It is time to end the essay and return to the quotation prefacing it. Even those who do not agree with the literal truth of Benno Müller-Hill's characterization of the situation in the history of human genetics have to acknowledge the disinclination to explore the subject which is in urgent need of cultivation. To do so requires, among other things, to examine the implications of the scientific method and logic of human genetics developed out of the fusion of Weismannian and Mendelian approaches to inheritance since the turn of the century. This is indeed a legacy which wants to be taken on board by historians as well as geneticists in order to throw light on to what extent it is correct to speak of 'aberrations', 'misuse', 'perversion' of human genetics not only in relation to its social application in Nazi Germany. This was something which weighed heavily on the mind of J. B. S. Haldane, that unique protagonist of the English eugenic tradition (criticized by Penrose). So, in conclusion, Haldane's opinion on the subject expressed shortly before his death is worthy of note:[67]

The plain fact is that human genetics is a very difficult branch of science, and has only been developing on scientific lines for about sixty years. So far it has only saved a few thousand lives and prevented the birth of a few thousand defectives. The evils done in its name by the National Socialist Party probably outweigh its benefits. But if one believes in evolution by any means other than divine intervention a knowledge of it is essential for the human race.

Evolution is, however, a very slow process compared with history, and we need not be dissatisfied because sixty years of work by a few hundred people have not yet given us the full understanding of the processes of human evolution, much less the power to control it.

NOTES

1 B. Müller-Hill, *Tödliche Wissenschaft, die Aussonderung von Juden, Zigeunern und Geisteskranken 1933–1945* (Reinbek, 1984). For a more accurate treatment, according to the author (personal communication), consult the English version translated by George R. Fraser: *Murderous Science Elimination by Scientific Selection of Jews, Gypsies, and Others, Germany 1933–1945* (Oxford, 1988).

2 B. Müller-Hill, 'Genetics after Auschwitz', *Holocaust and Genocide Studies*, 2 (1987), 11.

3 K. Diehl and O. von Verschuer, *Zwillingstuberkulose. Zwillingsforschung und erbliche Tuberkulosedisposition* (Jena, 1933).

4 O. von Verschuer, 'Twin research from the time of Francis Galton to the present-day', *Proceedings of the Royal Society* (B), 128 (1940), 62–81.

5 O. von Verschuer, 'Bemerkungen zur Gen-Analyse bei Menschen', *Proceedings of the Seventh International Genetical Congress*, 308–9, issued as a Supplementary Volume to the *Journal of Genetics*. In the full version of the paper, with the same title, in *Der Erbarzt*, 7 (1939), 65–9, there is no reference to the fostering of twin studies by the Nazi authorities. Actually in Edinburgh Verschuer did not deliver the short version in person – apparently H. J. Muller arranged that it was read in his absence. Probably recalled by the German government in view of the impending outbreak of war hostilities, he and other German delegates left the Congress before it terminated. Cf. E. A. Carlson, *Genes, Radiation, and Society: The Life and Work of H. J. Muller* (Ithaca, N.Y. and London, 1981), p. 265; see also *Der Erbarzt*, p. 65, n. 1.

6 Verschuer supervised Mengele's work. Cf. Müller-Hill, 'Genetics after Auschwitz', pp. 6–7. Previously Mengele was involved in the study of transmission of harelip and cleft palate in families at the Frankfurt-on-Main Institute headed by Verschuer. Cf. Verschuer, *Der Erbarzt*, p. 67.

7 O. von Verschuer, *Leitfaden der Rassenhygiene* (Leipzig, 1941), p. 127. Verschuer pointed to the three 'failed attempts', as he put it, to solve the Jewish question in the past: 1. absorption, for example, by the West Goths in Spain; 2. ghettos in

Europe (fifth to nineteenth centuries); 3. emancipation during the nineteenth century. Verschuer's formulation has to be viewed against the background of the Nazi 'final solution' (*Endlösung*) of the Jewish problem: genocide.

8   *Ibid.*, p. 130.

9   *Ibid.*, p. 11.

10   H. Grebe, 'Otmar Freiherr von Verschuer 60 Jahre alt', *Homo*, 7 (1956), 65–73. This includes a list of Verschuer's publications as well as thirty-six papers and other works published in honour of his sixtieth birthday.

11   O. von Verschuer,'Die Anwendung von Erkenntnissen der allgemeinen Genetik auf den Menschen und ihre Grenzen', *Akademie der Wissenschaften und der Literatur Abhandlungen der mathematisch–naturwissenschaftlichen Klasse*, 1950 (no. 4), 107–21.

12   In 1962 Verschuer considered 'degeneration' in man. He acknowledged that the hypothesis that the mixing of races was producing degeneration in mankind, and hence cultural decay, has not been sustained by science. Accepting that natural selection is of great significance to man, Verschuer observed that eugenic selection in aid of natural selection has taken a back seat, 'admittedly not least because of its political misuse'. Verschuer's presentation reads as though he had nothing to do, theoretically or practically, with the Nazi notion of the danger to 'racial purity' due to interbreeding of 'superior' and 'inferior' races. See O. von Verschuer, 'Gefähr-dung des Erbguts – ein genetisches Problem', *Akademie der Wissenschaften und der Literatur Abhandlungen der mathematisch-naturwissenschaftlichen Klasse*, 1962 (no. 3), 173–92.

13   E. Baur, E. Fischer and F. Lenz, *Menschliche Erblichkeitslehre und Rassenhygiene*, in 2 vols.: E. Baur, E. Fischer and F. Lenz, *Menschliche Erblichkeitslehre*, 1st–4th edn (Munich, 1921, 1923, 1927, 1936), I; F. Lenz, *Menschliche Auslese und Rassenhygiene (Eugenik)*, 1st–3rd edn (Munich, 1921, 1923, 1931), II. The edition referred to in this essay is the 3rd.

14   Verschuer, *Leitfaden*, p. 5.

15   Muller's review of E. Baur, E. Fischer and F. Lenz, *Human Heredity* (London and New York, 1931) appeared in *Birth Control Review*, 17 (1933), 19–21. The interested reader may find it convenient to consult the reprint in H. J. Muller, *Studies in Genetics: The Selected Papers of H. J. Muller* (Bloomington, Ind., 1962), pp. 541–4.

16   Muller's recent discovery that mutation rate could be immensely increased by X-rays had generated great excitement. Cf. his 'Artificial transmutation of the gene', *ibid.*, pp. 245–57; reprinted from *Science*, 66 (1927), 84–7. J. B. S. Haldane (himself a prominent figure in the field), surveying the work during the period 1895–1935, called this finding of Muller 'perhaps the last great discovery in genetics'. See J. B. S. Haldane, 'Forty years of genetics', in J. Needham and W. Pagel (eds.), *Background to Modern Science*, repr. (Cambridge, 1940), p. 236.

17   The term 'Mendelian' is not without problems; cf. R. Olby, 'Mendel no Mendel-ian?', *History of Science*, 17 (1979), 53–72, reprinted in his *Origin of Mendelism*, 2nd edn (Chicago and London, 1985), 234–58. When Muller wrote his review the term 'Mendelian', emanating from the work of the Moravian monk Gregor Mendel (1865), related to the particulate (genic) nature of inheritance. It is in this

sense that the term is used in this essay. Mendel himself was concerned with plant hybridization which he investigated by crossing pure strains of *Pisum*, the edible pea. Peas were distinguished by a contrasting pair of traits (characters) of which one was clearly dominant (e.g. round seed shape, yellow seed colour) and the other recessive (e.g. angular seed shape, green seed colour). Mendel's experimental work included studies of two- and three-trait differences. Analysing the inheritance pattern of the parental traits in statistical terms and finding that they retained their identity in successive generations, Mendel formulated the principles of heredity which bear his name: 'Mendel's rules (laws) of the segregation and of the independent assortment of characters'. Regarding the proportion of dominants to recessives in the first and subsequent hybrid generations, Mendel established the historically influential numerical relation of 3:1 and 1:2:1 respectively (the 'Mendelian ratio').

18 To refer to the vast literature on Mendel and the rediscovery of his work is not feasible. V. Orel, *Mendel* (Oxford and New York, 1984) is a brief portrait which, albeit marred by anachronisms, can serve as an introduction. For greater detail the already mentioned Olby's *Origin of Mendelism* (1985) should be consulted. It represents a careful study of the developments preceding the work of Mendel, placing the latter in the framework of mid-nineteenth-century biology, and reviews the controversies surrounding the neglect of Mendel's work and its rediscovery. This subject is also dealt with by M. H. MacRoberts, 'Was Mendel's paper on *Pisum* neglected or unknown?', *Annals of Science*, 42 (1985), 339–45; O. G. Meijer, 'Hugo de Vries no Mendelian?', *ibid.*, 189–232; and L. Darden, 'Hugo de Vries's lecture plates and the discovery of segregation', *ibid.*, 233–42.

19 'The science of genetics has had a meteoric rise' (C. Stern, *Principles of Human Genetics* (San Francisco, 1949), p. vii; 'Die Vererbungswissenschaft hat sich so stürmisch entfaltet . . .' (A. Barthelmess, *Vererbungswissenschaft*, Freiburg and Munich, 1952, p. v). The term 'genetics' was coined by William Bateson, one of the founders of the discipline. He had used it in private correspondence in 1905 and then in his Inaugural Address to the Royal Horticultural Society's Third Conference on Hybridization and Plantbreeding in 1906. Cf. L. C. Dunn, *A Short History of Genetics: The Development of Some of the Main Lines of Thought: 1864–1939* (New York, 1965), pp. 68–9.

20 E. Mayr, 'The recent historiography of genetics', *Journal of the History of Biology*, 6 (1973), 125–54.

21 Barthelmess, *Vererbungswissenschaft*, pp. v–vi.

22 A. H. Sturtevant, *A History of Genetics* (New York, 1965); Dunn, *Short History*.

23 Sturtevant, *History*, pp. 126–32.

24 Sturtevant's emphasis.

25 Sturtevant's emphasis.

26 The 1951 Unesco Statement on race asserted, among others, that race mixture was harmless. It was sent to 108 prominent social anthropologists and geneticists of whom 80 responded. Among them only Sturtevant questioned the validity of the assertion. Cf. W. B. Provine, 'Geneticists and the biology of race crossing', *Science*, 182 (1973), 790–6 (p. 796).

27 On this subject, the principal guide to the developments in the United States and

Britain during this period is D. J. Kevles, *In the Name of Eugenics: Genetics and the Uses of Human Heredity*, repr. (Harmondsworth, 1986). This study includes an invaluable 'Essay on sources'; in it the author calls attention to a fact pertinent to our inquiry: 'There is no comprehensive historical study of human genetics, and nothing more than a few fragmentary autobiographical reminiscences by its practitioners' (p. 399). The establishment and growth of the eugenic movement in Germany, and its function under the Nazi regime receives increasing scholarly attention. For recent accounts containing extensive references to primary and secondary literature, see J. Kroll's doctoral dissertation *Zur Entstehung und Institutionalisierung einer naturwissenschaftlichen und sozialpolitischen Bewegung: Die Entwicklung der Eugenik/Rassenhygiene bis zum Jahre 1933* (Tübingen, 1983); H.-W. Schmuhl, *Rassenhygiene, Nationalsozialismus, Euthanasie: Von der Verhütung zur Vernichtung 'lebensunwerten Lebens', 1890–1945* (Göttingen, 1987). Three other recent articles in English are also relevant: P. Weindling, 'Weimar eugenics: the Kaiser Wilhelm Institute for Anthropology, Human Heredity and Eugenics in social context', *Annals of Science*, 42 (1985), 303–18; S. F. Weiss, 'The race-hygiene movement in Germany', *Osiris*, 2nd ser., 3 (1987), 193–236 (I owe this reference to Dr Marsha Richmond); P.Weingart, 'The rationalization of sexual behaviour: the institutionalization of eugenic thought in Germany', *Journal of the History of Biology*, 20 (1987), 159–93. For a substantive treatment of this theme of broad scope, see P. Weingart, J. Kroll and K. Bayertz, *Rasse, Blut und Gene: Geschichte der Eugenik in Deutschland* (Frankfurt-on-Main, 1988).

28 Dunn, *Short History*, p. 214.
29 This is the year of publication of A. E. Garrod's paper 'The incidence of alkaptonuria: the study of chemical individuality', *Lancet* (1902, 2), 1616–20. Garrod, who was a clinician, studied alkaptonuria, discernible by the presence of homogentisic acid in urine which, if exposed to the air, becomes dark. It was generally accepted that the occurrence of homogentisic acid in urine was due to the abnormal metabolism of the amino acid tyrosine. Garrod was struck by the fact 'that of alkaptonuric individuals a very large proportion are children of first cousins'. This led him to think of alkaptonuria in genetic terms. W. Bateson, apparently, was first to suggest that this metabolic abnormality was an instance of a rare recessive condition which could be explained along Mendelian lines. See W. Bateson and E. R. Saunders' 'Experimental studies in the physiology of heredity', *Report I* (1902), pp. 133–4 (note in *Reports to the Evolution Committee of the Royal Society*, London, 1910).
30 This is the year of publication of W. Weinberg's paper 'Über den Nachweis der Vererbung bei Menschen', *Jahreshefte des Vereins für vaterländische Naturkunde in Württemberg*, 64 (1908), 369–82. For an English translation see S. H. Boyer, IV (ed.), *Papers on Human Genetics* (Englewood Cliffs, N.J., 1963), pp. 4–15. Weinberg, a practising physician, investigating the mode of inheritance of twinning developed a mathematical formula for the frequency of dominant and recessive traits under conditions of random mating. As for the inheritance of twinning, he concluded that his finding fitted with 'the assumption that the trait for twinning is inherited according to the Mendelian rule and is recessive'.

31 L. C. Dunn, 'Cross currents in the history of human genetics', *American Journal of Human Genetics*, 13 (1961), 1–13.

32 H. J. Muller, 'The guidance of human evolution', *Perspectives in Biology and Medicine*, 3 (1959), 1–43.

33 G. Pontecorvo, 'H. J. Muller as a teacher', in Muller, *Studies in Genetics* (no pagination).

34 'Men and mice at Edinburgh: Reports from the Genetic Congress', *Journal of Heredity*, 30 (1939), 371–4.

35 The emphasis is mine. The original seven signers were: F. A. E. Crew, FRS, J. B. S. Haldane, FRS, S. C. Harland, L. T. Hogben, FRS, J. S. Huxley, FRS, H. J. Muller, and J. Needham. The fourteen who subsequently signed it were: G. P. Child, P. R. David, G. Dahlberg, T. H. Dobzhansky, R. A. Emerson, C. Gordon, John Hammond, C. L. Huskins, W. Landauer, H. H. Plough, E. Price, J. Schultz, A. G. Steinberg, C. H. Waddington.

36 Muller, *Studies in Genetics*, p. 545–8.

37 The 'Manifesto' receives attention from D. Paul, 'Eugenics and the left', *Journal of the History of Ideas*, 45 (1984), 567–90 (p. 574). Also it is mentioned by Kevles, p. 184, and briefly dealt with by E. A. Carlson, 'Eugenics and basic genetics in H. J. Muller's approach to human genetics', *History and Philosophy of Life Sciences*, 9 (1987), 57–78 (pp. 75, 77).

38 Provine, 'Geneticists', p. 796.

39 J. Huxley, 'Genetics, evolution and human destiny', in L. C. Dunn (ed.), *Genetics in the 20th Century: Essays on the Progress of Genetics During Its First 50 Years* (New York, 1951), 591–621 (p. 616). For further passages quoted below, see pp. 613, 615, 642, 612.

40 J. S. Huxley and A. C. Haddon, *We Europeans; A Survey of 'Racial' Problems* (London, 1935). The authors suggested that the term 'ethnic group' should replace the word 'race'. It may well have been owing to Huxley's influence that in the 'Geneticists' Manifesto' the word appears in inverted commas.

41 H. J. Muller, 'Genetics in the scheme of things', in G. Bonnier and R. Larsson (eds.), *Proceedings of the Eighth International Congress of Genetics, 7th–14th of July 1948 Stockholm* (Lund, 1949), 96–127 (pp. 103–5).

42 *Ibid.*, p. 106.

43 J. B. S. Haldane, 'The rate of mutation of human genes', *ibid.*, 268–73 (p. 272).

44 L. H. Snyder, 'Old and new pathways in human genetics', in Dunn (ed.), *Genetics in the 20th Century*, 369–91 (p. 377).

45 L. S. Penrose, 'Genetics of the human race', in Dunn (ed.), *Genetics in the 20th Century*, 393–9 (p. 394). See also his 'Presidential Address – The influence of the English tradition in human genetics', in J. F. Crow and J. V. Neel (eds.), *Proceedings of the Third International Congress of Human Genetics, September 5–10, 1966 Chicago* (Baltimore, Md, 1967), 13–25; also 'Genetik und Gesellschaft', in G. G. Wendt (ed.), *Genetik und Gesellschaft Marburger Forum Philippinum* (Stuttgart, 1970), 3–9.

46 G. Wolstenholme (ed.), *Man and His Future: A Ciba Foundation Volume* (London, 1963), pp. 296–7.

47 For a critical interdisciplinary reappraisal of the issue by a neurobiologist, an

evolutionary geneticist and a psychologist, see S. Rose, R. C. Lewontin and L. J. Kamin, *Not in Our Genes: Biology, Ideology and Human Nature*, repr. (Harmondsworth, 1987).

48 A. Weismann, *Vorträge über Deszendenztheorie*, 3rd edn (Jena, 1913), vol. II, p. 33. See C. Stern, 'The continuity of genetics', *Daedalus*, 99 (1970), 882–908 (p. 888).

49 G. E. Allen, *Life Science in the Twentieth Century* (New York, 1975), p. 8.

50 See K. Sander, 'Stichworte zum Heft', in K. Sander (ed.), *August Weismann (1834–1914) und die theoretische Biologie des 19. Jahrhunderts Urkunden, Berichte und Analyse*, *Freiburger Universitätsblätter*, 24 (nos. 84/88, 1985), 21.

51 G. Robinson, 'August Weismann's hereditary theory', *ibid.*, 83–90 (p. 90).

52 F. B. Churchill, 'Weismann's continuity of the germ-plasm in historical perspective', *ibid.*, 107–24 (p. 122).

53 The author refers here to his article 'August Weismann and the break from tradition', *Journal of the History of Biology*, 1 (1968), 91–112, and also to Gloria Robinson's *A Prelude to Genetics* (Lawrence, Kans, 1979), chs. 7–8.

54 E. Mayr, 'Weismann and evolution', *Journal of the History of Biology*, 18 (1985), 295–329 (p. 326). This is an expanded version of the author's lecture at the Weismann-Symposium in Freiburg.

55 For a discussion of the relationship of Galton's and Weismann's approaches to the continuity of germ plasm, see Ruth Schwartz Cowan's illuminating article 'Nature and nurture: the interplay of biology and politics in the work of Francis Galton', *Studies in the History of Biology*, 1 (1977), 133–207 (pp. 142–78).

56 Here it may be apposite to quote from N. W. Pirie, 'John Burdon Sanderson Haldane 1892–1964 Elected F.R.S. 1932', *Biographical Memoirs of Fellows of the Royal Society*, 12 (1966), 219–49: 'British geneticists have a tradition of polemical fervour surpassed only by that of Lysenko . . . when feelings are less heated the whole episode will repay detailed analysis' (p. 222). Also R. Young pleads for a changed approach in a survey of the writings at hand: 'Getting started on Lysenkoism', *Radical Science Journal*, 6/7 (1978), 81–105. A reasoned entry to the topic is provided by N. Roll-Hansen, 'A new perspective on Lysenko?', *Annals of Science*, 42 (1985), 261–78. Helpful are a number of published texts by J.-P. Regelmann: *Die Geschichte des Lyssenkoismus* (Frankfurt-on-Main, 1980); 'Die Aktualität Lyssenkos Historische Ergänzungen zu einer wissenschaftstheoretischen Debatte', *Zeitschrift für allgemeine Wissenschaftstheorie*, 12 (1981), 353–63; 'Lyssenko und der Lyssenkoismus – Hintergründe, Ausbreitung und Verfall einer biologischen Irrlehre', *Praxis der Naturwissenschaften Biologie*, 33 (1984), 1–22; G. Galinsky and J.-P. Regelmann, 'Einflussnahme eines politischen Systems auf eine Wissenschaft Trofim D. Lyssenko und die Wirkungen auf die Biologie in der Sowjetunion 1926–1959', *BU Der Biologie Unterricht*, 20 (1984), 65–96.

57 L. I. Blacher, *The Problem of the Inheritance of Acquired Characters: A History of a priori and Empirical Methods Used to Find a Solution*, English translation edited by F. B. Churchill (Washington, D.C. and New Delhi, 1982), p. 94.

58 Mayr, 'Weismann', p.313.

59 E. Mayr, *The Growth of Biological Thought: Diversity, Evolution and Inheritance* (Cambridge, Mass., 1982). For quotations below, see pp. 827–8.

60 T. Hunt, 'Introduction: The General Idea', in T. Hunt, S. Prentis and J. Tooze (eds.), *DNA makes RNA makes Protein* (Amsterdam, New York and Oxford, 1983), pp. vii–xiv. I am indebted to Dr John C Gray, Fellow of Robinson College, Cambridge, for bringing the volume to my attention.

61 J. Cairns, J. Overbaugh and S. Miller, 'The origin of mutants', *Nature*, 335 (1988), 142–5. I am indebted to Dr Brian J. McCabe, Fellow of Robinson College, for alerting me to this article.

62 It was formulated in 1911 by the Danish geneticist W. Johannsen. For a historical discussion of the subject, see F. B. Churchill, 'William Johannsen and the genotype concept', *Journal of the History of Biology*, 7 (1974), 5–30; N. Roll-Hansen, 'The genotype theory of William Johannsen and its relation to plant breeding and evolution', *Centaurus*, 22 (1978), 201–35.

63 J. M. Smith, *The Problems of Biology* (Oxford, 1986), pp. 21–2.

64 For an earlier critique of DNA's position of superiority, see N. W. Pirie, 'Patterns of assumption about large molecules', *Archives of Biochemistry and Biophysics Supplement*, 1 (1962), 21–9 (pp. 23–4); S. Rose, *The Chemistry of Life*, 2nd edn (Harmondsworth, 1979), p. 206.

65 For what follows I draw on R. Lewontin, *Human Diversity* (New York, 1982), especially ch. 2.

66 R. C. Lewontin, 'Gene, organism and environment', in D. S. Bendall (ed.), *Evolution from Molecules to Men* (Cambridge, 1983), 273–85 (p. 277). This approach was explored by J. B. S. Haldane in his celebrated article 'In defence of genetics', *Modern Quarterly*, n.s., 4 (1949), 194–202: 'What is inherited is not a set of characters, but a capacity to react to the environment in such a way that, in a particular environment, particular characters are developed. It is, therefore, incorrect to speak of the transmission of a character, whether "acquired" or not' (p. 195).

67 J. B. S. Haldane, FRS, 'The proper social application of the knowledge of human genetics', in M. Goldsmith and A. Mackay (eds.), *The Science of Science Society in the Technological Age* (London and Toronto, 1964), 150–6 (p. 156).

ACKNOWLEDGEMENTS

Dr Kurt Bayertz, Professor Paul L. Farber, Dr Brian J. McCabe, Professor Benno Müller-Hill, Dr Roy Porter, Dr Marsha Richmond, Dr John Smith, FRS, and Professor Peter Weingart very kindly read the draft version of this chapter. I greatly benefited from their comments but, of course, the responsibility for the text is my own.

INDEX